Practical Case Studies in
Digitalising Operations

PIUS OBA • MICHAEL SONY

juta

Practical Case Studies in Digitalising Operations

© Juta and Company Ltd
First floor, Sunclare building, 21 Dreyer street, Claremont 7708
PO Box 14373, Lansdowne 7779, Cape Town, South Africa
www.juta.co.za

© 2022 Juta and Company (Pty) Ltd

ISBN 978 1 99896 225 9
ISBN 978 1 99896 229 7 (WebPDF)

Production Specialist: Zainub Gamieldien
Editor: Wilde Greene (James Ryan)
Proofreader: Rod Prodgers
Cover designer: Drag and Drop (Jacques Nel)
Typesetter: Wouter Reinders
Indexer: Ute Kühlmann

Typeset in Optima LT Std 10/13pt

CONTENTS

Chapter 8: Digitalising RTMC Driving Licence Renewal Operations Analysis and Improvement Proposals: A Viewpoint 127

Chapter 9: Practical Case of Digitalising a Leading Fast-Moving Consumer Goods (FMCG) Manufacturer 151

Chapter 10: Practical Case of Digitalising Public Hospitals in South Africa: A Viewpoint 182

FIGURES

Tables

DR PIUS OBA

Dr Oba is a leading engineer and seasoned operations management, digital technology and energy expert with over 25 years of high level technical, business, research and management experience in power, oil & gas, supply chain and manufacturing, both in South Africa and abroad.

Dr Oba holds a doctorate degree (PhD) in Industrial Engineering from University of the Witwatersrand, an MBA from the Wits Business School and LLB from Unisa, among other engineering certificates and qualifications. He is a registered professional engineer with the engineering council of South Africa (ECSA) and among the few engineers in South Africa registered in the International Register of Engineers (IntPE). Engineering, business and legal background has given him exposure and the capacity to work on highly complex projects. Presently, Senior Lecturer at the Wits Business School in the Technology and Operations Management (TOM) team.

Dr Oba started his career at Shell Petroleum Development Company, in 1992 as trainee engineer and progressed to senior engineer responsible for pipeline projects and new venture creation. Thereafter, he joined Wits University as a Lecturer in the School of Mechanical Engineering for about five years and from there to the CSIR. His experience at the CSIR and involvement within academia as a lecturer in the School of Mechanical Engineering helped him build strong research capacity and collaborations across industry. He then joined Eskom from the CSIR, where he managed a team of specialist and engineers as section manager and Chief Engineer and implemented knowledge sharing processes in a highly complex environment, as well as processes for optimal project management. In 2013, he joined General Electric (GE) – Oil & Gas, where he worked as African Region Manager overseeing capital drilling equipment remanufacturing. In the role, he re-engineered the machinery maintenance business model, saving the company huge amount of money. This model was then adopted in other territories of the business. In the role he was able to create strong teams of competent individuals who were focused on delivery.

Dr Oba has supervised a number of postgraduate students and published a number of papers in reputable journals. Dr Oba, has high level of business and technical competency, and is able to build strong relationships of trust with clients.

DR MICHAEL SONY

Dr Michael Sony is currently working as Senior Lecturer in Digital Business, WITS Business School. Prior to it he was working as Senior Lecturer in Industrial Engineering, at Faculty of Engineering, Namibia University of Science and Technology, Windhoek, Namibia since 2017. He has also worked with Government of Goa, India in the Goa State Electricity Department since 2008. He also has been consultant in Operation Excellence, Six Sigma, lean Six Sigma and Industrial Engineering having experience in power sector, mining, and metals. He holds academic degrees D.Sc. in Industrial Engineering, PhD degree in Operations Management, Master of Engineering in Industrial Engineering degree from Goa University, Goa, India. He is also a certified Energy Auditor with Bureau of Energy Efficiency, New Delhi, India. He is on the editorial board of the *International Journal of Lean Six Sigma* published by Emerald publications. He has authored two books on Quality management in Higher education. Besides, he has published around 70 research articles in various international journals. His publications can be assessed at https://scholar.google.co.in/citations?user=jB0Zp3kAAAAJ&hl=en. He is a member of South African Facilities Management Association (SAFMA)

His area of research interest are Production and Operations management, Quality management, Industry 4.0 and Quality 4.0.

Operations play a pivotal role in the success of the organisation. It plays a key role in the execution of strategy and helps in attaining a competitive advantage by creating products and services to meet customer needs. In a simplistic sense, it can be termed as a means of managing processes and resources. The Fourth Industrial Revolution has changed the manner organisations are managing their operations. From the erstwhile traditional operations, the modern-day operations are state-of-the-art with the latest technologies applied at various value creation activities. Modern technologies such as IoT, cyber-physical systems, cloud computing, augmented reality, additive manufacturing, robotic process automation and so on are applied to varying degrees in modern organisations. To be more specific, the digital transformation of operations has created new challenges and opportunities for organisations. In terms of opportunities, modern technologies have made it possible for operations managers to use large amounts of information both within and external to organisations to arrive at new optimums in operations performance. It has helped organisations redefine the market to create better quality products and services. From a macro perspective, digitalisation can be the leapfrog that will help organisations in Africa to jump ahead in the Fourth Industrial Revolution. Digitalisation, if implemented correctly, has the power to transform organisations that can compete at the global level. However, the challenge is to key operations which can be digitalised and gain the maximum advantage with minimum use of resources. Despite the popularity of digitalising operations, there is no book which deals with practical aspects of digitalising operations. Some of the key questions bothering both the practitioners and academicians are how to digitalise the operations. How to assess the current state of digital maturity of their operations? What should be the future state of digital maturity? How can you link the digitalising operations with organisational strategy? To deal with such wide-ranging questions, one needs a practical and easy to understand book with live examples so that users can understand how they can digitalise their operations for success. This book is devoted to making the users understand using practical case examples, how their organisations can digitalise their operations to thrive in modern markets. The authors use simple lucid, non-technical language to explain how organisations can implement digitalisation in their operations. They explain what the key pain points are where digitalisation should be implemented immediately, and which are the operations where the operations should not be digitalised. The concepts are explained concerning case studies from a practical perspective so that non-technical readers can understand how to digitalise their operations. This book will be beneficial to students, academicians, practitioners and senior managers in organisations as regards how to digitalise their operations.

Last, I commend the all the authors who have contributed to this unique book project. This book is a unique book with practical examples from organisations in South Africa.

I hope the readers will find this book an interesting read.

Editors:
P Oba
M Sony
November 2022

CHAPTER 1

Introduction

Digitising operations has become an important and critical lever of the business operations model. McKinsey (2017) identified five key levers that would constitute the next generation operating model, of which one of the levers is digitising operations. This lever will help companies to build value and provide compelling customer experience at lower costs – an operating model that provides a unique new way to run an organisation. It combines digital technologies and operations capabilities in an integrated, well thought out and sequenced way to achieve step-change improvements in revenue, customer experience and cost.

Digitising operations aim to digitise customer experience and day-to-day operations (McKinsey, 2017) by emphasising the use of tools and technology to improve journeys. The digital tools have the capacity to transform customer-facing journeys in powerful ways, often by creating the potential for self-service. The need for self-service capability has created tremendous opportunities to reach the customer and to involve the customer in executing operations. This provides the advantage of reshaping time-consuming transactional and manual tasks that are part of internal journeys, especially when multiple systems are involved.

Digitising operations has opened up opportunities towards achieving operational excellence in the need to satisfy the customer by providing seamless operational capabilities and integrations of processes. These are useful in product development and product leadership, process efficiencies in most cost-effective delivery of products and services, process effectiveness by better utilisation of inputs, channel access and overall exceptional operational performance. Bajaj (2018) states that operational excellence is the execution of the business strategy more consistently and reliably than competitors, with lower operational risk, lower operating costs and increased revenues relative to its competitor. Achieving operational excellence through execution excellence is the target of digitising operations. It is critical to bear in mind that operational excellence is not only about continuous improvement methods but is more about a long-term change in organisational culture.

Having identified the opportunities and factors linked to the need for digitisation, it is imperative for organisations to strategically prepare for the imminent technological disruption which has an impact on operational structures, culture and workforce skills. The crafting of optimal process designs needs to consider employee explicit and implicit knowledge management of the workforce and harness new digital technologies to achieve operational excellence.

The accelerated changes in the global market are placing enormous pressure on most industries and organisations to deliver on their strategic objectives with minimal operational cost, reduced risk and high revenue while remaining highly competitive (Bajaj, 2018). The advances in digital technologies are the cause of disruption, used to augment business processes to achieve large-scale automation and business insights. At the centre of this change is a more informed customer with high expectations of service and product quality. Customers can easily compare the quality of service and product against competing companies and make an informed decision based on peer reviews rather than relying on a company's marketing campaigns. Customers have become prosumers and are directly or indirectly involved in the manufacturing process. This means that organisations need to place their customer's need and expectations right at the fore of their business strategy. Digitising operations will help provide the capability to achieve this goal.

Boute & Van Mieghem (2021) provided the approach to digitising operations so that a company's workflow (that is, its sequence of activities) is digitally supported, if not fully digital. The steps consist of:
1. Before digitising or automating, *value stream map*, *streamline* and *standardise* your workflows; *reduce waste* by humans and machines; and *optimise* your workflows (*otherwise you automate waste*).
2. Focus on *data quality and quantity* – develop a *data strategy* that will allow you to collect and capture, organise, store and maintain data.
3. Prepare your organisation for a data-driven culture which *augments* human work.
4. Invest in *new human capabilities* – invest in different knowledge and skills.

Presented in this book are several examples of digitising and digitalising operations and its application in different sectors and operations. These are examples compiled from information obtained from the public domain. These examples are fictitious, and do not depict in any way the state of affairs in the organisations or the way an organisation is being managed. These fictitious examples are created so that readers understand how digitisation and digitalisation will help in improving the operations. In order to maintain a high degree of reader engagement, some names may resemble identifiable organisation. However, these are merely coincidental and these are practical examples will help to obtain a practical dimension.

REFERENCES

Bajaj, V. (2018). Business Transformation & Operational Excellence Key Challenges – Operational Excellence Society. Retrieved April 26, 2020, from https://opexsociety.org/body-of-knowledge/business-transformation-operational-excellence-key-challenges/

Boute R. N., van Mieghem, J. A. (2021). Digital Operations: Autonomous Automation and the Smart Execution of Work. *MBR Journal*. https://mbrjournal.com/2021/01/26/digital-operations-autonomous-automation-and-the-smart-execution-of-work/

McKinsey (2017). Next Generation Operating Model. Retrieved June 27, 2022, from https://www.mckinsey.com/~/media/McKinsey/Business%20Functions/McKinsey%20Digital/Our%20Insights/Introducing%20the%20next-generation%20operating%20model/Introducing-the-next-gen-operating-model.ashx

Practical Case of Operations Optimisation for Public Hospitals through Intelligent Automation (IA)

INTRODUCTION

The health industry in South Africa is now ready for a shift brought about by emerging technologies that disrupt the industry's roles, capabilities, partnerships and procedures. The digital transformation will affect every element of the healthcare practice especially in the public sector hospitals. This will include the practice from clinical, patient, supply chain management, as well as the institutionalisation of the healthcare system and public health policy that will provide oversight based on new ways of working within public hospitals (Chokkalingam, 2022). For public sector hospitals, digital transformation in healthcare is more than new technological advances. This will include the optimisation of business operations for public sector hospitals. The need to be customer-centric and to provide valuable services to patients will be necessary if improvements are to be made in the government hospitals (Willie, 2020). New developments will therefore provide a roadmap for attaining customer-centric public sector hospitals in South Africa through operations optimisation and smart automation.

BACKGROUND

The South African healthcare industry is based on a two-tiered system, comprising the public sector mainly supported by government, and the private health sector – which is profit-driven (Buswell, 2022). Public health services are classified into primary, secondary and tertiary health facilities and are managed by the provincial departments of health. The provincial departments are the direct employers of the health workforce, while the National Ministry of Health is responsible for policy development and co-ordination. The public health care services cater for over 84% of the South African population. This system has experienced gross mismanagement of hospitals, massive migration of skilled professionals either to the private sector or to other countries and, despite government spending close to 10% of GDP on healthcare, the majority of facilities within the public sector are severely underfunded and ill-equipped to offer acceptable level of healthcare (Lavers, 2020). Even though the public health sector has myriad of problems as described above, the syndicate can make a meaningful contribution to the body of knowledge through this assignment. The focus of the assignment will be to develop a model that will bring about effectiveness and efficiencies in the operations of public sector hospitals when implemented.

PROBLEM STATEMENT

The healthcare system in Gauteng is under severe strain with challenges that make a visit to the hospital tiring and daunting. The waiting time for an out patient at a government hospital in Gauteng is excessively long. Patients wait for 6 hours and 44 minutes at the SB hospital to receive medical attention on average (Sicetsha, 2019).

The waiting time is broken up as follows:
- Time to register: 2 hours
- Time to see a doctor: 2 hours and 46 minutes
- Time to collect medicine: 1 hour and 58 minutes

The long waiting times may lead to negative results, including patients leaving without receiving medical attention, increased human error and low staff morale. It is therefore important for the Gauteng Health Department to improve operations to reduce waiting times.

According to the 2021 Gauteng Health Annual Report, the digital transformation of health operations has been slower than expected, leading to process inefficiency as demand often exceeds supply in the health sector. Supply chain management irregularities, theft and wasteful expenditure have also been reported (Gauteng Provincial Government, 2021).

The aim of this assignment is to analyse and improve the quality of the healthcare system by reducing the time a patient waits to receive medical attention. Through digitisation of operations the sector will be able to allocate resources efficiently, predict demand and eradicate wasteful expenditure. The operations at the SB hospital were analysed and used as a basis to make recommendations to optimise processes and digitise operations using the DAS model.

Note the high-level process view of the typical process for an outpatient customer to a government hospital (Figure 2.1).

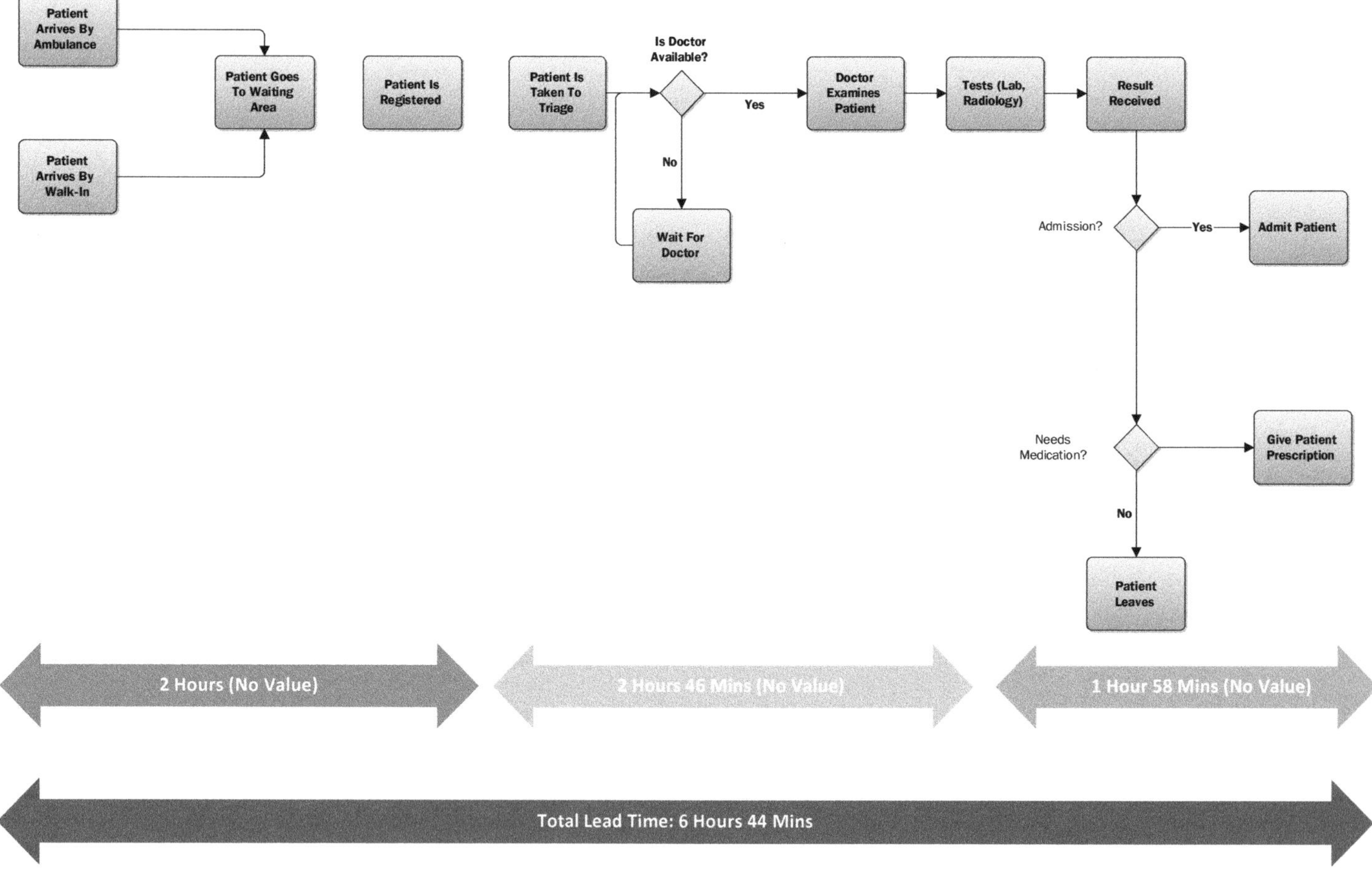

Figure 2.1 High Level Current View of Hospital Outpatient Process

Process Map of Operations — "As Is" Outpatient Business Process

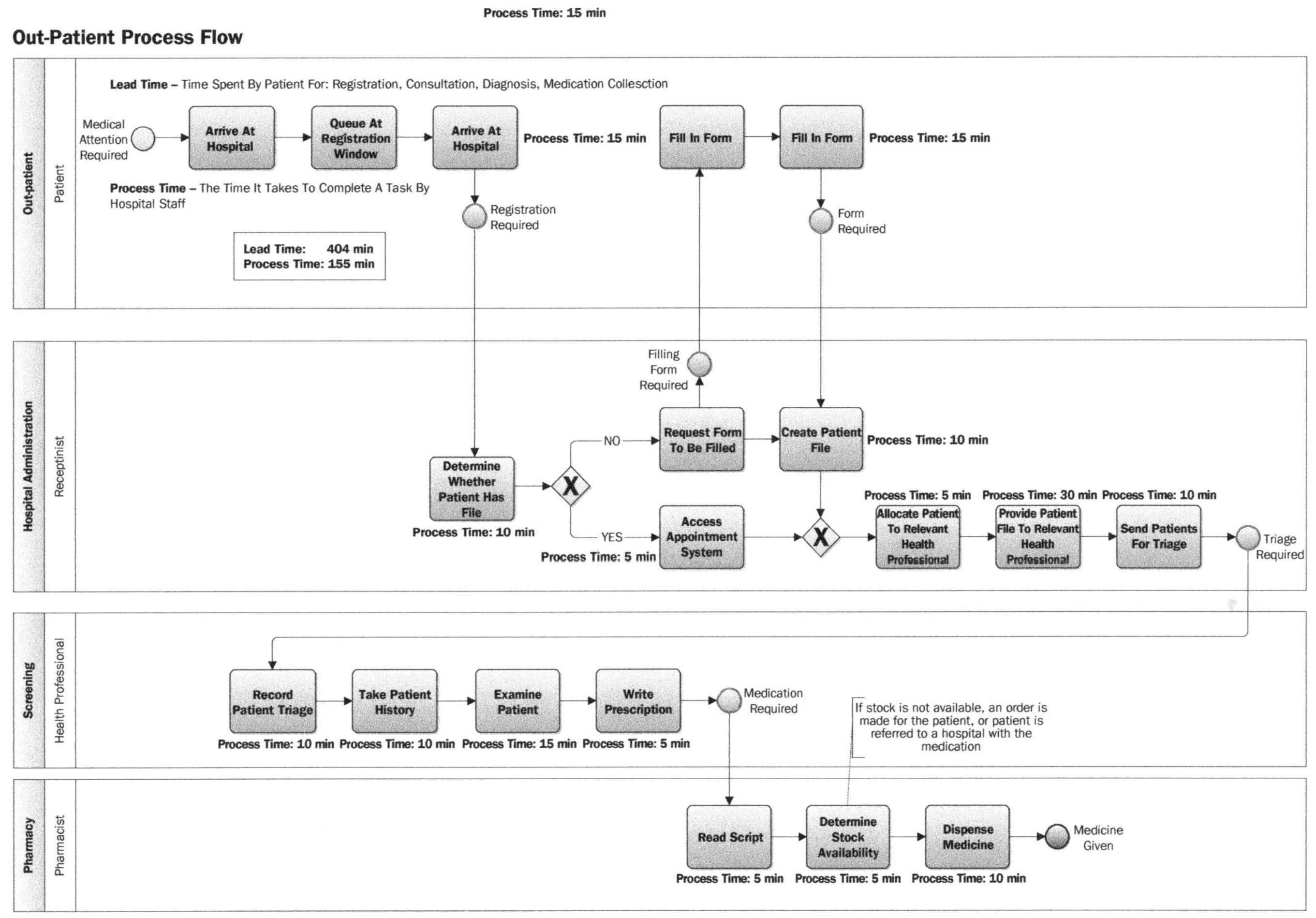

Figure 2.2 Government Hospital — Operations Processes

Process Map of Operations — Future State Outpatient Business Process

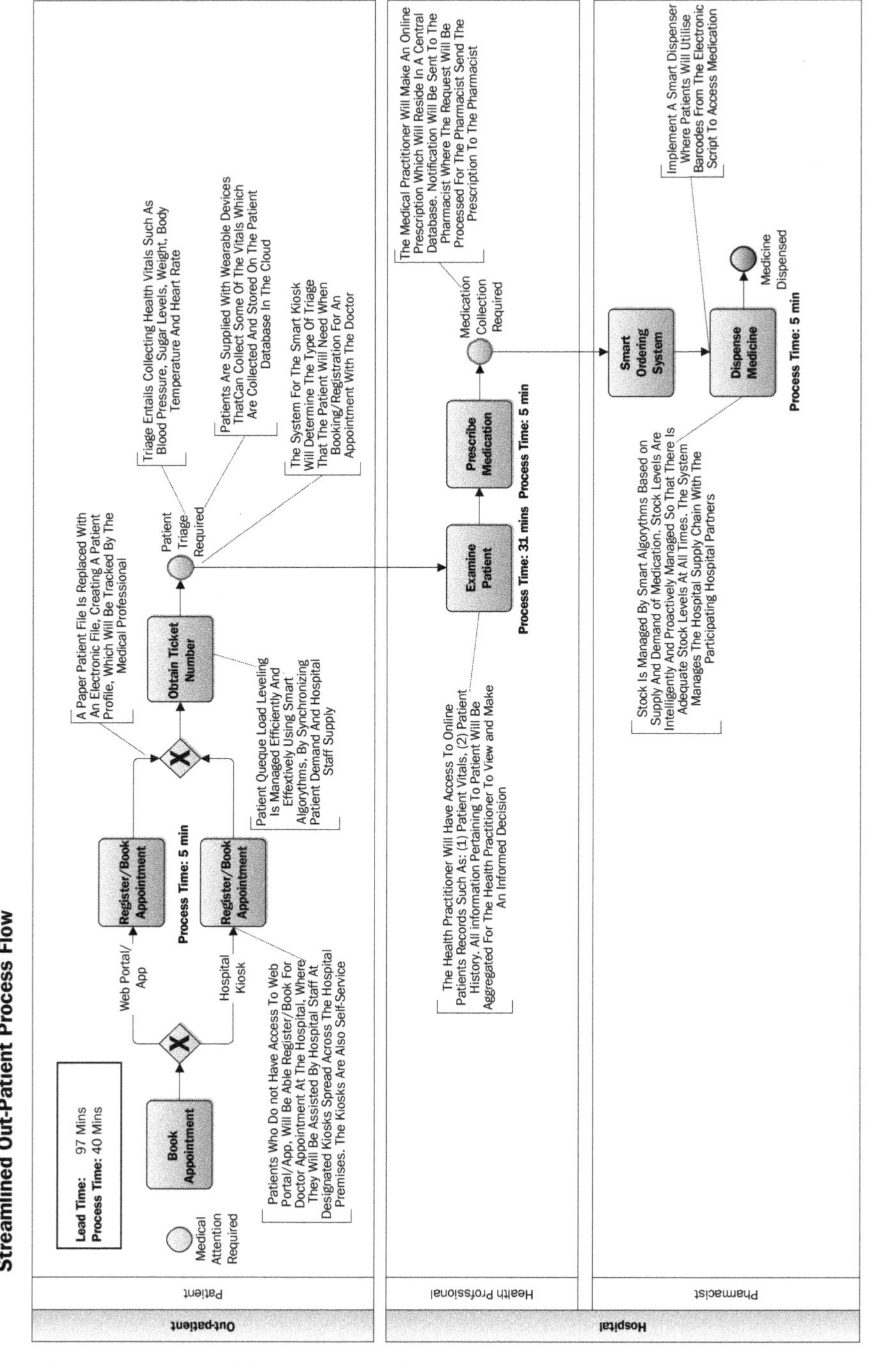

Figure 2.3 Process Map of Operations — Future State Outpatient Business Process

Value Stream Map Analysis

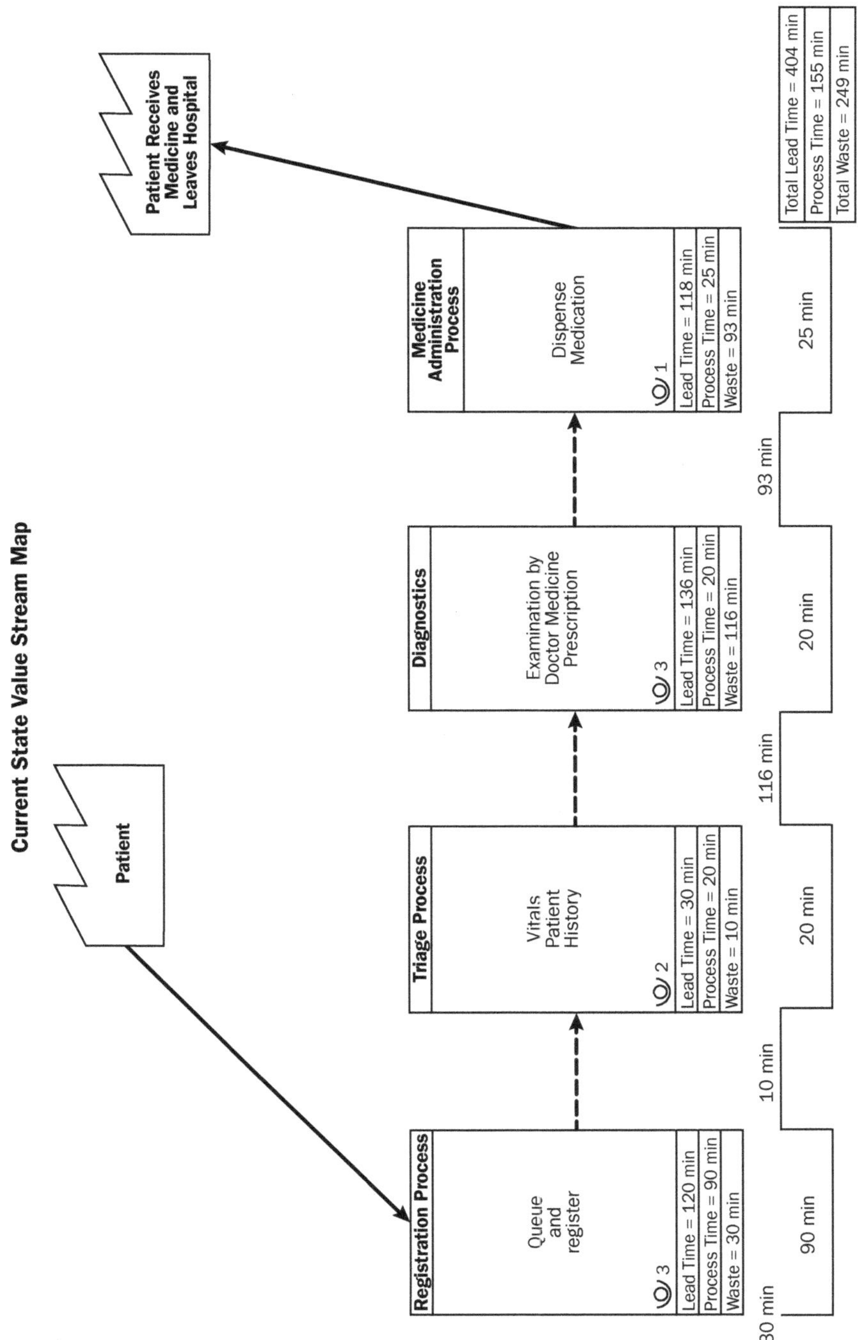

Figure 2.4 Current State Value Stream Map

Value Stream Analysis

Performance Objectives

Effective and efficient operations performance play a vital role for patients who will be experiencing the services offered by the hospital. The performance objectives will play a crucial role in guiding the business process improvement initiative that will be undertaken. The performance objectives that will guide the analysis are (LaMarco, 2019):

- **Cost** – Establish the productivity levels of the health and support staff while providing services to patients.
- **Dependability** – How dependable is the hospital service delivery from a customer perspective?
- **Flexibility** – How flexible are the internal operations in being able to adjust to high demand?
- **Quality** – How do patients perceive the quality of services rendered to them?
- **Speed** – How efficient are the hospital internal processes (Nigel Slack A. B.-J., 2019)?

Removing Non-value-Adding Activities (Waste)

The following non-value-adding activities will be identified in the processes under consideration:

- **Waiting** – How can we remove non-value-adding activities from the process, so that we can decrease the patient waiting times?
- **Transportation** – How can we remove non-value-adding activities that move patients from one department to another?
- **Defects/Mistakes** – How do we minimise something being done wrong and fixing it later e.g. wrong test being ordered, wrong diagnosis?
- **Overprocessing** – How do we prevent hospital staff, including the patient, from doing more work than is needed, e.g. asking patients to fill in duplicate forms, ordering and completing unnecessary laboratory tests?
- **Motion** – How do we prevent hospital staff from moving unnecessarily within the hospital premises?
- **Overproducing** – How do we prevent producing more than is needed? e.g. delaying patient discharge?
- **Inventory** – How do we prevent the build-up of patients waiting for services, e.g. patients waiting for admission (Ronald G. Bercaw, 2018)?

Optimised/Streamlined Processes

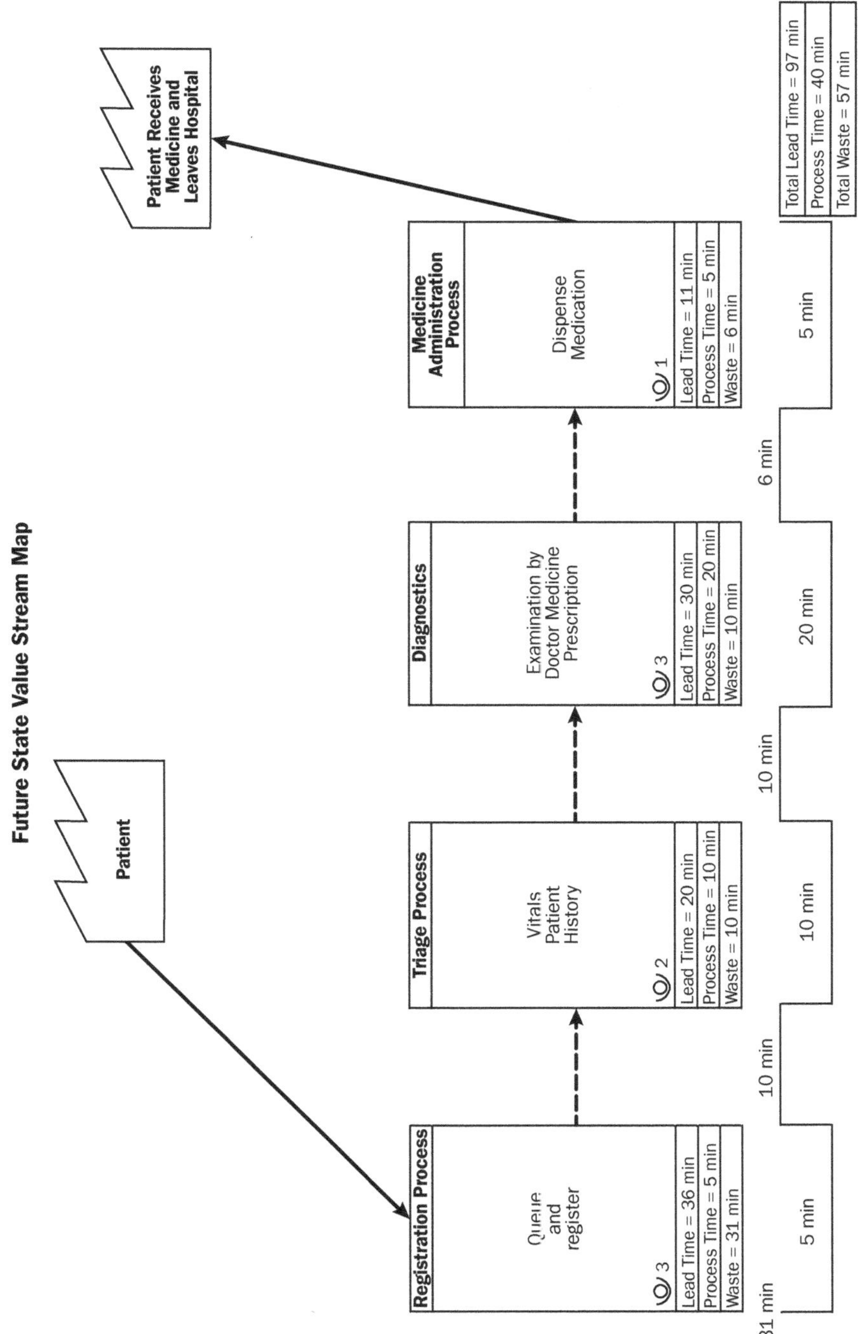

Figure 2.5 Future State Value Stream Map

GAP ANALYSIS

Table 2.1 Current Business Process

Description	Times
Total lead time	404 minutes
Process time	155 minutes
Waste	249 minutes

Table 2.2 Future State Business Process

Description	Times
Total lead time	97 minutes
Process time	40 minutes
Waste	57 minutes

Step 1: Identification for areas of improvement: Reduction of average outpatient waiting time from 6 hours and 44 minutes to 1 hour and 37 minutes.

Step 2: Analysis of the current state: In most government hospitals patients are unhappy with the long waiting times they are subjected to before they can get the needed medical attention. Table 2.1 shows a waiting time of 6 hours and 44 mins. This is an indication of business processes that need to be streamlined.

Step 3: Definition of end goal: The end goal is to have efficient and effective business processes at government hospitals. Outpatients should at most wait for 1 hour 21 minutes.

Step 4: Understanding the gap: The gap will involve closing the gaps between current business process and future state business processes as shown in Tables 2.1 and 2.2 above.

Step 5: Determining plan of action: A project will be set up to enable the transition from the current state to the future state. Key activities will involve:

- Streamlining the current outpatient process so as to reduce non-value-adding activities.
- Digitising the operations after streamlining the outpatient process.
- Facilitation of effective change management, including new ways of working and cultural change to a culture that is customer-centric.
- Consider the use of lean-six sigma in managing the operations while embracing a culture of continuous improvement (Izquierdo, 2022).

JUSTIFICATION FOR DAS MODEL

Many of the hospital processes are manual, data is hard to find in real-time and there is a lack of co-ordination among the health professional within hospitals (Kumar, 2018). With the vision of providing responsive and value-based health care digital transformation is required to improve the healthcare system. A digitally enabled health care system will provide efficient services to the patients (Akhter, 2017).

The DAS model allows us to analyse the extent to which the operations in the health department are digitalised and to guide the strategic decisions to digitalise operations.

The aim is to provide smart and automated patient-centric operations that improve the journey of the patient. The smart operations include patient satisfaction feedback, efficient healthcare, real-time health records, activity tracking, early warnings and a centralised system where data can be sourced. The expected outcome is improved efficiency in hospital operations, improved treatment and reduced patient waiting times at hospitals.

ATTAINING PERFORMANCE IMPROVEMENT

To improve performance of the Gauteng Health department we have used the Lean approach to optimise operations. The objective is to be customer centric, provide customers with value and eliminate waste in processes. Amazon is a perfect example of successful application of Lean operations as one of the most customer-centric companies in the world (Ruane, 2022).

The key areas of concern in Gauteng hospitals are the long waiting times of patients, irregular expenditure and wasteful expenditure. In the value stream analysis, it was identified that there is a lot of waste in the current processes. The operations were then streamlined to eliminate waste and smart automation was recommended.

The proposed solution includes smart operations where the patient journey can be tracked with timestamps to measure the time spent. The operations also include patient satisfaction feedback, which will assist in continuous improvement in areas of frustration. The operations will also include an automated dispenser with smart ordering, which will ensure medical supplies are always at the expected levels. The smart kiosks will determine the type of triage patients require and ensure queue load levelling. The operations will be integrated to ensure data is centralised – this will result in a synchronised flow.

IMPLEMENTATION PROJECT PLAN

Project Goals
The goal of this project is to optimise patient registration and consultations.

Assumptions
- **Executive support and advocacy** – Leadership team will commit to the project and support the implementation team.
- **Resource allocation** – People with skills and expertise will be allocated the project for the duration they are required.
- **Health professionals' availability** – Staff will be made available to participate in the project activities such as requirement gathering and process review and documentation. They will also be released to attend training and other enabling activities which will assist in efficient execution of their future tasks.
- **Budget** – An estimated budget will be made available to resource the project.
- **Service providers** – They will be available and allocate skilled resources to the project.

Project Stakeholders
Stakeholders for this project are defined as individuals and or institutions which will be impacted by this project or have input or vested interest. These have been summarised in the table below.

Table 2.3 Stakeholder Matrix

Low impact, high influence	High impact, high influence
Gauteng Department of Health Health Minister National Treasury	The Board Exco Project Team Service provider
Low impact, low influence	**High Impact, low influence**
Media Medical aid and insurance companies	Patients Health Professionals Hospital Managers

Project Duration
Planned duration for this project is 15 months.

Table 2.4 Project Plan

Project phase	Activities	Duration
Initiation	Define project scope	3 months
	Obtain budget	
	Resource the project	
	Conduct stakeholder analysis	
Design and build	Conduct as-is process analysis	6 months
	Identify processes to be streamlined	
	Define streamlining approach	
	Conduct technology gap assessment	
	Design to-be business process	
	Acquire required technology, licensing and subscriptions	
	Develop to-be processes	
	Streamline processes	
Implementation	Digitise identified to-be business process	6 months
	Test the processes	
	The technology implemented	
	Perform systems integration testing	
	Train the employees	
	Deploy the streamlined process into the environment	
Close out	Document the project close out report	1 month
	Hand over the project to the business	
	Roll the project resources off the project	
Post implementation	Provide user support to ensure transition into the new ways of work	3 months

Table 2.5 Resource Plan

Resource Requirements	Type of Resource	No. of resources
Project Team	Project Manager	1 senior, 1 junior
	Solution Architect	2 seniors
	Business Analyst	2 seniors
	Process Engineer	1 senior

Resource Requirements	Type of Resource	No. of resources
	People Change Manager	1 senior
	Data Engineer	2 seniors
	Software Developer	1 senior, 1 junior
	BI Specialist	2 seniors
	Security Specialist	1 senior
Technology	Hardware	
	Software and subscriptions	
	Infrastructure	

Project Budget

Total budget allocated to this project is **R160 000 000** and this will be allocated as follows:

Table 2.6 Project Budget

Project item	Cost (R)
Project management (professional fees)	25 000 000
Human Resources – hiring new staff members	15 000 000
Technology – hardware	40 000 000
Technology – software and subscriptions	50 000 000
Technology – infrastructure	23 000 000
Training	5 000 000
Post implementation support	2 000 000
Total	160 000 000

Risks and Mitigation

The following risks have been identified and will need to be mitigated to ensure successful delivery of the project. This will depict the possible risks and mitigation strategies.

Table 2.7 Risks and Mitigation

Risk	Mitigation
Third-party security breach	Develop SLA and OLA in line with data privacy policies to manage the contracts
Lack of buy-in and commitment from the project executive stakeholders	Include the project role as part of the KPIs
Budget constraints	Ensure that appropriate funds are approved and released into the project
Delay in project timelines due to delays in technology delivery challenges	Have contracts with multiple service to enable effective supply chain processes

WHAT IS ACHIEVED?

Reduced Patient Waiting Times

The streamlined and digitised operations will ensure wastages are removed – this will lead to quicker process times, which means the time patients spend at the hospital is reduced.

Improved Doctor–Patient Co-ordination

Digitisation means hospitals can maintain digital health records of patients. Electronic health records eliminate the need for physical files, which may be damaged or lost. Electronic health records may be stored on the cloud so doctors can access patient records as they need them (Rutkevich, 2019).

Automated Administrative Tasks

Having automated administrative tasks allows medical practitioners to spend more time attending to patients. Much of the time spent by the staff in hospitals is on administrative tasks which add no value to the patients. Automating these tasks therefore reduces the burden on staff, freeing up time for them to do valuable tasks (Rutkevich, 2019).

Data Security

Data security in any digital system is important, and it is no different in health systems. Implementing data security will not only protect sensitive patient data but also ensure that the data is only accessed by authorised personnel (Rutkevich, 2019).

Real-time Health Information

A patient's medical history will be readily available to doctors to allow them to make quick decisions when attending to patients (Krohn, 2020). The hospitals in the Gauteng Health Department will be integrated to ensure quick data flow among the different systems.

CONCLUSION

The proposed solution considered the challenges facing the Gauteng health sector including resource limitations, long patient waiting times and dissatisfaction, and current legacy systems. The main objective is to solve the patient's problem and make their visit to the hospital easier.

In line with the performance objectives the proposed operations will ensure that the costs of providing health care to patients are kept low by limiting supply chain irregularities and wasteful expenditure. Speed will be enhanced to ensure that waiting times are reduced – this will be achieved by speedy movement of required materials, data and decision-making. Using the feedback received, the care provided to patients can be kept consistent with their expectations. The operations will be flexible to adapt to the changing requirements of the patients. The proposed operations will also ensure timely delivery of services as promised to the patients.

ACKNOWLEDGEMENT OF CONTRIBUTORS

- Mamakhethe Zulu
- Mzwandile Mdladla
- Dalitso Chindongo

(All are affiliated to the Wits Business School, University of the Witwatersrand, Johannesburg).

REFERENCES

Akhter, S. (2017, October 18). IoT will make healthcare more accurate, consistent and affordable: Chris Sulliva. Retrieved from https://health. economictimes.indiatimes.com/: https://health.economictimes.indiatimes. com/news/industry/iot-with-make-healthcare-more-accurate-consistent-and-affordable-chris-sullivan/61111297

Buswell, G. (2022, July 8). The healthcare system in South Africa. Retrieved from https://www.expatica.com/za/healthcare/healthcare-basics/healthcare-in-south-africa-105896/

Bercaw, R., Knoth, K. A., Snedaer, M. B. A. (2018). *The Lean Electronic Health Record.* Boca Raton: CRC Press.

Chokkalingam, V. (2022, April 1). Digital Transformation in Healthcare in 2022: Key Trends. Retrieved from transcenddigital: https://www.transcenddigital.com/blog/digital-transformation-healthcare-2022

Gauteng Provincial Government. (2021). *Gauteng Department of Health Annual Report.* Johannesburg: Gauteng Provincial Government.

Izquierdo, R. (2022, May 18). How to Execute a Gap Analysis. Retrieved from https://www.fool.com/the-ascent/small-business/project-management/articles/gap-analysis

Krohn, R. (2020, July 30). The real-time health system: Adapting healthcare to the new normal. Retrieved from https://www.healthcareitnews.com/blog/real-time-health-system-adapting-healthcare-new-normal

Kumar, S. (2018). Digitization of Hospital Services and Operations: A Conceptual Framework. *International Journal of Healthcare Education & Medical Informatics*, 1–5.

LaMarco, N. (2019, August 3). Objectives of Operational Performance. Retrieved from CHRON: https://smallbusiness.chron.com/evaluate-companys-performance-67095.html

Lavers, J. (2020, September 9). South African healthcare industry and digital transformation. Retrieved from https://www.itweb.co.za/content/DZQ58MVPLkmvzXy2

Ruane, J. (2022, May 1). *What Is Lean Operations and How Can I Use It to Save Money?* Retrieved from https://www.beekeeper.io/blog/lean-operations/

Rutkevich, J. (2019). 5 Benefits of Digitization in the Healthcare Industry. Retrieved from Digital Health Buzz: https://digitalhealthbuzz.com/5-benefits-of-digitization-in-the-healthcare-industry/

Sicetsha, A. (2019, July 17). Here's how long patients wait to get assistance at Gauteng hospitals. Retrieved from https://www.thesouthafrican.com/news/gauteng-hospitals-how-long-patients-wait-to-get-assistance/

Slack, N., A. Brandon-Jones, A., Johnston, R. (2013). *Operations Management,* 7th edn. Harlow: Pearson.

Slack, N., A. Brandon-Jones, A. (2019). *Global and Southern Africa Perspectives Operations Management.* Cape Town: Pearson.

Virtua. (2021). Hospital queue management system. Retrieved from https://virtuaq.com/healthcare: https://virtuaq.com/healthcare

Willie, M. M. (2020). Digital Transformation In Healthcare – South African Context. *World Medical Journal*, 35–38.

CHAPTER 3

Digitalising Operations for the Electoral Commission*

INTRODUCTION

As a democratic country, South Africa allows participation in free and fair elections, which means all inhabitants 18 years of age and older are legally eligible to vote. The national and provincial elections are held once every five years at polling stations across the country.

The Electoral commission was established by the Constitution of the Republic of South Africa as an independent body to ensure the election process is fair and citizens are allowed to exercise their votes in such a manner. The Electoral commission is only subject to the Constitution and the law. This independent commission must operate impartially by exercising its powers and performing its functions without fear, favour, or prejudice. The Electoral commission is responsible to the National Assembly.

Who constitutes the Electoral commission?

The commission consists of commissioners appointed through a public process and officiated by the President of South Africa for seven years, renewable once. The Electoral commission comprises five members, one of whom is a judge (Electoral Commission, 2022).

What is the Electoral commission responsible for?

The Electoral commission:
- Oversees elections of national, provincial and municipal legislative bodies;
- Confirms that the elections are free and impartial;

---

* This case has been compiled by the contributors based on information available in the public domain. This case is just a practical depiction how digitalising can improve the operations.

- Declares the results of the elections;
- Compiles and maintains a voters' roll; and
- Maintains a register of parties.

The Electoral commission also undertakes electoral research matters and develops and promotes the development of electoral expertise and technology in all spheres of government. Noting this undertaking of continuous improvement, we have developed a proposed solution to integrate the above elements into a technology-driven solution which will address some critical concerns that the Electoral commission currently faces:

- The manual voting process allows for a high error rate, increased corruption, loss of votes;
- Queueing physically at polling stations;
- Counting of ballots allows for human error;
- Duration of time taken to count ballots physically;
- Corruption in the process of measuring and favouring political parties; and
- The elderly and differently abled must queue in line to vote when unique votes are not requested well in advance.

CURRENT PROCESS MAP

The current process illustrated below in Figure 3.1 was retrieved from the Electoral commission website (Electoral Commission of South Africa, 2014). The process depicted has been converted into an infographic, which has been redone using Lucid to demonstrate the process for voting using the standard process mapping symbols.

The first step involves the individual registering for voting in their designated voting district. This is done before the presiding government publishes the confirmed election dates. It is noted that re-registration is required if one has changed domicile, even if this is a short distance, as it might have changed the voting district one falls within (Electoral Commission of South Africa, 2022).

On the confirmed dates scheduled for voting, individuals must go to the voting station and follow the defined process illustrated in Figure 3.1. They present their South African Identity Document (ID), which could be the green bar-coded ID book, smart ID card or a temporary ID certificate, to the official. The official must check that their names appear on the voters' roll. If they are not on the voters' roll but have proof that they have registered (e.g. registration sticker), the Presiding

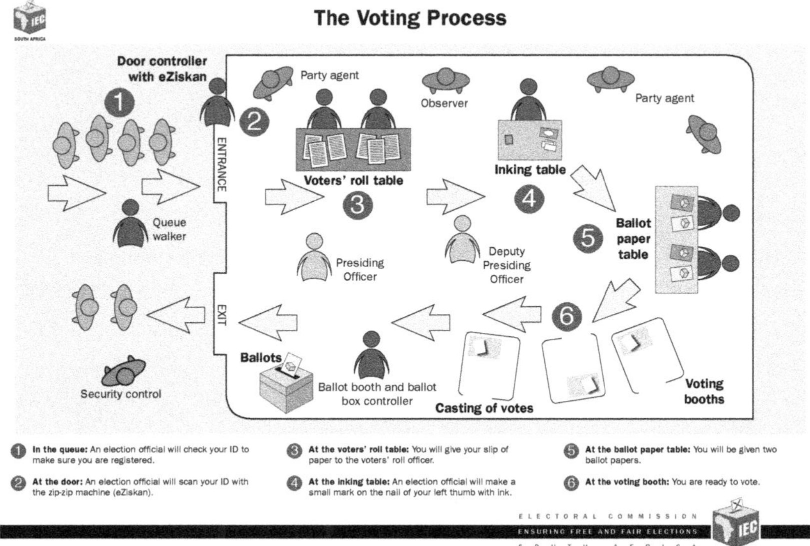

Figure 3.1 The Voting Process

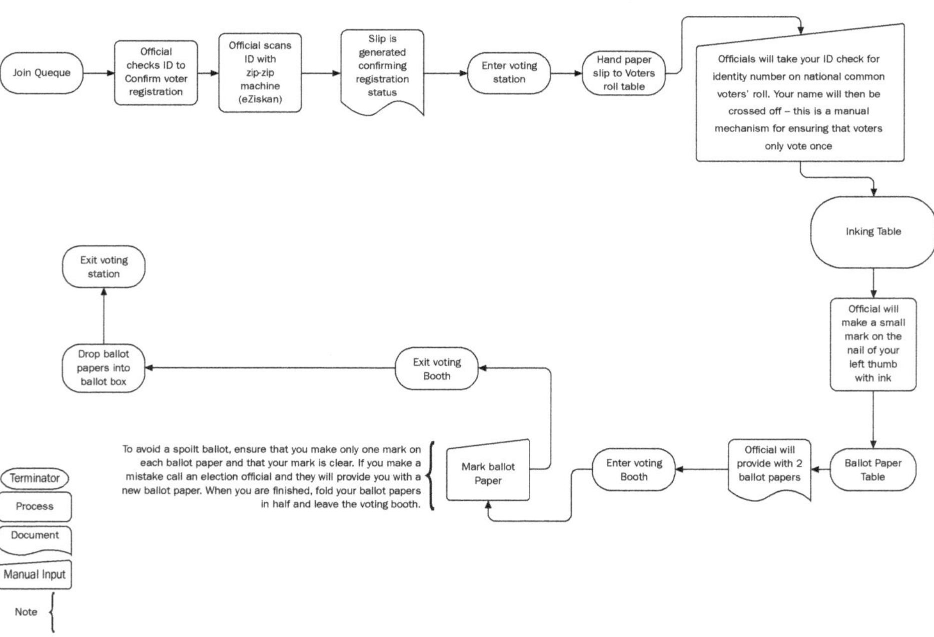

Figure 3.2 The Voting Process (Lucid Process Map)

Officer must validate the proof of registration. If he or she is pleased with the evidence, prospective voters must complete a VEC4 form (national elections) or MEC7 form (municipal elections). They will then be permitted to continue as ordinary voters (Electoral Commission of South Africa, 2022).

Once the voting officer is pleased that a voter has the correct ID, is a listed voter and has not previously voted, their name is marked off the roll, and their thumbnail is inked. The voting officer imprints the back of the accurate number of authorised ballot papers (one per election) and provides them to the voter. Voters take their ballot paper/s to an empty ballot booth, mark the ballot paper, fold it so their choice isn't visible and place the ballot paper in the ballot box.

VALUE STREAM ANALYSIS

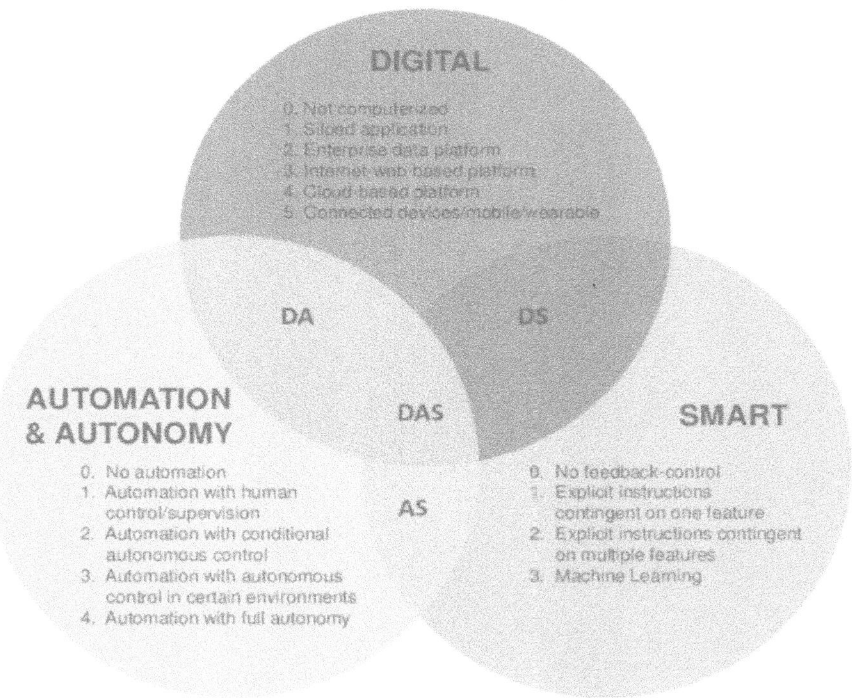

Figure 3.3 DAS Model

Using the DAS model to assess the Electoral commission and the current process for the public to vote, we notice they are low on the scale, and significant improvements can be made.

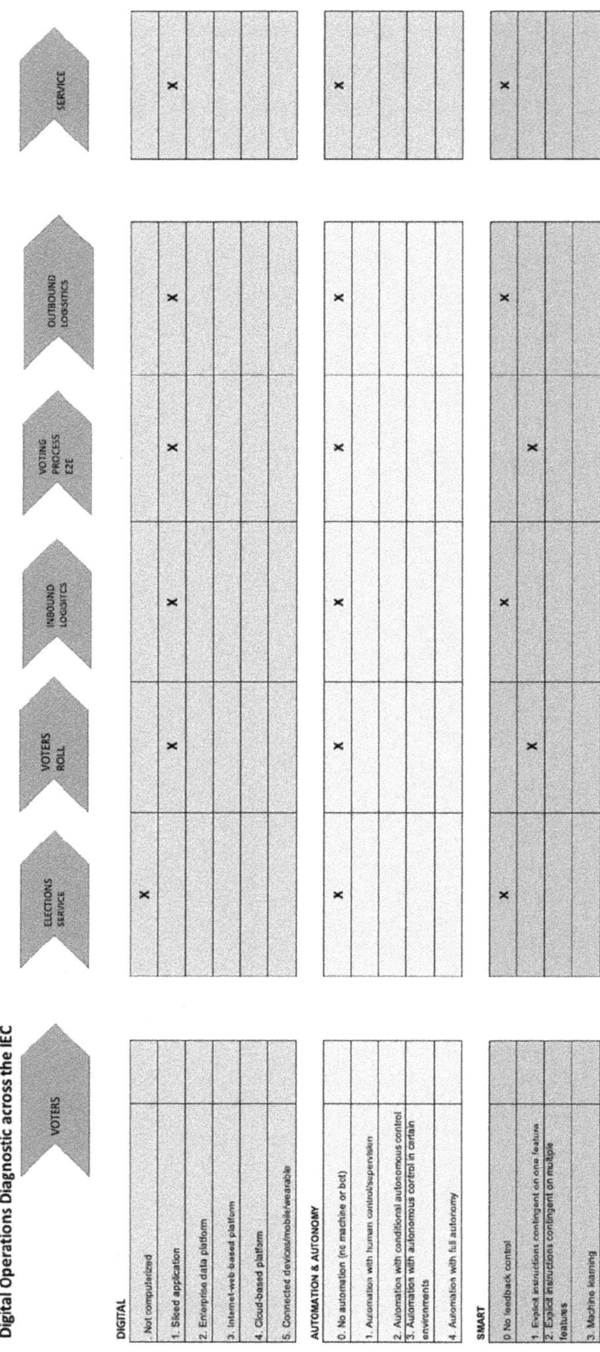

Figure 3.4 DAS Analysis

IDENTIFICATION OF THE PROBLEM AND THE PROPOSED SOLUTION

The global pandemic has forced South Africa to re-evaluate how our nation functions and highlighted how government and private organisations adapted to digital change. Logically, our problem statement is voting and elections in South Africa through the Electoral commission, which has raised concerns about the viability of manual paper-based elections. In our interpretation of the problem, introducing the digital voting (e-voting) system in South Africa will solve many problems; however, the electronic system produces differences of opinion.

THE CURRENT ELECTORAL LANDSCAPE

In 2020, the Department of Home Affairs (DHA) introduced the Electoral Laws Amendment Bill (Electoral Bill), which introduced requirements allowing the Electoral commission to propose a digital method of voting for national, provincial, and local elections. Section 38 of the Electoral Act 73 of 1998 and the Municipal Electoral Act 27 of 2000 explains the voting process: a registered voter presents their identity document to a designated Electoral commission officer, who validates the voter's identity and verifies that their name appears on the voters' roll. The voter's fingernail is then marked by an agreed method, and then the voters are allowed to cast their ballot paper using manual paper-based procedures.

The concerns raised in response to the proposal of an electronic voting system include:

- Parliament delegated its constitutional authority to the Electoral commission, which allows the committee to decide on voting procedures through legislation.
- In South Africa's current economy, implementing e-voting would be expensive, as it would require the government to purchase hardware and software for catering to the entire voting population.
- From a security perspective, the e-voting system may be susceptible to manipulation and could increase the possibility of democratic fraud.
- If there are inadequate verification processes, genuine concern with e-voting is that any political party may manipulate the outcome.
- Lastly, communities without access to digital technologies cannot be overlooked and need to be catered for.

OUR PROPOSED FUTURE ELECTORAL LANDSCAPE

Estonia, a country in northern Europe neighbouring the Baltic Sea and the Gulf of Finland, piloted digital voting in 2005 for its elections. Voters were invited to log onto the online system using their identity cards; however, the system conceals each voter's identity until their vote reaches the Electoral commission for calculation. Voters were also provided with the option of altering their votes. By implementing the digital system, Estonia reported that the system had saved the state 11 000 working days (Team, 2022).

Our primary argument in favor of e-voting is efficiency. As the country of Estonia has demonstrated, e-voting reduces manual labour and decreases human error during the electoral process, explicitly during vote counting. Using digital systems would enable the Electoral commission to announce results faster, if not immediately. A digital voting system has also demonstrated the ability to assist illiterate or disabled voters. An example of the technology used as an audio interface may be made available to visually impaired voters. In our opinion, digital voting systems could enhance the electoral experience and enable the constitutional right to vote if adequately implemented.

A clear and comprehensive legal framework is necessary if South Africa incorporates digital voting technologies. However, there are international standards on e-voting technology to take into consideration. In 2004, the Council of Europe developed and adopted recommendations on standards of e-voting (updated in 2017). Some of their suggestions, outlined in 'Democracy 2.0: Digital voting systems', are:

- the electronic voting interface should be easy to understand and use;
- where e-voting and non-electronic voting channels are used during the same election, there should be a protected and dependable method to aggregate all votes;
- voters' identification should be verifiable;
- the components of the e-voting system should be disclosed for verification and certification purposes; and
- only individuals sanctioned by the electoral committee shall have access to the central infrastructure, servers, and election data.

DIGITISED VOTING PROCESS OPTIMISED

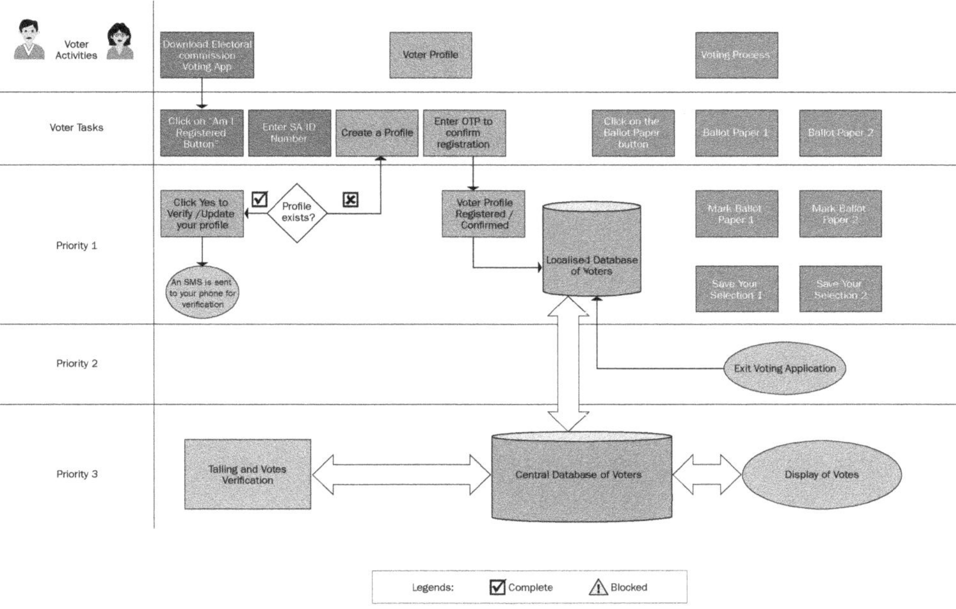

Figure 3.5 Digitised Voting Process Refined

Voting technology has evolved throughout the years, and the Electoral commission find itself in a unique position to stay pertinent and keep up with the digital revolution. This was spurred on by the pandemic and recent challenges faced within South Africa. The new proposed voting platform for conducting elections online would enable all eligible voters to cast their votes from any location.

Identity authentication secures the voting process when the voter logs into the system. The use of a unique South Africa ID number, which the voter types in at the login page, prompts the system to send an OTP (One Time Pin) to their mobile device; only after they have entered the OTP will they be allowed into the system. After that, the voter can cast their vote securely, and the system will flag the ID number in the database and automatically log them out as they click submit after they select the candidate of their choice.

PERFORMANCE IMPROVEMENT

Voting Process - Manual versus Digital

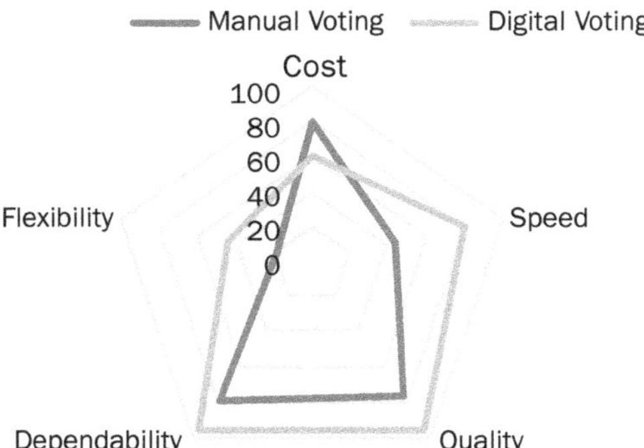

Figure 3.6 Polar Diagram of Manual Versus Digital Voting Process

The polar graph above compares the current manual voting process and the proposed digitised voting process for the Electoral commission. Using the five operations management benefits, our analysis is as follows:

Cost: At the start of digitisation, the price will be high as the Electoral commission would need to purchase digital devices used in the process. Overall, there would be the benefit of not printing ballots as voters would be using their digital devices to vote (cell phones, computers, and tablets) and minimal transportation cost of devices from stations to voting sites.

Speed: A digitised voting process gives the Electoral commission the advantage of providing fast and efficient results to voters as there is no manual counting and tallying of votes. This would minimise the disputes between political parties and the risk that votes get lost or damaged during transportation, commonly referred to as 'spoilt votes'.

Quality: A digitised voting process avoids tampering with votes. The Electoral commission can check whether a person has attempted to vote more than once and reduce the possibility of counting errors as results can be calculated automatically.

Dependability: Voters in urban areas will benefit from digitised voting due to the accessibility of internet networks. Rural areas may experience challenges when it comes to locations. According to Makwakwa (2021), the digitisation of elections might address the issue of voter turnout, particularly among young people. Blockchain technology will secure the votes, addressing cyber security concerns.

Flexibility: (USA.gov, 2018) noted that the ability to vote from the comfort of your home reduces the need to travel to the polling station for sick voters and those with disabilities have any disability. As much as digitised voting is convenient, it also brings some concerns related to usability, fraud, secrecy, and other security issues (Bam et al., 2016).

ASSUMPTIONS

The individual user's vote will be guaranteed confidentiality as the ID document verification is not linked to the ballot but only used as the control check to allow the user to cast their vote.

The digital voting system will also cater to assist illiterate or disabled voters.

Reduced numbers of voters at polling stations will allow for the elderly and people without access to smart devices to be assisted by the Electoral commission officials.

Smart devices to assist the elderly at polling stations will need to be developed linked to DHA to validate ID numbers and eliminate duplicate votes – biometric-enabled.

Hybrid operating models began with digital voting via smart app and polling stations with devices to assist those without access to devices.

Political party adoption is imperative so that the processes can be free and fair.

International and local observers will have access to the audit logs for verification of no external factors influencing the voting process (Electoral Commission of South Africa, 2022).

PROJECT PLAN

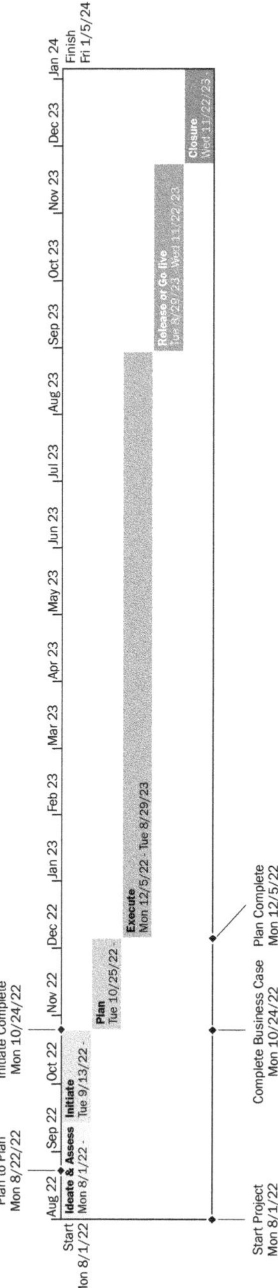

Figure 3.7 Project Plan

The high-level assumption for completing the project is estimated at 359 days, starting on 1 August 2022, as depicted in the Gantt chart in Figure 3.7 above, which addresses digital operational advancements. Subsequent change management must continue to post the technology change to ensure the refined process is adopted.

RESOURCE REQUIREMENTS

Funding for Development: The app and website will require funding from the government to develop, train, and roll out nationally and internationally for ex-pat voting.

Software Development Capability: The Electoral commission would need technical resources to develop and maintain an application platform to build the voting app and secure website.

Software and Hardware Infrastructure: The infrastructure required to facilitate the online voting will need to be purchased. This includes a data management facility (e.g., AWS and Fortinet as cloud and security tools).

Training and Development: This involves user engagement, understanding issues throughout the testing phase and the ability to convert negative sentiments into optimistic consumers of the service.

CONCLUSION

While some advantages and disadvantages come with the adoption of technology in any industry, the Electoral commission will only improve their service delivery to greater South Africa by introducing an e-voting platform that promotes a free and fair election service. Globally electronic voting technology intends to speed the counting of ballots, reduce the number of staff needed to count votes manually and provide improved accessibility for voters (Benefits and risks of e-voting and on-line voting, 2020).

The investment in this new system is expected to pay off in the long term, as running expenses are anticipated to decrease significantly and save time and costs for the current and future voters of South Africa.

ACKNOWLEDGEMENT OF CONTRIBUTORS

- Frank Ramabale
- Prema Arunajalam
- Trevor Naidoo
- Wesley Naidoo

(All are affiliated to the Wits Business School, University of the Witwatersrand, Johannesburg).

REFERENCES

Bam, Dr. B., Soudriette, R., Quraishi, D. S.Y., Jega, Dr. A. M., Zurita, Dr. L. V., DeGregorio, P., Lasham, C. (2016). 'The Future of Elections'. The International Elections Advisory Council. Retrieved from The International Elections Advisory website: http://www.thefutureofelections.com/ download/the-future-of-elections-report.pdf

Benefits and risks of e-voting and online voting. (2020, November 2). Retrieved from https://decentralization.gov.ua/en/news/12905

Electoral Commission of South Africa. (2014, February 5). Retrieved from https://www.elections.org.za/pw/Downloads/Documents-Election-Guides.

Electoral Commission of South Africa. (2022, July 7). Retrieved from https:// www.elections.org.za/pw/Voter/How-To-Vote.

Electoral Commission of South Africa. (2022, July 11). *About Us.* Retrieved from https://www.elections.org.za/pw/About-Us/Organogram.

Electoral Commission of South Africa. (2022, July 7). Moved since you registered. Retrieved from https://www.elections.org.za/pw/Voter/Moved-Since-You-Registered.

Electoral Commission of South Africa. (2022, July 11). Observers. Retrieved from https://www.elections.org.za/pw/Elections-And-Results/Observers.

Elections | South African Government. (2022). Elections South Africa. https:// www.gov.za/taxonomy/term/711.

Electoral commission Home – Electoral Commission of South Africa. (2022b). Electoral commission. https://www.elections.org.za/pw/.

Electoral commission Organogram - Electoral Commission of South Africa. (2022). Electoral commission. https://www.elections.org.za/pw/About-Us/ Organogram

Makwakwa, T. (2021, November 2). Calls to digitise the elections grow as local government election results filter through. Retrieved July 11, 2022, from https://www.iol.co.za/dailynews/news/kwazulu-natal/calls-to-digitise-the

elections-grow-as-local-government-election-results-start-filtering-through-396a1fa3-e684-497f-b883-8f06f849664f

Polar Diagram Definition PDF | What is Polar Diagram? & Explanation | MBA Supply Chain Management. (2022). What Is Polar Diagram? Retrieved 2022, from https://techleens.com/mba/scm/what-is-polar-diagram.php.

USA.gov. (2018). Absentee and Early Voting | USAGov. Retrieved July 9, 2022, from https://www.usa.gov/absentee-voting

CHAPTER 4

Practical Case of Operations Optimisation for Insurance Claims: A Viewpoint

INTRODUCTION

The key to ensuring that the customer, strategy and technology all work together to generate maximum value across the value chain is having a robust operations ecosystem (PricewaterhouseCoopers, 2018). The digitisation of business operations provides organisations with opportunities to improve the efficiency of workflow processes and the quality of interactions with customers (Verhoef, Broekhuizen, Bart, Bhattacharya, Qi Dong, Fabian, & Haenlein, 2021). However, Chan and Shukor (2018) suggest that this can only be accomplished if an organisation possesses the necessary competencies, alliances, technology and a plan to accelerate efficiency and effectiveness.

The management of operations is critical to the survival of any organisation. The technology available in the twenty-first century provides organisations with numerous opportunities to develop and produce innovative products, services and experiences tailored to the market's ever-changing needs. Outdated operating models can make it difficult for the organisation to keep up with industry advancements.

The purpose of this case study is to assess the internal processes of an insurance company, more specifically the process followed by the claims department, to evaluate how digitisation might enhance processing times and overall workflows.

INDUSTRY OVERVIEW

The large volumes of paperwork that insurance companies typically process hinder everyday operations, speedy processing of customer claims and organisation workflows (Nkosi, 2020). The insurance industry is under pressure as consumers adopt new technologies. To thrive in the industry, insurers need to anticipate and embrace change (Kweilin Ellingrud, Kimura, Quinn, & Ralph, 2022).

In the past, it was standard practice for insurers to conduct in-person underwriting and claims processing evaluations. In the coming years, it is anticipated that the insurance industry will utilise advanced data analytics techniques to gain insights from consumer data. The insights gathered will then be exploited to enhance customer experience, underwriting and claims management (Kweilin et al., 2022). The promise of automated underwriting and claims processing, according to Phaneuf (2022), is that information collection may now be streamlined, resulting in fewer human touchpoints.

LIMRA (2020) reports that 25% of insurance companies have increased their use of automated underwriting practices. McKinsey (2021) states that 50% of claims activities have already been replaced by automation and 65% of insurance leaders anticipate spending more on robotic process automation in 2022 (Deloitte, 2021).

Due to the increased use of artificial intelligence (AI) and digitised claims, insurers have streamlined the previously disjointed claims management practices. This, in turn, leads to faster processing and reduced wait times for claims, ultimately resulting in more products being sold to customers.

INSURANCE COMPANY BACKGROUND

South Africa's political, violence and terrorism (PVT) insurance market has four main insurance pillars: terrorism and sabotage (S&T); strike, riot and civil commotion (SRCC); political violence; and war, including civil war. Commercial and private insurers in South Africa do not cover political or social unrest events because of the country's troubled history. Instead, traditional short-term insurers offer a Insurance Company (IC) cover option (Cupido, 2022).

The political instability in South Africa in the 1970s was a significant factor in the formation of Insurance Company SOC Ltd. Insurance Company is the only South African non-life insurer that offers protection against unique risks such as civil unrest, public disorder, strikes, riots and terrorism and has held a monopoly for 35 years (Molokoane, 2021). This protection extends to anyone who owns property in South Africa, whether an individual, a business, or a government (Mushai & MacGregor, 2016).

Insurance Company operational structure consists of a membership network pool comprising registered Short-Term Insurance Companies that underwrite the fire hazard and these insurers manage the distribution of Insurance Company products (Cupido, 2022). The Financial Sector Regulation Act also provides a comprehensive framework within which Insurance Company, along with all other insurance companies in South Africa, operates (Molokoane, 2021).

CLIENTS	COVERS	CLASS OF BUSINESS
• Individuals • Corporate • Municipalities • Small Business • Tertiary Institutions	• Primary Cover: asssets are insured for up to R500 million • Excess of Loss: additional cover for up to R1 Billon	• Material • Money • Goods in transit • Motor • Business interuption • Construction risk

Source: Authors' own

Detailed below is an analysis of Insurance Company 4Vs of operations:

PRODUCTS AND SERVICES

Volume (Medium to Low)
Insurance Company volume fluctuates between medium and low depending on different external factors such as riots, political instability etc., for example, the July 2021 riots increased the volume of claims being registered and their insurance cover caters to a variety of customer categories, including individuals, businesses and corporations, small business and tertiary institutions

Variation (Medium to Low)
Although insurance company offers two standard covers, the level of protection/cover varies based on the size and nature of the asset insured. IC also covers various types of special risk such as civil unrest public disorder, terrorism etc.

Variety (Medium)
Insurance offers two forms of coverage for special risks, however the levels of coverage vary between R500 million and R1 billion, and the cover options vary from material damage, motor, money, goods in transit and construction risk cover.

Visibility (Low)
Insurance company has relatively low visibility, but clients can still customise and expand their coverage at an additional fee. Among the options for extension are inflation of cover, claims preparation costs and security expenditures, etc.

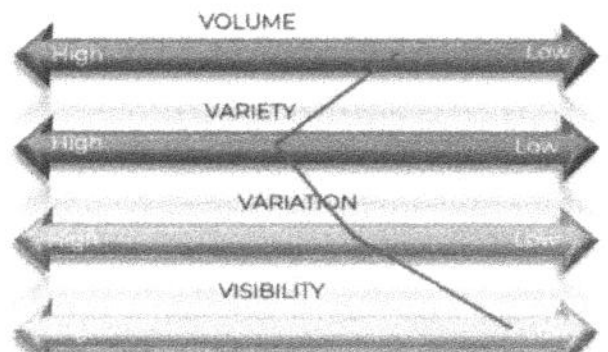

Source: Authors' own

SITUATION ANALYSIS

Current Situation

Typically, Insurance Company processes 25 claims a day. However, like most South Africans, Insurance Company was significantly affected by the civil unrest of July 2021, which saw them registering up to 70 claims daily (Insurance Company Communications, 2021). Consequently, a record number of claims were filed. According to Insurance Company communications (2021), 21 000 claims totalling R32 billion necessitated that Insurance Company increases its internal capacity and the mandate of its agents to process claims, assisted by their internal Underwriting and Legal team who assist with policy interpretation concerns.

Even though some claims have been resolved, a significant number remain outstanding for a variety of reasons, including Insurance Company needing to wait for clients to provide accurate information so that the claim can be quantified, clients experiencing difficulties in formulating claims, resulting in delays and policy interpretation (Insurance Company communications, 2022). Given the rise in the number of claims, Insurance Company has also had to deal with instances of fraud and claim inflation. The significant challenges faced by the organisations are best summarised as:

- Unstructured data generated by emails requesting registration of claims;
- Inadequate internal capacity to handle claims;
- Lack of required documentation for registering claims;
- Fraudulent claims; and
- Delays in registering and settling claims

The Claims Process

The Claims department is responsible for registering, evaluating and paying claims. The department consists of 25 full-time equivalents and ten part-time equivalents brought in specifically to help with the increased claims volumes. Due to the growing backlog of unregistered claims, this assignment's analysis of the claims registration process was the focus.

Swim lane mapping is a popular tool for illustrating a step-by-step business process and its associated role players by combining a flowchart with a swim lane (ProcessMaker, 2020). The end-to-end claims registration process and the actors responsible for each activity were mapped and identified using swim lane mapping.

AS-IS Process Description

The claims registration comprises three actors, i.e., the Insurance Company client, broker, or agent, the Claims Management System (CMS) and Claims

Administrator and they are represented by a swim lane. The term 'actor' is taken from the Unified Modelling Language (UML) and specifies the role played by a person, software, or hardware in the context of a system (Object Management Group, Inc, 2007). See Appendix 4.A for a process narrative of the end-to-end process depicted below.

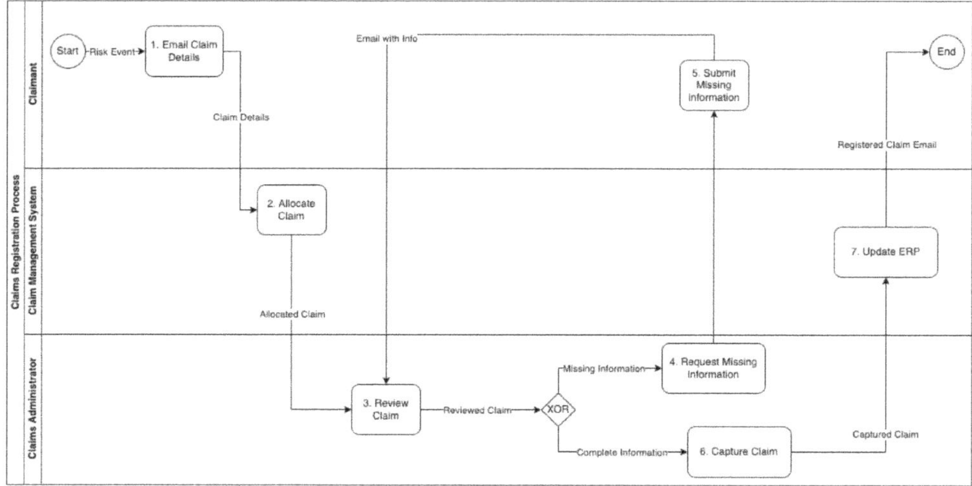

Figure 4.1 AS-IS Claims Registration Process

Understanding the Process Through Operations Process Objectives

It is imperative to have a tightly defined set of objectives when running an efficient operation. This is achieved by measuring the operation or process against five performance objectives: speed, cost, dependability, flexibility and quality (Slack et al., 2017). Speed refers to doing things fast. Costs assess how cheaply things get done. Dependability measures whether things are done on time. Flexibility indicates the extent to which the operation can respond to changes, e.g., volume and delivery. Finally, quality indicates how well the product or service is delivered (Slack et al., 2017).

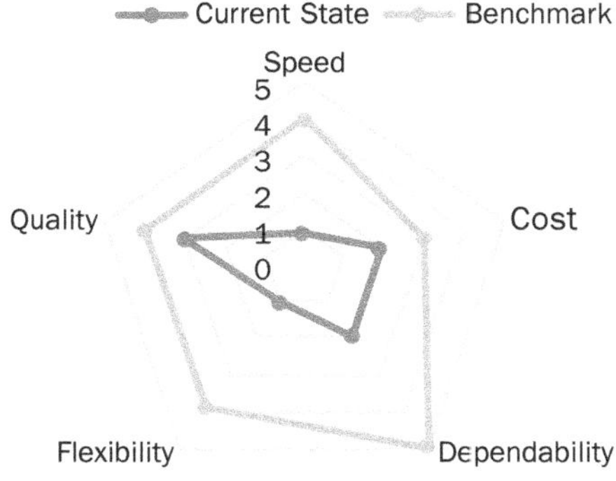

	Current State	Benchmark
Speed	1	4
Cost	2	3
Dependability	2	5
Flexibility	1	4
Quality	3	4

Figure 4.2 Current State Performance Objectives

When analysing the operations performance objectives through the polar diagram, it is apparent that the current claim registration operation underperforms the benchmark in every metric apart from cost. The process is expensive, slow, constantly breach internal service level agreements, unable to scale with demand and executes with mediocre quality.

Analysing the Claims Registration Process

The American Society for Quality (ASQ) defines Value Stream Mapping (VSM) as a lean tool for identifying waste in a process, reducing process cycle times and implementing process improvement (American Society for Quality, n.d.). VSM was used to understand better the causes of inefficiency in the claim registration process and analyse the process to optimise it accordingly.

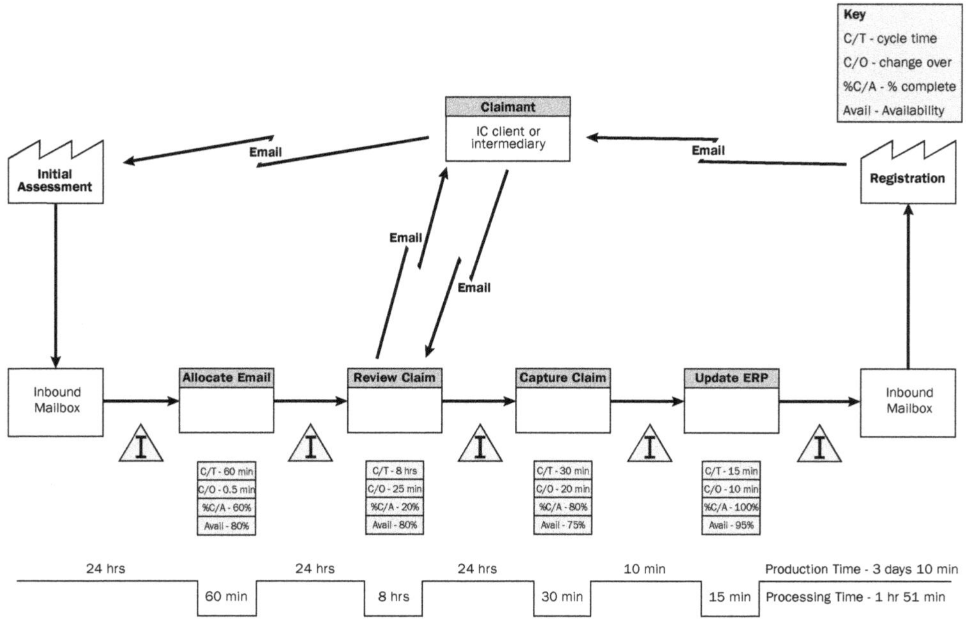

Figure 4.3 Current State Value Stream Map

Through the VSM analysis, it is observed that the clients submitting claims via email could wait up to 24 hours before it is allocated to a Claims Administrator for review. The allocation process completes within an hour, and the potential claim waits another 24 hours before it is reviewed. This wait is due to the system round robin assigning claims without regard for a Claim Administrator's queue depth or availability. It is also the reason behind the allocated claim process yielding a low complete and accurate percentage (%C/A) because the supervisor would have to reassign cases. On average, the review claim process takes eight hours to complete primarily due to incomplete information and the resultant activity to obtain the missing data. A reviewed claim could wait another 24 hours before it is captured on the system. The total production time of a submitted claim is three days and 10 minutes, while the processing or value-adding time is approximately two hours.

OPERATIONS SOLUTIONS

Haris (2016) defines the digital era as 'a period where a shift occurs from industrial-based to an information-based economy using a computer or other technology devices as medium of communication'. Insurance Company can achieve operational excellence by applying process design and digital (era) technology.

Internet Of Things (IoT)

IoT makes it more accessible, fast tracks insurers' decisions based on data and speeds up process times. It also enables clients to submit claims through mobile apps by taking pictures instead of filling out forms. Biometric and environmental sensors are examples of connected devices that make it easy to measure risk and change policy in response to new information (Morgan, 2021). Insurance Company can deploy IoT sensors to aid in monitoring infrastructure and through the creation of new channels to streamline the claim registration process.

Robotic Process Automation (RPA)

RPA in the insurance sector context would enable bots to perform the repetitive work of employees, such as collecting client data, extracting information from claims and performing background checks. RPA bots and web portals help accelerate the end-to-end claims procedure (Williams, 2021). By automating the claims filing activities process, Insurance Company can free up their employees' time to focus on addressing more pressing issues and disputing challenging claims.

Artificial Intelligence (AI)

Artificial intelligence can assist Insurance Company in risk assessment, fraud detection and minimising human claims processing errors. AI technology can automate processes to streamline the administrative process (Soberanis, 2021). Employees have more time to focus on challenging claims because machine learning algorithms can quickly identify warning signs in fraudulent claims and risk management data.

Big Data Analytics

It can take much time to collect, arrange and analyse data throughout the life of a claim, especially when handling several claims at once (Karle, 2019). When new information on a case is recorded, predictive analytics has the potential to provide real-time updates and notify claims management of any adverse developments (Karle, 2019). Insurance Company should ensure that a claim is handled by a person with the appropriate level of experience to find ways to reduce costs and resolve the claim as quickly as possible. Insurance Company will be able to swiftly identify the claims that are likely to be complex or expensive and take preventative measures to mitigate severity due to the use of AI and predictive analytics to rate claims by risk and severity (Smith, 2021).

Drones

Although this is not central to the solution at present, in future, assessors at Insurance Company can employ drone technology to improve access to damaged areas. An inspection requires multiple trips and can take up to two weeks; however, a drone can gather all the necessary information in just a few hours. The assessor will also be able to match footage from claims with footage from the original policy to determine the actual damage to confirm that an appropriate claim has been lodged.

TO-BE Process Description

The TO-BE claims registration process is re-engineered using process design and technology. An Insurance Company client can now register a claim using either a Chatbot solution or Online Portal integrated into the Claims Management System (CMS) using a Claims Robot. Where a claims administrator was validating received information and documents and then capturing the claim on CMS, this will now be carried out by the Claims Robot. See Appendix 4.B for a process narrative of the TO-BE process depicted below.

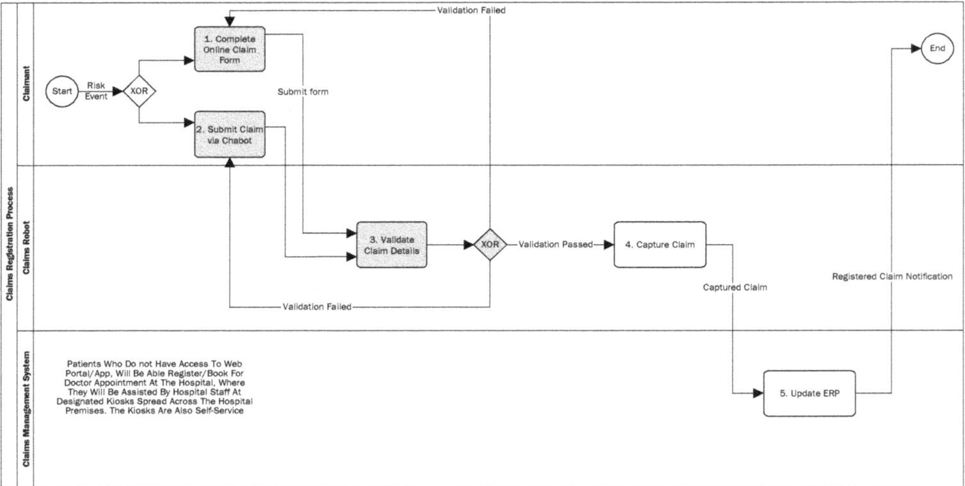

Figure 4.4 To-BE Claims Registration Process

TO-BE Value Stream Map

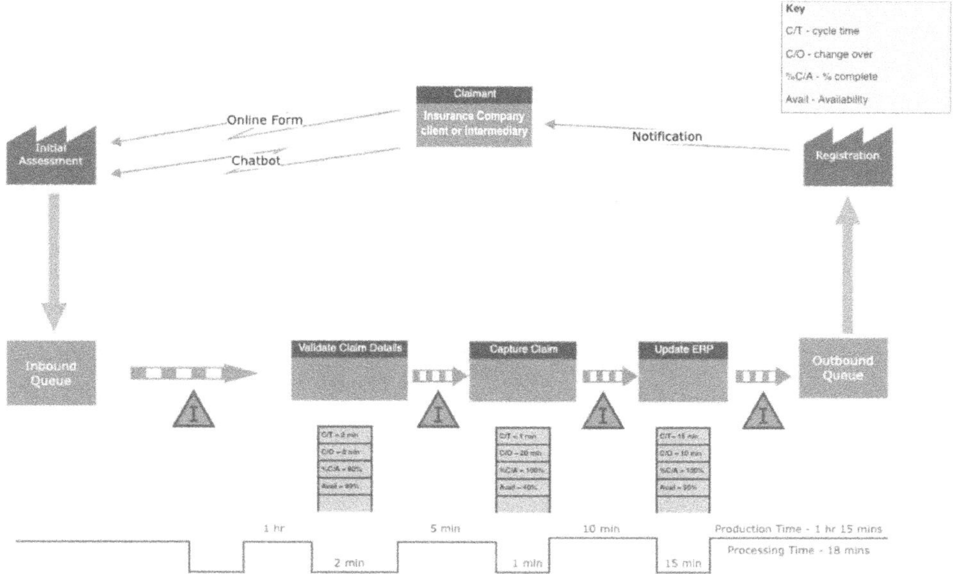

The standardised, lean and optimised TO-BE process was performance tested through the future state VSM to measure the overall process improvement. The introduction of intelligent digital channels eliminated one activity (Allocate Email) with a lead time of one day and a cycle time of one hour. In addition, the need to review claim applications was replaced by an AI and machine learning validation process that provides claimants with immediate feedback to ensure quality and structured data is collected at the source. The process changes coupled with the introduction of digital technologies resulted in a 98% reduction in total lead time and an 85% reduction in total cycle time. Noteworthy is that the Update ERP process was untouched because it was already optimised.

Future State Operations Performance Measures

By automating elements of the claims registration process and introducing intelligence into the process, the operations performance experienced a dramatic improvement. Insurance Company improved processing speed, cost efficiency and process dependability when viewed through the five performance measures. Other benefits of the solution include introducing process flexibility to scale up to down in line with market demand and ensure quality throughout the process. When measured against the market, it is clear that the new improvements bring Insurance Company on par with the market.

DIGITAL MATURITY

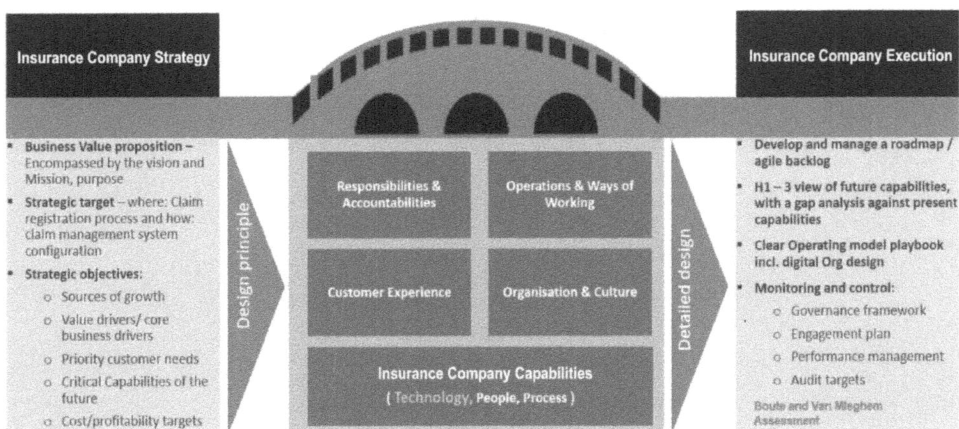

The Boute and Van Mieghem model is a maturity model focused on technology capability. Viewing Insurance Company's digital maturity through this lens allows a holistic view of the business's changes from a process perspective. It provides a view of how the business delivers value to customers and operates from a claims processing perspective (detailed design).

This is informed by the process map, which has been unpacked. By using the digital assets at Insurance Company's disposal, the organisation can avoid duplication efforts in the value chain and ensure an efficient process from start to finish that can aid in delightful customer journeys.

Digital transformation has a dependency on organisational structure and governance. To support the digital maturity analysis, the Evans Digital Maturity Model highlights the Process and Governance pillar, which aligns with the focus identified in Insurance Company old and new claims process.

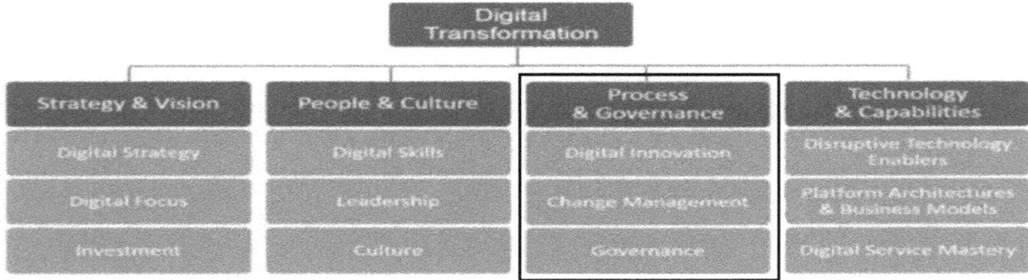

DAS FRAMEWORK

Although leveraging on digital and intelligent deployment, there is an important role that is to be played by frontline staff in the customer journey. Humans still want to know that there is a human being at the other end of the digital asset or platform ready to troubleshoot any issues that arise.

The intersection of digital and intelligent operations brings the Insurance Company value chain into focus. It allows the organisation to readily establish the areas that need improvement, not only from a process perspective but also by looking at the end-to-end customer journey, solving any pain points and managing the way the customer feedback loops will be closed off.

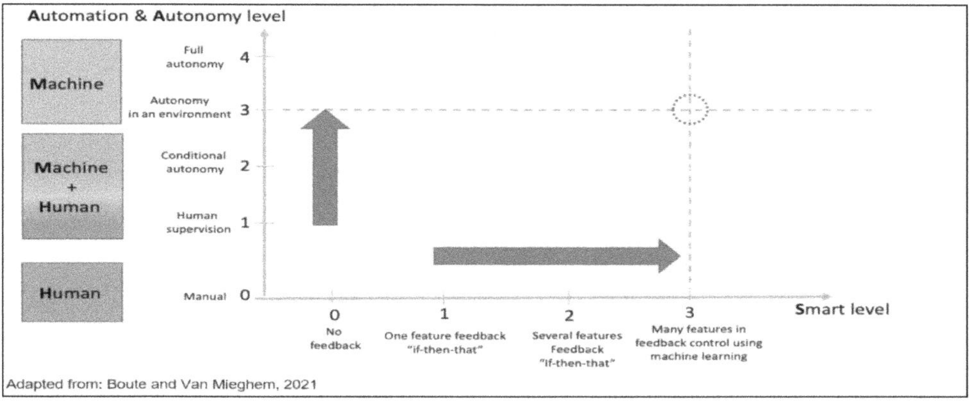

Through the elimination of the inefficient business activities and decommissioning of old systems, the organisation will not only ensure process efficiency from a Lean Kaizen perspective – eliminate, optimise and standardise (Grzelczak & Werner-Lewandowska, 2016) but will also ensure that their profit and loss (P&L) margins are increased.

Further analysis of the case gaps identified within the Insurance Company claims submission department showcased the need for a fully optimised tool to decrease repetition, eliminate human error and ensure efficiency in terms of turnaround time for customer feedback on claims. The Digital Operations Diagnostic across the chain maps out as below in the Insurance Company business case:

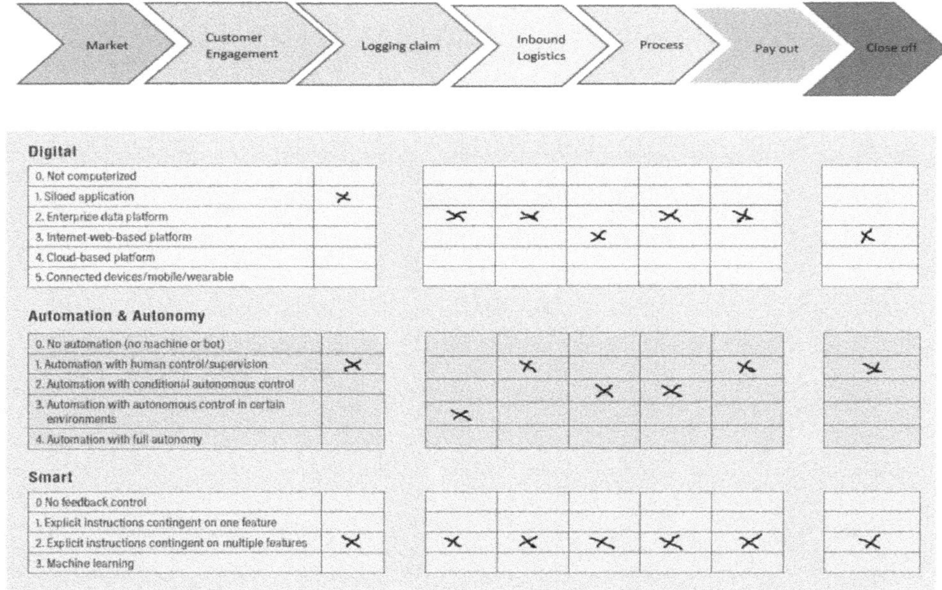

IMPLEMENTATION PLAN

Insurance Company aims to automate the Claims Registration process using RPA, integrating it into their Datawarehouse for AI Capabilities and decision-making. The organisation has approved a budget of R15 million. This includes procuring licences and resource costs. The project team consists of a Project Sponsor, a Project Manager, a Governance/Risk Specialist and Development Team, which will be outsourced due to limited resources and internal capabilities. Some assumptions are that no significant changes will be made to the project team's current registration process, commitment and availability, having chosen an Automation Platform and secured licences. Risks impacting the project delivery could be significant events like the July 2021 CAT event, procurement and regulatory risks. The detailed implementation plan is found in Appendix 4.C.

Only suppliers on the Central Supplier Database will be used to mitigate procurement and regulatory risks by following Insurance Company guidelines and internal risk measures. Due to the above reasons, there are existing budget constraints and the project team is expected to deliver the automation within the project timelines and approved budget. The project team will follow the Agile methodology to implement the project. The scope and goals are limited to automation, streamlining the registration process and building the online Portal and Chatbot solutions. CMS was implemented in December 2020 to replace a legacy claims application built for Insurance Company. As a modern solution,

CMS is relatively easy to integrate, configure, use and maintain. The project team is not expected to make any changes to CMS but to integrate the Chatbot and Portal for any validation activities required for claims registration. There is an expectation to upskill and grow the capabilities of the internal development team and hyper-care after the solution is delivered.

CONCLUSION

This report aimed to propose a redesign of an existing Insurance Company claims process. This endeavour began with a comprehensive analysis of the current claims process design and operation. Consequently, a redesign of the business claims procedure has been developed. The proposed claims process demonstrates an operational enhancement to achieve the desired objectives.

Insurance Company remained reliant on cumbersome and time-consuming documentation workflows for a considerable amount of time. These procedures resulted in less efficient management throughout the life cycle of the claim. This led to longer open claim periods, less accountability and less precise claim data. The South African financial services industry has evolved and is now focused on eliminating time-consuming manual labour and lengthy workflow obstacles. The paradigm shift is that processes should serve the users (administrators) rather than work against them (Holmes, 2021). This change presents numerous advantages.

The first step in automating the Claims Management System (CMS) involved organising and structuring the data entry, storage and distribution processes. Utilising technologies such as RPA and Machine Learning increased the accuracy of input data and produced a more comprehensive depiction of a claims incident, resulting in a 98% reduction in total lead time and an 85% reduction in total cycle time. The proposed 3 X 3 DAS automation level promises to enhance customer engagement and experience, as well as improved claim accountability. Embedded algorithms also hold the promise of enabling Insurance Company to track claims data in an organised, manageable format, which will increase the speed of data entry, processing claims requests and claims reviews. This will result in an immediate reduction in the number of claims administrators from the current 35 to 25. The ten part-time equivalents that were hired to assist with increased claim registration can now be reassigned to the payment processing department and retrained with new skills to focus on other crucial activities within the organisation.

Digital technologies play a transformative role in achieving operational excellence, but technology alone will not guarantee success. In order for organisations to get the most out of their value stream activities, they must optimise their operations through process design and process technology, as well as understand their processes through the use of swim maps and DAS frameworks etc., in an effort to standardise processes as much as possible, eliminate waste and optimise for performance, all whilst reducing costs. All of these proposed changes rely on a well-structured implementation plan in order to remain agile and competitive.

APPENDICES

Appendix 4.A

#	Activity Name	Activity Description
1	Email Claim Form	An Insurance Company client or intermediary will send an email to newclaims@Insurance Company.co.za containing the claim details.
2	Allocate Email	Once the email is received, an acknowledgement email is returned to the sender and the CMS automatically creates a case and allocates the email to a Claims Administrator.
3	Review Claim Details	The Claims Administrator opens the case and reviews the details to determine if all the required information was provided.
4	Request Missing Information	If some details are missing from the case, the Claims Administrator will initiate an email to the claimant requesting the outstanding information.
5	Submit Missing Information	The claimant responds to the request for information via email with the requested additional information.
6	Capture Claim	Once the Claims Administrator has all the required information, they proceed to capture the claim details in the CMS. The capture claim activity is a composite process comprising other activities such as checking if a duplicate claim exists, capturing the loss estimate and uploading any supporting documentation.
7	Update ERP	The process ends with another composite activity where the CMS automatically executes several steps that culminate in the sending of an email to the claimant containing the claim number and claim controller. Other steps in the process include generating a claim number, updating the ERP system and assigning a claim controller.

Appendix 4.B

#	Activity Name	Activity Description
1	Complete Online Claim Form	An Insurance Company client or intermediary will capture a claim using an online portal accessible over the internet.
2	Submit Claim via Chatbot	An Insurance Company client or intermediary will capture a claim using WhatsApp, WeChat or Telegram.
3	Validate Claim Details	An Insurance Company Claims Robot validates the information coming through from the Portal and Chatbot. This includes AI capabilities and integration to backend internal (CMS) and external applications and APIs. e.g., Google Maps and PBVerify (Credit Bureau). The Claims Robot seamlessly integrates with the Portal and Chatbot to keep the capturing of the claim interactive and intuitive.
4	Capture Claim	The Claims Robot then captures and registers the claim on CMS. A claim confirmation notification is also sent to the client using the selected channel and email.
5	Update ERP	CMS is integrated into D365, in this step the CMS updates the ERP system with a record of the claim and allocates a generic estimate (loss value/exposure).

Appendix 4.C

		Project Title					
		Autonomous Claims Registration					
Budget		**Start Date**	**End Date**	**Project Duration**		**Stakeholders/Resources**	
R15 000 000.00		1022/07/04	2023/02/06	156 Days		Project Owner/Sponsor	
						Governance, Risk & Comp	
						Project Manager	
						Development Team	

Key								
Status	**WBS No**	**Task Name**	**Status**	**Assigned To**	**Start Date**	**End Date**	**Duration**	**Comments**
Not Started	1	Project Conception & Initition	**Complete**	Project Owner/Sponsor	2022/07/04	2022/07/06	3	Research, Stakeholder Mapping & Project Charter
In Progress	2	Project Definition & Planning	**Complete**	Project Manager	2022/07/07	2022/07/08	2	Scope, Budget, Goals, Methodology & Communication Plan
Complete	3	Project Launch & Execution	**Complete**	Project Owner/Sponsor & PM	2022/07/11	2022/07/23	3	Status, KPI's, Tracking
On Hold	4	Requirements Gathering	**In Progress**	Development Team	2022/07/13	2022/07/28	12	As-is Process & to-be process has identified, analysed & documented
	5	Solution Design	**In Progress**	Development Team	2022/07/15	2022/07/29	11	Architecture/Security Design completed, Solutions Design in progress as new requirments are received
	6	Development	**In Progress**	Development Team	2022/07/18	2022/10/21	70	Team has Demo'd a to the Project Team & Continuing with Development
	7	User Acceptance Testing	**Not Started**	Development Team	2022/10/10	2023/01/13	70	Team has started to design test cases based requirements & design
	8	Training	**Not Started**	Development Team	2023/01/16	2023/10/27	10	User manuals & project handover documentation drawn from existing documentation & requirements
	9	Deployment & Hypercare	**Not Started**	Development Team	2023/02/03	2023/05/31	84	Environments ready based on approved archtecture
	10	Project Performance & Monitoring	**In Progress**	Project Manager	2022/07/04	2023/02/06	156	Effort & Cost Tracking, Quality Deliverables, Project Objectives

ACKNOWLEDGEMENT OF CONTRIBUTORS

- Asiphe Mtingane
- Zimkhitha Mathunjwa
- Olebogeng Mataboge
- Leroy Barnes
- Asiphe Mtingane
- Thabani Msibi

(All are affiliated to the Wits Business School, University of the Witwatersrand, Johannesburg).

REFERENCES

American Society for Quality. (n.d.). Value stream mapping tutorial – what is VSM? | ASQ. Retrieved July 19, 2022, from https://asq.org/quality-resources/lean/value-stream-mapping

Balasubramanian, R., Ari Libarikian, McElhaney, D. (2021, March 12). Insurance 2030—The impact of AI on the future of insurance. Retrieved July 18, 2022, from McKinsey & Company website: https://www.mckinsey.com/industries/financial-services/our-insights/insurance-2030-the-impact-of-ai-on-the-future-of-insurance

Boute, R., van Mieghem, J. (2021, September 2). Digital Operations: Autonomous Automation and the Smart Execution of Work. *Management and Business Review*. Retrieved July 17, 2022, from https://papers.ssrn.com/sol3/papers.cfm?abstract_id=3916455cial_Intelligence_in_Financial_Services

Burger, S. (2022). Cyber, electricity, riot insurance risks becoming increasingly complicated to manage. Retrieved July 18, 2022, from https://www.engineeringnews.co.za/article/cyber-electricity-riot-insurance-risksbecoming-increasingly-complicated-to-manage-2022-03-01

Davison, A. (2022, April 8). What the changing nature of risk means for your business – IT-Online. Retrieved July 18, 2022, from https://it-online.co.za/2022/04/08/what-the-changing-nature-of-risk-means-for-your-business/

Chan, A. and Shukor, R. (2018). Digital Operations. Retrieved July 20, 2022, from https://www.pwc.com/my/en/services/digital/digital-operations.html

Evans, N. (2017, August 15). Assessing your organization's digital transformation maturity. Retrieved July 18, 2022, from https://www.nicholasdevans.com/assessing-your-organizations-digital-transformation-maturity/

Grzelczak, A., Werner-Lewandowska, K. (2016). Eliminating Muda (Waste) in Lean Management by Working Time Standardization. *Arabian Journal of Business and Management Review*. Retrieved July 20, 2022, from https://www.hilarispublisher.com/open-access/eliminating-muda-waste-in-lean-management-by-working-time-standardization-2223-5833-1000216.pdf

Haris, A. (2016). Issues in Digital Era. Retrieved July 18, 2022, from https://www.researchgate.net/publication/328528038_Issues_In_Digital_Era/

Insurance Company Communications. (2022). A year since last July unrest, Insurance Company has made significant progress in settling claims. 13 July. Retrieved July 20, 2022, from https://www.Insurance Company.co.za/a-year-on-since-last-july-unrest-Insurance Company-has-made-significant-progress-in-settling-claim

Insurance Company SOC LTD. (2021). Insurance Company Integrated Report 2021. Retrieved July 17, 2022, from https://www.Insurance Company.co.za/wp-content/uploads/2022/06/Insurance Company-Integrated-Report-2021.pdf.

Insurance Company SOC Ltd. (2022). A year on since last July unrest, Sasria has made significant progress in settling claims. Retrieved from https://www.Insurance Company.co.za/a-year-on-since-last-july-unrest-Insurance Company-has-made-significant-progress-in-settling-claims/

Karle, V. (2019). 9 Ways Predictive Analytics in Insurance Claims is Helping to Achieve Better Outcomes. Retrieved July 20, 2022, from https://www.ventivtech.com/blog/9-ways-predictive-analytics-in-insurance-claims-is-helping-to-achieve-better-outcomes.

Lee, A. (2021, July 14). OPINIONISTA: A question of insurance: Insurance Company is there — but can it cover all losses suffered in the looting? Retrieved July 18, 2022, from Daily Maverick website: https://www.dailymaverick.co.za/opinionista/2021-07-14-a-question-of-insurance-Insurance Company-is-there-but-can-it-cover-all-losses-suffered-in-the-looting/

Manhood, A. (2019). Automation of Claim Processing System. Retrieved July 20, 2022, https://www.researchgate.net/publication/338153010_AUTOMATION_OF_CLAIM_PROCESSING_SYSTEM/link/5e02b7134585159aa4984ee9/download

Morgan, B. (2021, April 12). Here's How IoT Will Impact The Insurance Claims Process. *Forbes*. Retrieved from https://www.forbes.com/sites/blakemorgan/2018/05/16/heres-how-iot-will-impact-the-insurance-claims-process/?sh=4a6bfa6b366e

Napier, G. (2022, March 14). Key trends in the short-term insurance industry -

Moonstone. Retrieved July 18, 2022, from https://www.moonstone.co.za/key-trends-in-the-short-term-insurance-industry/.

Object Management Group, Inc. (2007, November). UML superstructure specification (V2.1.2). Retrieved from https://www.omg.org/spec/UML/2.1.2/Superstructure/PDF

Performance Improvement Partners. (n.d.). Digital Maturity: What It Is, How to Achieve It, and the Digital Maturity Model to Drive Business Transformation. Retrieved July 18, 2022, from https://www.pipartners.com/digital-maturity/

PricewaterhouseCoopers. (2018). Digital Operations. Retrieved July 20, 2022, from https://www.pwc.com/my/en/services/digital/digital-operations.html

ProcessMaker. (2020, December 21). What Is a Swimlane on a Process Map? Retrieved from https://www.processmaker.com/blog/what-is-a-swimlane-on-a-process-map/

Slack, N., Brandon-Jones, A., Singh, H., Phihlela, K., Johnston, R. (2017). *Operations Management*, 3rd edn. Pearson.

Smith, M. (2021, September 7). Data and analytics: Unlocking the power of claims. Retrieved July 20, 2022, from https://home.kpmg/xx/en/home/insights/2021/08/data-and-analytics-unlocking-the-power-of-claims.htm

Soberanis, L. (2021, September 13). From underwriting to claims management, artificial intelligence will transform the insurance industry. Retrieved July 20, 2022, from https://www.ibm.com/blogs/watson/2021/09/ai-will-transform-insurance-industry/

The importance of drones in insurance. (2021). Retrieved July 20, 2022, from https://fia.org.za/blog/the-importance-of-drones-in-insurance/

Williams, P. (2021). The Case for Robotic Process Automation (RPA) in Insurance. Retrieved July 20, 2022. Retrieved from https://www.ibm.com/cloud/blog/robotic-process-automation-in-insurance

2021 Insurance State of the Market. (2021). Retrieved July 18, 2022, from https://aon.co.za/insights/2021-insurance-state-of-the-market/

CHAPTER 5

Practical Case of Digitalising the Post Office: A Viewpoint

BACKGROUND AND PROBLEM STATEMENT

Background of the Post Office

The Post Office serves the Republic of South Africa as the primary conveyor of written communication domestically and internationally. In essence it provides essential services accessible particularly to disadvantaged communities and vulnerable citizens, which allows them to be economically and financially included (South African Post Office, 2020).

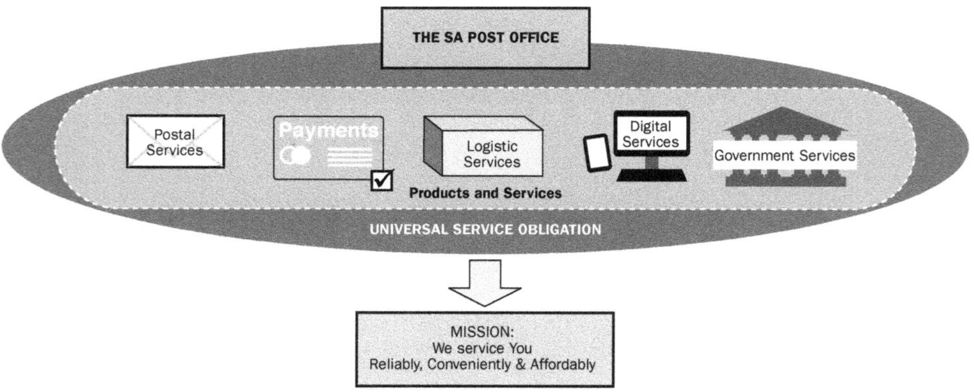

Figure 5.1 The Post Office Services Portfolio

The Post Office customer value proposition includes five key capabilities: postal services, payments, logistical services, digital services and government services (South African Post Office, 2020). The Post Office aims to transition into a trusted exchange channel of service delivery in South African and be respected for their relevance, reliability, reach and resilience (South African Post Office, 2020). There are, however, several challenges impacting the effectiveness and efficiencies of the Post Offices to deliver on its strategy.

South African Post Office Problem Statement

The Post Office has the following fundamental challenges:

- It is currently experiencing declining revenue due to shifting customer needs and demands. This decline stems from rapid adoption of digital technologies and e-commerce platforms that have driven customers away from the Post Office as the entity cannot provide customer satisfaction. Thus, the trend is exacerbated by the erosion of physical mail volumes and the income generated (The South African Post Office Corporate Plan, 2020).
- The negative income generation has impacted the Post Office cash flows severely wherein operational costs continue to escalate with rising employee, fuel, property, security and information technology costs as the primary drivers (The South African Post Office Corporate Plan, 2020). That means liabilities exceed current assets as postulated by the Post Office Corporate Plan (2020). For example, the Post Office services contribution of 63% in the FY 2019/20 was reduced to 47% in the next FY of 2020/21. That represents a net loss of R1,3 billion as this net loss remains unfunded.
- There is inadequate investment in modernising ageing postal office infrastructure.
- The impact of Covid-19 and the slow growth of the economy have impacted negatively on the Post Office.
- The slow and weak implementation of pertinent programmes and projects have further exacerbated the future growth of the institution.

INDUSTRY TRENDS

Postal Industry Trends

The global trends dictate that the postal industry or global postal operators are faced with the choices of continuing to operate in their current traditional role of conveyor of letters or transform their operating model into a modern business that seeks to position these entities into long-term viable businesses (The South African Post Office Corporate, 2020). According to the South African Post Office Corporate Plan (2020), external factors drive the need for change. Digital convergence and substitution, increasing competition, labour conditions, environmental impact and evolving customer expectations impact the Post Office negatively, thus drive the need to modernise its business.

These trends indicate that, globally, the postal service industry has been undergoing a shift in how they operate. It is therefore transitioning from relic to a facilitator of exchanges of goods and messages in the age of global internet connectivity. Henceforth, the postal operators will find themselves at a critical juncture that requires a review of their role within society's various ecosystems and the economy (The South African Post Office Corporate Plan, 2020).

Figure 5.2 highlights global trends that impact the Post Office.

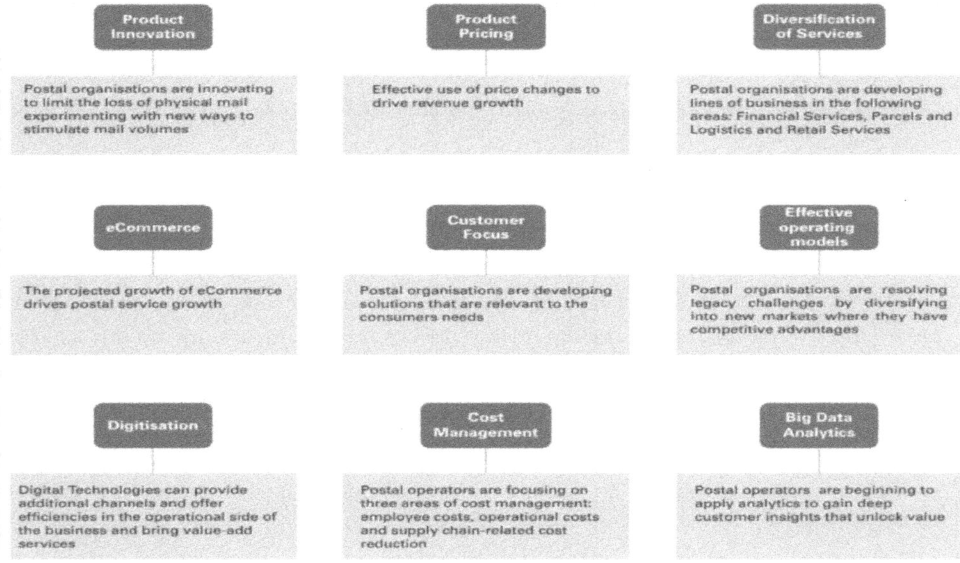

Figure 5.2 Global Postal Trends (Post Office Strategic Plan 2019/20 — 2021/22)

PESTLE, SWOT & TOWS ANALYSIS

PESTLE Analysis

The PESTLE analysis is a strategic tool that will assist in providing an overview of issues impacting the Post Office.

Table 5.1 PESTLE Analysis - the Post Office

Political	Economic	Social
• The Department of Communications and Digital Transition rationalised the State-Owned Entities • The mandate of the Post Office was changed to include digital services • There's a need to turn around the Post Office as it plays a key role in society	• The impact of COVID-19 on the economy, which resulted to low growth projections • The South African Macro policies set to provide new growth opportunities through the SA economic recovery and reconstruction plan	• Alternative shopping trends, consumers opting out to shop on-line • Unemployment increase impacts consumer spending
Technology	**Legal**	**Environmental**
• Upward surge of on-line shopping • Cashless payment solution preferred for example: digital wallets etc.	• Changes in the mandate of the Post Office through regulatory requirements	• Societal focus on green technologies

SWOT Analysis

Table 5.2 provides an industry analysis of the Post Office by focusing on the strengths, weakness, opportunities, and threats.

Table 5.2 SWOT analysis — Post Office

Strengths	Weaknesses
• Consumers still choose the Post Office • products and services • A national footprint that has a presence in the remote and rural areas • Commitment towards the modernisation of the Post Office • Pockets of excellence within the Post Office • The Post Office as one of the SOE's with platforms that aid distribution of goods, money and information • Strategically positioned to support developmental objectives of the Republic of South Africa	• High operating costs of the Post Office due to labour, security, logistics and Information Technology • Weaknesses in the management of product and capabilities • Low staff morale across the organisation • Vacancies not filled especially for critical skills • Unstable organisation due to service delivery • Low maintenance of infrastructure and the aging workforce • Productivity of employees very low due to limited tools of trade
Opportunities	**Threats**
• Shift of consumers to utilise other shopping alternatives and opting for cashless payment solutions, i.e. digital wallets	• Stiff competition from the private sector • Adoption of digital technologies by customers and business

PROCESS MAP & VALUE STREAM ANALYSIS

As-Is Process: Postal Services

The process types that the Post Office has are a combination of batch and mass processing (Slack, Jones, & Johnston, 2017). Therefore, for us to understand the above process types we need to firstly have an overview of what are process types. The process types are the position of a process on the volume–variety continuum that shapes its overall design and the general approach to managing activities (Slack, Jones, & Johnston, 2017). Thus, the As-Is Post Office processes illustrated below in Figure 5.3 assume a combination of batch and mass processing. The mass processing are processes that produce items in high volumes and relatively narrow variety, whereas batch processes are processes that produce more than one item at a time and have periods when the process repeats itself (Slack, Jones, & Johnston, 2017).

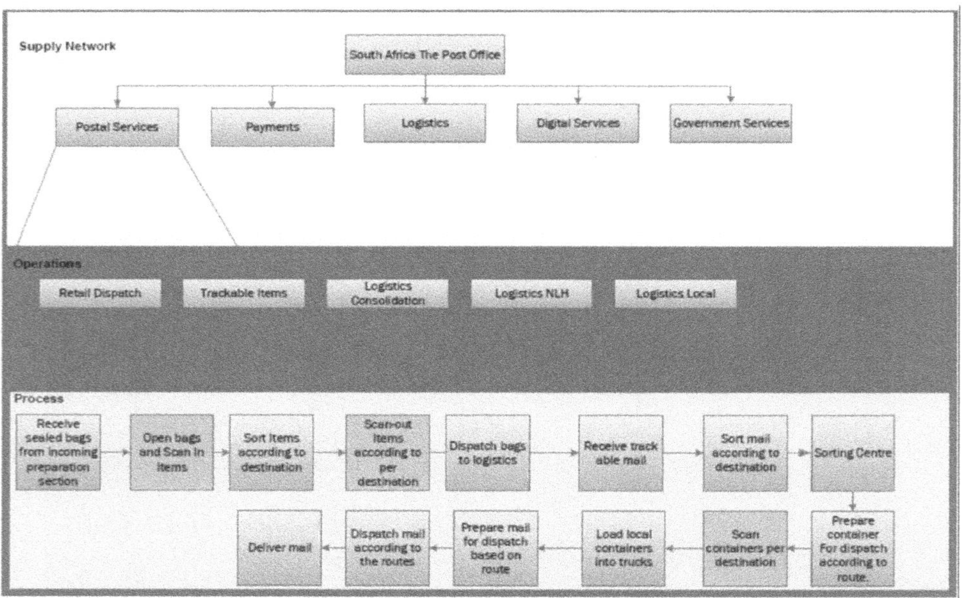

Figure 5.3 The Post Office Postal Services Processes (Slack, Jones, & Johnston, 2017)

Process Flow — As-Is Observations

The overall As-Is postal services processes are siloed and not integrated in the processing of mail and parcels. This leads to high inefficiencies and long cycle times just to process mail and parcels. In essence this makes the Post Office inefficient and non-competitive as it can't compete with its competitors as it cannot adhere to some of the operational principles of speed and dependability.

The processes are not flexible and the reputation of the Post Office is largely tainted. The processes are repetitive and not cost-effective as the entity is impacted negatively, which it results to losses of R1,3 billion as cited (The Post Office Corporate Plan, 2020).

The operating model of the institution is not supportive to the business processes of the organisation, hence within the operational processes there are a lot of inefficiencies caused by such an anomaly. The delivery of mail is still defined by old archaic processes of having a conveyor belt in the national and local sorting centres. This leads to errors as there's minimal investment in digital technologies.

The overall process, including collection point straight through to the consumer receiving registered mail/parcel phase, amounted to 50 hours maximum (five days). Industry standard is 36 hours. The main objective of this analysis is to reduce the time in between. The identified bottlenecks are between the inbound and domestic sorting centre, where repetitive work and time wastage takes place.

Value Stream Analysis

The purpose of the value stream analysis is to increase the efficiency of the process design (Slack, Jones, & Johnston, 2017). The To-Be processes will assist the Post Office in reducing its cycle time in delivering mail and parcels. This will enable the Post Office to grow its revenue streams from these processes as the entity generates revenue from this section. The optimised To-Be processes are intended to seamlessly integrate different functional areas within the logistic department with the branch and interface with the customer at retail offices. As a result, this will be the beginning of the alignment of operational processes with the operating model of the entity. This seamless integration assists the Post Office in reducing the cycle time to 36 hours. Therefore, by integrating the processes and the flow of parcels/letters in different functional areas i.e. logistics, sorting distribution areas, branches and retail office/branches will ensure that the entity will converge on organisational information-related platforms like IT and operational technologies that will enhance the functionality of these business processes. The shaded steps are those processes that will be automated.

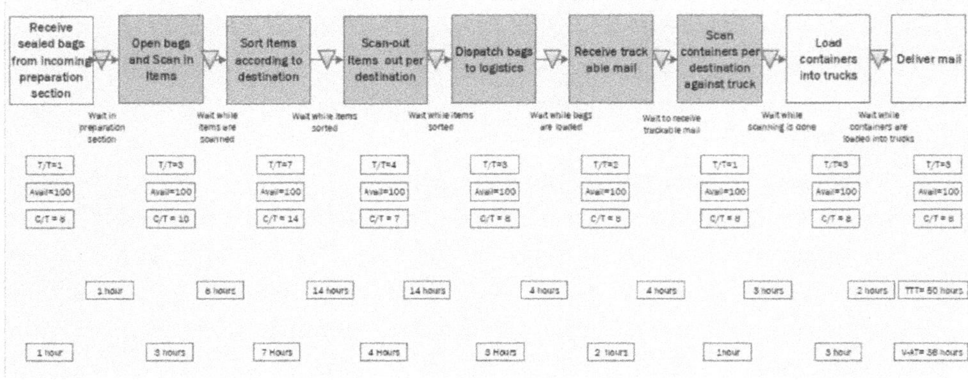

Figure 5.4 The To-Be Processes (Slack, Jones, & Johnston, 2017)

Identified Gaps and Solutions

To identify the gaps in the "As-Is" processes, we applied the Polar diagram to visually depict how the automation of certain level 3 processes would contribute to Quality, Speed, Dependability and Flexibility. We furthermore illustrate the gaps in the 4Vs model that considers Volume, Variety, Variation and Visibility. Lastly, using the DAS model, we were able to understand the digital maturity levels of the Post Office and provide recommendations in line with the Future state process recommendations.

Polar Diagram

The Polar diagram indicates that the implementation of Robotics Process Automation and other recommended technologies will improve:

- **Quality**: For the Post Office to improve quality our solution will allow for active monitoring of their customer satisfaction through Net Loyalty scoring and feedback. Allowing the Post Office to use non-conformance practices to identify gaps in their overall processes as part of their overall Quality Management System.
- **Speed**: The throughput and cycle times to process and scan records of registered mail at the inbound centre and that of the domestic sorting centre will be reduced from 50 hours to 36 hours. Allowing parcels to be received on the predicted delivery times.
- **Dependability**: The automation of repetitive work reduces the human error rate and waste in the process i.e. a person moving from one sorting bin to another. This solution will improve turnaround time and monitor performance. Allowing more time for quality assurance and efficient forecasting and planning in preparation for peak periods.

60

- **Flexibility:** The process needs to accommodate unexpected events and gear up for the e-commerce strategy to take effect. Furthermore, the Post Office should explore Internship opportunities to close the capability gaps in their environment by contributing to the unemployment rate and using these strategic young talent programmes as a future feeder pipeline for talent.
- **Cost:** The cost of running the business remains high given the current economic challenges. This is the only trade-off that will initially still remain high until returns are realised year on year through the increase in volumes and outputs brought about by automation and revenue streams.

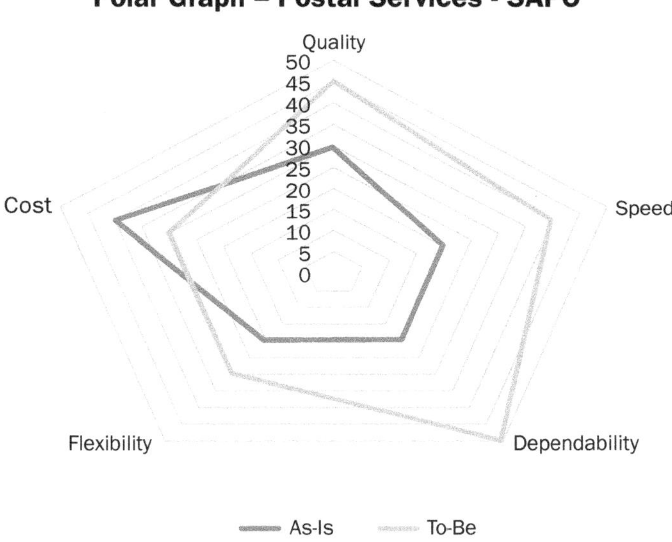

Figure 5.5 Polar Diagram — As-Is & To-Be- The Post Office

4Vs

The 4Vs were applied to the Post Office.

- **Volume** – High – Utilisation on average remains high as 70% irrespective of private courier operators entering the market, given the spread and footprint of the Post Office in rural areas.
- **Variety** – Low – Limited offerings given the separation of the Post bank partnership and the lack of e-commerce offerings.
- **Variation** – Low – Forecasting and planning are lacking and not in touch with the supply and demand due to manual inputs and lack of an intuitive solution.

- **Visibility** – Low – the Post Office's brand is not strong, and customer satisfaction has also been impacted due to the drive in e-commerce offerings by private operators and adoption of digital solutions.

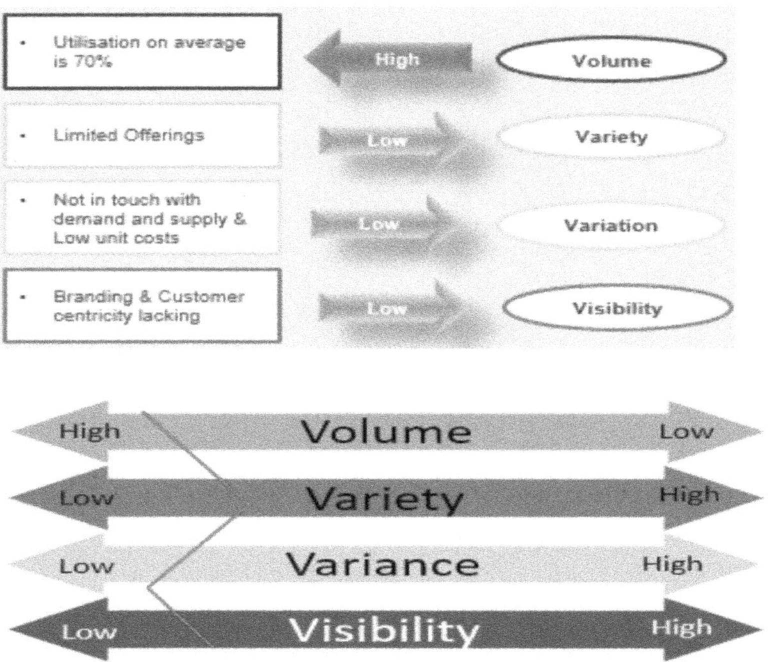

Figure 5.6 4Vs — The Post Office

Solutions and Benefits

To achieve this, the Post Office will invest in technologies like Inventory Bots, Wireless Sensors and Indoor Location Tracking, Wearable Barcode Readers.

- **Inventory Bots:** The inventory bots will allow the Post Office to utilise their employees' skills better by freeing up their time to focus on specialised tasks. The bots will help in optimising sorting centres, employee workloads and fulfilment process.
- **Wireless Sensors and Indoor Location Tracking:** The wireless sensors indoor location tracking will help to locate mail and parcels or people in real-time, generate tracking reports and monitor performance overtime. Sensors can also communicate with one another. A wireless sensor that lives on a shelf or pallet can talk with those around the building so that you can locate items more easily. Overall, sensors modernise how you manage your distribution centre, helping things to run smoothly with less hassle.

- **Wearable Barcode Readers Robotic Process Automation (RPA):** The RPA will be used to automate repetitive tasks done on the backend systems which comprise among others, planning and route management system, vehicle tracking systems and SAP system to speed up operations.

DAS Model—Optimisation & Streamlining

The following covers the DAS model and where the Post Office is rated at in terms of their existing digital platforms against the "As-Is" Level 3 processes:

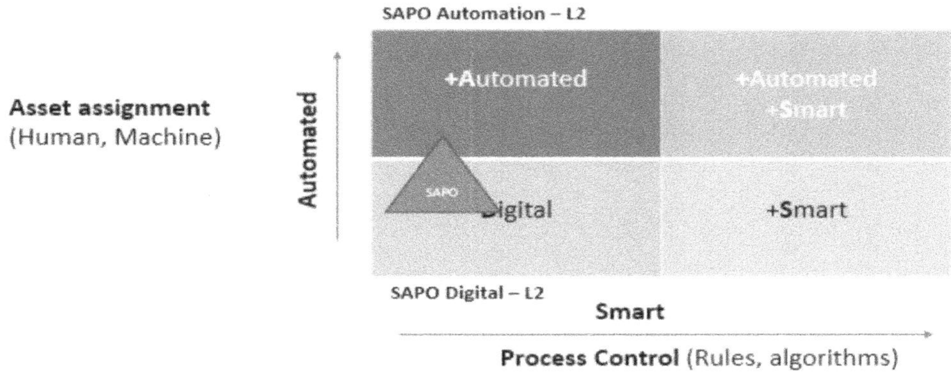

Figure 5.7 The Post Office DAS Model

The Post Office scores indicated the following:
- Digital – L2 – the Post Office's workflow and data are on an enterprise platform which is integrated to limited activities. Recommendation that wide-scale adoption to move operations to L3 using a platform over the internet which include web-based access to a central platform, which allows for remote assistance and communication of digital work instructions.
- Automation – L2 – the Post Office's existing platform allows for machine autonomy in certain conditions but requires human intervention in others. The system requests human intervention in the approval decision. Some repetitive tasks can be moved to L3 Automation & Autonomy which is fully autonomous in a given environment.
- Smart – L0 – The existing platforms do not have Machine Learning and Artificial Intelligence.

Our proposed solution will improve the Post Office's Digital maturity to a level 3 – which includes both Automated and Smart technologies into their eco-system.

PROPOSED SOLUTION ROADMAP FOR INTEGRATION

Programme Management Approach

To ensure successful delivery of the digital solutions for the Post Office, the Delivery Team has recommended adopting a phased approach across the project lifecycle.

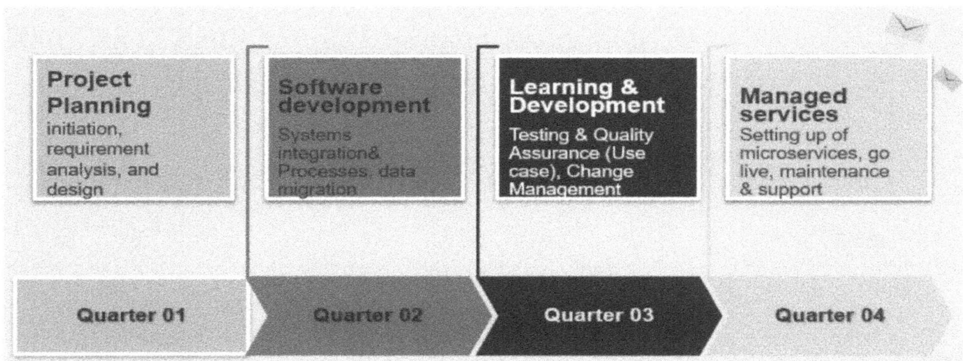

Figure 5.8 Programme Management Approach

Project Governance

The programme will have formal governance structures which will form part of the decision-making body in the project roll-out. The Project Team will report to a Provincial Level Steering Committee, which consists of primary vital stakeholders, the project sponsor, project owner and representatives of the Post Office.

Project reporting structure is illustrated in Figure 5.9:

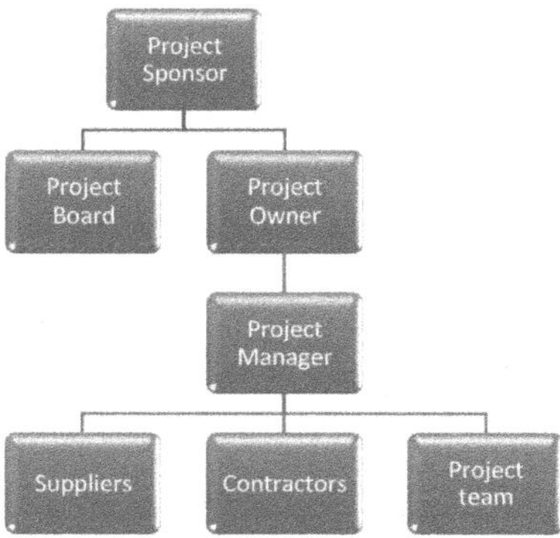

Figure 5.9 Project Governance

Further to this, the roll-out of these proposed solutions will require a formal Approval Process and Approval Authority to ensure the nature of the transaction is carried out transparently. The Project Team has signed off on the agreed approval process below (Figure 5.10).

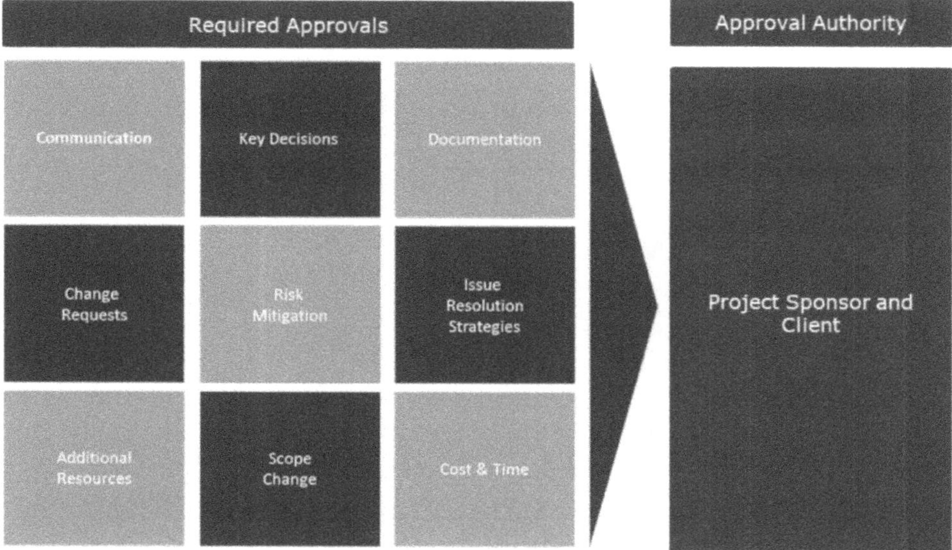

Figure 5.10 Approvals Framework

Project Charter and Scope

The project charter in Table 5.3 will serve to formalise the approval for the project to begin and authorises the project manager to apply resources to the project.

Table 5.3 Project Charter

Objectives	Critical Factors of Success	Key Activities	Resources
• Digitalisation of the Post Office mail and parcel operations • Successful implementation of RPA technology in the South African Postal Services operations environment • Reduce process time • Eliminate waste • Increase efficiencies	• Successful integration in the Post Office ERP environment using Microsoft Azure digital technology • Buy-in from key stakeholders ranging from Shareholders to employees • Access to network and coverage infrastructure • Achieve seamless interoperability between technologies and software • Access to local resources that can ensure the maintenance of local infrastructure and services • Reduce operational costs • Increase efficiencies	• Establishment of Project Consortium	• Post Office stakeholders • Clients • Employees • Contractors • Suppliers
Scope	**Deliverables**	**Constraints**	**External Dependencies**
• Increase efficiencies and reduce delivery time in order to reduce operational costs and increase revenue • Gauteng-based metropolitan area • Inbound and domestic sorting centres of the South African Postal services • Business process re-engineering • Process Mapping • Process Automation	• Digitalise the mail and parcel operation by optimising and streamlining the process and automating the workflows • Microsoft Azure licensing and software installation • RPA modeling • Testing and Quality Assurance • Cloud storage centre • Marketing, social and digital strategy • Onboarding sessions • Upskilling	• Limited Skills resources • Budget	• Labour • Policy and regulation • Competitive environment • Economy and political environment • 4IR technology & impact on the Post Office

Project Budget

The costs are broken down into Solution and capability / support costs:

• The solution costs amount to R12.6 million and the Capabilities a further R6 million bring the total investment to R18.6 million.

• The Development and support costs could vary based on the job scope and need, other alternatives could be exploring internship opportunities and receiving rebates for such strategic youth unemployment programmes.

Table 5.4 Project Budget

Cloud services (480 hours)		Monthly	Annually
Azure IoT Edge		R0.00	R0.00
Azure ExpressRoute		R4,229.50	R50,754.00
Virtual Machines		R300,033.04	R3,600,396.48
Azure Functions		R58.44	R701.33
Azure Machine Learning & RPA		R36,913.54	R442,962.46
Azure IoT Hub		R38,450.00	R461,400.00
Azure Stream Analytics		R2,276.24	R27,314.88
Service Bus		R2,214.72	R26,576.64
Azure DevOps		R14,611.00	R175,332.00
Azure Blockchain Services		R4,921.60	R59,059.20
Azure Monitor		R24.61	R295.30
		R403,732.69	R4,844,792.28
Development & Support		Monthly	Annually
IoT Project Manager		R93,264.00	R1,119,168.00
Solutions Architect(Enterprise)		R85,166.67	R1,022,000.00
Data Analytics Engineer		R78,691.00	R944,292.00
Data Scientist		R60,075.42	R720,905.00
Software Developer(Full-Stack)+DevOps		R85,868.92	R1,030,427.00
Business Analyst		R47,166.67	R566,000.00
Infrastructure Engineer		R49,970.83	R599,650.00
Support (Level 1)	200	R16.67	R200.00
Support (Level 2)	480	R25.00	R300.00
Total Monthly (VAT Exclusive)		R500,245.17	R6,002,942.00
Detail Costs			
Active RFID Readers / Antennas	50	R30,000.00	R1,500,000.00
RFID Software / Middleware	50	R42,000.00	R2,100,000.00
Inventory Bot	50	R30,000.00	R1,500,000.00
Wearable Barcod reader - Smart Pallet	20	R7,000.00	R140,000.00
Once Off (VAT Exclusive)			R5,240,000.00
Service Revenue	Per user	Monthly	Annually
Maintenance / Reportng / Analytics	16800	R50.00	R840,000.00
Licensing	16800	R100.00	R1,680,000.00
Total Monthly (VAT Exclusive)		R150.00	R2,520,000.00
Total Cost for Solution			R12,604,792.28

CONCLUSION

With the solutions recommended, the Post Office will be able to drive down operational cost and increase revenue opportunities through reducing waste in the process and automating workflow and tasks. These solutions will be scalable to reduce disruption on the operations. Customers' experience will be enhanced through actively managing detractors and keeping customers informed in real time throughout the delivery journey. Finally, digitalising operations will allow employees to focus more on strategic work.

ACKNOWLEDGEMENT OF CONTRIBUTORS

* Faheema Wannenburg
* Patrick Sithole
* Segofatso Thepa
* Ellek Blom

(All are affiliated to the Wits Business School, University of the Witwatersrand, Johannesburg).

REFERENCES

Boute, R. N., Mieghem, J. A. (2021). *Digital Operations: Autonomous Automation and the Smart Execution of Work*.

Office, T. S. (2020, July 20). *SAPO Corporate Plan*. Pretoria: South African Post Office.

Office, T. S. (2020). *The South African Post Office Corporate Plan*. Pretoria: SAPO.

PMG. (2022). Committee meeting. Retrieved from https://pmg.org.za/committee-meeting/29317/.

SAPO. (2022). *SAPO_Corporate_Plan FY21-22*. Pretoria: South African Post Office.

Slack, N., Jones, A. B., Johnston, R. (2017). *Operations Management*. Harlow: Pearson Education Limited.

CHAPTER 6

Practical Case of Digitalising Operations for a Property Management Company

INTRODUCTION

Company XYZ is a property management group specialising in commercial property management. The company offers a wide range of investment services focusing on increasing asset value and real estate performance. While offering comprehensive real estate solutions to clients, the company encourages ongoing innovation and service excellence. The property management division has over 900 employees and manages over 1 200 properties. Core services include comprehensive property management, lease renewal negotiations, vacant space management, retail leasing and consulting among others. XYZ is a proudly South African company with an extensive footprint in Africa.

The Covid-19 pandemic has had a significant impact on the property industry and in turn this has affected the way XYZ group handles the leasing process. According to Ramdass (2021), the pandemic forced businesses to adapt and digitise. The real estate sector had been advancing toward digitising processes and developing services that were digitally enabled for users and tenants before the crisis. Physical separation and the closure of physical places had practically overnight increased the significance of digitisation, especially when considering factors like tenant and customer experience (Gujral, Palter, Sanghvi & Vickery, 2020). Digitalisation in the property management sector can improve efficiency, transparency and ultimately deliver a great customer experience (Ramdass, 2021).

SITUATIONAL ANALYSIS

Macro-environmental Analysis

Some of the significant macro-environmental challenges faced by XYZ property group include the following:

- Over the past year, Gauteng, KwaZulu-Natal, and the Western Cape's premier office markets have experienced a severe supply–demand imbalance, greater vacancy rates, and falling rents (Ramdass, 2021). In some instances, tenants are still in arrears accumulated during the Covid-19 lockdown restrictions and subsequent economic fall-out (Price-Bailey, 2021). According to Bizcommunity (2021), industrial space weathered the economic downturn most effectively with lower vacancy rates, while retail and office spaces were hardest hit. Based on a report by the South African Property Owners Association vacancy rates in the office sector are at their highest levels ever at 15,4% (Bizcommunity, 2021). From a property management perspective, it has become more important than ever to quickly convert leads into paying tenants and keep existing paying tenants in place. In addition, there is a need to become more cost efficient.

- An enduring trend has been the change in leasing structures of commercial property because of 'work from home' trends and other factors (Nkate, 2022). This includes the rise of shorter term and flexible leasing options. Property managers should be willing to adapt their leasing spaces to the needs of their anchor tenants who lease larger spaces over longer terms (Nkate, 2022). The partnership between a landlord, property manager and a tenant in a commercial setting is more than just a legal one; the success of each business depends on the fulfilment of duties by the others (Singh, 2021). Wasting time on mundane admin-related issues in the leasing process means that the property managers don't have sufficient time to apply themselves to these important new changes and focus on relationship building.

- The fundamental structure of the commercial property industry has significantly shifted. There is high demand for industrial property rental for use as datacentres (due to remote working and cloud-based applications), logistics and e-commerce hubs/distribution centres. As online shopping continues to grow, there has been a rise in the need for last-mile logistic facilities, with underperforming office and retail properties being repurposed to support these inner-city centres (Ramdass, 2021). Businesses that are looking for office space are moving towards greener spaces that allow for improved physical and mental well-being of employees. As a result, mixed-use properties are in high demand (Broll, 2022). In addition, more tenants are looking for green buildings to end dependence on the Electricity Company Grid (Bizcommunity, 2021). Once again, property managers need to spend their time understanding these changes and adjusting their approach, not on routine admin-related processes.

- Digitisation is an important factor to consider as the commercial property landscape continues to evolve. By digitising, property managers will have more time to spend on other processes and tasks.

Stakeholders

According to Gujral, Palter, Sanghvi & Vickery (2020), in certain cases such as rental of offices and retail store space, property managers and landlords (property owners) should develop a deeper relationship with tenants and engage them directly to navigate the post Covid-19 situation. Engaging tenants directly and being quick to respond will significantly contribute to preserving relationships and value. The following stakeholders are relevant to the leasing process:

- **Property management team** – the portfolio executive, project manager and leasing administrator. This team within XYZ property group are required to keep the properties they manage occupied as much as possible and avoid vacancies while staying within budget parameters.
- **Landlord** – this is the property owner. They require the property management firm to deliver on agreed rental income and profits. In addition, they require that vacant buildings are occupied as quickly as possible with minimal delay.
- **Tenants (customers)** – these can include commercial retailer groups (such as Shoprite, Woolworths and others), smaller retailers ('mom and pop' stores) and businesses (for office space rental for a variety of business needs and industrial applications). These customers want quick responsive service from the rental agent and flexibility in terms of contract terms and space usage.

Problem Statement

Based on the macro-environmental and stakeholder analysis the following problem statement has been identified:

- The commercial property industry is under tremendous pressure to adjust to the significant changes brought about and accelerated by the Covid-19 pandemic. However, due to the manual, admin-intensive leasing process, property managers are spending more time managing this process rather than building relationships and working with clients and tenants to come up with creative leasing solutions.

The aim of this assignment is to streamline and digitise the leasing process for XYZ property group since this is a high value process that has potential to significantly impact on the efficiency and effectiveness of the business. By implementing technology into the process, the quality, speed, dependability and flexibility of the process can be improved (Slack et al, 2017).

THE CURRENT PROCESS

The As-Is process

The current leasing process in place by company XYZ is both tedious and resource-heavy for both the prospective tenant and the managing agent. In a nutshell, a prospective tenant will identify a potential space that they would like to specify and enquire with the property management company. The property agent will then provide them with an offer to lease and ask them for FICA documents. Once the FICA documents have been verified then the negotiation over the leasing terms happens between the stakeholders. After the negotiations are successful, the rental contract is prepared and manually goes through approval processes between the different stakeholders. This approval process is time-consuming and very admin-intensive and involves printing, signing and scanning the contracts several times with the various stakeholders. The final lease is then uploaded to the property management system and linked to the billing. A request for deposit payment is made to the tenant and after the money is received, then the on-site inspection of the property happens between the tenant and the property manager. Where defects of the property are noted with pictures as evidence, this information is then stored in the client file in a cabinet on site.

The main activities in this process include:

- location/rental space scouting by the tenant;
- negotiations between the stakeholders; and
- onsite inspection process.

The activities above consume a lot of hours, and this can be improved by optimising the process and digitising these activities. The current leasing process is highlighted in depth in the As-Is process map in Figure 6.1.

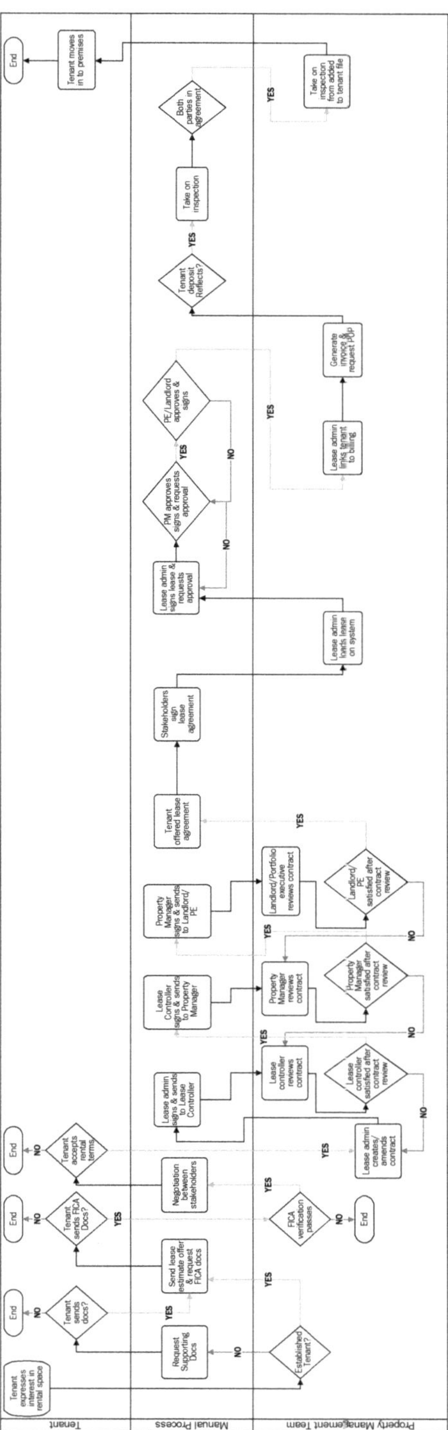

Figure 6.1 As-Is Rental Leasing Process

The Value Stream Map

The value stream is outlined in Figure 6.2. The current value stream has a lot of waiting time due to the highly manual process. This increases the total throughput time, which is currently 232 hours (29 days). Ideally this process should be reduced to better service customers and improve turn around time from initial interest in a property to final handover of the property to a paying tenant. In particular, the lease negotiation process and rental contract signing are time-consuming processes. There is also a lot of wasted 'wait-time'.

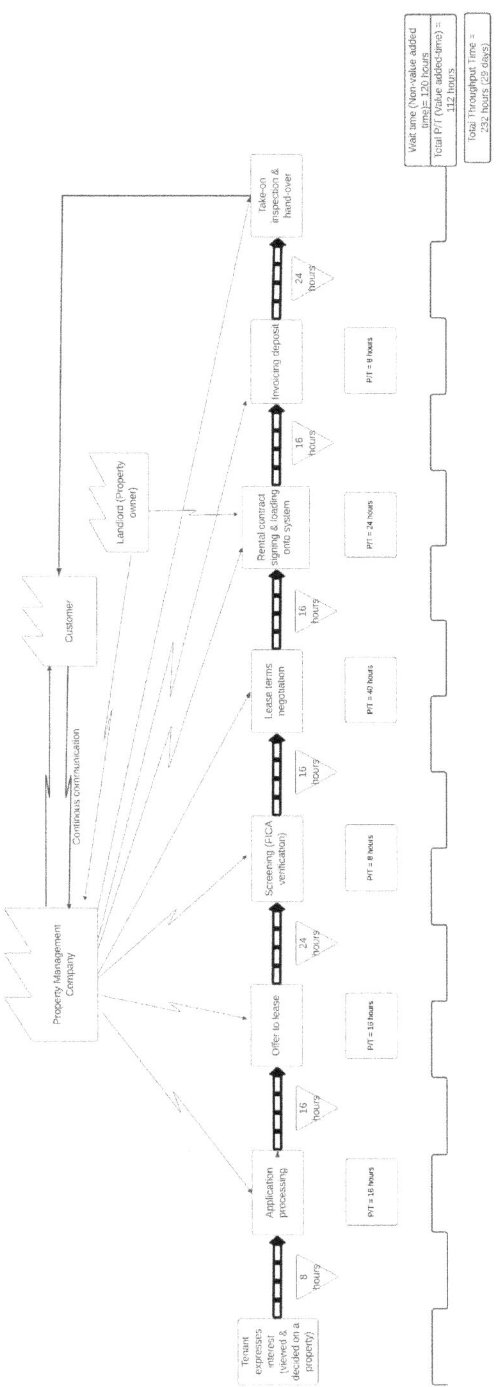

Figure 6.2 As-Is Value Stream Mapping

THE DAS MODEL

To further understand the current lease application process of XYZ property group, we make use of the DAS framework (Figure 6.3), which according to Boute and Van Mieghem (2021), is a tool that aims to segment operational functions into three layers for assessment and facilitates gap-identification, inefficient processes and enhancement opportunities in the current workflow. The layers of the framework are digital, automated, and smart. Ticks have been used to indicate the current situation while arrows have been used to show how the new digital process will move the leasing process.

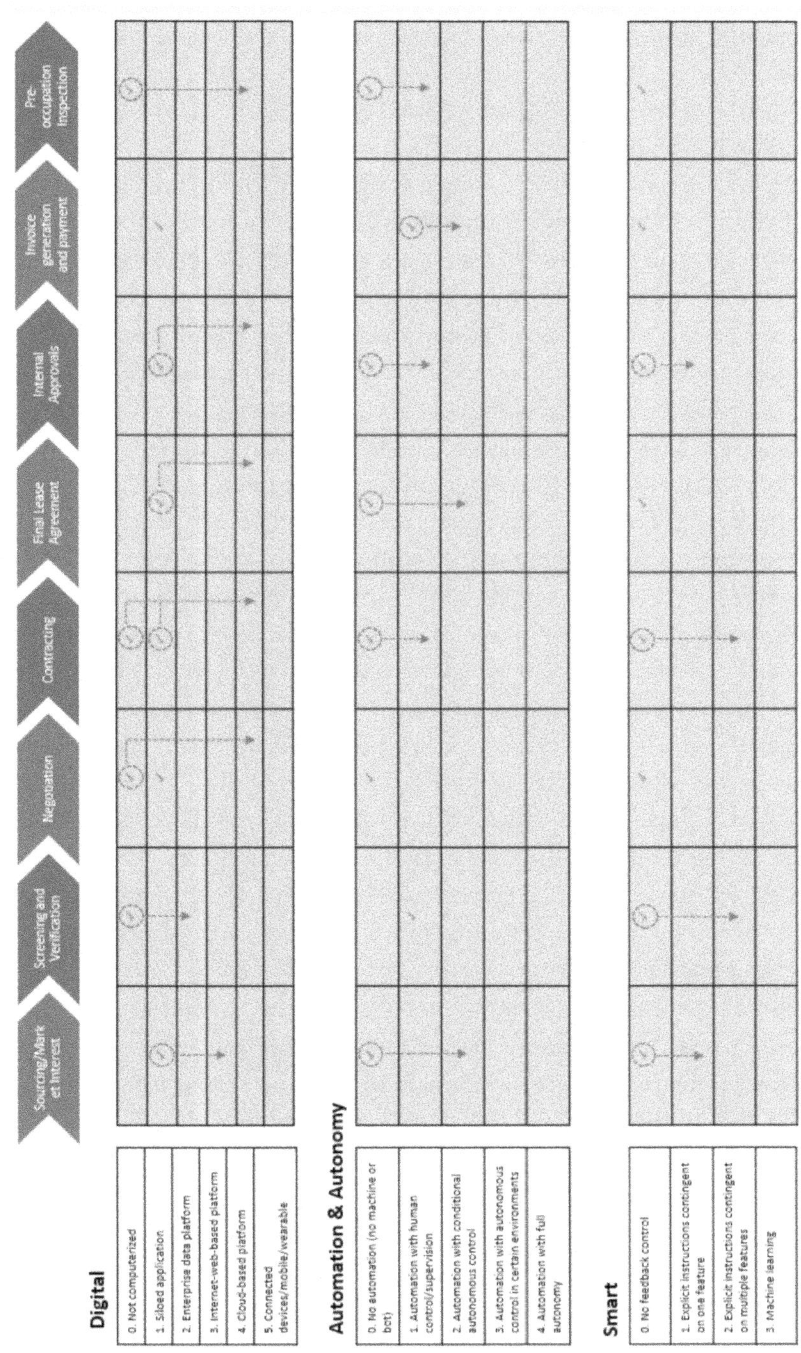

Figure 6.3 The DAS Model for XYZ Property Management Company

For easier interpretation of the DAS framework on the current process, the application has been summarised into seven main steps of the value chain, which the analysis of the digital, automation, and smart will be based on:

1. Sourcing/Market Interest
   - Digital and Automation – a potential tenant that identifies or is in search of rental space follows a manual call-to-action process where they can either call the property leasing agent or populate a 'call-me-back' form on the company's website with just a request for contact details. This process emulates a siloed application approach and is not intuitive, interactive nor does it connect to any customer relationship management system. With a response being dependent on a human resource picking up the 'call-me-back' request – the result is missed opportunities, especially where feedback is delayed. An opportunity to introduce a chatbot is presented, which will facilitate interactive engagement and initial unpacking of customer need, guiding them through the application process before handing over to a specialist. Viewing of the prospect property is available physically or by static images uploaded on the company's advertising page – a virtual walkthrough/tour (video) of spaces to let can be incorporated in the adverts to support a remote, internet-based viewing experience.
   - Smart – with the customer expressing interest through 'call-me-back' form regarding advertised space, there is still a gap to smartly use the captured details or website visits by applying search engine optimisation (SEO) and remarketing to improve conversion, and this can only be possible through digital interactions and touchpoints gathered from the prospect-customer activity supported by platform integration.

2. Screening and Verification
   - Digital – FICA and other supporting documents required for this step of the process are submitted on email and are not standardised (e.g., Standard Business Plan template) in format to enable robotic process automation (RPA), supported by optical character recognition (OCR).
   - Automation and Smart – the current activities in this step entail a combined fulfilment of a human resource and system integration for screening checks and verification, however there's an opportunity for enhanced automation as outlined in the gaps identified under 'Digital'. Standardisation in the collection of customer information can allow vetting rules to be written in the system that ultimately create efficiencies (faster) in the verification process.

3. Negotiation
   - This is a manual step in the process, where all parties get to engage through email and telephone to try to reach an agreement regarding the preliminary key terms (rent, estimated levies, rates and taxes) of agreement as outlined in the leasing offer. Although there isn't any current link to a system, this feature can be embedded in a cloud-based platform/system solution that can host an end-to-end leasing application process, for better tracking of changes and recording, eliminating risk of inconsistencies with the final drafted lease agreement.

4. Contracting
   - Digital and Automation – a paper-heavy activity, consisting of multiple printouts, manual signing and scanning of the drafted lease agreement. The lease administrator is also required to capture some detail input fields into the agreement, therefore having a platform-based fulfilment process, including a digital signature feature will eliminate the need for paper, risk of manipulation, and finger-errors.
   - Smart – currently a manual decision process. Hosting the contract on a system-based platform will enable the incorporation of referral logics where there are disagreements and deviation from standard process, in a more controlled and easier tracked environment.

5. Final Lease Agreement
   - Digital – where all the necessary signatures (approvals) have been obtained, the leasing administrator can proceed with loading the lease agreement on the property management system; however, the human intervention aspect can be avoided if the leasing process were to occur in a digital environment. Digital signatures can also be introduced, which will consist of a multi-factor authentication feature to bridge the legal concern of the verification of the authorised signatory (witnessing), as well as offer security in respect of confidentiality (TPN, 2021).
   - Automation – standardisation of all forms and required submissions will enable RPA, which in effect can allow for pre-population of information into the agreement.

6. Invoice Generation and Payment
   - Digital and Automation – the leasing administrator links the billing to the agreement (manual) which allows the relevant invoice to be generated. The human resource aspect can once again, be avoided in a digitised process. With payment gateway technology, payment can also be done on-platform, discarding the need for emailing or printouts of invoices.

7. Pre-occupation Inspection
    - Digital and Automation – this is a paper-based, physical walkabout inspection of the rental space by the property manager and the tenant before the latter party officially occupies the premises. The inspection form would include noteworthy points regarding the condition of the property at the time of occupation, which both parties sign on agreement, and the form would then be stored in a cabinet on the premises. An opportunity to link this activity to the overarching leasing process is presented, where a digital version of the form, available for access and editing on a mobile device (tablet), and connecting to the system, can be rather populated and stored digitally.

THE DIGITISED PROCESS

Based on the improvements outlined in the DAS process, the new digitised process has been outlined in Figure 6.4.

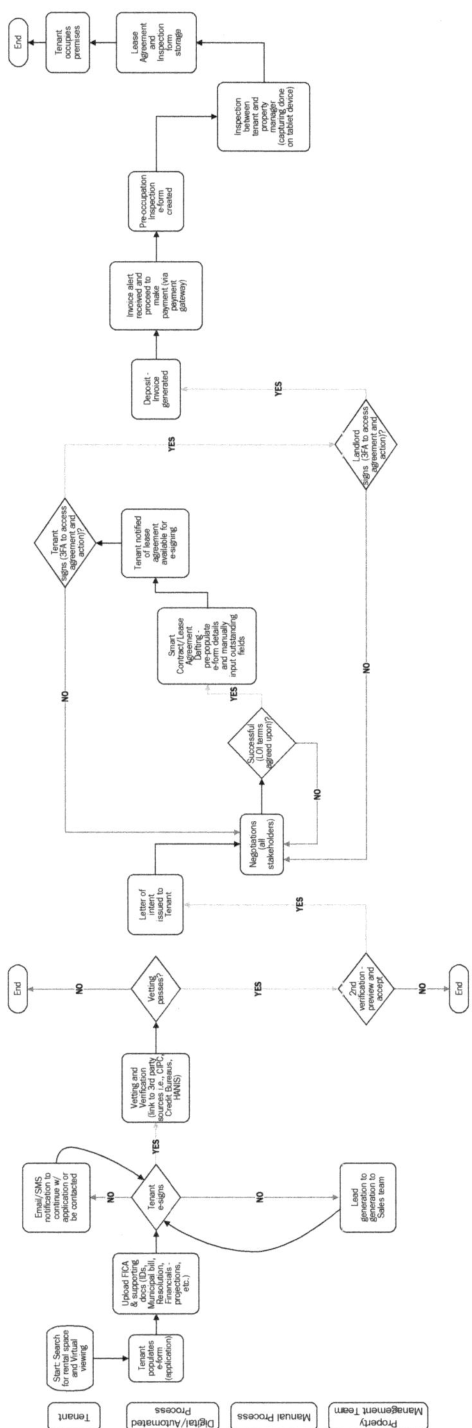

Figure 6.4 The Digitised Process

Note: The digitised process enhances the property management system through use of cloud-based property management software, and although it still involves most parties from the original approach, it is more tech-enabled, streamlined (no longer fragmented) and removes waste derived from the heavy use of paper. From when a prospective tenant expresses interest in rental space, to assessment, to signatures, handover inspection, and document storage, the entire process can be tracked and fulfilled seamlessly on a single digital platform by all mandated parties. The primary approach to operational improvement used is 'lean', where there has been more emphasis on the smooth flow in the leasing process through synchronisation, elimination of waste, savings on cost and a faster process created (Slack et al., 2017). With the removal of manual processes and limited human intervention (manipulation), thus avoiding finger-errors as well as allowing for systematic detection of exceptions, 'Total Quality Management' is achieved as a secondary approach to operational improvement.

PROCESS OPTIMISATION

The success and sustainability of any business is dependent on how best its running costs are managed. Unfortunately, old legacy systems and manual processes contribute to inefficiencies which result in revenue limitations and cumbersome manageability of businesses. The property lease management business is not exempted from the aforementioned. People, processes and technology, amongst others, are some of the factors that need to be taken into consideration when optimising property management operations.

- **People**: The adoption of digital solutions and ensuring that property management admin workforce is well trained to use such is critical in bringing about optimisation within the organisation. Re-skilling the staff will make it easier for them to monitor for outputs and intervene where necessary to ensure a quick and smooth process workflow.
- **Process**: The number of processes that were followed from the time a prospective tenant shows interest to finalising the lease agreement or contract has been reduced. For example, the submission of applications and issuing offer to lease for the potential tenant has now been integrated. Quick and easy to follow optimised processes increase delivery of services and therefore cut down on unnecessary delays due to manual processing of data and lengthy manual processes.
- **Technology**: Adoption of new technology in optimising processes is seen to be a challenge in that it threatens the employees, job security instead of it being an enabler in driving efficiencies within businesses. The introduction of online document collaboration systems for the ease of lease negotiation

shortens the negotiation process as changes are made online without a need for printing and signing documents to track changes.

Company XYZ can look at the introduction of digital solutions like e-forms which can be completed online, share-point for online editing of documents and digital signing of documents will help in optimising and improving the lease agreement processes. Once the contracts have been agreed upon and signed, they will be digitally stored and backed up in the cloud in compliance with the protection and processing of personal information regulations.

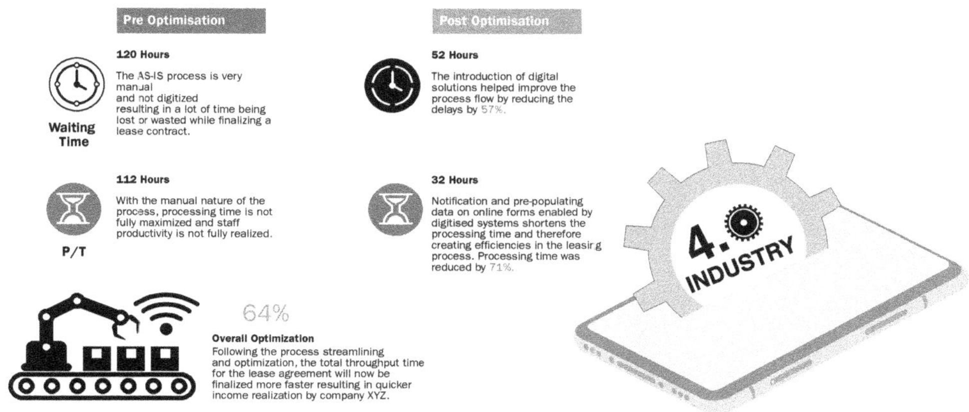

Figure 6.5 Pre and Post Optimisation

Investing in property management software will also help company XYZ streamline the leasing process because it will allow direct online interaction with the tenants and suppliers, uploading of important documentation, easy accessing and viewing of contracts and so forth.

Property management software makes it easier to manage multiple facilities across cities and extending to multiple countries as well. Company XYZ has properties in many countries outside South Africa therefore property management software will be beneficial for the seamless management of these and growing the property portfolio for even better returns.

Property maintenance is also a big challenge for landlords and property managers. Most of the defects can be prevented through routine property maintenance work that can be scheduled and communicated to the contractors, preventing issues that can lead to customer dissatisfaction.

PERFORMANCE IMPROVEMENT

All operations should be expected to improve their company's bottom line through cost management, revenue growth, risk mitigation, more efficient investment, and the development of long-term competencies (Slack et al., 2017).

There is a lack of understanding, managing, embracing and implementing digital transformation in the commercial property industry. Commercial property is one of the most conservative sectors in the economy, so transforming into a digital enterprise is a considerable challenge. Cost reduction (through process changes and process automation) and revenue growth will be part of the solution, but first there must be a paradigm shift (Stratforce Group, 2013).

Leasing is a time-consuming process. Advertising, responding to leads, handling showings, collecting and processing applications, and ultimately preparing a lease all require a lot of manpower. By automating this process, manual functions can be eliminated. Digitalising the leasing process will improve customers experience and motivate XYZ team. The process of digitisation will include virtual viewings, online lease applications, and electronic leases with digital signatures to make the process much more efficient for everyone involved (Jones, 2017).

The cloud-based portal which XYZ company and its customers will use to process the lease-agreements will commence after the initial process of virtual and physical viewing of the advertised property. Mobile phones and other browser-enabled devices can be used to sign and return documents when the process is automated. Documents no longer need to be printed, signed, scanned, and sent back separately. In the digital process, storage problems, transportation issues, and courier service problems will be eliminated.

In property management, technology is underused but can reduce expenses while increasing the quality of service. Every tiresome procedure or process needs to be automated or streamlined (Jones, 2017).

Additionally, it's critical to remember that in business, being able to track documents back to their source is essential for internal records as well as for transparency, compliance, and the security of company information (Signiflow, 2022).

The system will enable both users to:

- upload documents;
- track documents;
- update information;
- digitally sign;
- store documents;
- credit check; and
- have remote access with mobile compatibility.

Improved Performance Objectives

With reference to the five basic objectives of performance as outlined in Slack et al. (2017), the following areas of improvements will be realised from the digitisation process:

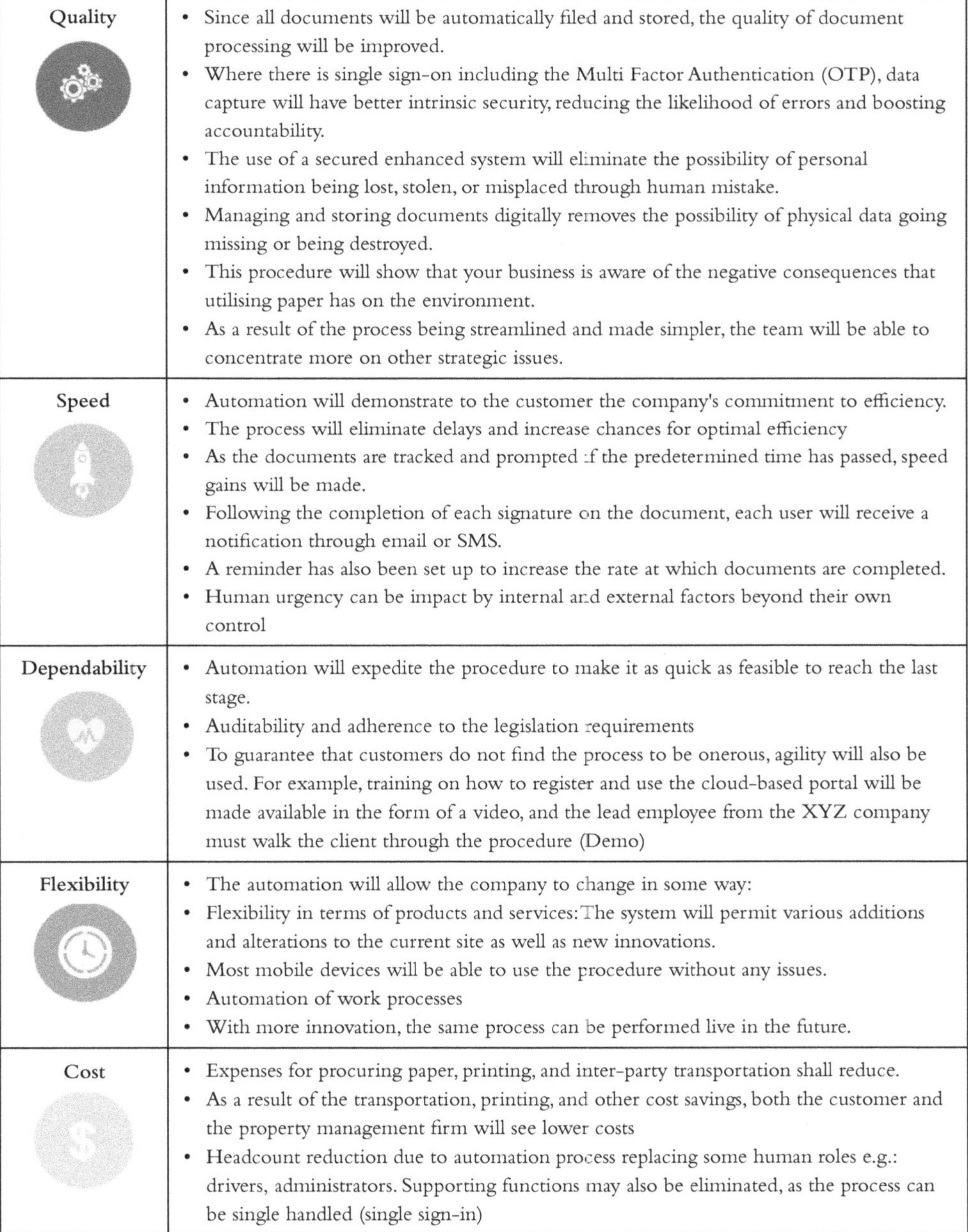

Quality	• Since all documents will be automatically filed and stored, the quality of document processing will be improved. • Where there is single sign-on including the Multi Factor Authentication (OTP), data capture will have better intrinsic security, reducing the likelihood of errors and boosting accountability. • The use of a secured enhanced system will eliminate the possibility of personal information being lost, stolen, or misplaced through human mistake. • Managing and storing documents digitally removes the possibility of physical data going missing or being destroyed. • This procedure will show that your business is aware of the negative consequences that utilising paper has on the environment. • As a result of the process being streamlined and made simpler, the team will be able to concentrate more on other strategic issues.
Speed	• Automation will demonstrate to the customer the company's commitment to efficiency. • The process will eliminate delays and increase chances for optimal efficiency • As the documents are tracked and prompted if the predetermined time has passed, speed gains will be made. • Following the completion of each signature on the document, each user will receive a notification through email or SMS. • A reminder has also been set up to increase the rate at which documents are completed. • Human urgency can be impact by internal and external factors beyond their own control
Dependability	• Automation will expedite the procedure to make it as quick as feasible to reach the last stage. • Auditability and adherence to the legislation requirements • To guarantee that customers do not find the process to be onerous, agility will also be used. For example, training on how to register and use the cloud-based portal will be made available in the form of a video, and the lead employee from the XYZ company must walk the client through the procedure (Demo)
Flexibility	• The automation will allow the company to change in some way: • Flexibility in terms of products and services: The system will permit various additions and alterations to the current site as well as new innovations. • Most mobile devices will be able to use the procedure without any issues. • Automation of work processes • With more innovation, the same process can be performed live in the future.
Cost	• Expenses for procuring paper, printing, and inter-party transportation shall reduce. • As a result of the transportation, printing, and other cost savings, both the customer and the property management firm will see lower costs • Headcount reduction due to automation process replacing some human roles e.g.: drivers, administrators. Supporting functions may also be eliminated, as the process can be single handled (single sign-in)

Figure 6.6 Performance Objectives

Polar Diagram Reflecting Current and Improved Performance Status

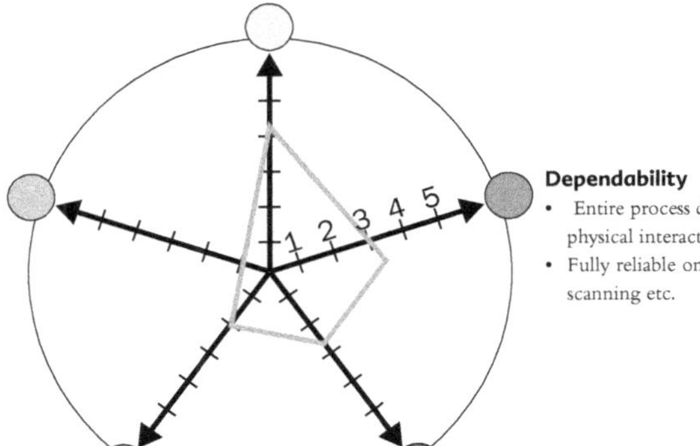

Figure 6.7 Polar Diagram Reflecting Current and Improved Performance Status

New Value Stream Map

The new value stream map is outlined below. Initially the process had eight steps; this has been reduced to seven steps

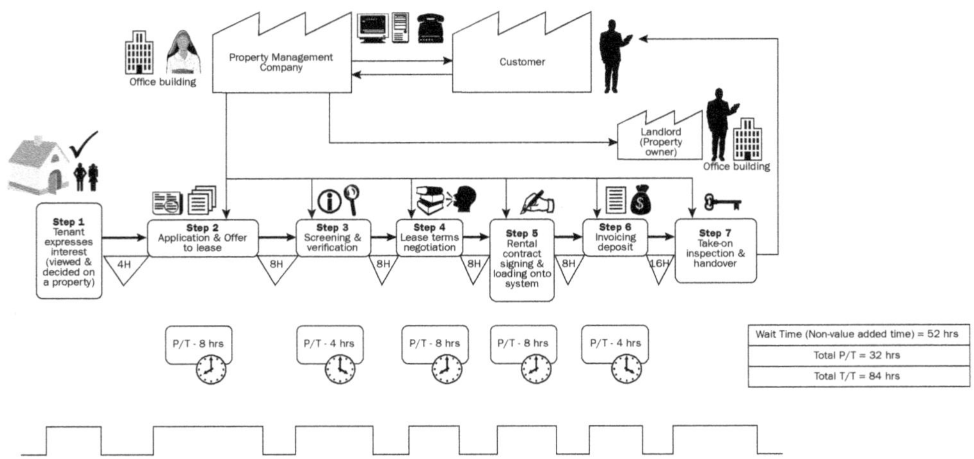

Figure 6.8 New Value Stream Map

Performance improvement summary	Current Value Stream	Digitised Value stream
Wait time (Non-value added time)	120 hours	52 hours
Processes time (Value added time)	112 hours	32 hours
Total Throughput time (hours)	232 hours	84 hours
Total Throughput time (days)	29 days	10.5 days

The improvement in non-value and value-added times by a total of 18.5 days is because of the streamlining of the processes and removal of unnecessary steps as well as the use of digitisation to improve wait times and processes times. Wait time from when the tenant expresses interest to when the application is processes has been reduced due to the use of a chatbot (two days to four hours). This creates faster response times and assists customer with initial application process. This also results in all the correct information being captured electronically (due to the chatbot's assistance).

Steps 2 and 3 (application processing and offer to lease) have been combined due to the use of an electronic form and chatbot. This is standardised and therefore RPA can be used to process the form, reducing both the processing time and wait time. The client uploads all the documentation at initial application process and therefore there is no need to request additional information from the client.

The processing time of the screening step is also reduced. Verification and exception rules are written into code, therefore verification can be streamlined and time reduced.

One of the big wins of the new process is the reduction in lease term negotiation (from 40 hours to 8 hours). This can be significantly reduced due to the cloud-based solution. Negotiation is no longer a physical process, therefore can be sped up as all parties can negotiate remotely at their own convenience through the online platform. Therefore, wait time between lease negotiation and contract signing is also reduced.

Contracting has been reduced (from 24 hours to 8 hours) due to the new digital signature system and this results in better tracking of versions and reduction of manual printing, signing and scanning. The improvement of the leasing step eliminates errors or risk of inconsistency in the terms agreed in the negotiations and effectively reduces the need for redrafting of contracts. Time is also saved since contracts no longer need to be transported to various parties for signatures. Wait time between steps is also reduced due to the digital system.

With payment gateway technology, the invoicing and deposit can also be done on-platform, reducing the time taken and the wait time in between steps, since there is no need to wait for payment to clear. Take-on inspection is also improved since this is now an electronic form.

RESOURCES AND IMPLEMENTATION PLAN

Resources

Focus Area	Process to be Improved	Proposed Solution	Benefit	Measurement	Cost	Timeline
Sourcing / Market Interest	Potential customer contacts the Company online or telephonically	**Online contact platform**	• Introducing an App to interact with the organization. • Realtime chatbot can be used for enquiries. • Online and telephonic enquiries entered into the App by person assisting with enquiry, App then used to send feedback (Pulling customer into App).	• Number of customer contacts via App and Chatbot • Number of customers successfully 'pulled' into App.	<200k ZAR initial investment for development, testing and implementation. <20k ZAR monthly management and maintenance cost	3-6 Months
Lease Negotiation	• Lease offer sent to prospective tenant. • Rental price and estimates of levies, rates &Taxes sent to potential tenant • FICA documents requested	**Digital Lease Offer**	• Digital Lease offer & FICA documents accessible from online repository. • Rental prices, estimates of rates & Taxes made available online	Reach zero documents outside of the digital exchange platform	None **Note:** Expected reduction in stationery costs.	Within 2 months of implementation
Screening and Verification	FICA and other supporting documents received & sent for verification.	**Digital Supporting documents upload**	• Electronic uploading of supporting documents. • FICA department could get a notification to check verify uploaded documents	Reach zero documents outside of the digital exchange platform	None **Note:** Expected reduction in stationary costs.	Within 2 months of implementation

Focus Area	Process to be Improved	Proposed Solution	Benefit	Measurement	Cost	Timeline
Final Lease Agreement and Internal Approvals	• Agreement document drafted, printed and signed by internal stakeholders sent to potential tenant. • Tenant makes manual notes and changes and sends document back. • Both parties print and sign final agreement. • Invoice printed, mailed through for payment.	**Online electronic agreement processing with electronic signatures**	• Agreement drafted and electronically signed. • Prospective tenant alerted to check and review document online. • Final agreement document electronically signed online.	Reach zero documents outside of the digital exchange platform	None **Note:** Expected reduction in stationary costs.	Within 2 months of implementation
Data Storage	• Hard copies of files stored in cabinets. • Risk of losing the documents • No backup copy of the original documents. • POPIA violation	**Digital storage and Backup**	• Store files in the Cloud • Backup and secure data • Cloud storage complies with POPIA	All old contracts and records to be scanned and uploaded into the cloud.	Initial costs relating to scanning and processing of manual documentation based on an estimation of 120-man hours. <60k ZAR once-off <10k ZAR per month for cloud storage facilities, backups and related security. **Note:** Should be partly offset by savings in physical storage location costs.	Within 6 months of implementation

Figure 6.9 Proposed Solution Implementation Criteria

Implementation Plan

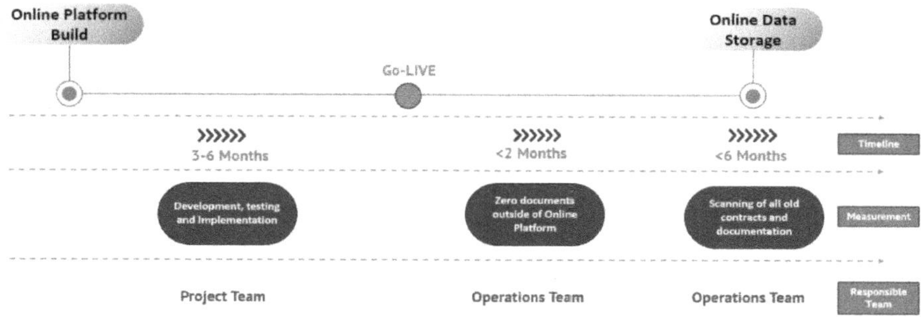

Figure 6.10 Implementation Plan

CONCLUSION

The commercial property industry has been drastically impacted by recent macroeconomic factors. This has necessitated the need for improvement in the customer experience. Property managers have had to adjust and move forward. Increased flexibility and adaptability are required. Currently the property leasing process is time-consuming and highly manual and well primed for digital improvement.

One of the key findings when analysing the current process was that there is a lot of wasted time in between processes (non-value-added time). In addition, processing time was very long for certain steps, in particular the lease negotiation and contracting processes.

It is therefore our recommendation that XYZ go through a lean transformation to streamline and enhance its processes. Any company that adopts a lean business structure does so primarily to concentrate organisational resources on reducing waste and streamlining operations to increase productivity (Do, 2017).

As mentioned, XYZ manages every rental property manually, utilising a variety of disconnected technologies like email, phone calls, paper, physical signing and delivery. Through the assignments analysis and suggestions, XYZ can improve operations and increase efficiency through digital transformation. The world's businesses are being transformed by digitisation. These initiatives are being driven by four main factors: increasing customer involvement, digitising products and investigating new business models, enhancing decision-making, and enhancing operational efficacy. Actions should be taken to continue eliminating all paper-based processes, giving all stakeholders access to digital capabilities. This ensures that systems are accessible from anywhere and enables instrumentation and virtual representation (Protiviti, 2022).

Digitisation will strengthen XYZ business processes, functions, and procedures through performance improvements with the goal of enhancing overall results as outlined in the five objectives. Continuous improvement is the process of identifying inefficiencies and working to decrease or eliminate them so that a business can compete effectively (BDC, 2021).

One of the key learnings from this assignment is that before embarking on any digital transformation strategy, it is vital to first understand the business processes and identify potential wastage or ineffective steps. Internal buy-in of new processes is an integral part of the digital transformation to ensure successful implementation. By improving the processes and implementing new technologies, reskilling should be considered to effectively utilise the current workforce, whose functions may have become superfluous. In addition, this frees up the property management team to focus on growing the business and exploring new opportunities. These efficiencies ultimately filter down to the bottom line.

Digitalisation is a continuous improvement process and by applying the principles of operations management, XYZ can ensure they are ready to adapt and move forward into the changing business world. Echoing the words of George Westerman, 'When digital transformation is done right, it's like a caterpillar turning into a butterfly, but when done wrong, all you have is a really fast caterpillar', XYZ property group can be transformed into a brave new butterfly, ready to fly into the future with confidence.

ACKNOWLEDGEMENT OF CONTRIBUTORS

* Mologadi Betty Maloka
* Atlegang Mosiman Ekgosi
* Joana Oberholzer
* Natasha Edie
* Sensi Masilela
* Philani Chili

(All are affiliated to the Wits Business School, University of the Witwatersrand, Johannesburg).

REFERENCES

Aquila. (2022). Your Guide to the Elements of a Commercial Lease (Terms, Definitions). Retrieved from https://aquilacommercial.com/learning-center/your-guide-to-the-elements-of-a-commercial-lease-terms-definitions/

BDC. (2021). Building continuous improvement into your business. Retrieved from https://www.bdc.ca/en/articles-tools/operations/operational-efficiency/continuous-improvement

Bizcommunity. (2021, December 15). 6 commercial property trends to watch out for in 2022. Retrieved from https://www.bizcommunity.com/Article/196/730/223437.html

Boute, R. N., & Van Mieghem, J. A. (2021). Digital Operations: Autonomous Automation and the Smart Execution of Work. *MBR Winter*, 1(1), 177–186. Retrieved from https://mbrjournal.com/wp-content/uploads/2020/11/32_Digital-Operations-.pdf

Broll. (2022). Increase in demand for Rosebank offices. Retrieved from https://www.broll.com/media-centre/latest-news/increase-in-demand-for-rosebank-offices

Do, D. (2017, August 5). The five principles of Lean. Retrieved from www.theleanway.net/The-Five-Principles-of-Lean

Gujral, V., Palter, R., Sanghvi, A., Vickery, B. (2020, April 9). Commercial real estate must do more than merely adapt to coronavirus. Retrieved from https://www.mckinsey.com/industries/private-equity-and-principal-investors/our-insights/commercial-real-estate-must-do-more-than-merely-adapt-to-coronavirus

Jones, T. (2017, September 8). Technology Is Evolving Property Management And Leasing – And Investors Need To Keep Up. Retrieved from https://www.forbes.com/sites/forbesrealestatecouncil/2017/09/08/technology-is-evolving-property-management-and-leasing-and-investors-need-to-keep-up/?sh=5037b92c45fd

Managecasa (2018, January 12). Dissolve Your Micromanagement Tasks/How to Reduce your Property Management Workload. Retrieved from https://managecasa.com/articles/dissolve-micromanagement-tasks-reduce-property-management-workload/

Nkate, S. (2022, February 15). Commercial real estate trends post-Covid. Retrieved from https://www.rmb.co.za/news/commercial-real-estate-trends-postcovid

Price-Bailey. (2021, October 5). The commercial property market during Covid-19: a reflection. Retrieved from https://www.pricebailey.co.uk/blog/commercial-property-market-covid-19/

Protiviti. (2022). Digital Transformation. Retrieved from https://www.protiviti.com/ZA-en/digital-transformation

Ramdass, N. (2021, July 30). Commercial property industry set to improve. Retrieved from https://www.engineeringnews.co.za/article/commercial-property-industry-set-to-improve-2021-07-16

Signiflow. (2022). Digital solutions. Retrieved from https://www.signiflow.co.za/digital-signatures/

Singh, S. (2021, February 21). The impact and effects of Covid-19 on commercial leasing agreements. Retrieved from https://www.wylie.co.za/Articles/Read/19/The-Impact-and-Effects-of-Covid-19-on-Commercial-Lease-Agreements

Slack, N., Brandon-Jones, A., Johnston, R., Singh, H., Phihlela, K., (2017). *Operations Management: Global and Southern African Perspectives*, 3rd edn. Pearson South Africa.

Stratforce Group. (2013, December 7). Commercial property as a sectoral case study for digital transformation. Retrieved from https://stratforcegroup.com/commercial-property-as-a-sectoral-case-study-for-digital-transformation/

TPN, (2021). The end of the property paper wars. Retrieved from https://blog.tpn.co.za/2021/11/the-end-of-property-paper-wars.html

Unissu. (2022, July 12). How to optimise your Property, & Asset management operations and generate new revenue in Residential and Commercial Real Estate. Retrieved from https://www.unissu.com/proptech-resources/optimise-property-asset-management-generate-revenue-residential-commercial-real-estate/

CHAPTER 7

Coal Value Chain Operational Optimisation and Digitisation Case Study

PROBLEM STATEMENT

The Electricity Company (EC) electricity baseload is almost exclusively coal dependent with more than 90 million metric tonnes (MT) of coal per annum being transported from various mines to the power stations through a complex road, rail and conveyor network. The current coal supply network and value chain is by and large manual. It is prone to energy leakage and reconciliation inaccuracies. There are also allegations of corruption around the coal supply chain where the right quality coal is not finding its way to the EC power stations.

Context

As a vertically integrated utilities provider in South Africa, EC owns and operates various coal-fired power stations which among them utilise coal of different quality specifications to generate electricity. The Primary Energy Division (PED), which is part of the EC generation business unit, is tasked with the responsibility to ensure effective and efficient supply of right quality at the right time to the power stations.

PED division owns the Primary Energy Business Value chain that deals with procurement, logistics management, quality management, storage and supply management of the coal to the EC. Coal being a key input into the power generation process makes the PED operation mission critical for successful operation of the EC and more so to ensure the EC is able to meet the country's energy demand effectively. To this end, accurate data is required on the movement of coal across the PED value chain, which includes but is not limited to coal available at mine, the quality of coal, coal stock levels at rail sidings, coal delivered to the power stations through various modes of transportation, coal stock levels at power stations and the volume of coal consumed in the production of electricity.

Management of the coal supply chain has been a persistent and key issue for the EC in the past and continues to be a challenge currently. Automation of the coal management process along with accurate record keeping of all the relevant data points across the value chain is important for audit, performance measurement, accounting, visibility and management of the coal operations.

Coal is delivered to power stations by the following modes of transport:

a. Conveyor belts
b. Rail transport
c. Road transport
    * A portion through EC Managed Contractors (FCA)
    * A portion through Supplier Managed Contractors (DEL)

A multi-dimensional technology-driven model solution making use of road and rail is required.

Currently very little automation is available for information gathering. Information is gathered using various means and consolidated into spreadsheets and other system such as Collops and Coal Stock System (CSS). Manual intervention is prevalent throughout all processes and most reporting is spreadsheet based.

Therefore, an automated process providing the user with a 'single source of truth' of the end-to-end movement of the coal volumes and coal quantities across the PED Coal Value Chain is required.

Below is a high-level capability view of the PED business process:

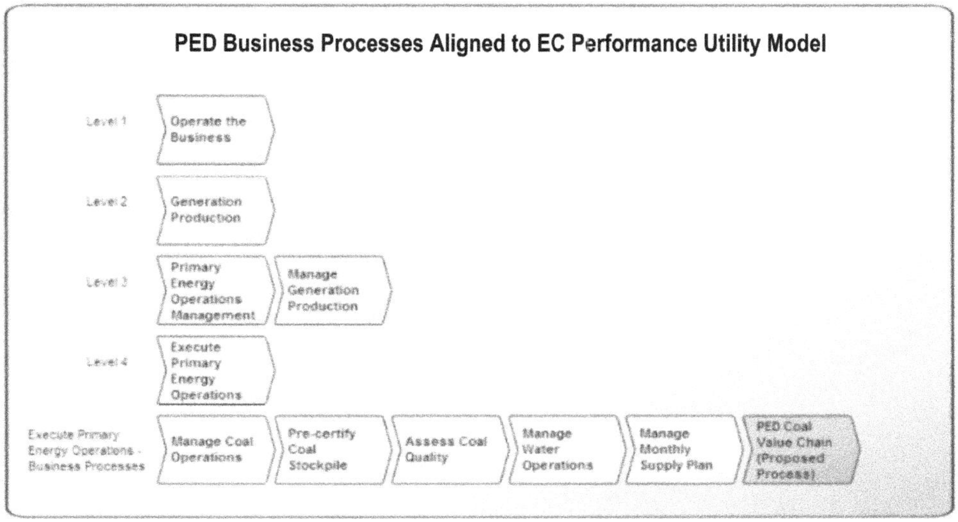

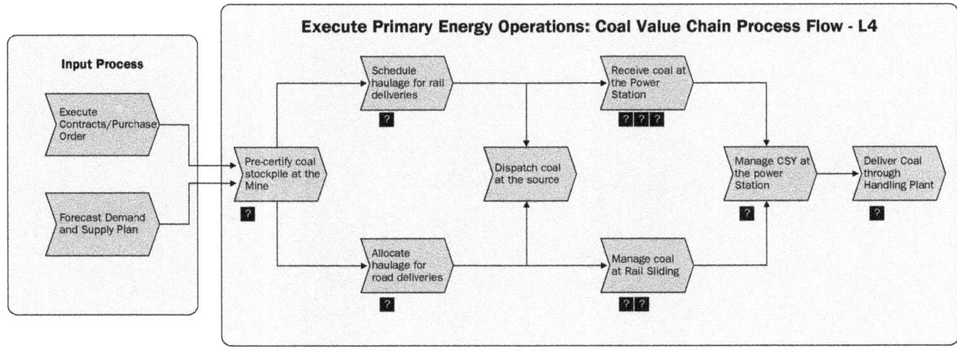

Figure 7.1 Electricity Company Utility Model

As demonstrated above Coal Value Chain is a new process that is being proposed to be included under the Level 4: Execute Primary Energy Operations capability, to ensure smooth operations of the coal supply and logistics management.

The Coal value chain process can be represented by the following level 4 process flow:

Figure 7.2 Coal Value Chain Process Flow—L4

This above level 4 process can be further represented as per the below As-Is process flow:

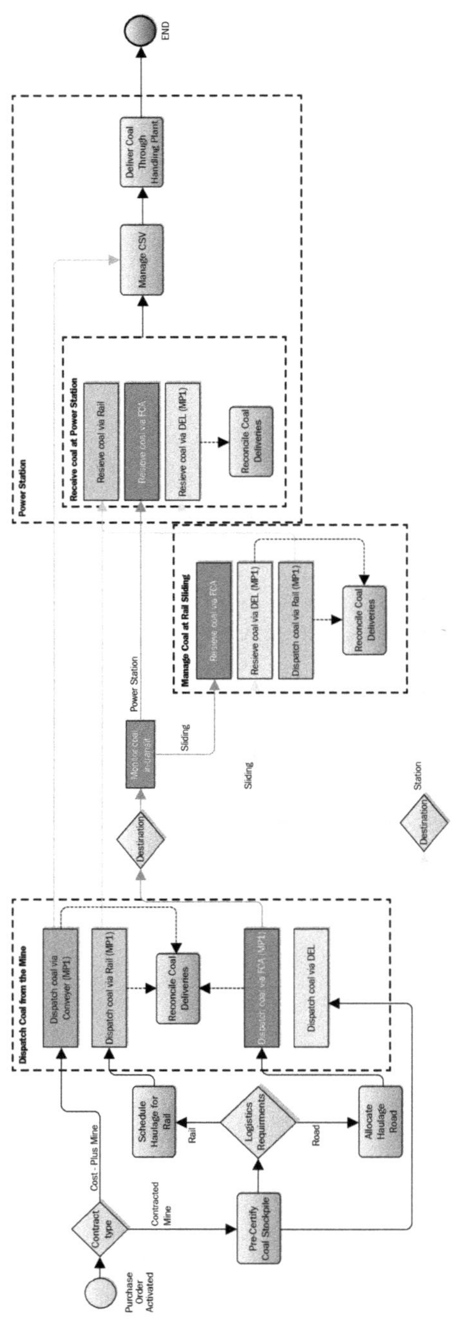

Figure 7.3 As-Is Representation of Level 4 process

As part of this assignment members of Syndicate 4 attempt to understand the As-Is situation of the EC PED's Coal Value Chain process while identifying the key value drivers and areas of strategic gaps with a view to enabling the EC to better control and operate its coal value chain. The scope of this assignment will be limited to the coal value chain process and excludes analysis of any input or output processes to the coal value chain process.

It is our assumption that the EC has already implemented required interventions to optimise the input and output processes to the coal value chain process.

BACKGROUND AND CONTEXT

According to the TIPS report, SA leads in the production of global coal by contributing 3.6% in comparison to 0.6% produced globally. This coal enables the EC to fuel over 80% of the electricity supply for SA. The EC alone uses 60% of SA coal. According to SCOA, coal prices have declined with decreasing coal supply avenues in SA. The shortage of coal supply could mean that the EC has to rely on other more expensive avenues (OCTGs) for power generation.

Domestic coal consumption in South Africa (DMR, 2015)

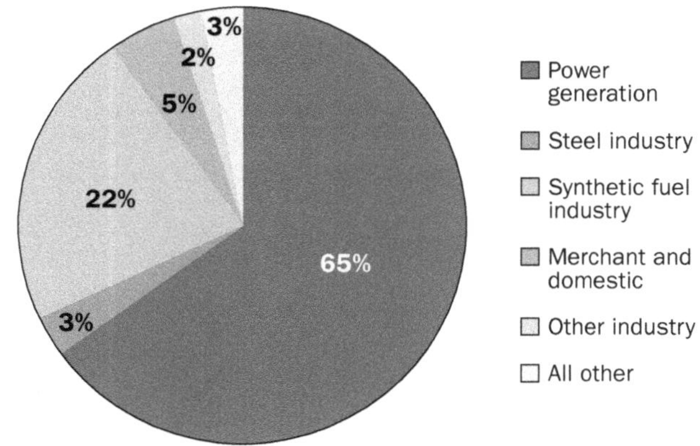

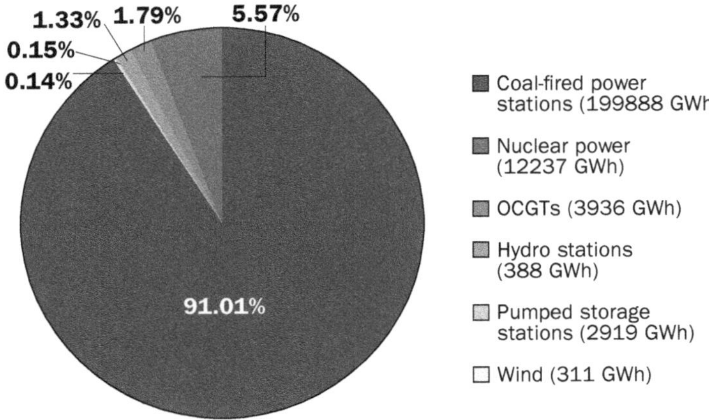

Figure 7.4 Coal Consumption Patterns

Coal Costs

According to the EC, in early 2000 the price of coal was averaging R60/t, by 2018 the costs had tremendously increased to R400/t. These financial increase changes are due to growth in inflation related to mining and coal mining in demanding geological conditions. In the past, the EC used low-grade coal. The consumed coal was supplied by closely built tied mines via the conveyor belt. This translated to a low costs transportation model. The long-term coal supplier agreements translated to the low cost of coal for the EC. The EC coal supplier chain is broken down to 60% conveyor delivered, 30% (equating to 40 mtpa) truck delivered increasing from 14%, and 10% delivered by rail.

	Arnot	Camden	Grootvlei	Hendrina	Komati	Kusile	Kusile (units 5 and 6)
O&M – ficex (R/kW/a)	638	686	686	638	868	959	959
O&M – variable (c/kWh)	6	66	6	6	6	8	8
Water (R/kl)	8	7	4	8	8	19	19
Coal – delivered (R/ton)	380	47	519	407	407	377	446

Figure 7.5 Summary of Costs

Electricity Company Current Coal Challenges/Problem Statement

- **Speed:** Security and transport breakdowns impact the speed that coal is supplied to the EC. Using suppliers located away from the conveyor belts also exacerbates the situation. The cumbersome supplier on-boarding process further contributes to the timely delivery of coal.

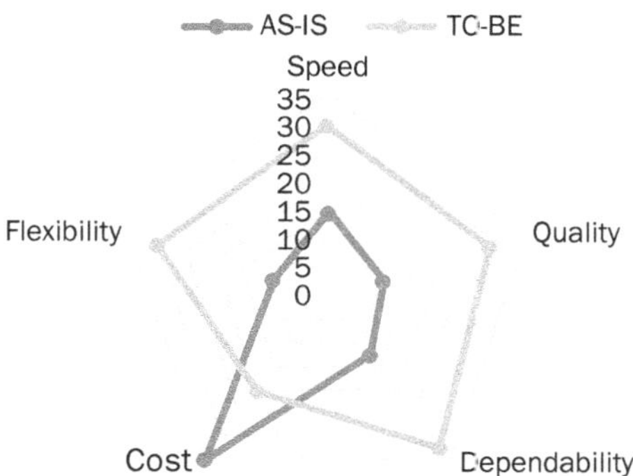

- **Quality:** Low-quality coal supplied (according to *Mining Engineering News*), lack of advanced technologies for weighing and evaluating coal quality.
- **Dependability:** Lack of tracking and visibility in the supply value chain. Manual processes result in unpredictable results.
- **Cost:** Supplier costs have increased due to an increase in truck-supplied coal, a decline in coal availability
- **Flexibility:** Ability to alter the demand and supply patterns based on internal and external forces that enable effective and efficient coal operation via scenario and proactive planning.

All of the above severely impact the EC's ability to generate electricity, which in turn has a key impact on power security nationally for South Africa.

AS-IS PROCESS MAP

Coal value chain process is part of the overall Execute Primary Energy Operations level 3 capability and has the process flow illustrated in Figure 7.6.

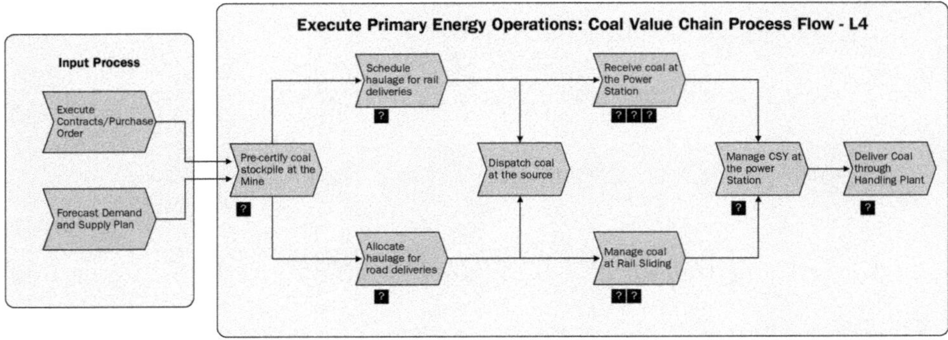

Figure 7.6 As-Is Process Map

As outlined in the process flow the coal value chain process has the following key process areas:

Pre-Certify Stockpile – That deals with management of coal quality on both the mine and power station side.	
Schedule Coal Haulage for Rail Deliveries – That deals with rail transport scheduling management for coal delivery.	
Allocate Haulage for Rail Delivery – That deals with allocation of specific rail vehicles as per the schedule and quantity requirements.	
Dispatch Coal from Mine (Rail) – Deals with the process of dispatch planning for transportation of coal from Mine via Rail.	

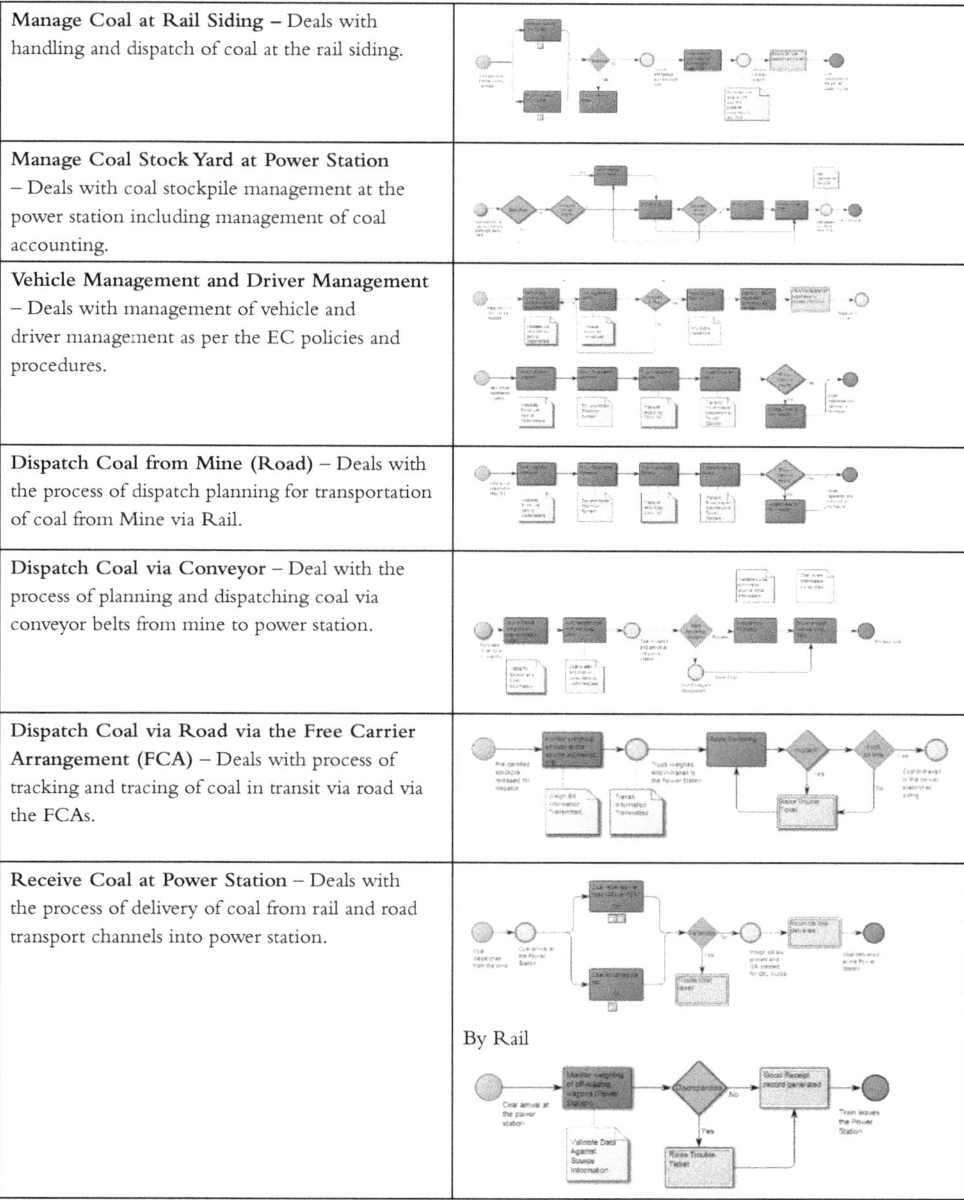

Manage Coal at Rail Siding – Deals with handling and dispatch of coal at the rail siding.	
Manage Coal Stock Yard at Power Station – Deals with coal stockpile management at the power station including management of coal accounting.	
Vehicle Management and Driver Management – Deals with management of vehicle and driver management as per the EC policies and procedures.	
Dispatch Coal from Mine (Road) – Deals with the process of dispatch planning for transportation of coal from Mine via Rail.	
Dispatch Coal via Conveyor – Deal with the process of planning and dispatching coal via conveyor belts from mine to power station.	
Dispatch Coal via Road via the Free Carrier Arrangement (FCA) – Deals with process of tracking and tracing of coal in transit via road via the FCAs.	
Receive Coal at Power Station – Deals with the process of delivery of coal from rail and road transport channels into power station.	By Rail

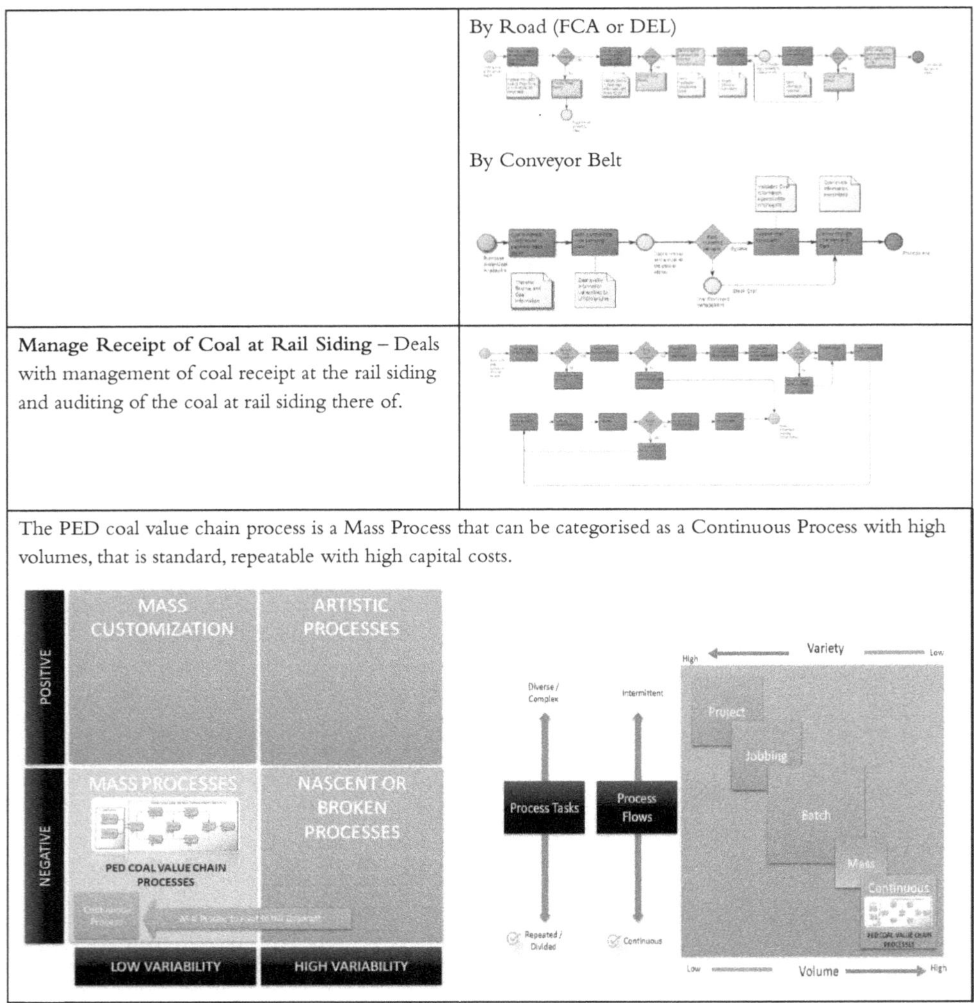

By Road (FCA or DEL)
By Conveyor Belt

Manage Receipt of Coal at Rail Siding – Deals with management of coal receipt at the rail siding and auditing of the coal at rail siding there of.

The PED coal value chain process is a Mass Process that can be categorised as a Continuous Process with high volumes, that is standard, repeatable with high capital costs.

Based on the above process flows it is key and vital to note the level of automation across all the processes and sub-processes needs to mature for effective management of operations of the identified coal value chain. There are multiple interventions required from an operations digitalisation perspective to achieve the required level of efficiencies and address the key challenges:

Figure 7.7 Current Pain Points

Based on Figure 7.7 we propose and have adopted a Business Process Re-Engineering approach to enable the EC to realise dramatic improvements in its performance by radically embedding automation into the coal value chain processes as an initial phase. Once the processes are re-engineered and automation is implemented, we propose that the EC follow a Lean Sigma process to achieve waste reduction and fast throughput time while leveraging on data-driven rigour and variation control to achieve operational excellence in the PED value chain.

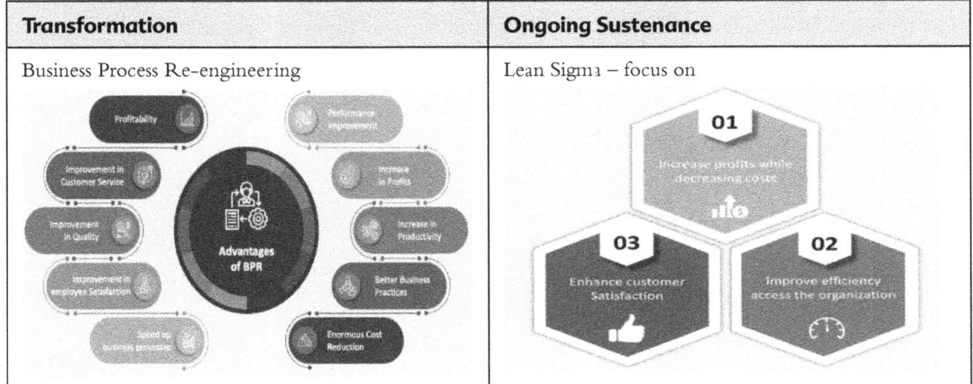

Figure 7.8 BPR and Lean-Sigma Approach

We propose that that PED value chain would require the following key capabilities as part of the automation opportunities:

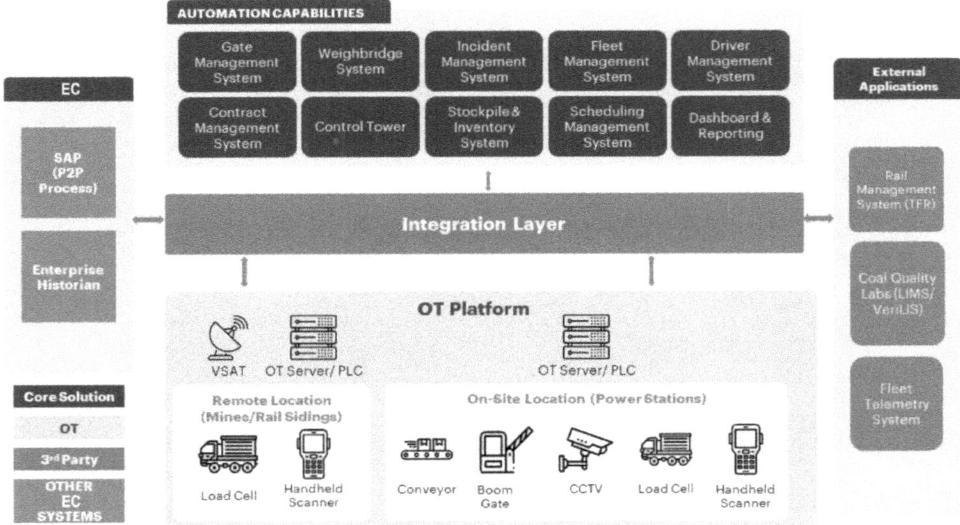

Figure 7.9 Proposed Automation

The following information must be captured and/or sourced from existing/ future systems:

- Coal volumes at the mines, located in the EC stockpiles, are being built and the stockpiles that have been quality assessed and are opened for delivery to the power stations;
- Quality of the coal of the EC stockpiles that have been quality assured;
- Pre-certified coal availability information at mines and sidings on a continuous basis;
- Coal volume delivered to power stations via conveyor;
- Road delivery transactions at sources (mines);
- Road delivery transactions at destination (power stations and sidings);
- Rail collection transactions at sources (mines/sidings);
- Rail delivery transactions at power stations;
- Coal stock levels at power stations and rail sidings; and
- Coal volumes burnt by the power stations.

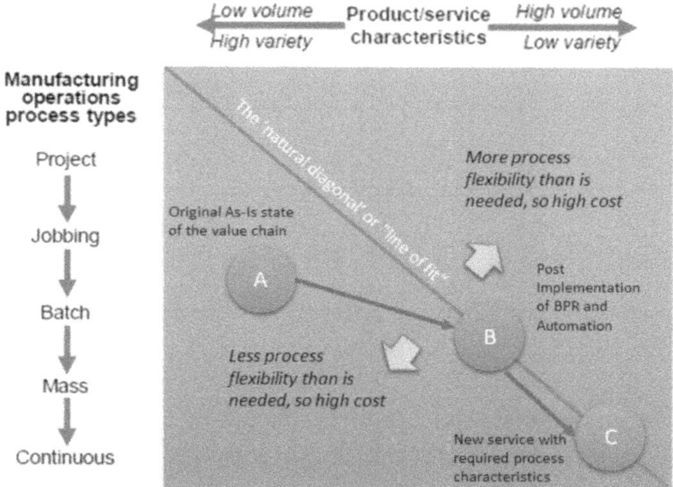

Current Scenario: Primary Energy is currently dependent on a lot of manual capturing of data regarding coal quantities and qualities across the value chain and information is captured and reported by means of spreadsheets. Although the files are stored on a central network, it is not an accurate and secure system with limited traceability.

The product process matrix on the left outlines our approach towards the proposed process improvement for the coal value chain.

VALUE STREAM MAPPING

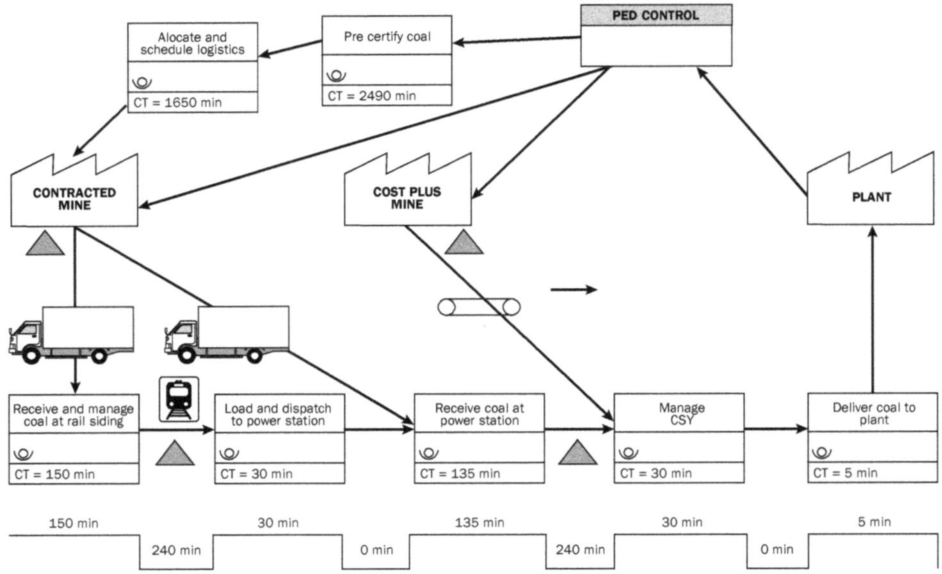

Figure 7.10 PED Value Stream

From the information in Figure 7.10, there are three main modes of coal transport namely: road, rail and conveyor systems. The conveyor system is the most efficient mode of transport from the mine as there are no double handling activities in between. The road transport has one stockpile at the station and the rail has two stockpile activities at the rail siding and the power station. The below process maps provide further details into the processes for each transportation mode.

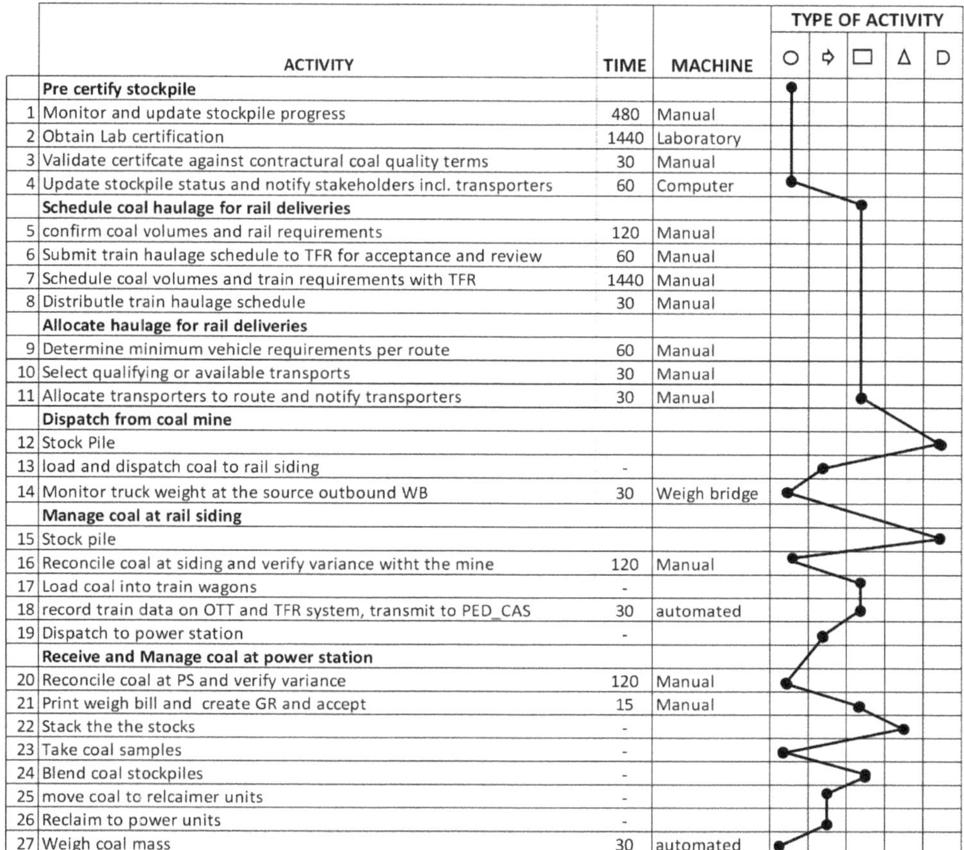

ACTIVITY	TIME	MACHINE	TYPE OF ACTIVITY				
			O	⇨	□	Δ	D
Pre certify stockpile							
1 Monitor and update stockpile progress	480	Manual	●				
2 Obtain Lab certification	1440	Laboratory	●				
3 Validate certifcate against contractural coal quality terms	30	Manual	●				
4 Update stockpile status and notify stakeholders incl. transporters	60	Computer	●				
Schedule coal haulage for rail deliveries							
5 confirm coal volumes and rail requirements	120	Manual			●		
6 Submit train haulage schedule to TFR for acceptance and review	60	Manual			●		
7 Schedule coal volumes and train requirements with TFR	1440	Manual			●		
8 Distributle train haulage schedule	30	Manual			●		
Allocate haulage for rail deliveries							
9 Determine minimum vehicle requirements per route	60	Manual			●		
10 Select qualifying or available transports	30	Manual			●		
11 Allocate transporters to route and notify transporters	30	Manual			●		
Dispatch from coal mine							
12 Stock Pile							●
13 load and dispatch coal to rail siding	-			●			
14 Monitor truck weight at the source outbound WB	30	Weigh bridge	●				
Manage coal at rail siding							
15 Stock pile							●
16 Reconcile coal at siding and verify variance witht the mine	120	Manual	●				
17 Load coal into train wagons	-			●			
18 record train data on OTT and TFR system, transmit to PED_CAS	30	automated			●		
19 Dispatch to power station	-			●			
Receive and Manage coal at power station							
20 Reconcile coal at PS and verify variance	120	Manual	●				
21 Print weigh bill and create GR and accept	15	Manual			●		
22 Stack the the stocks	-					●	
23 Take coal samples	-		●				
24 Blend coal stockpiles	-				●		
25 move coal to relcaimer units	-			●			
26 Reclaim to power units	-			●			
27 Weigh coal mass	30	automated	●				

Figure 7.11 VSM for Rail Transport

Figure 7.11 represents the rail transportation mode where coal is first moved from the mine to the rail siding using road transport. The coal is temporarily stored at the rail siding before loading into train wagons for haulage to the power station where it is again stored temporarily before being moved to the power station. There are inefficiencies in the process of transporting the coal to the power station as it is temporarily stored twice en route. There is also a lot of inspection/quality assurance activities during this process.

	ACTIVITY	TIME	MACHINE	TYPE OF ACTIVITY				
				O	⇨	□	Δ	D
	Pre certify stockpile			●				
1	Monitor and update stock pile progres	480	Manual	●				
2	Obtain Lab certification	1440	Laboratory	●				
3	validate certifcate against contractural coal quality terms	30	Manual	●				
4	Update stockpile status and notify stakeholders incl. transporters	60	Computer	●				
	Schedule coal haulage for road deliveries					●		
5	Confirm coal volumes and truck requirements	120	Manual					
6	Schedule coal volumes and truck requirements with transporters	60	Manual					
7	Distributle road haulage schedule	30	Manual				●	
	Dispatch Coal via road							
8	Stock Pile							●
9	Load and dispatch coal via road	-	Manual		●			
10	Monitor truck weight at the source outbound WB	30	Weigh bridge	●				
	Receive and Manage coal at power station							
11	Validate fleet and schedule at arrival	15	Manual					●
12	Monitor weighing of truck at inbound WB	30	Weigh bridge	●				
13	Offload at CSY	-			●			
14	Weigh empty truck at outbound WB	30	Weigh bridge	●				
15	Reclaim to power units	-			●			

Figure 7.12 VSM for Road Transport

Figure 7.12 represents road transportation directly to the power station, where coal is temporally stored before being moved to the power station. As with the rail transport, although not as many, there are a lot of quality assurance activities that prolong the process, and these can be optimised.

	ACTIVITY	TIME	MACHINE	TYPE OF ACTIVITY				
				O	⇨	□	Δ	D
1	**Purchase order receive**							
	Dispatch coal via conveyor				●			
2	Weigh coal in transit	-	In line scale	●	●			
3	Auto sample coal with sampling plant	-	Automated	●	●			
4	Bypass to coal handling plant or stack coal	-	semi automated		●		●	
5	Deliver through coal handling plant	-			●			

Figure 7.13 VSM for conveyor transport

Figure 7.13 represents conveyor transportation of the coal; the process is a lot more efficient with no double handling activities in between. The coal is transported straight into the power station from the mine with inline quality monitoring systems.

GAP ANALYSIS

VALUE STREAM	CURRENT STATE	DESIRED STATE	GAP	IMPACT
1. Precertify coal at Mine (contracted mines)	Precertification process takes long at 2490 mins.	Pre-certification to take 120 mins.	EC has no definite recorded and audited knowledge of volumes (stock levels) of coal produced in mines in real time to enable swift decision-making. There is also no capability to keep track of the weight of stockpile of coal. EC is currently not tracking stockpile completion date, labeling of stockpile & obtain stockpile certification and update stockpile labeling. No means to fully certify and record for audit purposes, the quality of coal produced in mines against contractual requirements.	Reduction in process time and quality monitoring
2. Allocate and schedule logistics	Allocation and scheduling of trains and trucks takes too long (1650 mins) and too many engagements.	Automatic scheduling and notification of trains and road transport services.	The process lacks the capabilities to monitor volumes of coal delivered via the conveyor/truck/road. EC has no automated process to calculate required delivery trucks for the route, select available qualifying transporters, allocate to qualifying trucks and digitally share route and loaded trucks with the EC receivers.	Reduction in process time
3. Load and dispatch coal (Contracted mines)	Exposure to coal theft and delays in getting to the EC plant should there be any mechanical failures that are not immediately remediable due to late notification and late dispatch of needed help.	Control and real time monitoring of haulages	The coal is not monitored in transit from the mine to the EC, even though it can be precertified, the EC has no single view of the truth that they are receiving the same quality and volume of coal that was dispatched. The trucks/goods trains have no digital real-time monitoring capabilities. Conveyors: No real-time monitoring capability on conveyor meters and feed mines cumulative tons throughout the day. Lack of recorded quality and volumes	Availability and quality

VALUE STREAM	CURRENT STATE	DESIRED STATE	GAP	IMPACT
4. Receive and manage coal at siding	Manual receipt and management of coal volumes	Automation of siding activities including the quality	The coal volume and quality levels at station are manually measured with digital real-time capability of interconnected devices and people to make sound financial decisions, prevent theft and record for audit purposes with ability to make predictive analysis on when to raise the next Purchase Order (PO), what mines to get the coal from who are producing the required volumes at the time and are in close range.	Reduction process time
5. Manage CSY	Manual inventory management, reconciliation and blending	Digitalisation of coal inventory management	There is manual process to validate the vehicles delivering the coal, the control access is not effective. Manual recording of time of entry, exit and gross and net weight of the load delivered and validity of the PO. Lack of real-time feedback mechanisms to improve experience of the drivers, personnel on site, conditions on equipment and overall EC process satisfaction.	Reduce coal waste and ensure that there is accurate billing to the EC
6. PED control	Fragmented oversight and control of PED activities	Single view and control of all PED activities in real time	No real-time capability reporting across the value chain. Inability to keep digital data and insights over five years as required by audit regulations. No interconnected systems to view and custom draw reports as and when needed.	Overall process efficiency will improve

110

OPTIMISATION AND DIGITILISATION PROPOSAL

Based on our understanding of the challenges faced by the coal value chain process and inferring from the knowledge of the As–Is process and automation levels, we believe an integrated coal value chain automation system that aims at automating various manual tracking tracing and data collection points is key as a foundation to ensure the EC has a single source of truth view across the entire value chain. Ensuring such a system integrate into a control tower concept provides the EC the ability to monitor and control the entire value chain while acting proactively to avoid theft, losses and avoid corruption.

We propose the EC automate the coal value chain by leveraging on a BPR approach that streamlines various manual processes and ensures the EC is able to reduce the overall cycle time. Furthermore, the BPR approach needs to consider automation in such a way that enables the EC to gather data and analyse data in real time across the coal value chain, thereby increasing visibility and transparency across the value chain. We propose that the EC consider implementing a coal value chain automation system with following capabilities:

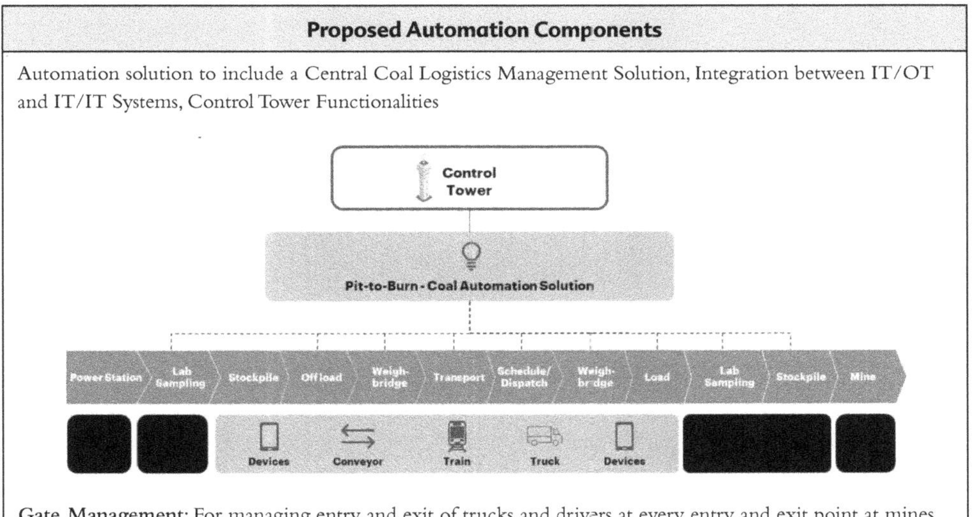

Gate Management: For managing entry and exit of trucks and drivers at every entry and exit point at mines and power stations.

Incident Management: A central view of all incidents across the coal logistics value chain, so that the relevant operations teams can take co-ordinated response and mitigating actions.

Fleet Management: A portal-based functionality for the fleet companies to interact with the central coal value chain automation system to upload fleet-related information and respond to the published trip schedules.

Driver Management: A portal-based functionality for the fleet companies to interact with the central coal value chain automation system to upload driver-related information and respond to the published trip schedules.

Inventory Management and Coal Accounting: An automated coal accounting system that provides the EC a single point view of coal at hand, coal in transit and coal on conveyor going for burn; thereby providing real-time auditable insights of its coal position per power station and/or mine.

Weighbridge System: A central functionality that reconciles all the weighbridge readings across all mines, rail sidings and power stations to provide an accurate view of any deviations or loss of coal either in loading, transit or off-loading.

Schedule Management System: A central scheduling functionality that allows schedulers to automatically generate optimised schedules based on their current coal position (burn rate – stock in hand – demand). This module also enables the schedulers to alter the schedule based on contract volumes and residual contract volumes and/or duration.

Contract Management System: A functionality that is integrated with coal value chain automation system to provide accurate view of the current coal and fleet contract positions.

Control Tower: A central and/or per site interactive dashboard-based functionality that provides the control tower operator a cockpit view of all the individual functions of the coal logistics value chain. The operator will be able to click through on an interactive dashboard to understand and visualise the end-to-end value chain while proactively monitoring and resolving issues and incidents. This will also include cockpit views for PED executives and power station managers

Dashboard and Reporting: The coal value chain automation solution will have capabilities of producing both transactional reports directly from the Coal Logistics Management Solution (LMS) and will also have a dashboarding capability that will sit on top of the core backbone to produce interactive dashboards.

Integration and Workflow Orchestration: EC's coal value chain automation platform will need to integrate to several 3rd party systems such as SAP ERP, Electricity Company LIMS, Historian, a variety of fleet telematics systems and Transnet's rail management platform. The high-level automation solution needs to make provision for these integration points.

Voice Assistance: A voice recognition-based engine that will allow for automation of incident reporting and management across the coal supply chain. This will enable end-to-end incident traceability across the solution

QR Code: QR codes will be used as a manual back up for transmitting of trip, vehicle, driver, load, quality and schedule related data that will get encoded as a QR code on the truck and can be scanned via a hand-held reader to retrieve in case system connectivity is down between mine and central coal value chain automation system.

Proposed OT Solution Components

The OT solution includes PLCs at each weighbridge (mines, rail sidings and power stations), PLCs at mass meters, Hand-help devices for gate management, VSAT based communication layer, Site OT Servers.

All the mines, power stations and rail sidings will have PLCs installed which will be used as data interfaces between the mass meters, weighbridge electronics and any other field sensor devices. Each local site will be fitted with an operational technology (OT) server. The OT server will act as the local gateway between the central coal value chain automation solution and local OT equipment such as PLCs, sensors etc. Break-out communications from the sites will be by means of VSAT at 3rd party sites such as the mines and rail sidings and via the Electricity Company business LAN for power stations. Local operators at the sites will be equipped with rugged mobile devices to enable the onsite functionality of the coal value chain automation. Each process such as weighbridge operations, stockpile operations and gate management will have a custom developed app that will be installed on the mobile devices. The data from the individual sites and the various equipment will be transmitted to the central coal value chain automation software platform in a near real-time mode.

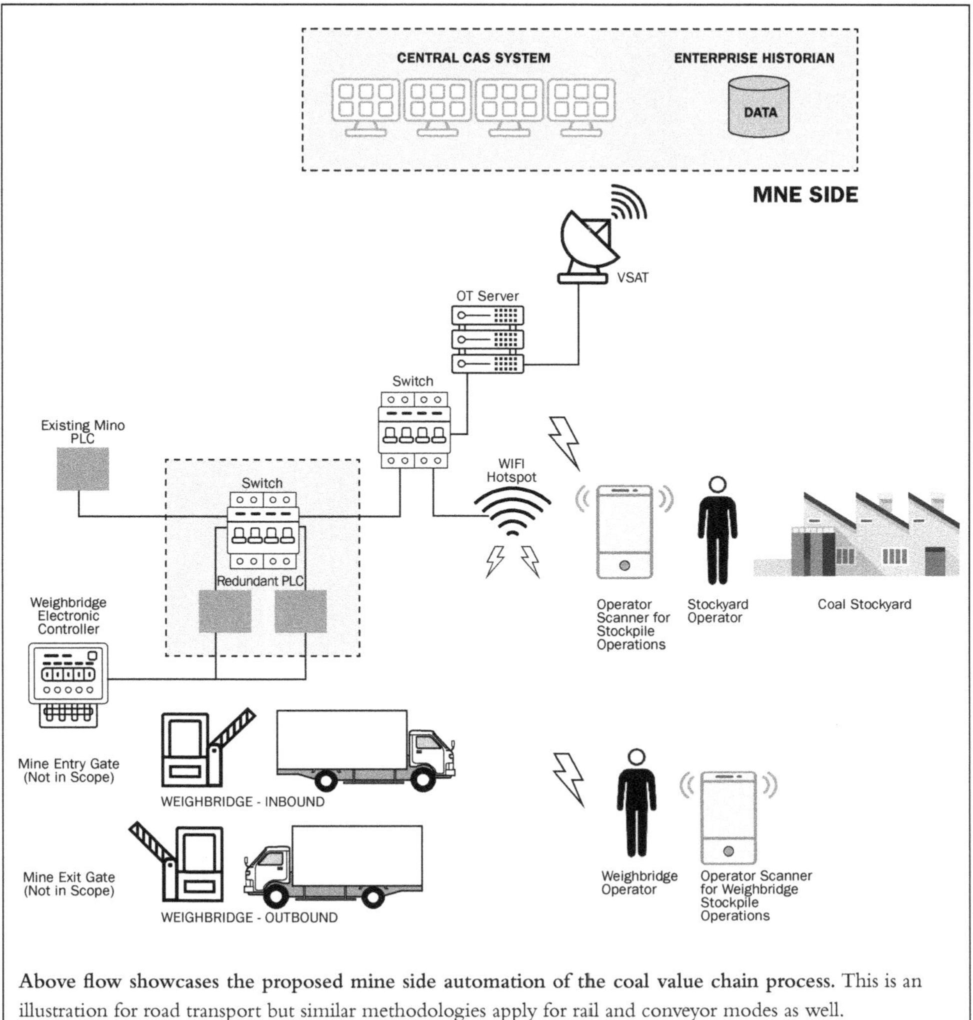

Above flow showcases the proposed mine side automation of the coal value chain process. This is an illustration for road transport but similar methodologies apply for rail and conveyor modes as well.

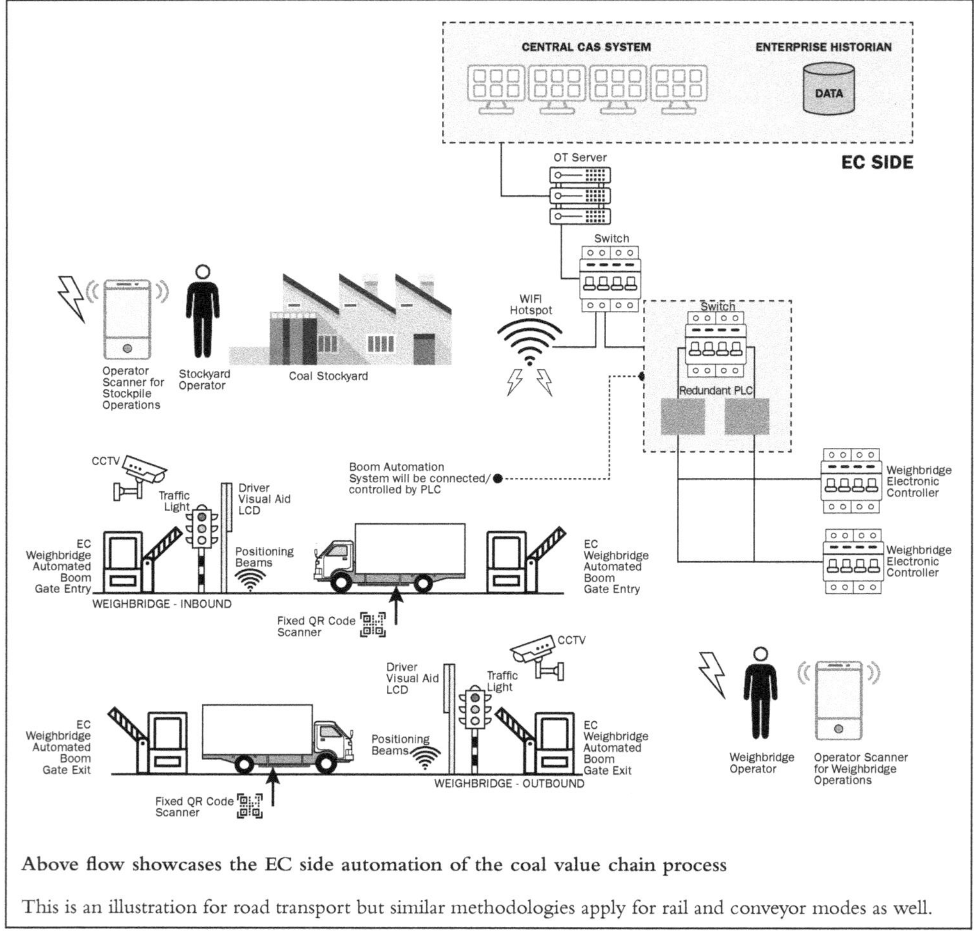

Above flow showcases the EC side automation of the coal value chain process

This is an illustration for road transport but similar methodologies apply for rail and conveyor modes as well.

Figure 7.14 Proposed Automation Approach

OPTIMISATION BASELINE AND METRICS

Salient PED Process Activities	Optimisation Baseline Metrics				
	Quality	Dependability	Flexibility	Speed	Cost
Pre-Certify Coal Stockpile (Mine and Power Station)	• Inventory Management and coal accounting system *(IMCAS)* • Real-time, auditable view of coal levels per power station and mine, including weight sensing	• Reliable insights on real time knowledge of coal stockpiles improves long term planning initiatives • Shortages and re-stocks of coal identified well in advance	• Operational Technology (OT) Solutions implementation will improve Coal levels assessments in real-time, with the PLCs installed across sites to actively monitor any variances	• Automation results in reduction of stockpile level assessment time • Reporting of inputs is electronic through **IMCAS**	• Cost reduction from reduced manual (Human) input requirements
Allocate and schedule logistics (rail and road)	• **Schedule Management System** • Reduces costs of unnecessary trucks and rail carriers/coaches for coal • Improves contractual obligation adherence and minimises exceptions	• PED will have a more stable and reliable schedule for coal deliveries	• Automation reduces time lag, from demand assessment, to reschedule additional loads of coal for transportation. • Improves agility *(flexibility)*	• Better planning through **Schedule Management System** ensures deliveries are timeous	• Reduction of undue or unnecessary trucks at less optimal coal carriage levels, per load

115

Salient PED Process Activities	Optimisation Baseline Metrics				
	Quality	**Dependability**	**Flexibility**	**Speed**	**Cost**
Load and dispatch coal	• integrated **Incident Management system.** • Real time centralised view of all incidents across value chain to limit	• Ensuring security of coal in transit, reduces costs of replenishment.	• Ability to introduce enhanced Technology solutions for better Coal load/dispatch management, in line with Energy demand.	• **QR Code** technology will ensure real-time monitoring and tracking of Load/dispatch levels.	• Mitigation of Loss or Theft of Coal will directly reduce PED sunk/wastage costs.
Receive and manage coal at siding	• Integrated **Weighbridge System** • Improves accuracy of Coal in receipt. • Eliminates manual (Human) inputs for recording of Coal amounts.	• Elimination of manual (Human) input which is prone to error. • Integrated reporting of Coal levels via **Control Tower**	• Integrated **Weighbridge System** • Immediate identification of discrepancies in requisite coal levels. • Improved response rate to Coal shortages.	• Integrated **Weighbridge System** • Improved response rate to Coal shortages.	• Accurate and auditable reporting of Coal levels reduces PED cost provisions. • Integrated **Weighbridge System**
Receive and manage coal at Power Station	• Integrated **Weighbridge System**	• Elimination of manual (Human) input which is prone to error.	• Integrated **Weighbridge System** • Improved response rate to Coal shortages.	• Integrated **Weighbridge System** • Improved response rate to Coal shortages.	• Accurate and auditable reporting of Coal levels reduces PED cost provisions.
Manage CSY	• Integrated **Gate Management system.** • Preservation of coal delivered. • Eliminates risk of theft or loss of coal.	• Integrated **Dashboard and Reporting** ensures real time and auditable levels of coal.	• **Contract Management System** • Improved contractual negotiation terms, in line with CSY levels.	• The **Voice Assistance** technology will ensure up to minute reporting of incidents.	• Automated **Driver Management** system to improve accuracy in reporting entry/exit from CSY

116

Salient PED Process Activities	Optimisation Baseline Metrics				
	Quality	Dependability	Flexibility	Speed	Cost
PED Control (Value Chain)	• Centralised Control Tower. • Interactive dashboard that allows live visualisation of the end-to-end value chain.	• Automation will improve EC's overall ability to deliver reliable Power.	• Integration and Workflow Orchestration • Ability to leverage third-party systems.	• Centralised Control Tower. • Live visualisation of the end-to-end value chain.	• Integration and Workflow Orchestration reduces costs of multiple system license and operator requirements.

DIGITAL MATURITY ANALYSIS (DAS MODEL)

Digital Levels	
Not Computerised	0
Siloed Application	1
Enterprise Data Platform	2
Internet Web-based platform	3
Cloud-based	4
Connected Devices Mobile & Wearables	5

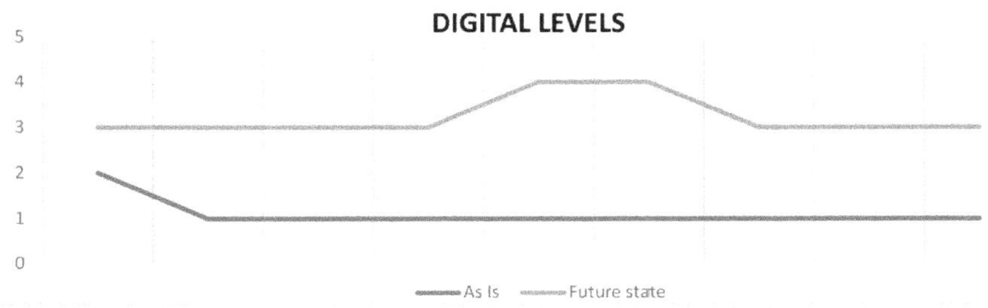

We believe the current maturity level of the EC in terms of digital levels of the DAS model is predominantly level 1. Based on the proposed automation using the coal value chain automation platform we believe the EC can reach a web-based platform and cloud platform levels when it comes to digital maturity. This will enable the EC to manage and control the entire value chain effectively.

Automation & Autonomy	
No Automation	0
Automation with human control	1
Automation with conditional autonomous control	2
Automation with conditional autonomous control in certain environments	3
Automation with full autonomy	4

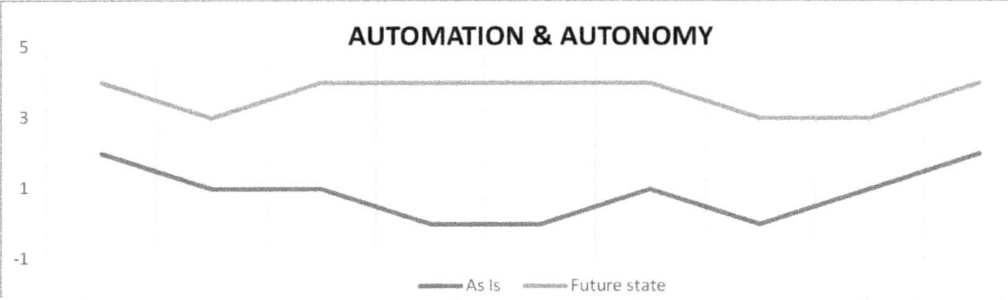

We believe the current maturity level of the EC in terms of Automation and Autonomy of the DAS model is predominantly level 0 across the coal value chain. Based on the proposed automation using the coal value chain automation platform we believe the EC can reach an Automation with conditional autonomous control in certain environment level of maturity. This will enable the EC to respond proactively to coal-related challenges across the entire value chain.

Smart	
No Feedback Control	0
Explicit instruction contingent in one feature	1
Explicit instruction contingent in multiple features	2
Machine Learning	3

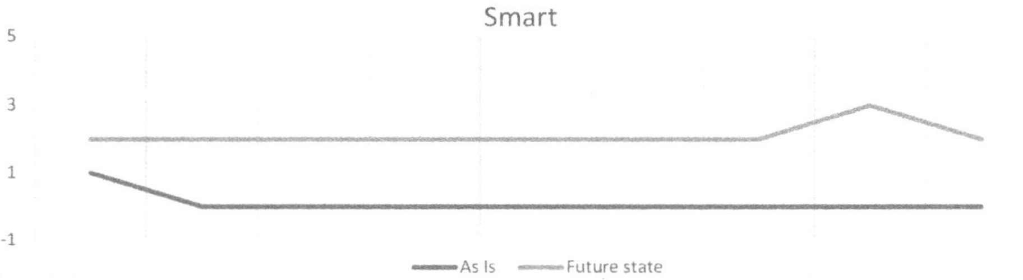

We believe the current maturity level of the EC in terms of Smart criteria of the DAS model is predominantly level lower than 0 across the coal value chain. Based on the proposed automation using the coal value chain automation platform we believe the EC can reach an explicit instruction contingent in multiple features level of maturity. This will enable the EC to increase transparency and make effective decisions across the entire value chain.

Summary of As-Is and To-Be Levels of the Electricity Company Coal Value Positioning on DAS Model

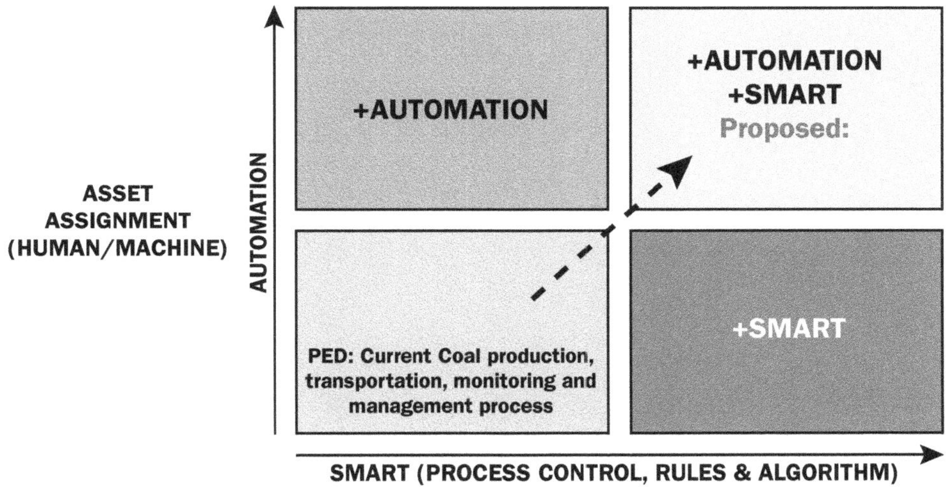

Figure 7.15 DAS Model

WHY THE DAS MODEL?

According to (Kane 2017):
Digital maturity is defined as the process of an organisation learning how to respond to a competitive digital environment. The definition of digital transformation is like the definition of digital maturity, but digital maturity can be seen as a structured way for an organisation to digitally transform.

The integration of digital technologies into the running, managing and planning of organisations is growing steadily. We have developed a framework to structure our understanding of what digitisation means for the operations of individual companies. Operations refers to the repetitive activities that organisation's use to carry out day-to-day business.

It cannot be ignored that the DAS model has been developed to help organisations to stay true to the ability to measure how the organisation is transforming digitally across the value chain. It helps depict areas of improvement and areas where the organisation is fully transformed across the functions of the value chain. The DAS framework can serve as a diagnostic, allowing organisations to assess the current state of their digital operations. This assessment can focus on any number of specific processes, or even the entire value chain, evaluating each task along the three dimensions and assessing them across the three dimensions of Digital, Automated and Smart.

Given that we are attempting to optimise the entire coal value chain and identify automation opportunities to unlock business value across all related processes and sub processes, DAS model provided a solid foundation and a structure approach to assess the As–Is maturity of the value chain and envision the To-Be state of the automation to help the EC unlock business value in a sustainable manner.

This is the reason we adopted the DAS model as an analysis framework to analyse the Primary Energy Coal Value chain.

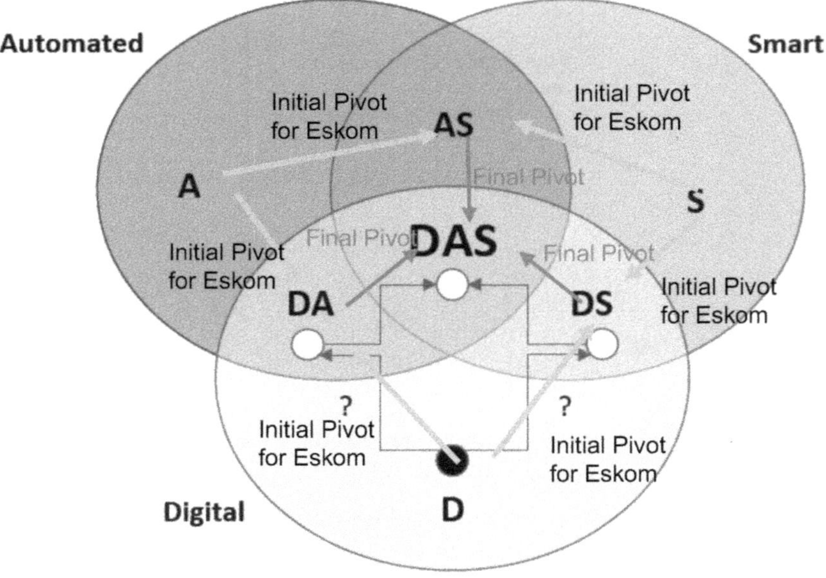

Figure 7.16 Application of DAS Model to the Electricity Company- PED

DIGITISATION REPRESENTATION AND IMPLEMENTATION

Based on the proposed implementation of a BPR lead automation effort we believe the coal value chain within the EC's PED will transform, and the EC will be able to leverage large-scale benefits in terms of lower coal losses, theft and better coal quality. The To-Be model of the proposed automation can be visually represented as follows:

*CAS — Coal Value Chain Automation System

Figure 7.17 Proposed Automation Model

The model shown in Figure 7.17 will enable end–to-end visibility across the coal value chain thereby optimising the EC's ability to collect key data points and correlate the same to make strategic decision, in time that could impact the entire value chain in an effective manner.

We propose that the above automation be rolled out in a phased manner across all the mines and power stations of the EC. A phased rollout ensures we are able to limit operational and organisational impact and ensure gradual transformation and are able to study the lessons during the transition to the new ways of working.

We further propose that the EC follow an initial due diligence phase to study the impact of the proposed BPR and automation before embarking on implementation and furthermore adopt an iterative prototyping model as proposed below to ensure the re-engineered processes and automation meets the PED requirements.

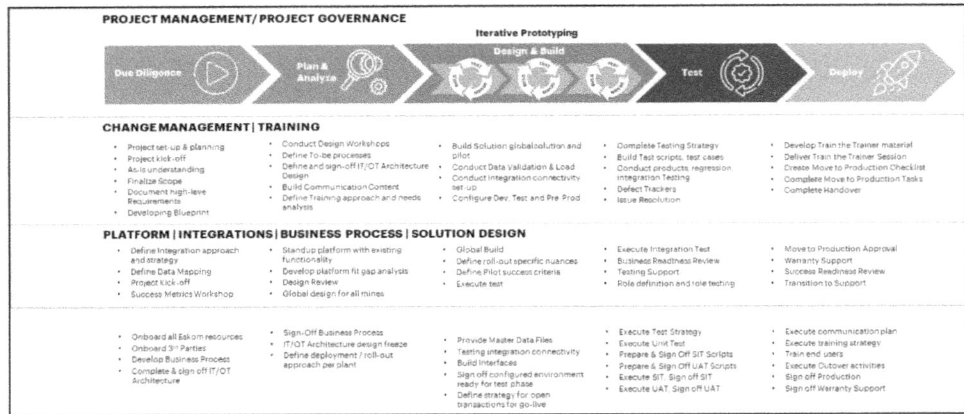

Figure 7.18 Implementation Approach

IMPLEMENTATION PLAN

As outlined in the above section we propose a phased-in implementation methodology for embarking on the identified operational transformation of the EC coal value chain for PED and we propose the following implementation plan for roll out of the identified automation:

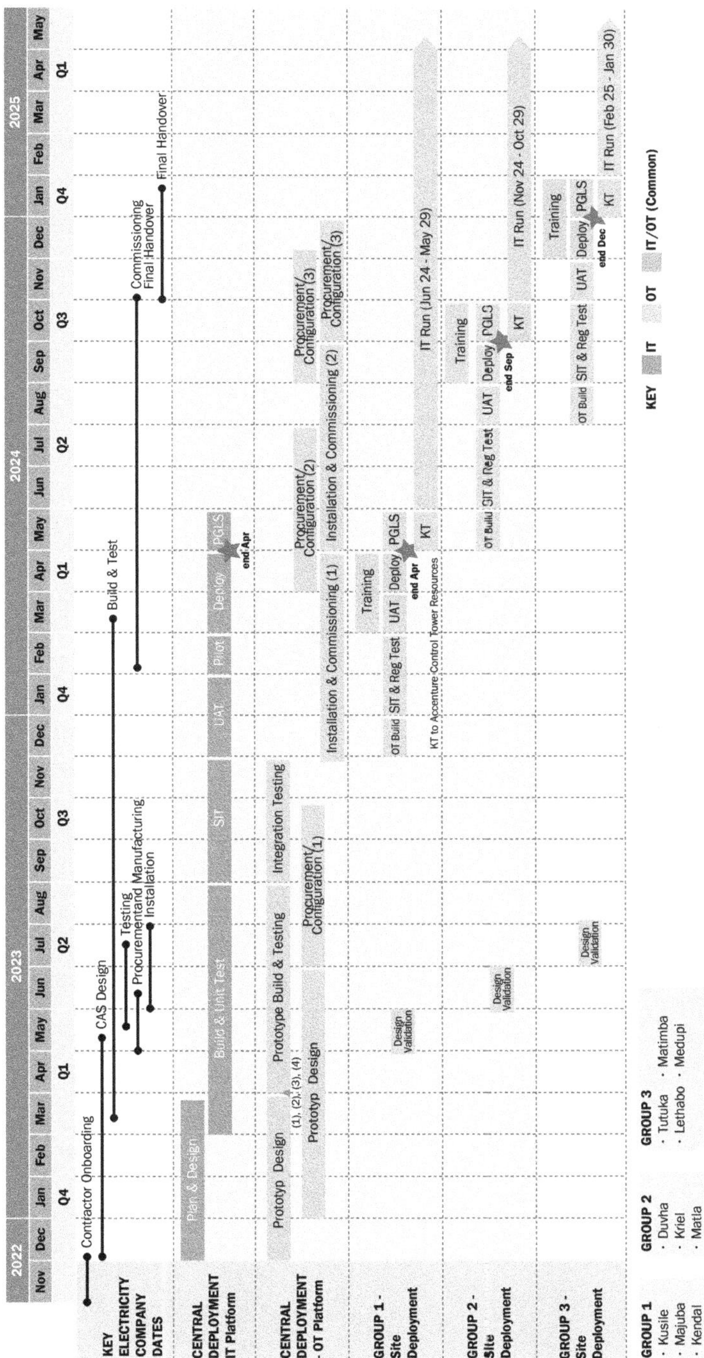

Figure 7.19 Implementation Plan

Above proposed approach ensures phased rollout with a prototype and pilot phase to ensure the deployed system meets the PED requirements and is able to effectively and efficiently automate the operations while streamlining the processes. The data gathered by this system post-initial phase-in will be leveraged to adopt a lean sigma ongoing quality improvement approach across all identified mines and power stations with an intention of reaching the best-in-class process and quality maturity over the implementation lifecycle.

SO-WHAT JUSTIFICATION

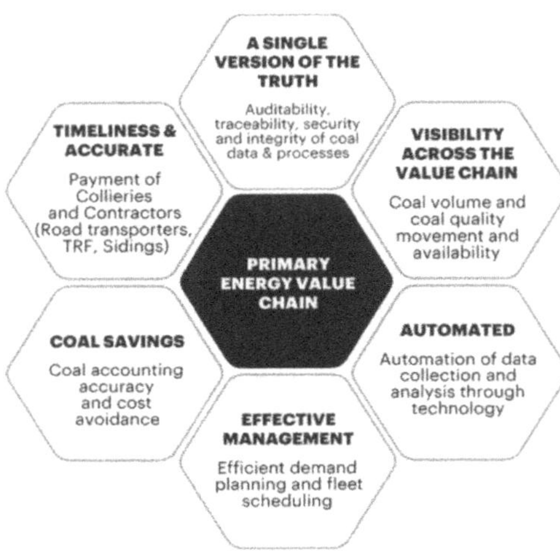

Figure 7.20 Value Realisation

The proposed BPR and Automation process will ensure that the EC is able to improve visibility and effective management of the Primary Energy Value Chain while maturing their Digital, Automation, Autonomous and Smart levels from 0 and 1's to 4-5's. These proposed improvements will impact the PED department positively as illustrated in the diagram on the left. These proposals are further supported by two well-researched studies done by Deloitte (The Future of Mining in Africa), and Accenture (Accenture-Extracting-Value-And-Building-Resilience-With-Data-Led-Mining-South-Africa) as listed in our references.

The proposed improvements will manifest as follows:

Improvement Dimensions	Anticipated Improvements	Improvement Index
SPEED	More than 200% cycle time improvement across the entire value chain	★ ★ ★ ☆ Major Improvement
QUALITY	Real-time integration with LIMS and VERI LIMS systems will ensure supply of right quality of coal each time and every time.	★ ★ ★ ★ ★ Transformational Improvement
DEPENDABILITY	Data and insights driven actions increase dependability across the value chain and will improve the effectiveness of the value chain multi folds.	★ ★ ★ ★ ☆ Transformational Improvement
COST	Better planning, just in time delivery, better quality control, lesser break downs of the supply chain and increased efficiencies in the power stations all lead to lower cost of operations and better profitability for the EC.	★ ★ ★ ★ ★ Transformational Improvement
FLEXIBILITY	Automated processes and insights-based planning and decision ensure flexibility and proactiveness at all levels of the value chain.	★ ★ ★ ★ ☆ Transformational Improvement

ACKNOWLEDGEMENT OF CONTRIBUTORS

- Dalson Modiba
- Dominic Moloto
- Fulufhelo Nepfumbada
- Yolanda Kope
- Ramaprasad Deepal Belur
- Simon Darko

(All are affiliated to the Wits Business School, University of the Witwatersrand, Johannesburg).

REFERENCES

https://www.jacarandafm.com/news/news/gordhan-lecture-descends-chaos-told-he-must-resign/ accessed on 26 July 2022

https://www.dailymaverick.co.za/article/2022-05-11-eskoms-biggest-challenges-are-a-poorly-performing-coal-fleet-and-a-62-energy-capacity/ accessed on 19 July 2022

Day_064_-_U4._Brakfontein_Bundle_-_Part_03_(12.03.2019).pdf

TIPS_report_The_coal_value_chain_in_South_Africa_July_May_2021%20(1).
pdf

https://www.parliament.gov.za/storage/app/media/PBO/Analysis_of_Eskom_
finances_Report_to_SCOA_presented_8_March_2017.pdf accessed on 23
July 2022

http://meridianeconomics.co.za/wp-content/uploads/2017/11/Eskoms-
financial-crisis-and-the-viability-of-coalfired-power-in-SA_ME_20171115.
pdf accessed on 25 July 2022

https://www.diva-portal.org/smash/get/diva2:1270797/FULLTEXT01.pdf
accessed on 21 July 2022

Digital%20Operations%20(MBR%20Winter%202021%20Boute%20%20
Van%20Mieghem)%20(003)%20(1).pdf

https://tenderbulletin. eskom.co.za/ accessed on 22 July 2022

240-151834455 Coal Automated Information System.pdf

https://www.researchgate.net/publication/354623339_THE_COAL_
VALUE_CHAIN_IN_SOUTH_AFRICA?enrichId=rgreq-
c1e37462b857652f53b2172c450d1ed1-XXX&enrichSource=Y292ZXJQ
YWdlOzM1NDYyMzMzOTtBUzoxMDY4NTcyODYwMjQ4MDY1Q
DE2MzE3NzkwMzE4NzM%3D&el=1_x_2&_esc=publicationCoverPdf :
TheCoalValueChaininSouthAfricaMakgetla2021.pdf accessed on 25 July
2022

Intersecting the three perspectives on operations-- digital, automated, and
smart---yields seven zones. Digital%20Operations%20(MBR%20Winter%20
2021%20Boute%20%20Van%20Mieghem)%20(003)%20(1).pdf

Process types –the volume-variety effect on process design

The Process Matrix: This simple tool can help managers categorise processes
and consider how they might or should change. Source:Hall, J. M., &
Johnson, M. E. (2009). When should a process be art, not science? Harvard
Business Review, 87(3), 58-65.

Slack, N., Brandon-Jones, A., Johnston, R., Singh, H., & Phihlela, K. (2017).
Operations Management: Global and Southern African perspectives (3rd
ed.), Cape Twon: Pearson

https://www.accenture.com/_acnmedia/PDF-126/Accenture-Extracting-
Value-And-Building-Resilience-With-Data-Led-Mining-South-Africa-
FinalV.pdf accessed on 18 July 2022

https://www2.deloitte.com/content/dam/Deloitte/za/Documents/energy-
resources/za_Future_of_mining.pdf accessed on 18 July 2022

https://www.engineeringnews.co.za/article/eskom-laments-poor-quality-of-
coal-2019-01-31 accessed on 20 July 2022

CHAPTER 8

Digitalising RTMC Driving Licence Renewal Operations Analysis and Improvement Proposals: A Viewpoint

INTRODUCTION

Governments have developed strategies to maximise the value of digital technologies for their populations since they first became available. Government services referred to as 'e-government' are intended to make online transactions more convenient, lessen people's dissatisfaction with the government, and save a lot of money and time (Garson, 2004). Despite tight resources and challenging restrictions like economic inequality, geopolitical unrest, and ageing populations, governments should still supply services that meet the growing requirements of people and businesses with the aid of digitalisation (Corydon, Ganesan, & Lundqvist, 2016).

The South African government has implemented initiatives in this area through the department of transport to facilitate access to official papers, data, information, and services. The South African population has expressed discontent with the present system, procedures, and practices for renewing driving licences due to their inefficiency and overall unhappiness (BusinessTech, 2022). Therefore, the purpose of this article is to put out a problem-based, technologically assisted solution for the improvement of the existing operational difficulties in the South African driving licence renewal procedure. In tackling the Covid-19 pandemic the government of South Africa imposed nearly two years of lockdowns, which resulted in limited public services. During this period the Minister of Transport issued a one-year grace period for driving licence renewals, which expired on 31 March 2022. During the lockdown the production of licence cards was stopped. This has resulted in the 597 000 backlog in the printing of licence cards (eNCA, 2022). This backlog is made worse as there is also a backlog of applications from drivers who could not go to Driving Licence Testing Centres (DLTCs) to apply for their licence renewal.

In order to eradicate these two backlogs, the entire driving licence renewal operation will have to drastically increase its rate of production and throughput. This report investigates the operations processes and proposes significant improvements that may help address the double backlogs. The improvements are based on gaining the advantages of digitalisations, automation and smart/intelligences.

ORGANISATION AND OPERATION SELECTION

The chosen organisation is the transport information system, which falls under the Department of Transport. Among other services, the transport information system is responsible for South African driving licence renewal (NaTIS, 2022). The selected operation to digitise is driving licence card renewals.

Background

The renewal of driving licences falls under the responsibility of the department of transport, which is responsible for the regulation and coordination of transportation in South Africa (Transport, 2022). In South Africa, the process of renewing a driving licence disc or card has been a problem for many years.

In April 2007 the Department of Transport moved from then current transport information system to a more modern, technologically advanced electronic transport information system. However, this system and the underlying processes have been a source of frustration, with citizens being compelled to miss work to visit the centres and having no way of knowing if they'll be successful when they do visit traffic departments (OUTA, 2021).

One of the recommendations by OUTA, a South African civil activist organisation was to optimise the online booking platforms to improve customer experience (OUTA, 2021). However, the recommendations made by OUTA do not contain any detail on how this can be achieved.

The following section of this chapter provides a critical analysis of the services provided by the department of transport and its current performance. This is then followed by a detailed recommendation on how these can be optimised using digital technologies.

The 4Vs (volume, variety, variation, visibility) shown in Figure 8.1 serve as a guideline to assess performance of operational processes and to categorise product/service type (Slack, Brandon-Jones, & Johnston, 2017). The process is analysed before and later, after digitisation, to test for optimisation in cost and efficiency.

4Vs

The operations have been assessed using the 4Vs framework as a means of getting an understanding of the nature of the current operation.

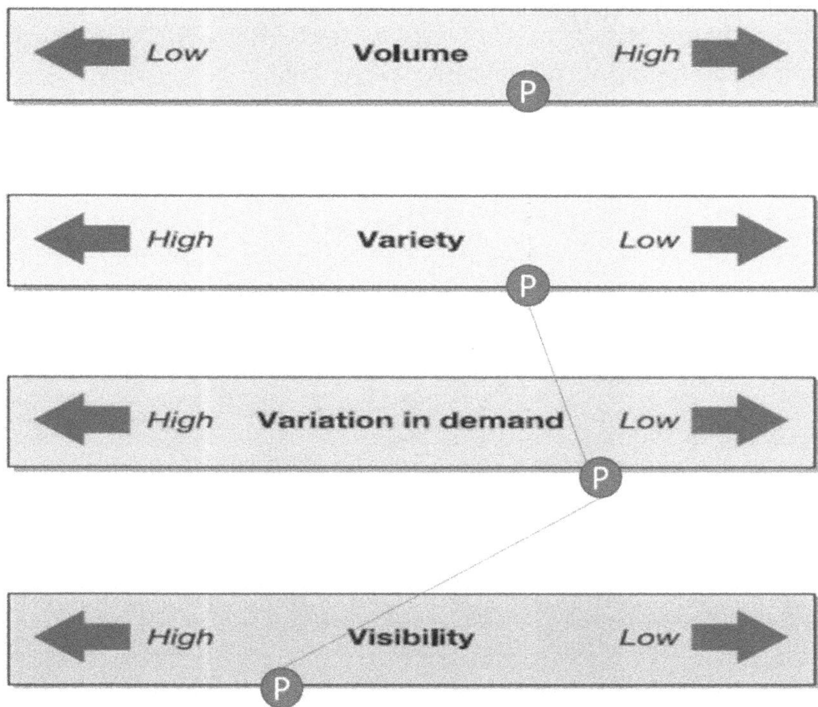

Figure 8.1 4Vs assessment of RTMC Licence Renewal Operations

Volume – Licence renewal is applicable to all South African driving but only every five years and is not a daily item like frozen food. The large quantity combined with the low frequency make the volume **moderate to high**.

Variety – The licence renewal process is standardised across all clients, with minimal variety. While licence cards all look the same, the end product is not fully standard (e.g., soap bar) and requires customer-specific information such as ID numbers and photographs, which adds a level of variety. Overall, variety is **low to moderate**.

Variation – Licences expire and require renewal all year round and there is no specific seasonality. Variation is **low**.

Visibility – All parts of the process except for database updates and licence printing is visible to and interact with the customer. Visibility is **moderate to high**.

PERFORMANCE OBJECTIVES

The performance objectives are represented on the polar diagram and explained below. The polar diagram provides a critical view of the current service levels in comparison with the customer's expectations. The expected customer service acts as a goal. The before state is plotted against expectations, and later the diagram will be remapped with post-digitisation positioning.

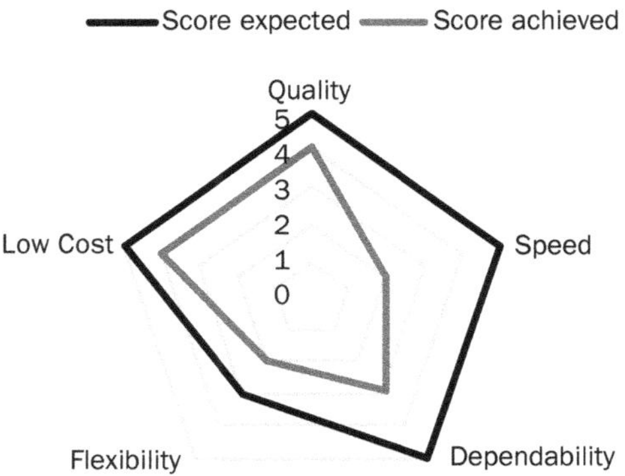

Figure 8.2 Polar Diagram of the Licence Renewal Operations showing applicant expectations versus achieved scores

Table 8.1 Expected Performance vs Achieved Performance

	Expected	**Achieved**
Quality	Durable, compact, high-quality driving licence accurately representing driver details. Executed through a streamlined process.	Quality as expected, except for temporary licences, which are paper documents with taped photographs. Process is not entirely streamlined.
Speed	Produce renewed licence in a short time with minimal application time and wait between processes.	Online booking time long due to inefficient booking system, full day presence at centre and 6–8-week collection period. Paper info capture leading to information transfer delay.
Dependability	Completed accurate licence disc in promised time period.	End product meets expectation; however; process often fails (eg might not receive service on the day, system offline).

	Expected	**Achieved**
Flexibility	Moderate flexibility required in processes to meet changes e.g., missed appointments, online vs in person payments, temporary licence if expiry out of collection period.	Limited flexibility as process is mostly standard. Delays and inconvenience is often caused when the expected cases occur.
Low cost	A basic government process should be fairly low cost and affordable to all drivers.	Pricing is reasonable but not necessarily cheap.

PROCESS MAP

The driving licence operations processes have been mapped (see below) to allow for an analysis to determine where and how improvements can be made. It is commonly acknowledged that such models can provide helpful, and relatively inexpensive, descriptions that can aid in the improvement and redesign of business processes (Biazzo, 2002).

The very first step is that an applicant must book an appointment. Recent improvements have resulted in the booking process now being online, as opposed to when applicants had to go to a DLTC and queue in the hope of being assisted. As shown in the 4Vs analysis the operation is highly visible once the applicant attends their renewal appointment at a DLTC. This visibility introduces a lot of inconsistency in the way the operation is executed depending on which DLTC an applicant goes to, and which official assists them on that day. Even the day-to-day changes in the mood and motivation of the officials introduce more inconsistency.

There are specific delays which are essentially built into the operations processes, especially where applicants must pass through a step where there is a natural limit of processing resources available. An example of this is the eye testing step. Each DLTC has a limited number of testing equipment so this creates a hold point where almost every applicant must pass through.

There are also data exchanges which need capturing by one or both parties. There is also some duplication of data exchanges such as the appointment booking process requiring data which is repeated on the paper form that applicants have to print and bring to the appointment for submission.

The analysis of the process map is shown with estimated average time/durations for key phases of the process. Those durations which are deemed inefficient are highlighted in red. These are areas in which interventions will be considered which can reduce this time. The critical outcome of this analysis is that reducing the time consumed by the applicant would be the key improvement sought. Improvement interventions should also seek broader improvements based on the operation's objectives, as outlined.

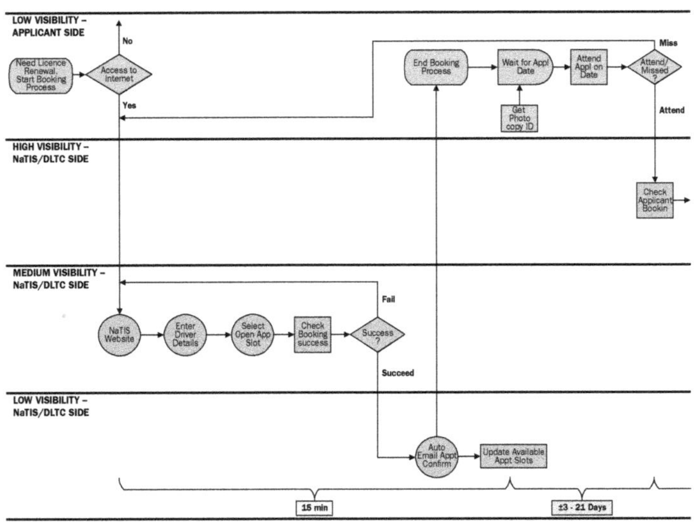

DLR Process: Booking Stage

Online hosted process but this may be a limitation as those without access will not be able to make use of this.

This limitation significantly affects process througput – refer to value stream.

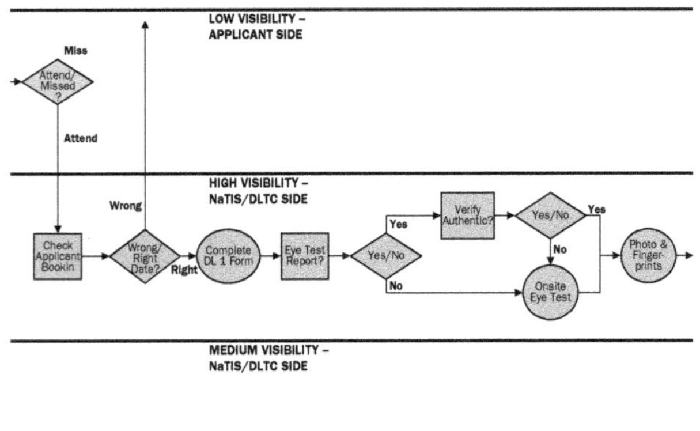

DLR Process: Data Capturing Stage

This is a high visibility portion of the operations process. Applicants directly interact with DLTC staff who are capturing data, including biometrics.

This is a time-consuming stage as this is bottlenecked by the number of eye test machines and operators available. Almost every applicant must pass through this point so a large amount of the time for this process is just spent in queueing rather than in the value producing activities.

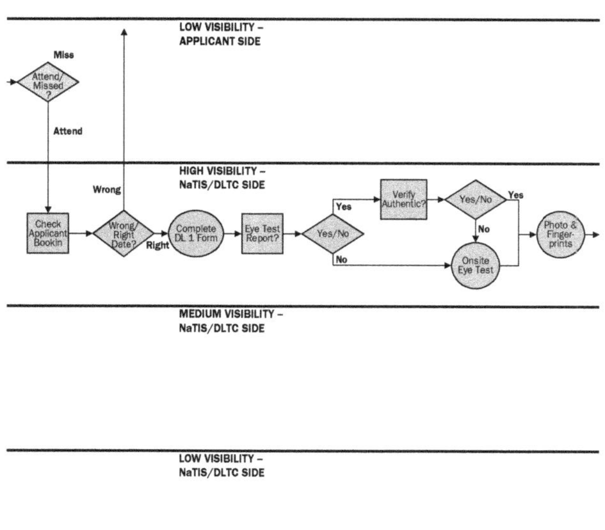

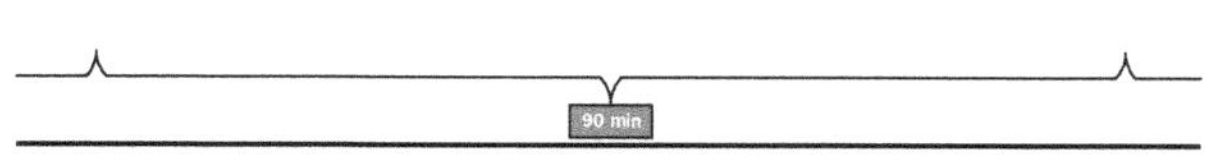

DLR Process: Data Capturing Stage

This is a high visibility portion of the operations process. Applicants directly interact with DLTC staff who are capturing data, including biometrics.

This is a time-consuming stage as this is bottlenecked by the number of eye test machines and operators available. Almost every applicant must pass through this point so a large amount of the time for this process is just spent in queueing rather than in the value producing activities.

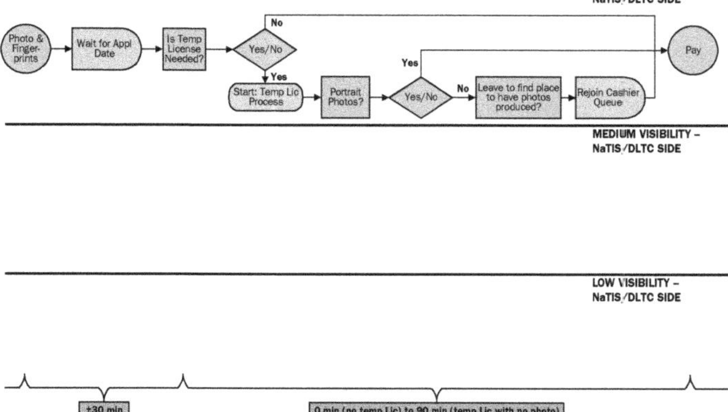

DLR Process: Payment/ Conclusion Stage

Also a high visibility stage where the applicant interacts with DLTC cashier in order to pay.

The current process has a check point to determine if the applicant requirs a temporary licence. If they do they must provide two B/W portrait ID photos. If you do not have them then you will have to leave the testing centre in order to get a photo. There are usually informal photo service providers, but they often require cash payments. If you cannot get a photo you must abandon the request for a temporary licence.

This stage also involves a significant queueing time which the payment based on the number of cashiers on duty.

Time will also be consumed if the applicant needs to leave to get photos.

133

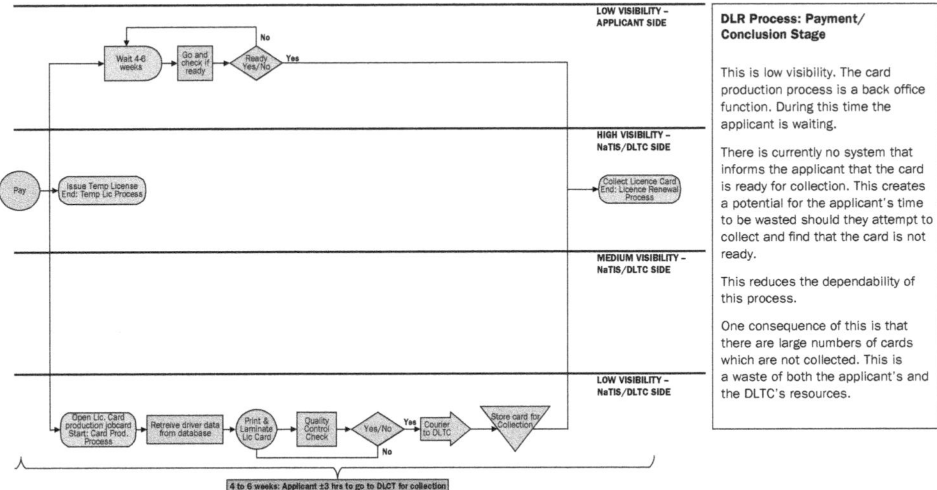

PROCESS OPTIMISATION

Value Stream Mapping

To identify if the transport information system process for driving licence renewal is optimum, the value stream model was used as shown in Figure 8.3 and Figure 8.4. In the analysis inefficiencies can be identified throughout the value stream of the transport information system causing an overall reduction in throughput of over +/-70%. A simplified assessment of the throughput of the operation has been conducted. Although not in the form of a full value stream map, the presented shows where the operation loses applicants, i e throughput blockages. This, combined with the durations indicated on the process map, indicates the performance of the processes underlying the operation.

What is apparent from the analysis is that there are two constraining steps in the value stream which negatively affect throughput. The first is the online booking process. In the case of an applicant who does not have internet access the alternative is for them to go to a DLTC and try to get a booking 'manually'. The other option is to use agents who can do this on their behalf. This introduces additional 'cost' to the process.

The second major constraining step is where an applicant required a temporary licence but did not come to the appointment with photos ready.

In designing interventions these two constraining steps are the areas of focus. The low throughput percentages point to the process not being optimised.

Original Process

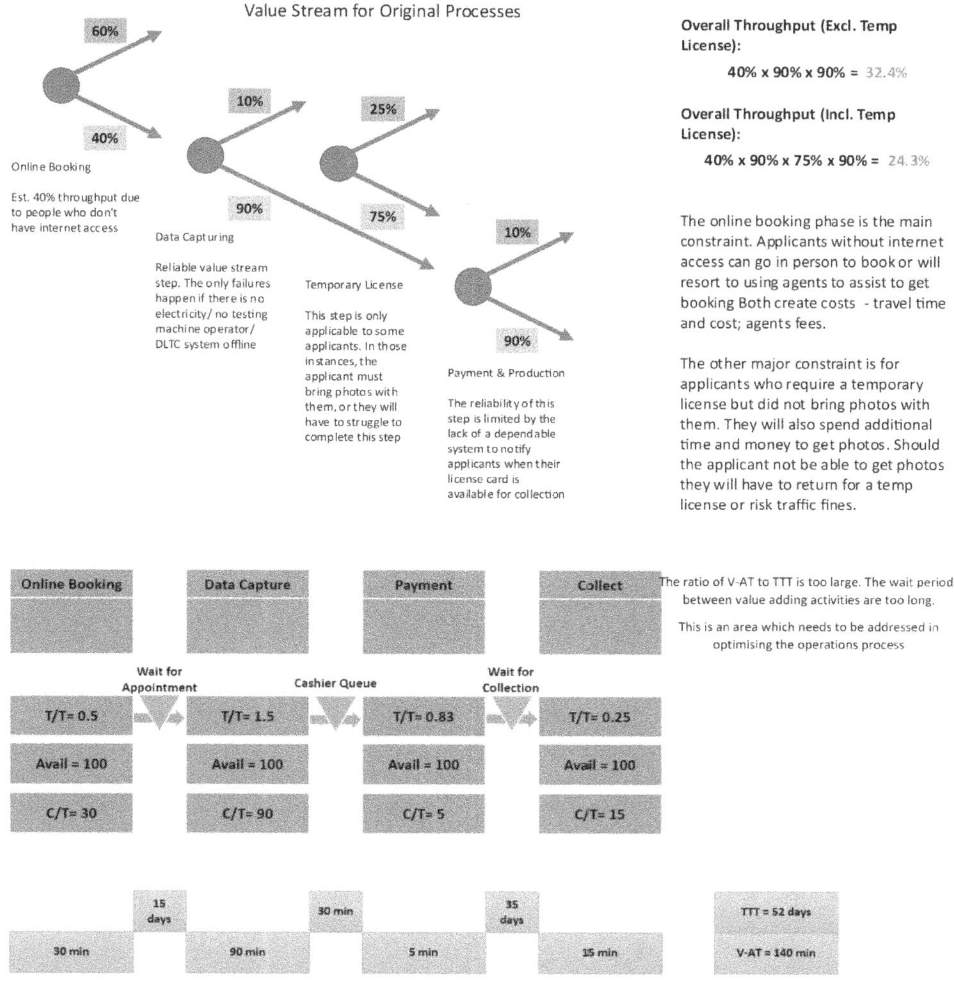

Figure 8.3 Current Value Stream Processes (Slack, Brandon-Jones, & Johnston, 2017)

Gap Analysis to Identify Problems and Provide Solutions

Table 8.2 is an analysis of the problems faced by the transport information system in servicing its customers.

Table 8.2 Problem Analysis

No	Problem	Proposed Solution
1	Driver is not reminded that licence is about to expire. Driver typically realises after receiving a fine at a roadblock.	Licence department to automate licence expiry date notification by sending SMS/email a month before expiry date. Notification could include a USSD that drivers can use to start their renewal licence application process.
2	Difficulty in obtaining a booking slot due to poor system structure, which does not make cancelled and held slots available again.	A smart system able to capture capacity and track availability of slots live, thereby releasing slots from cancellations and incomplete processes.
3	Duplication of information capture (booking and on-site) Driver-applicant completes the online form capturing identifying information	Prepopulating of existing personal and licence information from the transport information system and DHA website. Driver should only confirm or correct information to reduce the delay.
4	Driver-applicant is often unable to select a slot due to agents bulk-booking and selling slots	ID verification to only allow one booking per driver, preventing slot selling.
5	Non-digitised capture and submission of information. Documents emailed to be printed, filled and resubmitted instead of filled online. Supporting documents (ID copy, proof of address etc.) must be physical.	All forms to be completed online digitally and submitted. Supporting documents must be pulled from databases (and uploaded for proof of residence) and automatically linked to application, post verification.
8	If an applicant misses a slot (centre closed or not served on the day) then the applicant must restart from point 2.	Providing a reschedule option which automatically picks up documents from initial application, only providing a new date and venue.
9	Information from printed forms is recaptured by administrators on site, rather than automatically transferring from the application form.	On-site, existing data must be pulled up from application form and database, preventing duplicate capture.
10	Temporary licence process is a secondary process, not integrated into general renewal booking. The driver is only given the option of a temporary licence upon paying for the general and must go back to take photographs and resume the process. Temporary licence is not tamper-proof, it is a printed paper document with taped photograph.	Integrate temporary licence renewal process into main process, prompting user to opt for one if expiry is within a month of application. Utilise documents from main process (e.g., photos) and issue a fully printed temporary licence document.
	Poor payment options. No online payment option. Payment only allowed for driving licence, not temporary as this must be paid separately.	Online payment option. Combine payment of main and temporary licence.

No	Problem	Proposed Solution
11	No clear time frame on collection of licences, and no indication that it is ready to collect. The applicant told to come and check for a licence in four to six weeks.	Provide process tracking notifications Send notification to driver when licence is ready to collect. Provide a delivery option

Figure 8.4 shows how, by solving the problems identified above, the optimisation of the driving licence renewal process will increase the throughputs in the value stream to the customer.

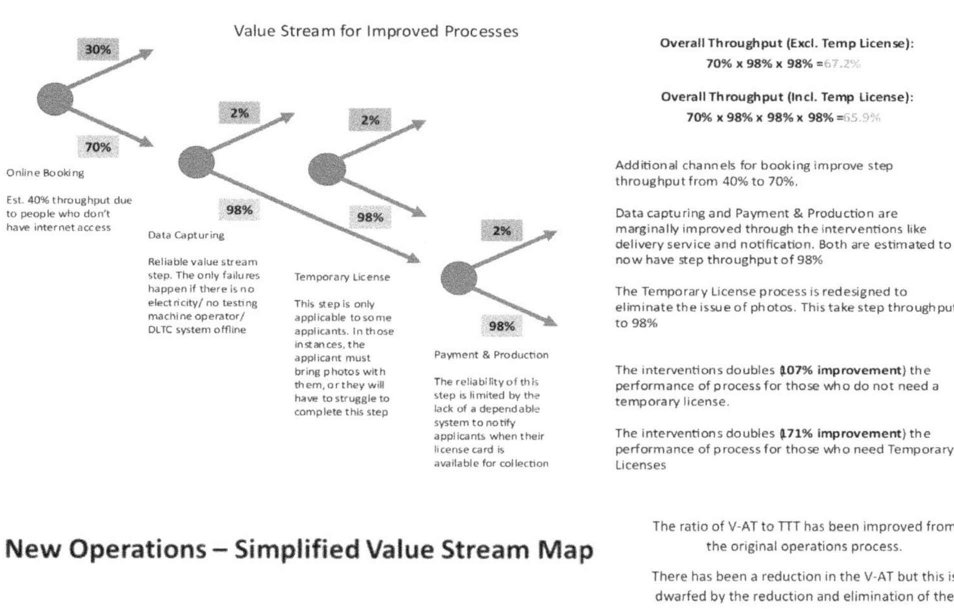

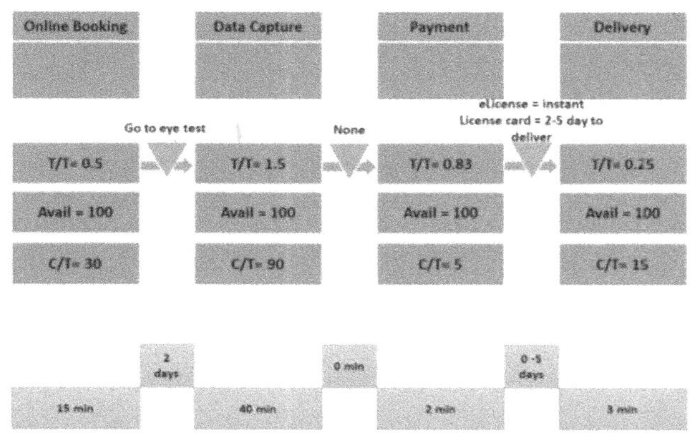

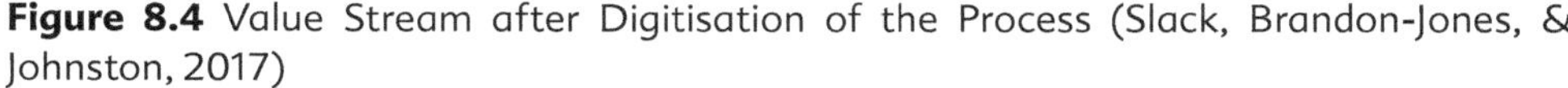

Figure 8.4 Value Stream after Digitisation of the Process (Slack, Brandon-Jones, & Johnston, 2017)

OPERATIONS DIGITAL MATURITY ASSESSMENT USING THE DAS MODEL

Digital maturity is how organisations systematically prepare to adapt consistently to ongoing digital change. Digital maturity draws on a psychological definition of 'maturity' that is based upon a learned ability to respond to the environment in an appropriate manner. Aslanova and Kulichkina (2020) state that, simply put, digital maturity is the ability to create digitally. It is therefore critical to understand the transport information system's current level of digital maturity to map out a desired state of digital maturity for the future using the DAS model. The DAS model is used because it provides a clear indication of the current stated of each of the main processes in the driving licence renewal process. This provides the basis for the proposed solutions detailed in the sections that follow.

The transport information system's digital maturity will be assessed by focusing on the following dimensions:

Customer – This is because customers cannot book with the traffic department at the time of their convenience, for example the best time for drivers to organise a booking is at 12:00 noon through the system, otherwise the customer must try another day at 12:00.

Digital supply chain – The digital supply chain is not seamless and prone to manipulation; there are marshals selling booking slots to drivers.

Marketing Personalisation – The transport information system warn customers when their Public Drivers Permit (PDP) is about to expire, so they do have the capability to market personally but this is currently very rudimentary with no actual service being derived from it by the drivers.

This proposal uses the widely used Digital Automate Smart (DAS) framework to assess the transport information system's digital operations level of competence as detailed below.

Table 8.3 DAS Model — Digital Score for Licence Renewal Operations Processes

Digital Ranking	Reminder	Booking	Renewal	Licence Production	Collection Notification	Collection
0. Not Computerised					x	x
1. Siloed Application	x		x	x		
2. Enterprise data platform						
3. Internet web-based platform		x				
4. Cloud-based Platform						
5. Connected devices/mobile/ wearable						

Table 8.4: DAS Model — Automation and Autonomy Score for Licence Renewal Operations Processes

Automation & Autonomy Ranking	Reminder	Booking	Renewal	Licence Production	Collection Notification	Collection
0. No Automation (no machine or Bot)		x	x		x	x
1. Automation with human control/ supervision				x		
2. Automation with conditional autonomous control						
3. Automation with autonomous control in certain environments						
4. Automation with full autonomy	x					

Table 8.5 DAS Model — Smart Score for Licence Renewal Operations Processes

Smart Ranking	Reminder	Booking	Renewal	Licence Production	Collection Notification	Collection
0. No Feedback control		x	x	x	x	x
1. Explicit instructions contingent on one feature	x					
2. Explicit instructions contingent on multiple						
3. Machine learning						

Very little of their current process is digital. It therefore difficult to automate and convert to smart. Therefore, the current process must first be digitised and then made smart and automated to move into the top right-hand quadrant as shown in Figure 8.4.

Reminder – Automatic advance warning of driving licence expiration with the ability to initiate the booking process. Data analytics should be used to predict demand and capacity planning bookings.

Booking – Customers must be able book for the required service after this has been initiated through the reminder via multiple platforms e.g., App, Telephone, USSD, WhatsApp and Web. Customers should also pay on multiple platforms, without the platform malfunctioning including temporary driving licences it is recommended that opensource software be used as it is cost-effective and secure (Slack, et al, 2017). This will enhance customer experience, efficiency, and security by cutting out current practices were marshals at the sites are able to sell booking slots.

Renewal – The renewal process must not include any paper trail for both walk-ins and digital applicants and use biometrics to authenticate for enhanced security. The driver receives a tracking number to track the production and delivery of their driving licence.

Licence Production – Fully automated once the renewal process is completed and the driver has met all requirements. Applications are sent automatically to the printers for production to commence.

Collection Notification – Automatically sent to the driver. The driver can track delivery to the address they provided or designated collection point.

Collection – Option of delivery or collection at a designated point.

DIGITISING THE OPERATION

The Fourth Industrial Revolution is making available technologies that can be used to enhance the products and services offered by an organisation (Baines et al, 2020). Technologies, such as biometrics and, face verification that uses deep learning models for online identity verification, have been successfully used for easy verification and identification of individuals to enhance security and non-repudiation (Mathew et al, 2020).

Major changes provided by the new system

Digital driving licence as a fully acceptable legal alternative to printed cards.

Flexible driving licence facility options. An alternative to the on-site process is a combination of online information capture (photographs, ID verification) and partnering with facilities (e.g., Dischem, Postnet) to perform eye tests and fingerprinting, making it more convenient.

DETAILED PROCESS

Overview

The new system provides flexible and accessible driving licence facilities and options, instead opting to partner with facilities to perform eye testing (e.g., Dischem, Clicks, Post Office). In addition to printed licence cards, it also uses digital driving licences, which are a fully accepted legal alternative.

Detailed Process

The star indicates optimised location on map in Figure 8.4. The circle indicates pre-optimised location.

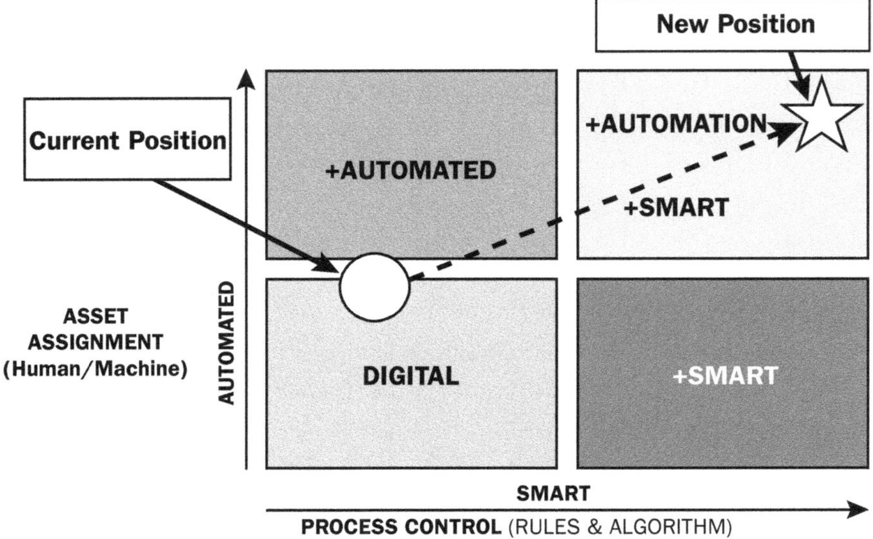

Figure 8.4: DAS Model Framework Showing the Predicted Outcome with Proposed Interventions

Driver receives licence expiry reminder

Reminder via SMS and email containing link to online application form at https://online.natis.gov.za

Reminder sent one month before expiry date

DIGITAL + AUTOMATED

Driver visits website

If applicant does not have internet, they visit their nearest SA Post Office branch, which contains computers where bookings can be made free of charge. Self-service computers configured to the transport information system's booking page with digital guidance.

DIGITAL

Driver fills in booking form for eye test + fingerprint scanning

Testing centre selection – system suggests closest testing centre to last known physical address (using location and maps in the backend). The user can either select one of the suggested locations or dismiss it and enter new location or testing centre.

142

DIGITAL + SMART

ML and Data Analytics to determine availability – the system uses historical data to determine availability of testing centres. Data includes average test duration, number of visitors per day etc to determine feasible capacity. Machine learning then predicts/forecasts occupancy, and therefore availability, and provides an available date.

AUTONOMY + SMART

Eye Test + Fingerprint Scanning

Eye test – performed at selected centre and certificate passed to the transport information system's database. Driver presents ID document as identity verification.

Fingerprint scanning – performed at eye test facility using fingerprint scanner.

Database update – results automatically passed from machine to the transport information system's database, triggering next step in process.

AUTOMATED

Test Success and notification prompt

Immediately after successfully completing the eye test, applicant receives an SMS and email notification indicating this. The SMS/email contain a link to resume the process.

DIGITAL + AUTOMATED

Online information capture

Driver clicks the link and reaches the transport information system website, which is prepopulated with information and progress to date (eye test)

ID – Driver scans ID barcode through the camera, and information is verified in the background.

Photograph – Driver captures photograph on phone/computer camera. The system is linked to the DHA (Department of Home Affairs) and the transport information system website. Verification is performed using AI to match person to DHA database image. Once verified it updates the image on both sites.

Existing information population – Based on the scanned ID, the system picks up existing driving licence information (driving licence number, initial issue etc.), which is displayed to the driver.

Signature – signature performed on screen.

Temporary Licence

The driver is prompted to select a temporary licence if expiry is within a month but is given the option. User either selects 'Yes' or 'No'.

DIGITAL + AUTOMATED

Digital vs Physical option

Driver selects if a physical licence card is required. A digital one will be provided either way at no extra charge, while the physical incurs a delivery fee.

Payment

Delivery – A standard delivery fee of R60 is added. Delivery is promised within 14 working days (partner with delivery operator such as Takealot or Fastway).

After successful information capture, the driver selects 'Next' to go to payment.

Online payment offered in the traditional online payment methods (cards, PayPal, Instant EFT, Ozow etc.).

Card printing

Card printing performed at key locations in each city, using standard printing equipment.

Database update

The transport information system website updated with info on completed driving licence.

RPA runs in the background to update databases and to transfer information between systems and stakeholders.

AUTOMATION

Delivery

Card is sent out for delivery.

Driver receives an SMS/email notification.

Driver receives licence.

The location on the autonomy vs smart curve is indicated in Figure 8.5. A justification to the scoring is also provided.

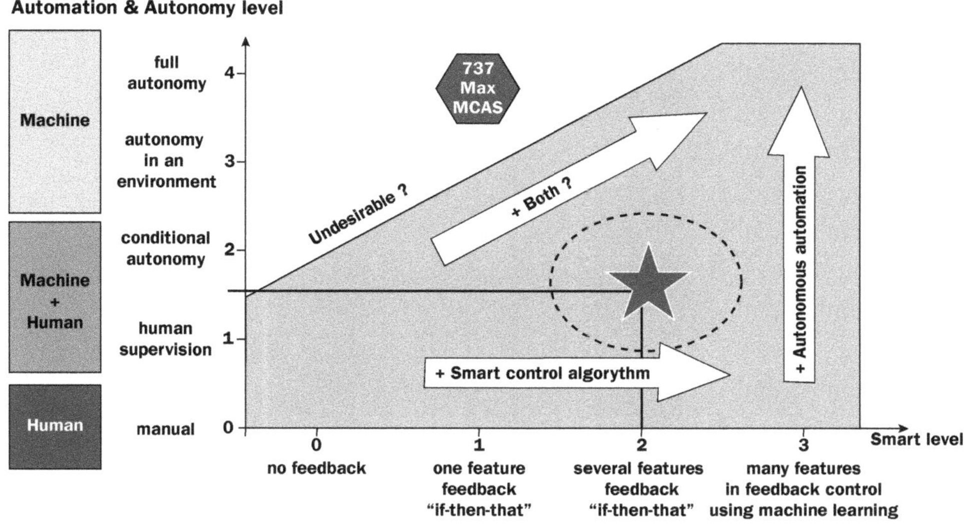

Figure 8.5 DAS Automation and Autonomy Level of Improved Operations

Autonomy: Between 1 and 2 – human supervision for eye tests and fingerprints etc. but also conditional autonomy for location suggestions, automated notifications etc.

Smart level: Feedback if expiry is less than a month etc and related conditional actions.

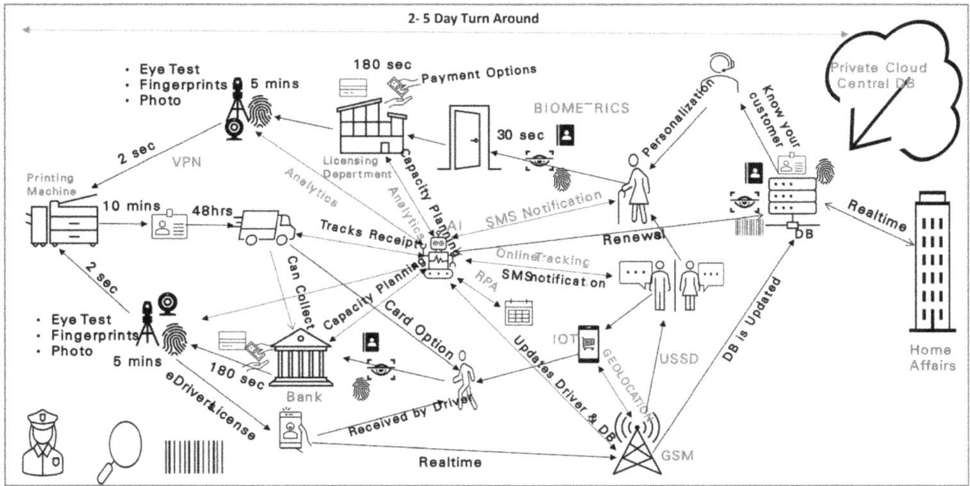

NEW EXPECTED PROCESS PERFORMANCE

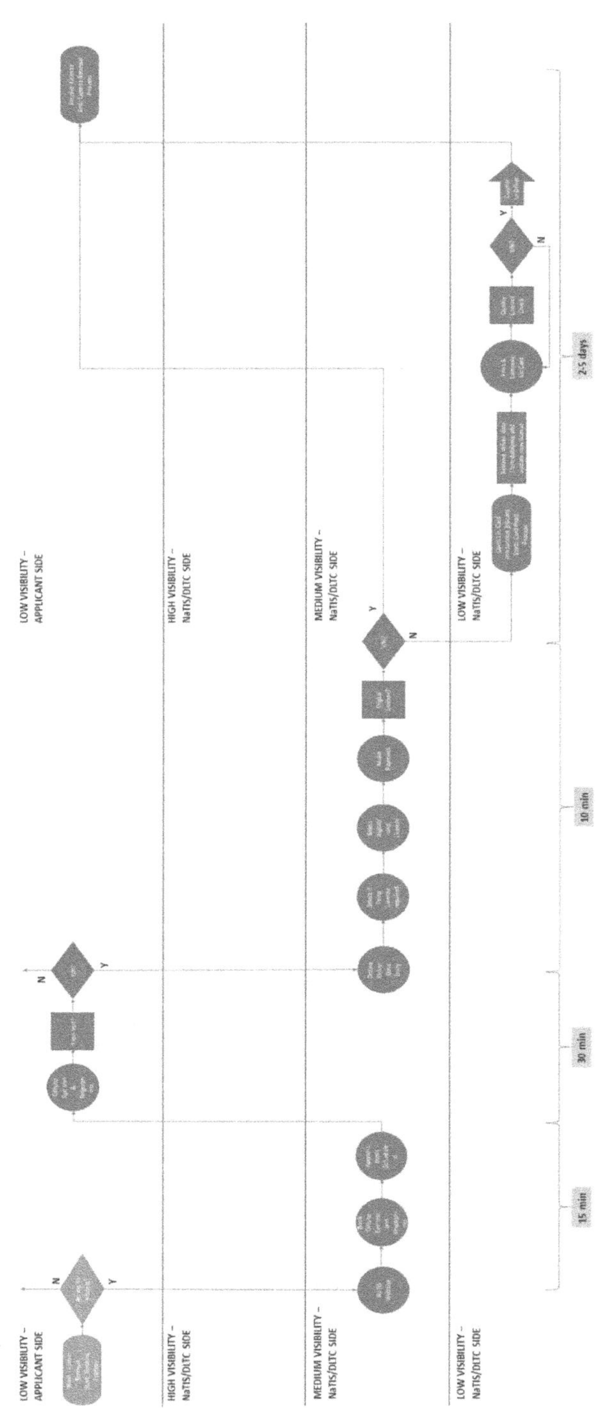

New Expected Polar Diagram

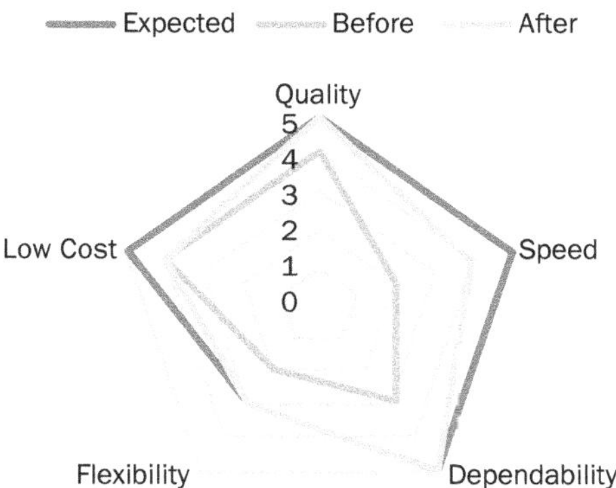

Figure 8.6 Post-Improvement Radar Diagram Showing Comparison with Original Operations

Table 8.6 Operations Objectives Scoring Comparing Pre- and Post-Improvement Operations

	Expected	Achieved			
		Before	**After**	**Dif**	
Quality	5	4	5	+1	Process streamlined.
Speed	5	2	4	+2	Short booking, no info transfer delay.
Dependability	5	3	5	0	No service issues resolved.
Flexibility	3	2	3	+1	Caters for temp licence. Missed appointments still not catered for.
Low cost	5	4	4	0	No need to visit centre (book leave).

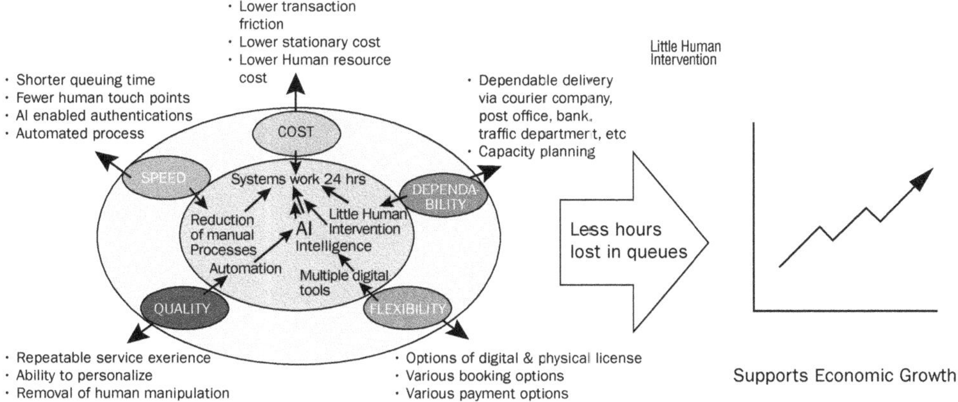

Figure 8.7 Benefits to the Economy

IMPLEMENTATION: RESOURCES AND PLAN

Table 8.7 Project Resources Phase 1

Resources	
Project Manager	R1 800/h
IT Specialist	R1 700/h
Web Developer	R1 300/h
Electrical Engineer	R1 900/h
Software Architecture	R1 500/h
Security and compliance specialists	R1 400/h
Business-technology liaisons	R900h
Technologists	R700/h
Marketers	R500/h
Implementation leads	R950/h
Automated Printing Machine	R50 000 000
Software	R10 000 000
Hardware	R5 000 000

High-Level Project Plan

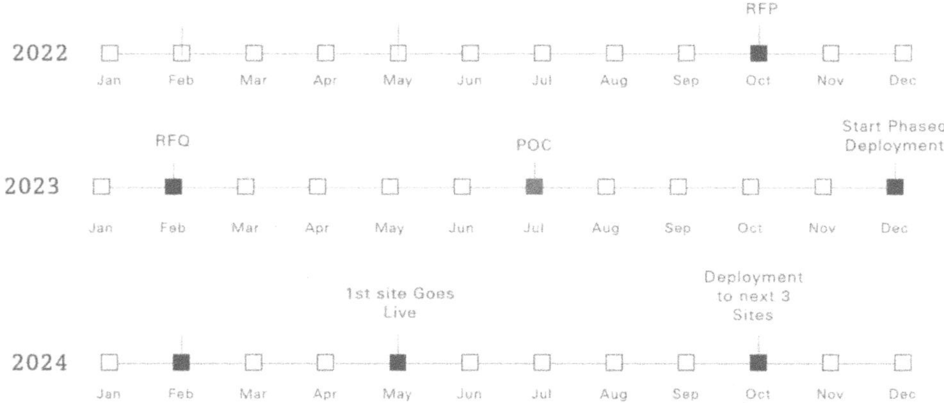

Figure 8.8 Project Plan Phase 1

ACKNOWLEDGEMENT OF CONTRIBUTORS

- Tafadzwa Mukwena
- Aasma Jaffer
- Matuma Mosidi

(All are affiliated to the Wits Business School, University of the Witwatersrand, Johannesburg).

REFERENCES

Aslanova, I.V., Kulichkina, A. I. (2020). *Digital Maturity: Definition and Model.* 443–449. Retrieved from https://doi.org/10.2991/AEBMR.K.200502.073

Baines, D., Nørgaard, L. S., Babar, Z. U. D., Rossing, C. (2020). The Fourth Industrial Revolution: Will it change pharmacy practice? *Research in Social and Administrative Pharmacy*, 16(9), 1279–1281. Retrieved from https://doi.org/10.1016/J.SAPHARM.2019.04.003

Biazzo, S. (2002). Process mapping techniques and organisational analysis: Lessons from sociotechnical system theory. *Business Process Management Journal*, 8(1), 42–52. Retrieved from https://doi.org/10.1108/14637150210418629/FULL/PDF

Big driving licence problem for South Africa. (n.d.). Retrieved July 21, 2022, from https://businesstech.co.za/news/motoring/571146/big-driving-licence-problem-for-south-africa/

BusinessTech. (2022). Driver licence headache for South Africa. March 17. *Businesstech*. Retrieved from https://businesstech.co.za/news/government/568930/driver-licence-headache-for-south-africa/

Corydon, B., Ganesan, V., Lundqvist, M. (2016). Digital by default: A guide to transforming government. Retrieved from https://moodle.ufsc.br/pluginfile.php/2784781/mod_resource/content/2/Digital-by-default-A-guide-to-transforming-government-final.pdf

eNCA. (2022, February 3). Mbalula: At least four months to clear driving licence backlog. Retrieved from https://www.enca.com/news/rtmc-says-drivers-licence-backlog-should-be-cleared-four-months

Garson, G. D. (2004). The Promise of Digital Government. Retrieved from https://services-igi--global-com.eu1.proxy.openathens.net/resolvedoi/resolve.aspx?doi=10.4018/978-1-59140-122-3.ch001

Mathew, V., Ramesh, K., Toby, T., Chacko, A. M. (2021). Face Verification for Person Re-Identification from Surveillance Camera and Drone-based Videos. *Journal of Computer Science*, 17(7), 639–656. Retrieved from https://doi.org/10.3844/JCSSP.2021.639.656

Mbalula: At least four months to clear driver's licence backlog | eNCA. (n.d.). Retrieved July 21, 2022, from https://www.enca.com/news/rtmc-says-drivers-licence-backlog-should-be-cleared-four-months

NaTIS. (2022). Natis Online Services. Retrieved from https://online.natis.gov.za/#/

OUTA. (2021). A Critical Analysis of the Driving Licence Renewal Process. Retrieved from https://www.outa.co.za/web/content/209155

Slack, N., Brandon-Jones, A., Johnston, R. (2017). *Operations Management*, 4th edn. Pearson.

South Africans are renewing their driving licences — and then not fetching them. (n.d.). Retrieved July 21, 2022, from https://mybroadband.co.za/news/motoring/444426-south-africans-are-renewing-their-drivers-licences-and-then-not-fetching-them.html

Transport, Department of (2022). Home – Department-of-Transport. Retrieved from https://www.transport.gov.za/

Uchenna, E., Raphael, O., Innovation, A. L., (2020). Overview of Technologies and Fingerprint Scanner Used for Biometric Capturing. Retrieved from https://www.sciencepublishinggroup.com/journal/paperinfo?journalid=623&paperId=10050872

Practical Case of Digitalising a Leading Fast-Moving Consumer Goods (FMCG) Manufacturer

EXECUTIVE SUMMARY

We are living in a world where rising oil prices and shortage of input materials used by companies to create their end products are resulting in a massive increase in supply chain costs (Reporter, 2022). To maintain profit targets, most companies have no option but to pass on this cost to end consumers. This, in turn, is impacting overall inflation and creating an environment where customers' disposable income is shrinking to a point where they need to cut down their spending on everyday consumables.

One company impacted by this negative cycle is RB, a leading fast-moving consumer goods (FMCG) manufacturer. The company needs to ensure its products are not only being purchased by consumers but also at a competitive price. To achieve this, it can adopt different strategies to adapt to market changes:
1. Increase the price;
2. Shrinkflation, where the size of the goods is decreased, but the price stays the same; or
3. Eliminate waste and optimise its operations.

RBB has selected the third option as it believes adopting new processes and digital technologies is vital to increase its performance objectives (Cloutier, 2021). Furthermore, they are confident that they will be in a better position than their rivals, who are using traditional methods in their operation. In both the short and long term, this is not the most efficient in the current economic environment.

RBB has begun this process by deploying a new Warehouse Management System (WMS) to increase picking productivity and reduce inventory losses. However, there are some inefficiencies they have seen during the deployment which require further investigation. The approach which will be outlined in this document is based on using the principles summarised below:

- Value Stream Mapping – a tool used in lean management that enabled the understanding of how the company creates a product end to end. Using this approach, we were able to identify challenges in their operations.
- Using the Five Whys as input to defining the problem statement
  - Why 1 – Unable to provide customers with estimated times of delivery and inform them of delays
  - Why 2 – Unable to plan distribution without picking being completed, no visibility of a planned time
  - Why 3 – Unable to load vehicles without completing picking first
  - Why 4 – Need to wait for the team to manually update the paperwork to understand which customers are being delivered to and the volumes to be delivered
  - Why 5 – Lack of a Transport Management System (TMS) to efficiently provide customers with planned times, route planning, fleet management, end-to-end monitoring, and automatic system updates.
- Waste identification and areas to optimise using MURA, MURI and MUDA. These lean principles were leveraged to identify waste across the value stream:
  - MUDA – The analysis identified mainly type 2 non-value adding activities, for example how they transport goods, waiting times or holding inventory levels.
  - MURA – It is clear that overproduction and waiting time are due to a lack of process standardisation and limitation in controls applied across the different systems. This has resulted in unevenness and irregularity. Therefore, the principles of lean synchronisation to optimise operations have been employed.
  - MURI – One of the challenges that has arisen due to manual ways of doing work and using paper to track operations has resulted in uneven distribution of work resulting in inefficient use of transport fleet and workforce, resulting in underutilisation and overutilisation.
- Using lean synchronisation to optimise operations
  - In the analysis conducted, it was found that the company's current processes for deliveries are not efficient as they are using the buffer approach for inventory management in their operations.
  - One of the reasons identified is that operations are conducted manually, and data cannot be gathered across the different stages to get the visual insights needed to monitor the end-to-end process.
  - The recommended solution optimised this by gathering data from the different stages using various technology solutions and enabling the team to view the complete process from a single pane of glass.

- This in turn has created an environment where teams can not only better plan for orders but also identify disruptions or bottlenecks across the value stream.
- The recommended digital technology solution has ultimately created an environment where the team can better plan and control day-to-day operations from a central system thereby, creating a pull system 'just in time' operations.
- The above has resulted in increased efficiencies across the value stream by improving the performance objectives such as flexibility. The team can now quickly adapt to changes in customer demand.

- Leveraging the DAS model to transform digitally and automate its operations while setting the foundations for the future.

BACKGROUND

RBB (RB) is a multinational consumer goods company. RB specialises in producing and distributing health, hygiene, and nutrition products. Some of their popular brands include Dettol and Vanish. RB is a company that constantly seeks to improve its internal operating processes. The company aims to use technology to provide greater visibility and improve efficiency by utilising data to provide them with a competitive edge in the market.

The following extract is sourced from RB's website, depicting the company's passion for its products:

TAKING CARE OF OUR WORLD

Now more than ever, we all understand the importance of hygiene. Cleanliness is at the heart of our own good health – for us, our families, friends, and communities. Here at RBB, we understand the huge role we play in this. We are committed to helping everyone take the best possible care of the world we all share. Every day, millions of people put their trust in our products. We work with relentless energy and innovation to make the best possible products we can. And then we make them even better. We protect, heal and nurture. It's how we make a difference. (Narasimhan, 2022)

RBB recently upgraded to a world-class WMS (Warehouse Management System) in SAP EWM. SAP EWM (Extended Warehouse Management) assists supply chains in managing high-volume operations. It can seamlessly integrate complex supply chain logistics and distribution processes. RB is keen to improve other elements of its distribution. This submission focuses on identifying processes that are not optimised and recommending solutions. The approach includes understanding the current processes, identifying process gaps, and identifying solutions to streamline the process using technology. The main objective is to identify one process optimisation solution that will provide the most significant benefit to RB.

CHALLENGE

The main challenge of the submission approach is identifying the biggest opportunity in RB's supply chain to add value, productivity, and efficiency while increasing customers. In understanding RB's current supply chain process, it has been identified that there is no Transport Management System (TMS). Therefore, the TMS system and its recommended implementation to optimise RB's processes is the focus of this submission.

PROCESS MAPPING

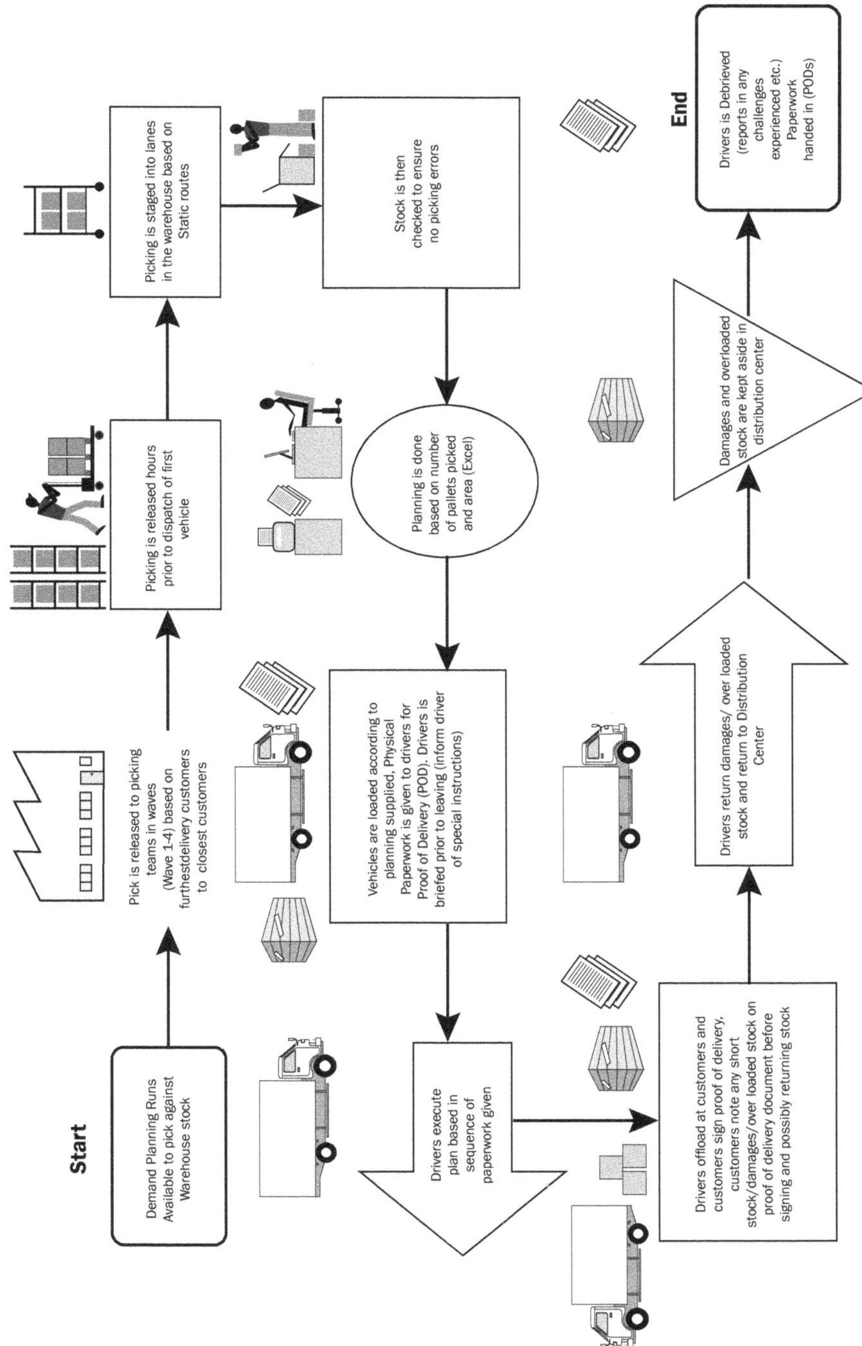

Figure 9.1 High-level Delivery Process

To provide further transparency to the process, we have provided a visual value stream map. The map highlights key process aspects, including time and effort spent during each stage of the process. The value stream process identified critical gaps that contribute significantly to waste. Key activities in stock planning, stock waiting to be delivered, stock waiting to be offloaded, and stock waiting to go back to inventory were identified as key focus points for improvement.

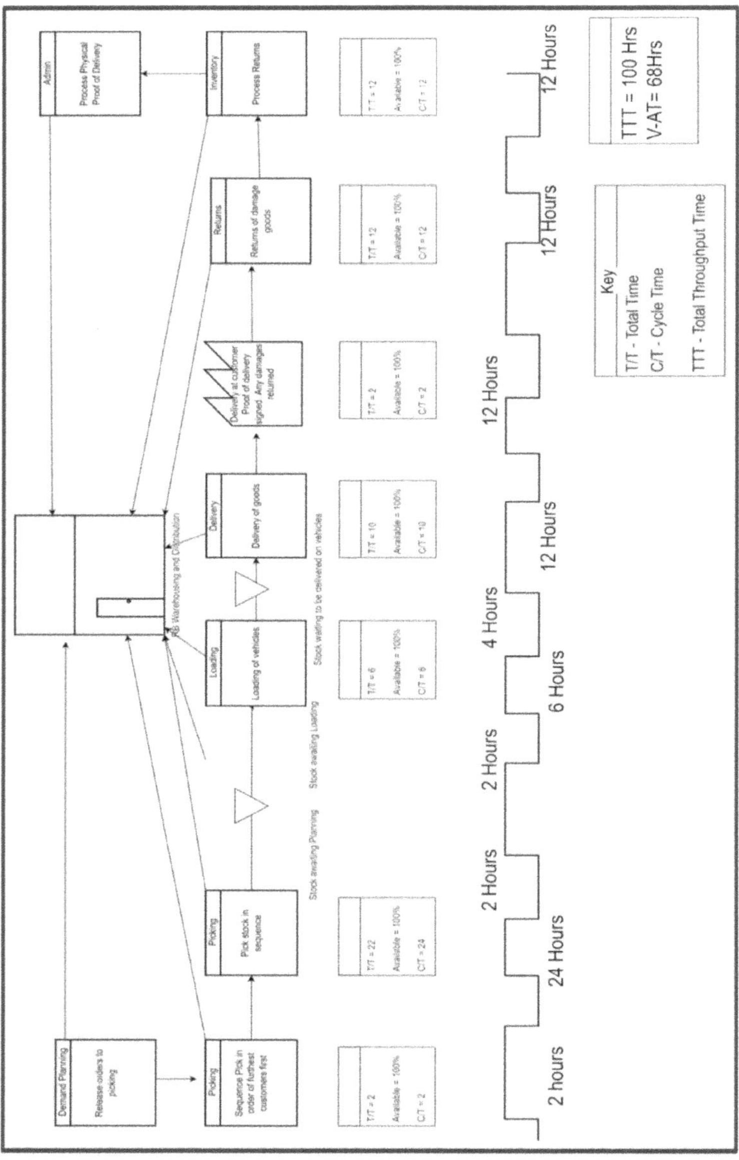

Figure 9.2 Mapping Physical Value Stream Process, Highlighting Waste and Causes

Process Gap Analysis

Table 9.1 is a high-level overview of the waste that has been removed from the process resulting in an overall reduction due to optimisation of the below equation. To guide our thinking during the analysis we had to reference multiple journal articles, which provided valuable input (Ramesh et al, 2008; Siregar, 2017; Sasikumar, 2013; Soliman, 2017)

Value-Added + Non-Value-Added Time = Total Process Time

Table 9.1 Efficiencies Added to Existing Process

Process	Gap	Optimisation	KPIs	Efficiency Added
Distribution Planning	Planning completed manually in Excel.	Deploy the Transport management system (TMS) to complete the planning	Planning cut-off time (measurement of the on-time release of plan)	2 Hours
Release of Picking	Picking was delayed due to the picking team needing to split picks according to distance	The TMS will automatically manage picking and release, prioritising the furthest routes	On-time picking start. Inter-department SLA to ensure on-time release of the pick when plan is complete	2 Hours
Stock waiting on floor until pick is completed	Stock waits on the floor until the pick is complete. This is to plan the number of pallets required	Pulling this process forward and utilising the TMS system results in the team loading vehicles as each route is completed. The TMS releases the pick by route and the picking team can complete a route allowing for vehicles to be loaded immediately.	• Stock on floor time • Loading turnaround time On time dispatch of vehicles	6 hours (time on floor and loading time)

Process	Gap	Optimisation	KPIs	Efficiency Added
Lack of distribution visibility	Lack of visibility of deliveries en route (unable to provide customers with ETA's, inform customers of delays, and manage deliveries exceptions)	The TMS will provide real time updates by using Internet of Things sensors to collect live data. Telematics will provide on route exceptions and turnaround (based on geo-fence in, geo-fence out) times and ETA's. RPA from the handheld devices will provide E-PODs for deliveries with sign-on glass.	OTIF (On time in full deliveries) All stock ordered is delivered according to the planned time from the TMS. Planned time is communicated to customers.	3 hours
Unable to manage drivers and fleet, to understand capacity and time utilisation	Unable to manage drivers and fleet by understanding wasted time by drivers Understand fleet capacity in both time and capacity	Exception reports to manage driver behaviour to ensure on-road discipline and driving efficiency (speeding alerts, unscheduled stops, etc.)	Time and capacity utilisation metrics (bench marking of ideal utilisation and measure planned versus actual against this)	To be understood when system is live
Reduce damages in transit	Drivers reckless driving can damage stock in transit	Exception management through IOT will score drivers on their driving. Therefore, if there are in transit damages, drivers can be held accountable.	Driving scoring KPI's	Reduces stock that needs to be returned due to stock damages

Process	Gap	Optimisation	KPIs	Efficiency Added
Long time to process damages and returns	Returns take a long time to process due to waiting for the applicable paperwork	Processing damaged goods that need to be returned will be quicker as drivers will trigger the RPA workflow. The work will be completed before the stock gets to the distribution centre. It simple needs to be scanned back to confirm	Turnaround times for processing damages	20 hours
Long turnaround times at admin due to manual processing of paperwork (working off physical documents)	Due to waiting for manual paperwork, the admin team takes time to process invoices	E-POD's will be generated instantaneously as deliveries are completed through the mobile devices using RPA (workflows). Goods short delivered or damaged will be marked off and the admin team can start processing invoices faster	Turnaround times for processing of paperwork (invoicing and credits)	To be identified on implementation
Using physical documents, risk involved in reconciling	Using manual proof of delivery documents poses risks as paperwork can get damaged or lost	All paperwork will now be electronic meaning less risk	Outstanding proof of deliveries % Target = 0%	No losses due to missing or damaged proof of deliveries
No data to analyse and use to improve transport operations	No data available to measure and improve or review gaps in transport operations	Data lake to be created that can provide live dashboard reporting to measure and improve operations	Planned versus actual OTIF, KM's, labour (hours), fleet and labour efficiency	Data to make informed decisions

In mapping the distribution process, it has been identified that there is a manual process that can be completed much earlier in the process. In addition, with the use of technology, the process can avoid waste, avoid errors, add efficiency and visibility.

Thereafter, a value stream mapping was completed to identify the parts of the process where time is wasted. This resulted in identifying the need to introduce a Transport Management System (TMS) to optimise the process. The system will not just optimise the delivery process but also the elements of the order picking process. In the FMCG environment, these processes are co-dependent.

The addition of the TMS system will pull the planning process forward given its use of Artificial Intelligence to determine the number of pallets to be delivered based on product pallet fill rate. The pallets will then be released to the warehouse to start with picking automatically once the plan is completed. The planning time will be significantly reduced, from four hours to one hour, provided the stock does not need to wait on the floor for loading while the plan is being completed. The plan will also be dynamic, taking into consideration the following factors to provide an optimal plan:

- available fleet;
- customer location;
- vehicle and labour costs;
- customer order size;
- customer delivery windows; and
- customer turnaround times.

The optimised planning process will also remove the need for the picking team to sort the sequence of picking. It will release the pick automatically based on furthest routes first and reduce the picking time by two hours. The optimised routes will reduce the time stock spends on vehicles since vehicles will be dispatched sooner due to the faster loading times.

Delivery times will also be reduced due to optimal routing as well as the execution model. As part of the TMS system, handheld devices (Internet of Things) with workflows will be deployed. These devices will have the Google Maps navigation feature to ensure drivers are on optimal routes. This will also result in faster offloading at clients as there is a standard workflow to complete on the devices. This will generate an electronic proof of delivery by utilising sign on glass, meaning the admin department can start processing these faster. The devices use Robotic Process Automation (RPA) to achieve this.

We will also use the telematics (Internet of Things) data from the vehicles to conduct a comparison between the planned times, the actual times (telematics) and the mobile time stamps. This is to provide customers with ETAs, inform them of possible delays, or call customers to understand why a vehicle at their location longer than planned. The TMS system will also manage the drivers based on performance expectations, travelling speed, entering high-risk areas, and making unscheduled stops. This means RBB can increase fleet efficiency.

160

By deploying this technology, a further 12 hours can be reduced from the Returns and Damages processes. The applicable TMS system that can be deployed is recommended as follows:

- **One Network** (Onenetwork, 2022)

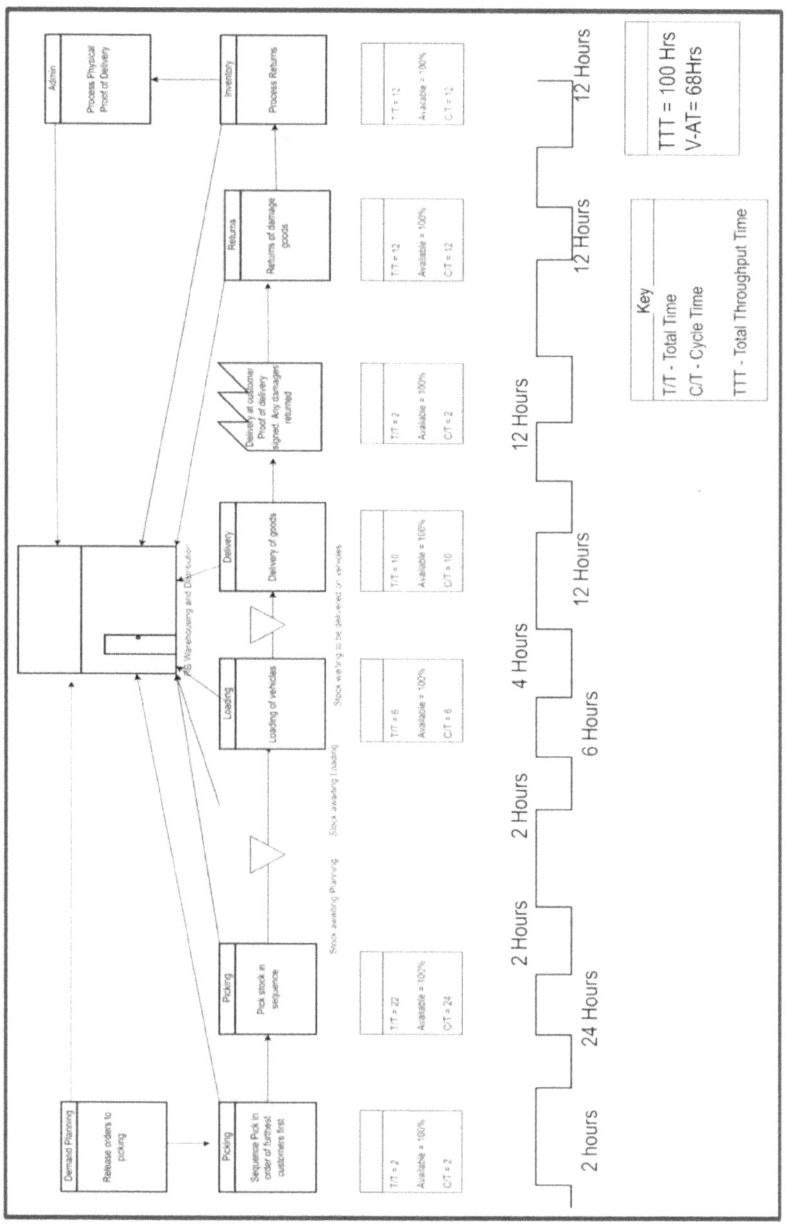

Figure 9.3 Optimised Process

BENEFITS OF TMS

Challenges like the capacity crunch, increased final mile delivery expectations and rising freight prices have shippers looking for ways to improve their supply chains. The solution to these problems is to implement a transportation management system (TMS). A robust TMS can speed up logistics operations, reduce waste and improve the company's bottom line. Here are a few of the main advantages and benefits of transportation management systems (TMS) (Turk, 2019):

- Approximately 10–20% saving on transport costs
- Provides ability to provide customers with ETAs on deliveries and other relevant data
- Route and fleet optimisation
- Visibility of SKU on vehicles to know stock location
- Generate live dashboard reporting to assist with en route exceptions.

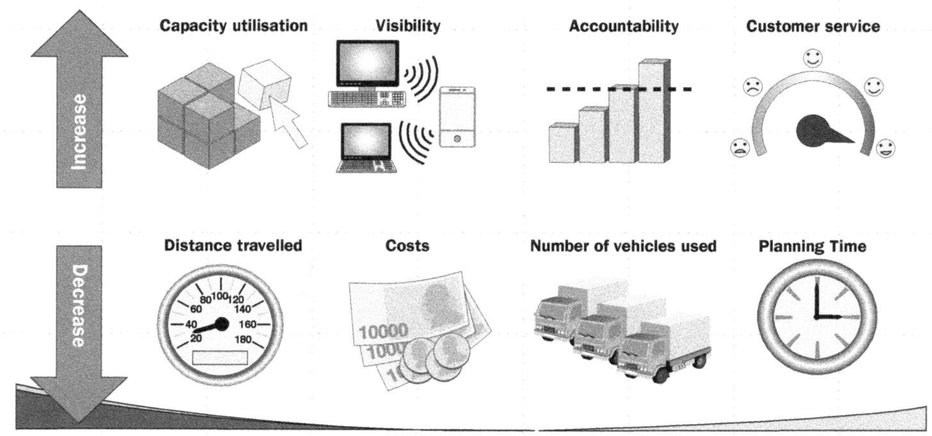

Figure 9.4 Benefits of TMS

OPTIMISING OR STREAMLINING THE PROCESS

A streamlined delivery process will benefit RB significantly. RB's idle stock problem requires creativity, an idea both central and key to innovation. Creativity will create a path for RB to move away from applying existing techniques, and breaking known rules and approaches in an effort to reduce idle stock (Nigel Slack, 2017).

To achieve this, it is important to streamline the process in its entirety before applying optimisation techniques. To measure how streamlined the Process Design should be considered by addressing the following key questions:

162

1. How is the current process designed?
2. What objectives should the design process have?
3. How do volume and variety affect the process design?
4. What are the effects of process variability?

To elaborate further on the above questions, additional literature has been referenced on the Lean Process and how that could further improve RB's processes.

RBB CURRENT PROCESS DESIGN

To understand how the current process is designed, an input–output model is used to highlight the required input resources required for the delivery process.

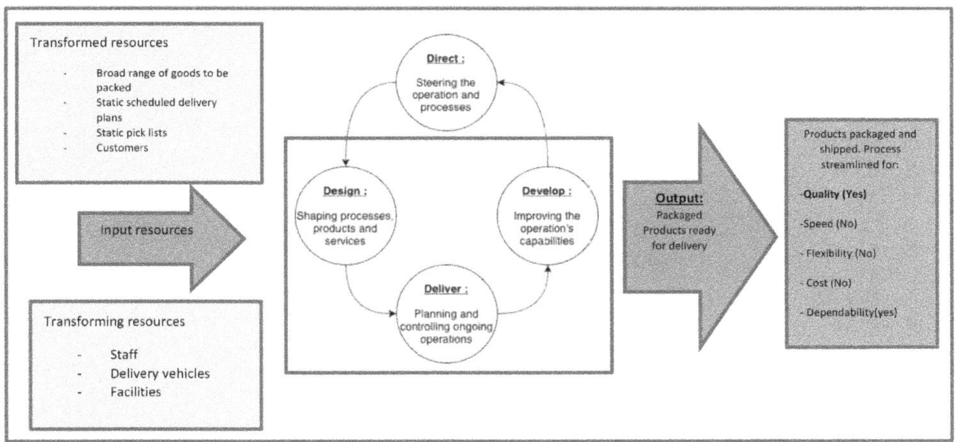

Figure 9.5 RB's Delivery Process Input–Output Model

OPERATIONS STRATEGY

The current delivery process is streamlined for quality and dependability. The Polar Diagram in Figure 9.9 visually depicts this observation, emphasising RBB's focus on ensuring good quality packaged goods for customers.

The process is considered high quality as it is consistent and has minimal errors. The output is consistent with each cycle and shift. It can be stated that the specification quality of design is consistent (Nigel Slack, 2017), resulting in delivered products that are predominantly free from errors. The strategy places a huge emphasis on specification quality with the main goal of each delivery meeting customer specifications. This is extremely important as incorrect deliveries result in further time wasted, effort, and cost implications due to returned orders. Additionally, the processes aim to be dependable, and with a proven track record in the industry, RB prides itself in continuously meeting customer needs.

Design

To get a detailed understanding of the delivery process before optimisation, a detailed process map has been used to detail all stages involved in the delivery process. By recording each stage of the process, improvement opportunities were identified along with a better understanding of how the process is organised in its entirety. The existing has multiple bottlenecks during various stages, the process delays between picking completion and loading the goods on trolleys due to unavailability of trolleys for loading resulting in increased waste. Tasks are organised and coordinated in a sequential process with proportional cycle-time allocated for each stage. This ensures task precedence and ensures that each sub-process can be optimised and monitored individually. Finally, as can be seen in Figure 6, the process experiences reduced throughput efficiency because of process bottlenecks by design.

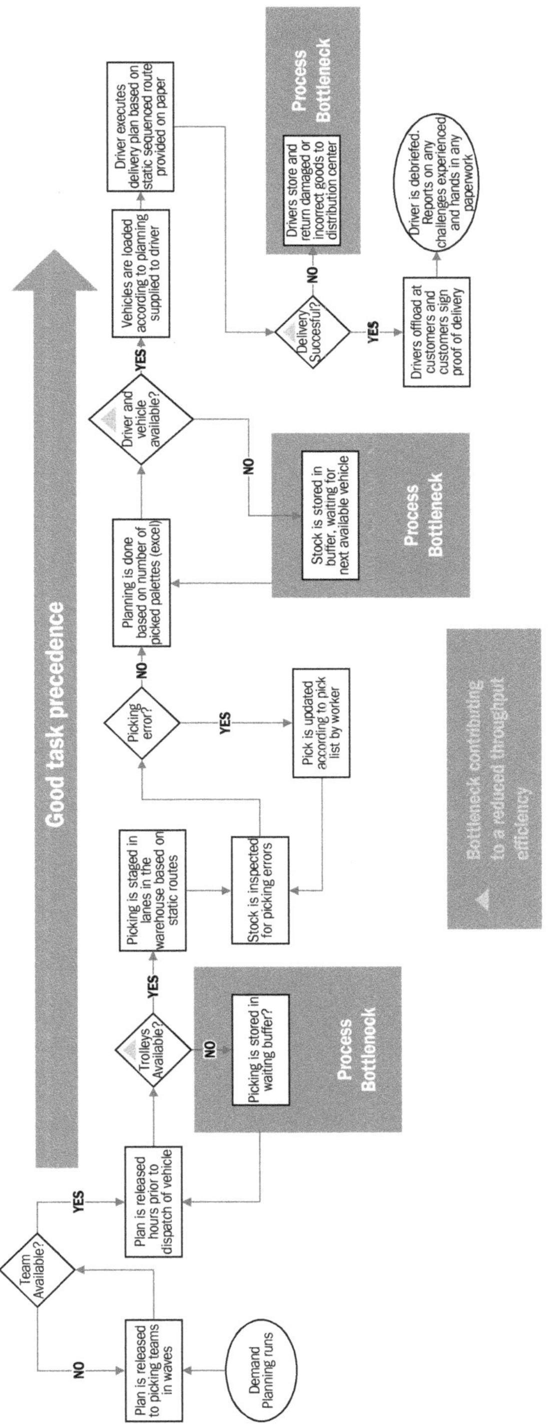

Figure 9.6 The Current Process Map

Impact of Volume and Variety on Process Design

There are several process types mainly categorised as either Manufacturing or Service Process Types. These process types are characterised by their different volume-variety characteristics. The Product-Process Matrix in Figure 9.7 depicts the relationship between a process's volume variety position and its design characteristics (Nigel Slack, 2017):

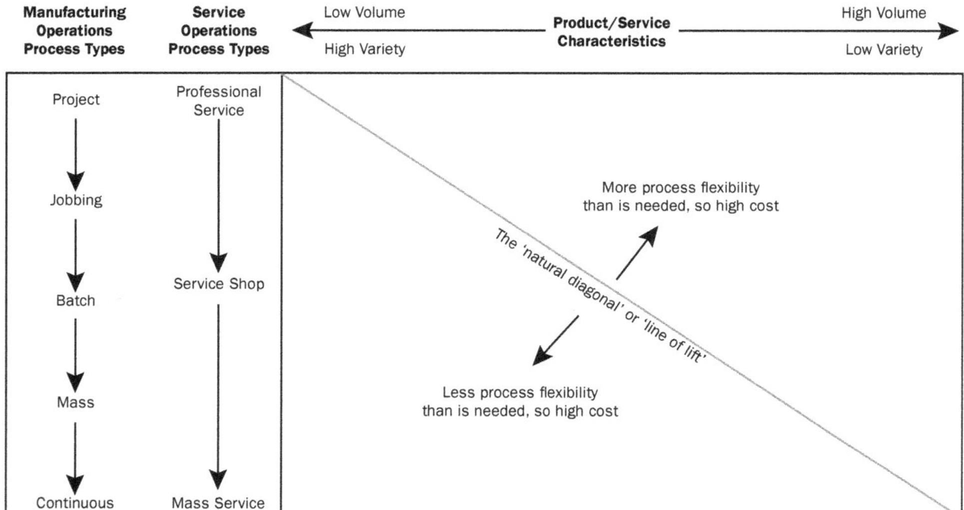

Figure 9.7 The Product-Process Matrix (Slack, 2017)

Ideally, all processes should be as close as possible to the Natural diagonal line as possible. This means that the flexibility of the process is optimised and therefore the overall cost of the process is optimised (Slack et al, 2017)

RB's delivery process is a service shop type process. The delivery process deals with a mixed level of variety and volumes given the nature of the goods delivered. The delivery process requires a high level of flexibility to adapt to the different types of products delivered through the process. Currently, as per the Polar Diagram in Figure 9.11, RB's delivery process is not adequately flexible to deliver the products according to the customer variety. Therefore, the process cost is higher compared to a more flexible process.

The optimised process proposed for RB's delivery service moves the process from its current position to an optimised position close to the natural diagonal line. This is depicted in the matrix of Figure 9.8.

166

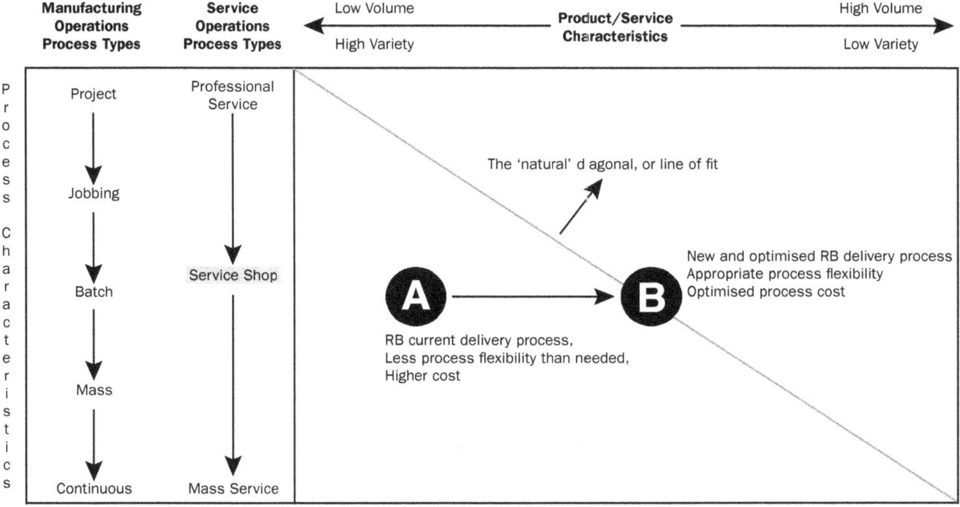

Figure 9.8 RB Product—Process Matrix for Its Delivery Service

Improvement

In summary, RB's process is streamlined as it results in producing the desired output of correctly packaged deliverable goods to a variety of customers. The process is, however, not fast, flexible, and cost-effective. The objective is to optimise the already streamlined process by introducing technologies and innovations that will result in a faster and more flexible delivery process.

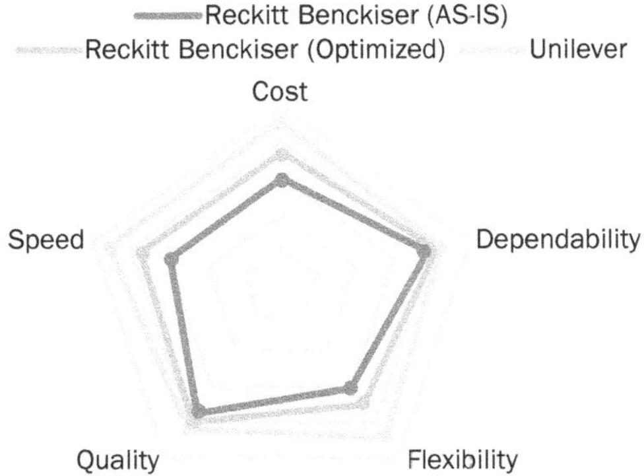

Figure 9.9 Polar Diagram

Table 9.2 Performance Objectives

Performance Objectives	Objectives	Current	Optimised
Cost	Low supply chain costs	High waste in value stream resulting in non-optimised cost	Optimised cost by reducing wastage in the value stream by leveraging digital enabling technologies
Dependability	Are goods delivered on time and our customers place their trust in our services	Optimised	N/A
Flexibility	The ability to produce different types of products, volumes and delivery flexibility based on customer requests	Due to the manual way of doing things and lack of insight, the team has challenges in making changes on the fly	With the implementation of the TMS and integration into WMS, the team can now use real-time data to visually view the value stream, which enables them to quickly make changes across the value stream based on customer demands.
Quality	Zero mis-packaging and damaged goods being sent to end customer	Optimised	N/A
Speed	Low stock kept in inventory by moving items as fast possible from input to output and finally to the customer	Speed is lower compared to competitors due to manual ways of working	Digitisation and automation have increased the speed across the value stream resulting in reduced inventory holding

DIGITAL MATURITY

To date, RB has implemented a world-class SAP EWM warehouse management system. This has simplified the management of complex high-volume delivery processes. The introduction of the SAP-based system has allowed for paper-based information to be converted into digital form. Digitising the core of its supply chain has removed restrictions the company previously faced. The introduction of the SAP system has made information more accessible, increased productivity, and contributed significantly to synchronised communication and information sharing between divisions. The system also improved decision-making.

Companies are embracing the digital world and all the opportunities it can bring to an organisation more than ever before (Malak, 2022). According to Malak, factors such as the simplification of data communication between both internal and external parties adds speed and convenience for all stakeholders involved. If leveraged correctly, customers could also benefit from an improved, transparent, and reliable experience.

RB has made significant strides in its digital journey. Working from the SAP EWMs system as the base, the existence and implementation of digital technology as an extension of the SAP system in the delivery process has been assessed. The addition of a SAP system allows for such scalability by creating a foundation from which predominantly clean and accurate information regarding orders and planned deliveries can be derived. The DAS framework of Boute and Van Mieghem was employed to position RB's level of digital maturity. The framework evaluates the following:

- A process level of reach;
- How far the process is on its digitisation journey; and
- Automation and smart control.

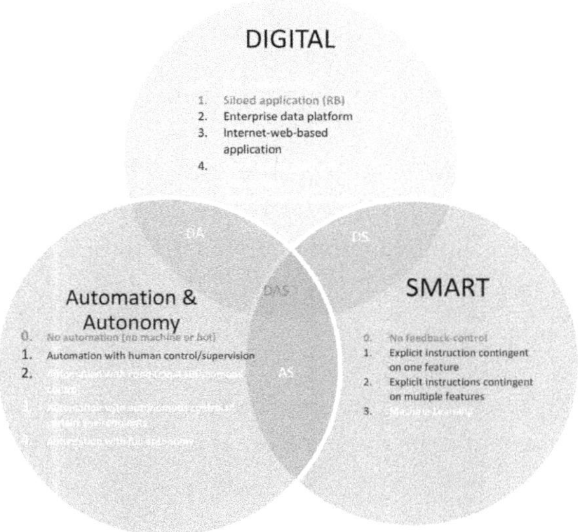

Figure 9.10 RB's Digital Maturity, As-Is DAS Framework

Digital

According to the assessed framework in Figure 9.8, RB's delivery process is currently on level 1 of its digital journey. The process is still predominantly paper-based with siloed applications providing information for:

- Picking orders,
- Packing orders,
- Delivery route planning,
- Driver staffing and route scheduling.

Spreadsheets are used to support the workflow (Boute, 2021). Scalability will require a shift to level 2 in the delivery process. This can be achieved through the extension of the SAP system into the delivery process as a foundation for further process optimisations.

Automation and Autonomy

Digital operations play a key role in the facilitation of automating processes. The introduction of machines such as robots or bespoke software applications that solve a particular problem provide significant benefits.

The approach to RB's process was to identify stages of the delivery process that could be automated (Boute, 2021). RB is currently positioned at level 1 in terms of autonomy. There is significant human intervention in the sub-processes involved in defining the following:

- Suitable picking schedules,
- Inspecting incorrectly picked items,
- Scheduling routing as well as organising vehicles for delivery.

The use of the TMS system, as well as scanners and sensors such as cameras for inspection points, will allow for control to be embedded in the sub-process above with little to no human intervention. Therefore, the process will be shifted to level 2 in its autonomy journey.

Smart

Smart control allows for numerous possibilities including the use of IoT based sensors. A typical use case is the use of cameras coupled with suitable edge devices to detect parcel defects prior to vehicles being loaded.

Control algorithms make it possible to develop adaptive, contingent, dynamic, and personalised control processes as part of any process (Boute, 2021). To date, RB uses a manual process with minimal feedback. This creates numerous challenges such as defective goods making their way to customers. Boute classifies smart control in three distinct levels.

The first level describing control rules or algorithms that consist of a sequence of explicit instructions that are contingent to one or numerous input features. For example, an inventory system used to measure idle stock and alert staff of increasing buffer sizes. To date, RB makes use of manual feedback loops and lacks such a system. In addition, stock spends a lot of time idling due to insufficient driver, and or vehicle allocations. A system that dynamically adjusts staff planning based on customer needs and available stock is essential. The second level classifies control rules into explicit instructions contingent on multiple features and the third level is use of machine learning.

APPLIED DAS FRAMEWORK

This section focuses on the future or desired state. To gain the intended benefits from digitalisation, it is important to ensure that the process is fully digital, and that waste is eliminated. The following steps can be taken for this digitalisation journey:

1. Digitising aspects of the delivery process such as the picking process by ensuring that picking instructions are digitally generated.
2. Introducing a Transport Management System (TMS) to ensure all aspects of the delivery process such as available drivers and dynamic route planning are represented digitally. It will also ensure they are repeatable and can be streamlined through tools and techniques such as advanced analytics in future.
3. The introduction of an internet-based web platform for route planning, visualisation, and monitoring will provide the much-required transparency and engagement with all stakeholders involved.

Digital

The introduction of the aforementioned tools and technologies will streamline and optimise workflow, by ensuring a fast and dependable delivery process. Using the Enterprise Data Platform, RB can move, synchronise, integrate, and share data across various departments. RB can use the data to support departmental activities. For example, supporting the delivery process by using the data for dynamic picking, real-time scheduling of delivery, and dynamic planning of activities. The implementation of said technologies and techniques will provide a suitable foundation to a digital future for RB (Boute, 2021).

The TMS system can collect and share transport and telematics from the delivery vehicles. By leveraging the system, RB will further shift up to level 3 on their digital journey. The implementation of such a system will act as a gateway to additional opportunities such as migrating to cloud computing systems in the future as part of level 4. This will take place after the successful implementation and rollout of an internet web-based platform. It will be used to connect picking and packing data with available resources and capabilities to fulfil customer demands in real time, dynamic scheduling and planning and transparency as part of the delivery process as part of level 3.

Automation and Autonomy

Introducing automation through software that can execute tasks without human intervention is key to creating a foundation for further levels of automation. The picking process can be considered a highly repetitive process with a high volume of products being packed daily by RB. In addition, the use of IoT sensors to monitor idle stock and dynamically allocate it to available delivery vehicles will save the organisation time and money. It will also reduce the high number of returns and damaged goods.

The introduction of an IoT TMS system allows for an automated, connected, and digitised process. When data is captured and stored at the level required by retailers and shared with them, it makes it possible for retailers to manage inventory efficiently (De Vass et al, 2020). De Vass et al (2020) further state that IoT-enabled integration of processes between business departments allows retailers to respond to market at a significantly faster rate. In summary, IoT provides much-needed flexibility at RB. This should be leveraged from the picking stage when orders are picked for delivery through to the planning and assigning of delivery routes to customers (De Vass et al, 2020).

The ability to sense, auto-capture, transmit, collect data and process more transparently throughout the business provides some advantages. These include improved security and added value to the delivery process by reducing waste due to idle inventory. Furthermore, adding connectivity throughout the delivery value-chain as well as additional visibility from added tracking. The introduction of a tracking-based system will take RB to level 2 when it comes to their automation journey for their delivery process.

Smart

Digital operations can potentially improve the intelligence of production line control rules. RB currently applies level 0 autonomy as part of their delivery process. The picking process, scheduling and planning processes are automated based on time execution. For example, the allocation of picking jobs to workers is completed in waves, with automation being highly dependent on time (i.e., every 5 minutes picking jobs are released in batches).

Although the process is functional and delivers results, there is minimal feedback. For instance, workers, allocated picking jobs in a static sequential order. The process has limited visibility on whether picking jobs are allocated as efficiently as possible. To introduce smart controls as part of the delivery process for RB, the recommended optimised process map requires the introduction of algorithms. These will provide explicit picking and packing instructions based on input variables such as:

- Availability of items for packing in the smart buffer;
- Releasing pick jobs passed on customer demand rather than forecasting; and
- Recommending optimal delivery routes.

The TMS system will allow for a transparent picking, packing, and loading process. In addition, IoT sensors will allow for a condition-based buffer in which the system maintains its buffer levels dynamically based on demand and incoming orders. These steps will elevate RB to levels 1 and 2 by introducing explicit instructions contingent on multiple features.

It is important that RB makes strategic decisions that are in line with moving towards a digital and automated process control environment, with smart technology as the foundation. To ensure a dependable and fast delivery process, while maintaining and improving the already existing quality, eliminating waste and digitising manual processes should be primary objectives of the optimisation journey. Using the TMS system will further introduce ways of capturing human interventions and errors such as incomplete orders being loaded for delivery.

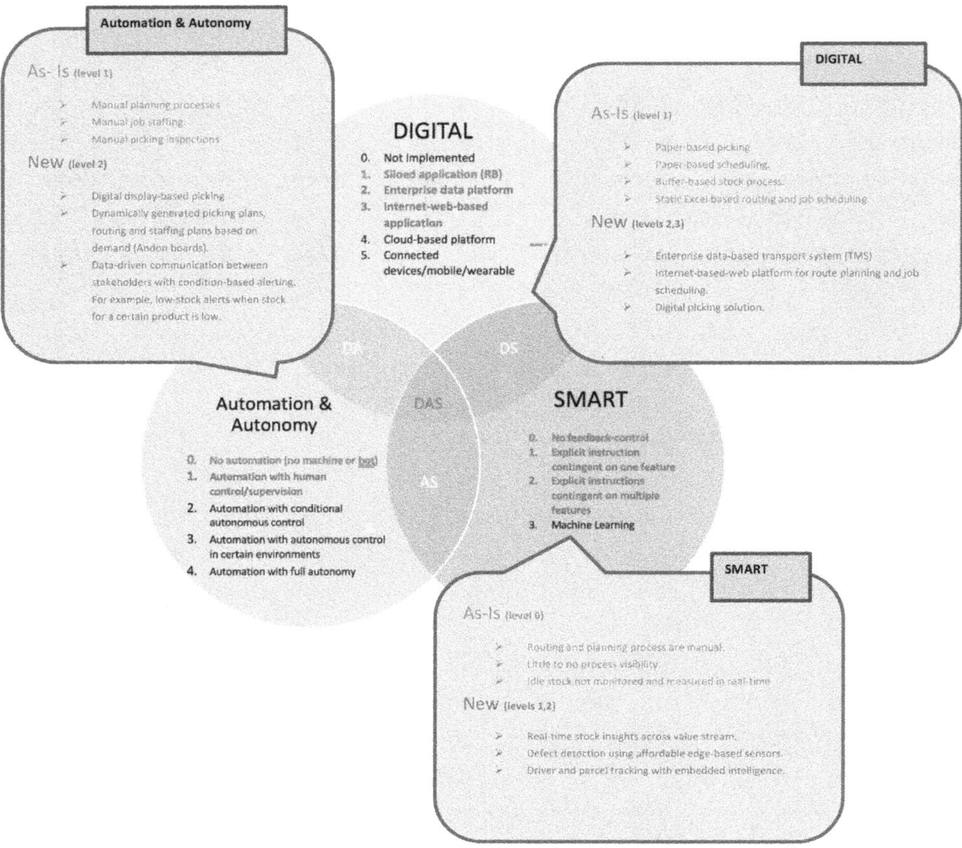

Figure 9.11 Applied DAS Framework (Boute, 2020)

In concluding the DAS framework assessment, before digitising, automating, and enabling a smart production environment, the approach was to first streamline the process through standardisation of techniques used as part of the process.

Ensuring streamlined workflows allowed for the reduction of waste and decreases cycle time for various sub-processes within the delivery process. The second objective of the recommendation was to ensure the collection of clean and dependable data from the delivery process (Boute & Van Mieghan, 2021). The clean data generated from the processes as well as the smart inventory buffer allowed the accurate augmentation of shopfloor activities. As stated by Boute and Van Mieghan (2021), reliable data is a pre-requisite for the effective implementation of smart control within a production facility. Finally, it is important that RB place strong emphasis on shifting the organisation's culture.

A data-driven mindset will allow for human work to be augmented, assessed, and improved over time. As it is early the stages of RB's digitisation journey, strong emphasis must be placed on the successful implementation of smart-control measures. Smart control will create the foundation for further automation and autonomy as well as the possibility to accurately leverage artificial intelligence to further optimise the process in future.

After eliminating waste attributed to idle stock, errors due to manual picking and static planning need to be addressed. This submission recommends the implementation of a Pull-Based system in which information is synchronised between the various stages of the process. Figure 9.12 shows the final state process map after implementing recommendations as outlined in the DAS framework assessment.

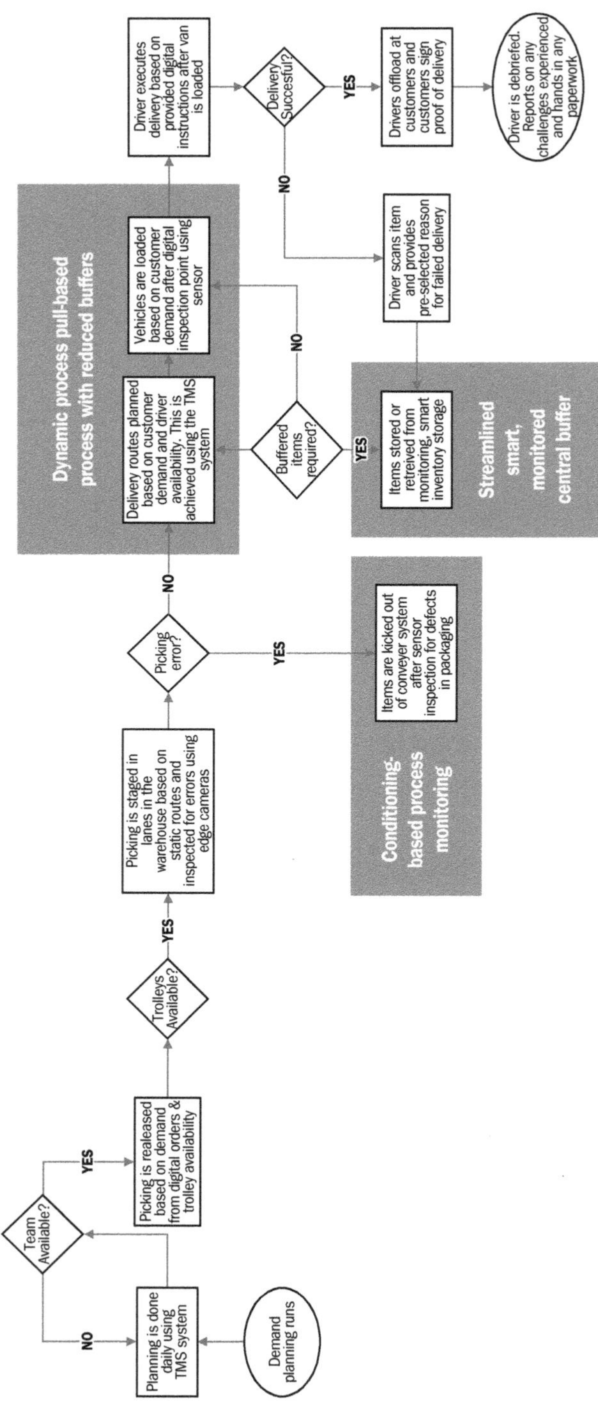

Figure 9.12 Optimised Pull-Based Lean Delivery Process Map

Rollout based on the DAS Model

The rollout of the DAS model will be completed in waves to ensure the optimisation of the existing processes. This will take place before moving to implementation of automation and autonomy of smart systems using techniques based on artificial intelligence.

It is required that the teams reach the level of maturity required to adopt digital solutions. Using this approach will enable the identification of any potential challenges to introducing a new process which can impact the rollout of the other waves, thus, mitigating any project risks which could arise in later waves. The goal is to first eliminate waste from existing processes using digital techniques, optimise the process as much as possible, standardise and disseminate across the organisation to ensure everyone understands the new ways of working. Once completed, the next step is automating and implementing smart systems to reduce human touch points.

At a high level, the approach below will be implemented:

- Wave 1 – Begin the digital transformation of the processes identified as creating unnecessary waste. The major deficiencies were around the team using paper or Excel to track tasks across the value stream. To address this, the TMS solution is deployed to digitise existing tasks.

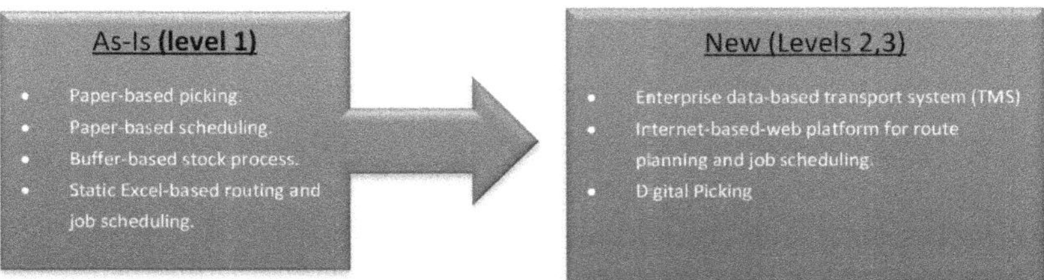

- Wave 2 – The implementation of the new system enabled the collection of additional data for processing. This is required to visually analyse the operations to enable smooth implementation of level 1 of Automation and Autonomy.

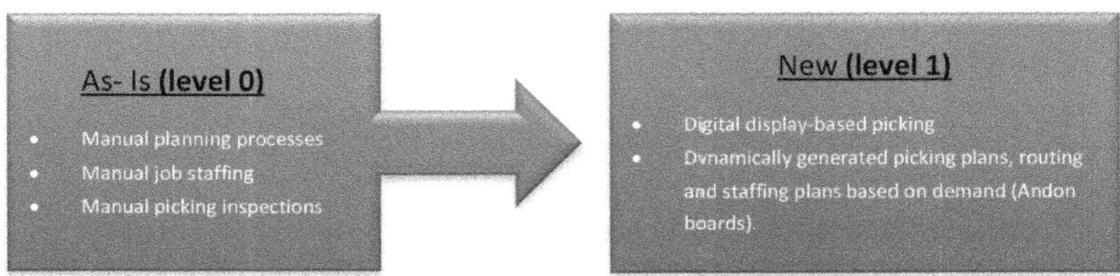

- Wave 3 – The foundations have been laid to begin implementing smart systems which can easily be introduce a higher level of maturity has been reached. The teams have become used to working in a digital first company. The process has also been aligned to allow for better adoption of new smarter digital solutions.

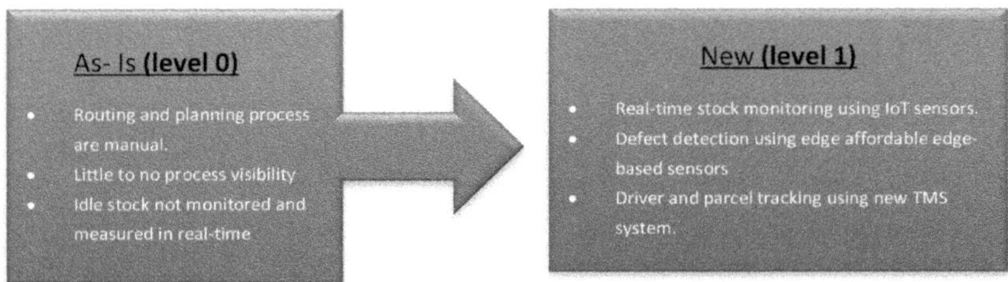

DEPLOYMENT PLAN

The deployment plan shows on a high level the implementation plan, which will be done in phases. Using an approach based on phases will ensure the plan realises the expected benefits of the solution (PMAlliance):

- The Assessment phase tasks create a deep understanding of the current environment, enabling us to develop our action plan and identify potential gaps. Some of the activities we will carry out include value stream mapping, problem-solving Five Whys strategy, and a high-level business case, including investments in skills and vendors.

- In Readiness & Planning, a detailed plan is put together while ensuring the organisation is ready to implement the new processes and technologies. One of the critical parts of this section is to ensure the teams have the right skills to carry out their tasks, and where gaps were found in the previous section, it will be supplemented by consultants or new hires.

- In the Execution, we carry out the project in different waves starting with the new TMS as detailed on page 179.

- Finally, we will do a detailed analysis of the impact of each wave while iterating and optimising where required.

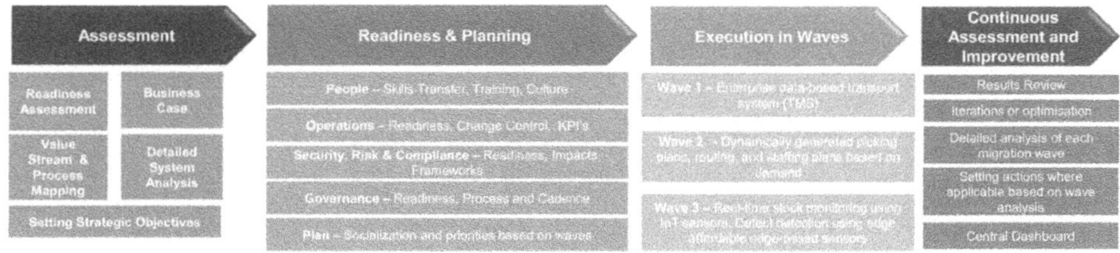

Figure 9.13 Deployment Plan

MILESTONES

The planned milestones for the TMS project are provided in Figure 9.14.

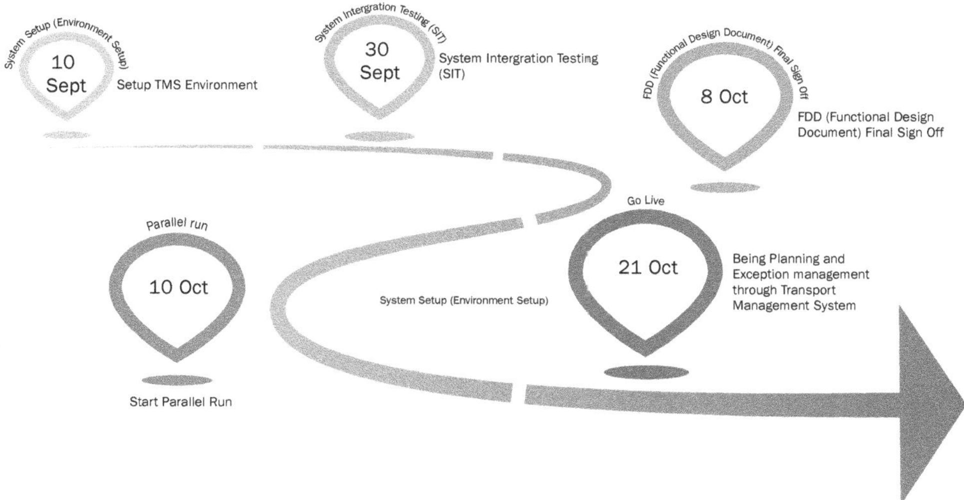

Figure 9.14 Time Management System Deployment Plan

SUMMARY

This case has proven how the digitisation of RB's standard processes and operations will enable the organisation to compete in an environment of high supply chain costs while also being prepared for unexpected disruptions in supply chains and customer demands. By deploying lean techniques such as Value Stream Mapping and the five Whys, we identified the opportunities to eliminate waste and improve time in the value stream and customer experience.

RB will now be delivering a first-in-class product and service. The next questions to ponder are:

1. Does this solve RB's challenge?
2. Does it fit in with the overall strategy?

The simple answer is a resounding yes! The TMS system provides RB the platform to become more efficient and more customer-centric. Overall, we have shown by making use of data and automation, RB can achieve the following benefits:

- Reduce waste in the value streams.
- Increase the quality of the delivery process.
- Optimise fleet operations which in turn reduces fuel and other operational costs.

179

- Reduction in inventory by applying a Pull System using data collected from across the value stream.
- Planning for the future using the DAS model which can introduce further benefits and increase digital maturity of RB.

> People all over the world are faced with tremendous challenges … helping communities to find sustainable solutions is what driver our portfolio not just to do well, but to do good. (Narasimhan, 2022)

Laxman Narasimhan is CEO of RB and Benckiser.

This case proves the approach to identify and deploy a sustainable solution fit into the RB model. This is through cost savings, improved customer service, and ensuring a reduced carbon footprint in:

- Reducing vehicles on the road through optimisation
- Reducing distance driven through optimisation

The above is in line with Narasimhan's vision depicted through the quote above.

By using the approaches proposed in this case, RB can become a digital first company, ready to embrace new technologies.

REFERENCES

Boute, R., Gijsbrechts, J., Van Mieghem, J. (2020). Digital Lean Operations: Smart Automation and Artificial Intelligence in Financial Services. *SSRN Electronic Journal.* https://doi.org/10.2139/ssrn.3747173

Boute, R. N., Van Mieghem, J,.A. (2021). Autonomous Automation and the Smart Execution of Work. *MBR*, 01(01), 177. https://mbrjournal.com/wp-content/uploads/2020/11/32_Digital-Operations-.pdf.

Cloutier, M. (2021). Building the factory of the future today. Retrieved July 29, 2022 from https://www.ibm.com/case-studies/RBB-group/

Malak, H. A. (2022). 10 Unbeatable Advantages Of Digitization. The ECM Consultant. May. Retrieved February 1, 2022 from https://theecmconsultant.com/advantages-of-digitization/

Narasimhan, L. (2022). Who we are. Retrieved July 27, 2022 from https://www.RBB.com/about-us/who-we-are/

Onenetwork. (2022). Transportation Management Systems (TMS) and Intelligent Logistics. Retrieved 29 July from https://www.onenetwork.com/

supply-chain-management-solutions/intelligent-logistics/transportation-management-systems-tms/

PMAlliance. (2022). A Phased Approach to Project Management Implementation. Retrieved July 27, 2022 from https://pm-alliance.com/phased-project-management-implementation/

Ramesh, V., Sreenivasa Prasad, K.V., Srinivas, T. R. (2008). Implementation of a Lean Model for Carrying out Value Stream Mapping in a Manufacturing Industry. *Journal of Industrial and Systems Engineering*, 2(3), 180–196. http://www.jise.ir/article_3977_1ba55d337aac4cf2cbf95806373c7710.pdf

Sasikumar, A., & Kumar, K. (2013) Value stream mapping in a manufacturing company. *International Journal of Commerce, Business and Management (IJCBM)*, 2(2), 2319-2828.

Siregar, I., Nasution, A., Prasetio, A., & Fadillah, K. (2017). Analysis of production flow process with lean manufacturing approach. IOP Conference Series: Materials Science and Engineering, 237, 012002. https://doi.org/10.1088/1757-899x/237/1/012002

Slack, N., Brandon-Jones, A., Johnston, R., Singh, H. & Phihlela, K. (2017). *Global and Southern African Perspectives Operations Management* (3rd ed.). Pearson Education South Africa

Soliman, M. (2017). A comprehensive review of manufacturing wastes: Toyota production system lean principles. *Emirates Journal for Engineering Research*, 22(2), 1–10.

Turk, V. (2019). *The Advantages and Benefits of Transportation Management Systems (TMS)*. Retrieved July 29, 2022 from https://www.kuebix.com/the-advantages-and-benefits-of-transportation-management-systems-tms-infographic/

de Vass, T., Shee, H., Miah, S. J. (2021). Iot in supply chain management: a narrative on retail sector sustainability. *International Journal of Logistics Research and Applications*, 24(6), 605–624. https://doi.org/10.1080/13675567.2020.1787970

Venter, I. (2022). Supply chain bottlenecks here to stay for 2022, goods prices to rise sharply. Retrieved July 27, 2022, from https://www.engineeringnews.co.za/article/supply-chain-bottlenecks-here-to-stay-for-2022-goods-prices-to-rise-sharply-cargo-compass-sa-2022-04-06

CHAPTER 10

Practical Case of Digitalising Public Hospitals in South Africa: A Viewpoint

CURRENT STATE OF PUBLIC HOSPITALS IN SOUTH AFRICA

Access to quality health care is a constitutional right, enshrined in the South African Constitution. Challenges such as poor record keeping and prolonged waiting times have plagued the South African health system, especially citizens at healthcare facilities. Poor record keeping causes unnecessary delays for patients, where sometimes the patient's folders are missing or lost, causing the patient to wait while needing medical treatment, and in worst case scenarios the medical history of the patient is lost, which can create issues leading to misdiagnosis or incorrect treatment due to lack of patient history, resulting in death. Although it is the best healthcare system in Africa, South African healthcare is regarded as one of the most unequal healthcare systems in the world. According to the National Health Department, about 84% of South Africans depend on the public healthcare system, with only 503 healthcare professionals for every 100 000 public healthcare users (Cleary & Low, 2020).

Some of the main challenges faced by public hospitals

We have evaluated the general admittance process based on research conducted at various hospitals.

As a result we discovered these challenges:

a. Lack of human resources with currently more than 10 000 vacancies for nurses and 1 300 vacancies for doctors not being filled (Maqhina, 2022).

b. Lack of strategic direction to implement technology that simplifies patient admission and record keeping.

c. The health records of patients are kept manually. There is also inability to co-ordinate patient information between hospital divisions. This does not inspire the confidence and freedom for patients to seek medical care at a public health facility knowing that their history will be available for more informed diagnosis and treatment.

d.   Shortages of medication, where tracking systems are not implemented within the operation process.

e.   The enforcement and standardisation of the code for patient care.

REITERATING THE STANDARD ADMISSION OPERATIONS PROCESS

The established standard admission process, while streamlined, still shows significant wastage and makes use of manual operational efficiencies as well as legacy systems for the management of patient information. The standard admission and patient documentation process is segmented into four main categories:

1.   Administration, where most of the patient credentials are managed prior to admission of the hospital.

2.   Transfer, which shows the highest volume of wastage and points of contention for patients waiting for beds to become available and needing to wait for nurse and doctor availability.

3.   Treatment, which only accounts for of time taken to get the patient through this and is a variable not contained due to the focus being primarily on admittance and patient information documentation and management.

4.   Discharge, where the patient has had treatment and their information is captured and the admittance process ends.

Patients are segmented into three categories:

1.   Emergency, which bypasses administration and primarily is admitted and would run through transfer, patient treatment and ultimately discharge.

2.   Elective existing patients who would need to access information at the front desk, which is generally manual and extracted from legacy storage (at times this is even a physical store room and file). They too are only then transferred, treated and discharged and during the course of the process spend most of the time waiting.

3.   Elective new patients, who need new files to be creaed in the admittance administration process and see the longest duration, averaging around 20+ hours from arriving to being discharged (*not accounting for treatment longer than an estimated four hours*).

UNDERSTANDING DIGITAL MATURITY

In order to understand digital maturity, we adopted the Deloitte Digital Maturity (DDM) framework so that we can address the holistic view of the hospitals with a key focus to improve the admission and patient record-keeping process and operations. And this is because the DDM can be used in each phase of the business transformation to help identify where the gaps are and to establish key areas to focus on and where to start.

We made use of the DAS framework as an audit to assess where the hospitals' admission and record-keeping process is now, and where it could be in the future. We scored the process on level 1 (Digital). However, after digitisation/process improvements, we re-evaluated and it had moved to level 2 (Automation and Autonomy).

DIGITALISATION OF THE PROCESS

The manual operation and management of information, as well as various legacy systems used for information storage, have an indirect impact on the health of patients. This can be attributed to long waiting periods which offer no value to the hospital's operation process. Based on the current patient admission process being ineffective and inefficient we've deduced that the process should be digitalised to ensure faster treatment and improved management of patient admission (which is the main output) needed for a public hospital.

The proposed main areas of focus for digitalisation are the Standard Operating Procedure for Patient Admission, Patient Record Management and Patient Identification. We propose improvement within these areas as follows:

Standard Operating Procedure

The key identified patients would be elective, either new or existing, as well as emergency patients, who bypass administration. Key consideration is that there is no standard operating procedure for these respective patients routed to the same area to wait prior to either opening new files or accessing their existing files, which are paper-based.

In order to reduce patient waiting time upon arrival at public hospitals, we propose an e-triage process at patient arrival to allow patients to be segmented according to their need – that is, whether they are in an emergency, following up on a consultation or have a new consultation. During this process a new client can electronically create a file through an online system via the hospital app. We propose a patient application (app) that would be integrated into a HIS (Hospital Information System) which would be integrated into a Customer

Relationship Management (CRM) system to manage patient information via cloud solutions.

We also propose a biometric system to identify existing clients that will eliminate the need for a hospital card. Existing clients will only need to input their fingerprint in the onsite biometric system for file retrieval (from the HIS). In addition to this RPA will be deployed to enhance the patient routing process following the patients, interaction with a medical chatbot to diagnose the severity of their injury/condition. Bed availability would be assessed via RPA as well as RFID tags and scanners.

Patient Record Management and Patient Identification

This calls for implementation of a Hospital Information System (HIS) that is centralised on a hybrid cloud solution integrated to a CRM system, which will eliminate record management issues. This information management system will directly store all information captured via the hospital patient registration app/site portal as mentioned above, and will be accessible by patients through utilising their ID/passport number when on hospital app or website or using biometrics when in hospital.

Doctors and nurses will utilise a staff application to access and update any patient information, which will be automatically stored to the cloud storage solution (HIS) when patient information is updated. Furthermore, having safely and digitally accessible patient data, storing this data digitally allows patient records to be shared as and when needed to other private/public hospitals and clinics through an Integrated Referral System. This in turn is linked to a National CRM system, giving a single view of a patient and ensuring tailored patient care derived from full patient history records across the country.

IMPLEMENTATION PLAN AND TIME FRAMES

Our implementation plan will follow the process outlined in Figure 10.1 underpinned by the PRINCE2™ project management methodology

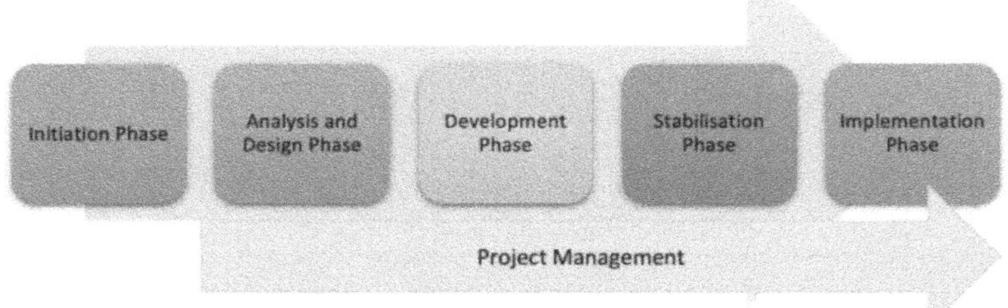

Figure 10.1 The PRINCE2™ Project Management Methodology Reworked

Analysis

An experienced project manager will co-ordinate workshop sessions with the relevant stakeholders within the Dept of Health to define the scope of the requirement. The output of this will be a functional design specification that will detail the business process: as-is and to-be, branding, documents to be digitised, migration, gap analysis and readiness of infrastructure and skills. The analysis stage will also take into account budget requirements and procurement plans as the project is envisaged to be rolled out over a period of five to seven financial years. During this stage of the project we will also focus on Training & Development to ensure user adoption once implemented.

Development

The development team will use the Agile methodology in developing the solution.

The key steps in the development process are listed below:
* Business Process Streamlining & Mapping;
* Server & Network Configuration;
* ERP Deployment;
* Custom Development;
* Content Migration; and
* Branding.

Regular demos and testing will ensure alignment to objectives.

Testing

The development team will do systems testing before handing over a User Acceptance document for User Acceptance Testing to ensure the solution can be tested against the requirements.

Implementation

Once UAT is complete the systems can be implemented in a phased approach.

Risk

Utilising the PRINCE2™ project management methodology a Risk Register will be developed from the start of the project and track all risks identified in conjunction with project impact. PRINCE2™ is underpinned by sound project governance, scalability and flexibility to satisfy individual project needs.

Resources

The following will be called for:

1. Technology where we make use of:
   (a) Scalable and secure compute & storage platform
   (b) Integrated cyber security solution protecting data and data access
   (c) Highly available nationwide network connectivity
   (d) Enterprise resource planning tool and customer relationship management tool customised for healthcare
   (e) Backup power solutions
   (f) Biometric solutions
   (g) Interactive kiosks/ticketing system
   (h) Medical chatbots
   (i) RPA
2. Human resources and skills through appointment of:
   (a) Business analysts
   (b) Database administrators
   (c) ICT engineers
   (d) Cyber security specialists
   (e) Governance officer
   (f) Training facilitators
   (g) Patient liaison officers
3. Strategy and culture:
   (a) The Enterprise Project Management Office will lead strategic strategy formulation and change management processes.
4. Training and development through:
   (a) Development of refined SOPs
   (b) Upskilling of staff (Instructor-led and on-the-job training as well as virtual training initiatives)
   (c) Patient/supplier education

Timeline

Associated timeframes considered are based on key phases starting with the Outcome Identification, Current Business Process Mapping & Streamlining and thereafter following a Request For Information (RFI) process to evaluate appropriate solutions.

Once an appropriate platform is identified the Proof of Value (PoV) will be conducted within a limited scope to evaluate the success criteria for successful completion.

The next step will be to carry out all the dependency mapping and gap analysis to ensure all the infrastructure, skills and training requirements are identified and planned upfront.

We envisage that due to the complex nature and vast geographic landscape the project will take around five years to be rolled out. Digitising of existing patient records and implementing new systems will start with District Hospitals then Regional Hospitals, Clinics and eventually Primary Health Facilities.

The scope is laid out in Figure 10.2:

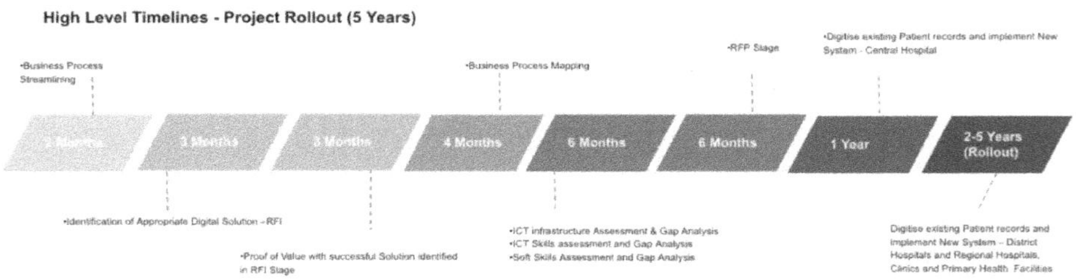

Figure 10.2 High Level Time Line

THE PROJECTED RESULTS OF THE DIGITALISED OPERATIONS PROCESS

The process and value stream mapping was re-evaluated following the implementation of digitisation and it was identified that all manual processes and waiting times, which were the largest contribution to wastage, had been removed.

Compared to the initial cycle time of the process a projected average 50% efficiency improvement was seen in the new cycle time in total and was around 10 hours and 25 minutes (previously around 20 hours). Efficiency measured between the initial cycle time and value added time was also accounted for and compared to a previous 40% of the cycle time being value added time, this grew by 53,89% and averaged a total 93,84%. This shows that through digitisation of the process, close to 100% of the cycle time was added value.

Having re-evaluated the DAS model as projected and forecast by the digital maturity framework an inclined shift to automation with partial human supervision was seen for admission, transfer and treatment where discharge moved into a level four of digital with components of cloud computing seen.

CONCLUSION

The purpose of our activity was to solve some of the pressing and operational issues affecting public healthcare operations in South Africa through digitisation and standardisation of the admission and medical records process on a centralised management system across public hospitals in the country.

Based on the analysis conveyed through value streaming the process map we were able to identify the inefficiencies as time wasted while patients are waiting, lack of standardised admissions procedure as well as a lack of integrated systems to store and to provide patients' information.

Our proposed solutions to tackling the process inefficiencies included process redesign, making use of emerging technologies and standardising some of the work procedures.

Looking at the assessment on the redesigned process plan, it can be concluded that the implementation of some of the emerging technologies as RPA, Cloud Systems, Biometric and Facial recognition is important for mitigation and speed improvement in bottleneck areas – thereby reducing inefficiencies.

ACKNOWLEDGEMENT OF CONTRIBUTORS

- Tyran De Beer
- Ravi Pillay
- Diveshan Deonarain
- Freddie Petje
- Esinako Makaluza
- Mendy Mufamadi
- Jerry Nematswerane
- Shandulo Joseph
- Keny Mutimbwa

(All are affiliated to the Wits Business School, University of the Witwatersrand, Johannesburg).

REFERENCES

Cleary, K., Low, M. (2020). Government strategy shows billions needed to avert healthcare worker crisis. Spotlight. Retrieved May 12, 2022, from https://www.spotlightnsp.co.za/2020/09/01/government-strategy-shows-billions-needed-to-avert-healthcare-worker-crisis/

Competition Commission South Africa. (2019). Health Market Inquiry. September. Retrieved from https://www.compcom.co.za/wp-content/uploads/2020/01/Final-Findings-and-recommendations-report-Health-Market-Inquiry.pdf

Department of Surgery Steve Biko Academic Hospital. (2019). Manual/Handbook Registrars/Medical Officers/ Interns. January. Retrieved from https://www.up.ac.za/media/shared/135/ZP_Files/2019-edition-surgery-manual-final-final.zp167210.pdf

Maqhina, M. (2022). Public hospitals have shortage of more than 10,000 nurses and 1,300 doctors. Retrieved May 12, 2022, from https://www.iol.co.za/news/politics/public-hospitals-have-shortage-of-more-than-10-000-nurses-and-1300-doctors-474f9729-2363-480a-b54c-72c1509760b4

Mlamla, S. (2021). Patients demand action over the long queues at day hospitals and clinics in Cape Town. Retrieved from https://www.iol.co.za/capeargus/news/patients-demand-action-over-the-long-queues-at-day-hospitals-and-clinics-in-cape-town-ce32c9fb-3c27-4a10-b0b7-845b8493653b

Palghat, S. (2020). Value Stream Mapping. Retrieved from https://wordpress.lehigh.edu/swp320/2020/12/07/value-stream-mapping/

CHAPTER 11

Digitalising Billing Operations in a Telecommunication Service Provider

INTRODUCTION

Service provider on-billing activation operations were chosen to digitise. On-billers are third-party partners that buy contracts from Service providers and resell them to customers at affordable rates that they would not have qualified for directly with service provider. Currently, on-billers do not have access to the service provider IT systems and therefore rely on a central Service provider team to activate the contract packages sold to the end consumer. The service provider dealer specialist team consists of four members who are responsible for the activation and processing of ± 6 500 monthly contract lines, with an average revenue per user of R135. There are manual and mundane steps involved in the activation of the contract packages, resulting in the need to achieve improved operational efficiencies so that the team can free up their capacity to focus their efforts on more strategic outputs.

INPUT-OUTPUT ON-BILLING TRANSFORMATION

Figure 11.1 represents the 'input-transformation-output' model applied to the on-biller activation process. The transformed resource Inputs identified is the use of Information to validate and process the activation; the transforming input resources entail both the staff who are responsible for the execution of the operations as well as the system facilities such as MS Excel and MS Outlook. The transformation process is initiated by the input resources which consist of extracting information per line item from Eppix, the consolidation of data into one Excel spreadsheet, the allocation of the subscriber number as well as uploading data onto the M2 system. The output of the on-biller activation process is a successful, activated contract that is communicated to the on-biller partner. The on-biller partner is the customer of the process and forms the input to as well as the output from the operation.

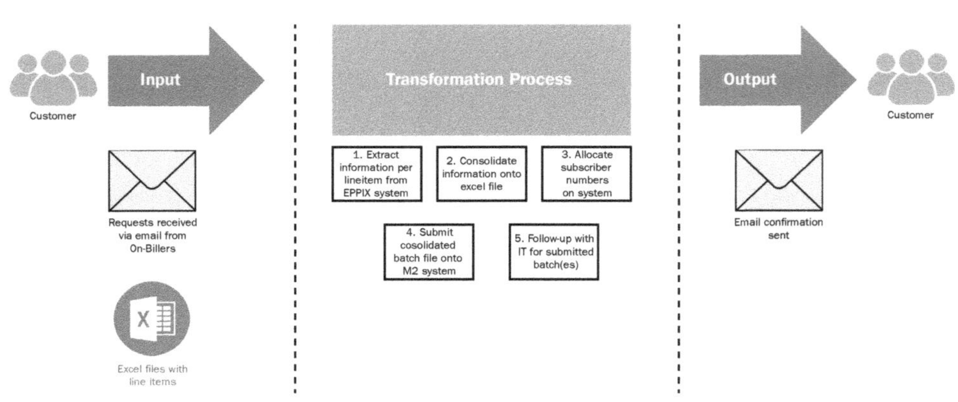

Figure 11.1 On-biller Input-Output Model

ON-BILLING SUBSCRIBER ACTIVATION VALUE STREAM MAPPING

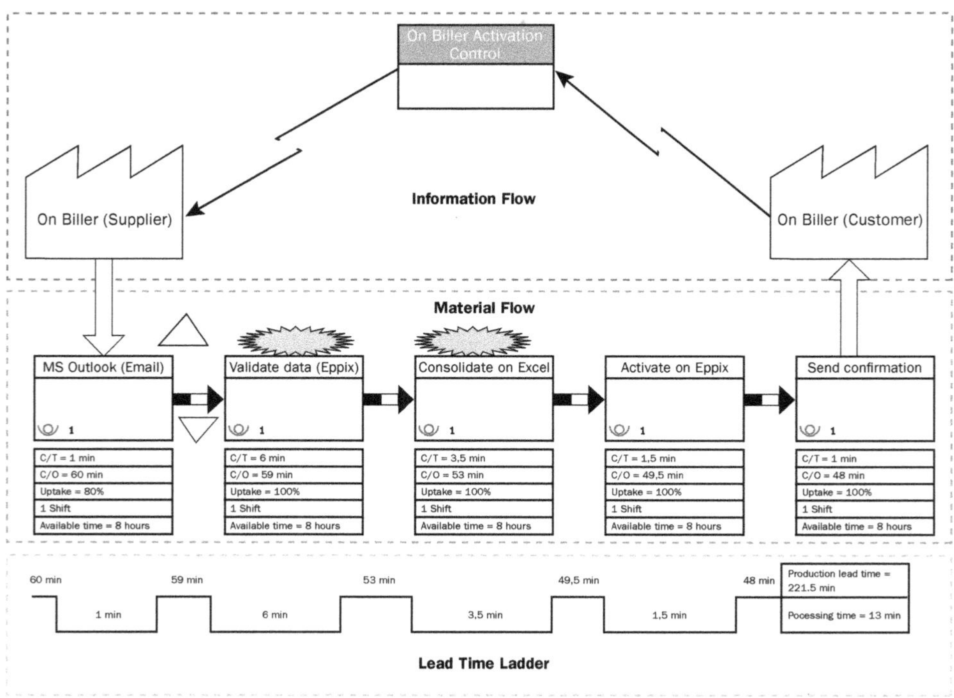

Figure 11.2 Value Stream Mapping

Our As-Is value stream mapping depicts the information flow between the on-biller and the agent via email.

192

The material flow shows a sequence of steps where we highlighted validation of data and consolidation thereof on Excel as the main areas for improvement.

The lead time ladder depicts the production lead time of 221 minutes and lastly the processing time of 13 minutes per line item.

ON-BILLING GAP ANALYSIS AND PROPOSED SOLUTION

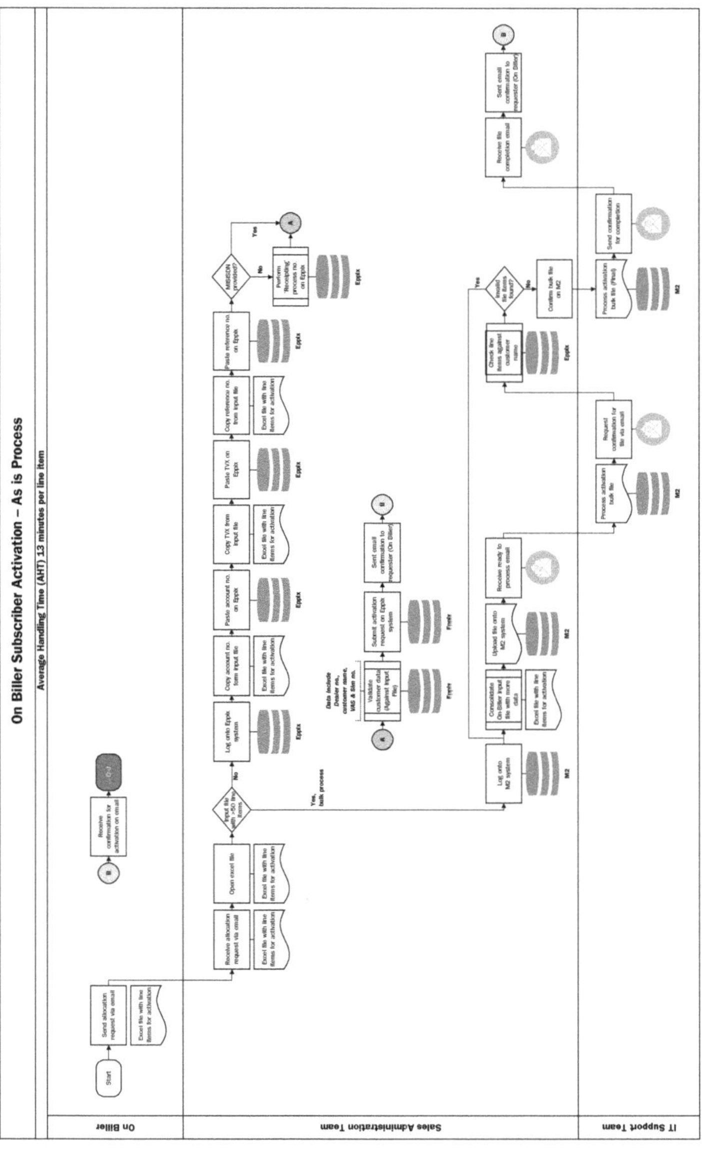

Figure 11.3 On-Billers Subscriber Allocation

The current state is triggered by an email containing an input file with details of the lines to be activated. The agent checks the number of lines in the file to know whether to follow a bulk process or manual line by line activation.

With the line by line activation, the agent will copy the account number, TVX and reference number to validate each line item on Eppix system before activating. The SLA here is six hours.

With the bulk process, the agent will first gather and validate customer information, then upload the file onto the M2 system.

Once the file is uploaded there are feedback loops between the agent and IT team until the file is successfully processed. The SLA here is 24 hours.

The agent would then send an email confirmation to the customer.

Table 11.1 Gap Analysis

Sub-Process	Challenges		Impact
Individual line by line processing	1.	Manual processing and navigating between MS Outlook, MS Excel and Eppix system.	Risk of missing emails or confusion with different input sheets.
	2.	Repetition of tasks for each line item	Risk of missing other line items.
Batch File Processing	3.	Manual gathering of data	Prone to errors with the copying and pasting of data.
	4.	Waiting for IT Support to process the batch file	Back and forth email follow-ups between Sales Admin team and IT Support to check progress of bulk processing.
	5.	Batch processing SLA of 24 hours compared to 6 hours for Individual processing	Non-standardised SLA's may create different impressions to the customers.

With the line by line activations, there is a risk that certain emails can be missed or confused with other input files. There is also another risk of missing line items within the same input file.

With the bulk file, this process is prone to errors due to the searching, copying and pasting data from one file to another. There is also back and forth follow-ups between the agent and the IT Support team until the file is processed successfully. The SLA for bulk processing is four times longer than the line by line activation.

CHECK IF THE PROCESS IS OPTIMISED/STREAMLINED

Table 11.2 Process Optimisation Validation

Component	Description
Excel Input File	The input file is received from multiple parties, and it is not standardised.
Gathering data	The data gathering is very manual and repetitive in nature.
Navigating between applications	The agents navigate between three different applications repeatedly until the process is completed.
Hand-offs	There are hand-offs between the agent and the IT Support team to confirm contents of the batch file
Follow-ups	Over and above the hand-offs, the agent would follow-up with the IT Support team to check the progress of the process conscious of the SLA.

We can therefore see that this process needs to be optimised due to its manual nature of processing.

DIGITAL MATURITY OF THE BUSINESS AND JUSTIFICATION OF DAS MODEL

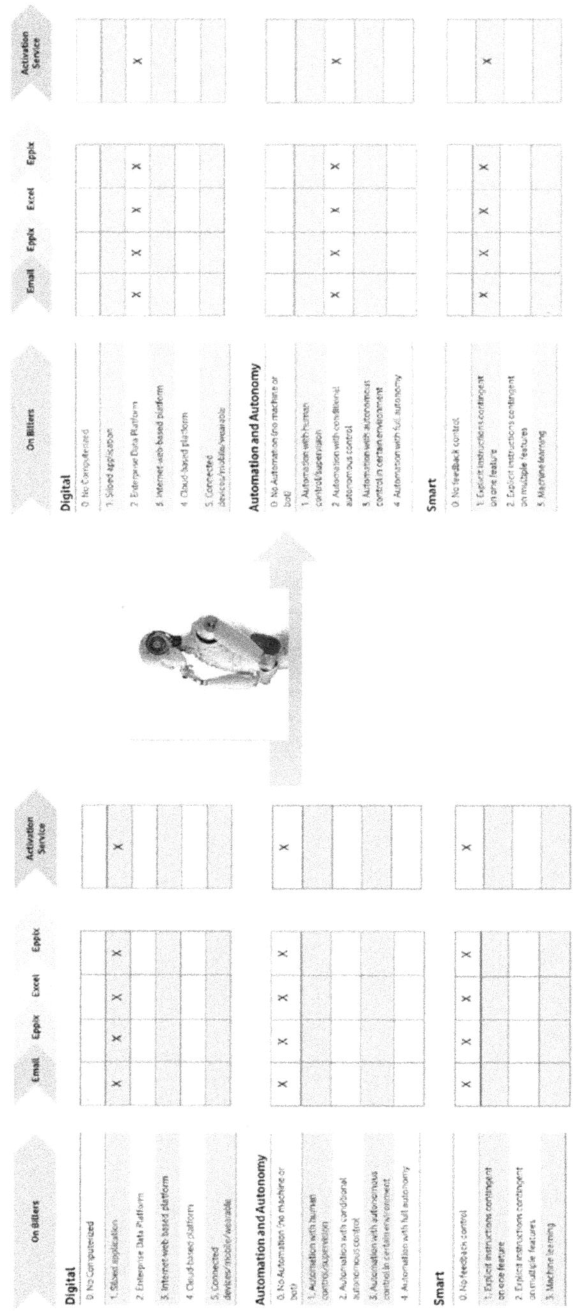

Figure 11.4 Digital Operations Diagnostic Across the Value Chain (Boute & Van Mieghem, 2021)

In the on-billers operations area there are multiple systems involved for the subscriber activation process. The activation process is currently very manually driven using siloed systems. The Microsoft Outlook (email) and Microsoft Excel systems are cloud based but still function in a very siloed mannered. The Eppix system is a legacy system which is positioned as a critical system within the operations processes to activate subscribers. The systems mentioned here are not integrated with each other to activate the subscribers. The digital level is therefore level 1, ie siloed applications (Boute & Van Mieghem, 2021).

Through the optimisation of the processes as well as the inclusion of RPA (robotic process automation) we will effectively integrate the systems within the operations process.

The application of robotics will enable the collection of data and the synchronisation of data across the systems. This will therefore provide an integrated workflow which will elevate the digital level of the on-billers subscriber activation to level 2 i e Enterprise data platform (Boute & Van Mieghem, 2021).

When it comes to the automation and autonomy level, the process is at level 0 as there is no automation across the value chain. Each step within the process requires a human to manage controls and take decisions at every process step.

Using robotic process automation, the process can be increased to level 2, which will allow for automation with conditional autonomous control. The robot will on exceptions in the process request for human intervention before further or final processing.

The current smart operations level is observed to be at level 0 with no adaptive feedback controls (Boute & Van Mieghem, 2021). With the application of robots, the instrumentation of control rules, which consists of a sequence of events across the on-billers value chain, can be set. Each system will require actions and through certain results the next step within the process can be handled until the final subscriber activation takes place.

The smart level can be increased to level 1 to deal with the subscriber activation feature only.

For all functions of the DAS model, the levels can be elevated above what has been reflected. What must be considered, however, is that the initial implementation of robotics must first be monitored to validate effectiveness and then adjusted where required, ie continuously improve the digital operations for on-biller's subscriber activation.

ON-BILLING DIGITISED OPERATION

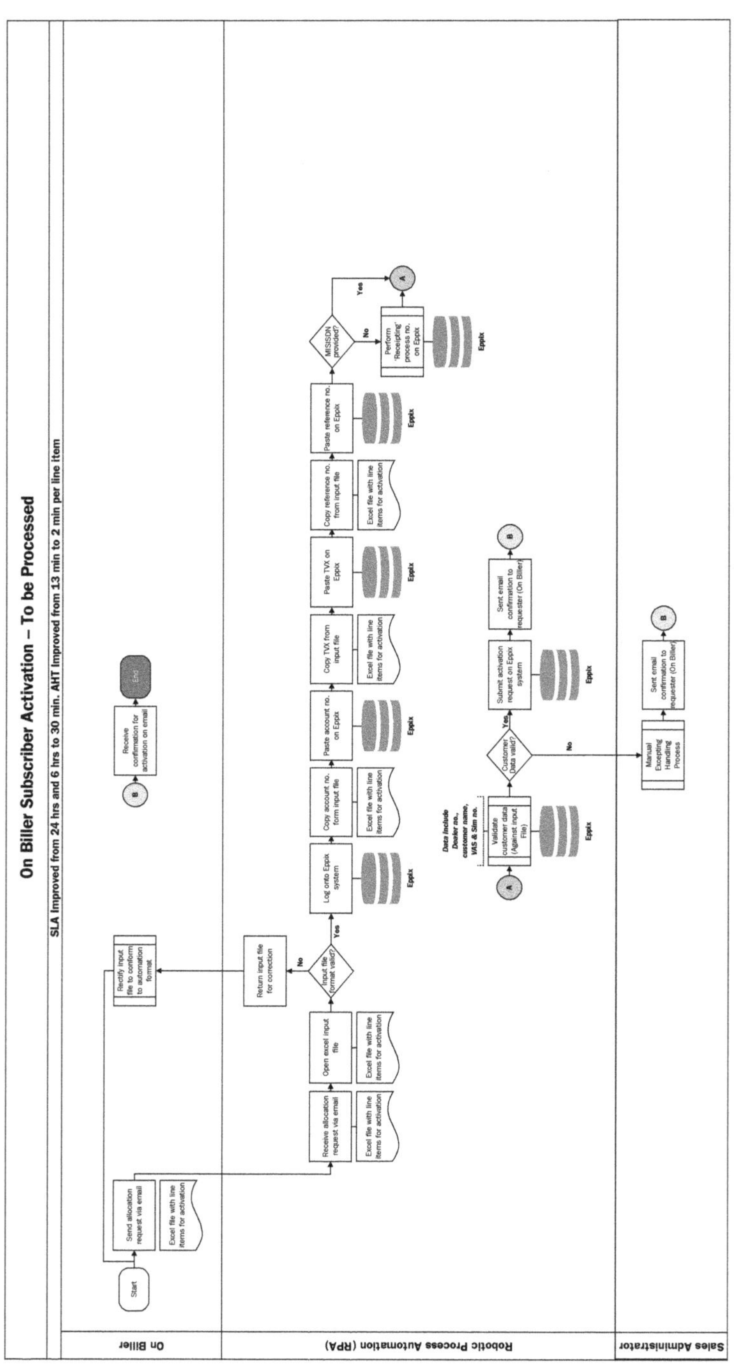

Figure 11.5 On-Biller To-Be Process

We have now standardised the input file by specifying the three key columns and configured the bot to reject inconsistent formatting and send feedback to the requestor. We have combined both sub-processes into one. This has eliminated the hand-offs with the IT Support team thereby improving the SLA. We have also kept the human in the loop to handle exceptions.

We have chosen RPA to process the activations and have combined both sub-processes into one. The bot will check the file format for consistency before proceeding with the process.

Key input data will be copied from the validated input file to search for a customer on the Eppix system. Based on the configured rules, the bot would determine whether to proceed with the activations.

Once completed, a confirmation email will be sent to the customer and the SLA Admin team. This process will improve the SLA to under thirty minutes per file received, therefore unlocking more time for faster activations.

CHECK IF PERFORMANCE IMPROVEMENT HAS BEEN ACHIEVED WITH DIGITISING THE OPS

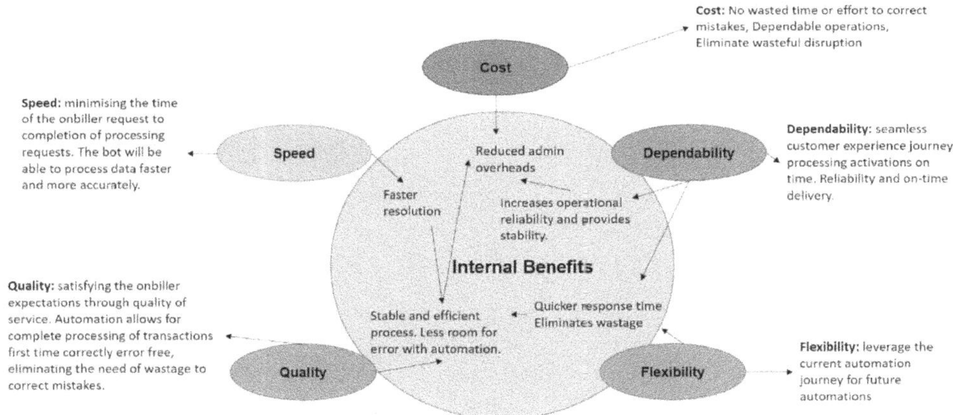

Figure 11.6 Performance Objectives

The opportunity is to replace manual repetitive activities and to augment the current process through automation. This is done through utilising operations management to efficiently automate a service to satisfy the on-biller demand. Performance improvement is based on the five key performance objectives of cost, quality, flexibility, dependability and speed (Slack & et al, 2017).

Quality: 'Doing things right'

Achieving a quality advantage by satisfying the on-biller expectations through quality of service. Automation allows for complete processing of transactions first time correctly error free and eliminating wastage to correct mistakes.

- External benefit is customer satisfaction.
- Internal benefit is a stable and efficient process. There is less room for error with automation.

Speed: 'Doing things fast'

A speed advantage is obtained by minimising the time of the on-biller request to completion of processing requests. The bot will be able to process data faster and more accurately.

- External benefit is customer service
- Internal benefit is a reduction in turnaround time for requests.

Dependability: 'Doing things in time'

Providing a seamless customer experience journey. Providing a dependability advantage through processing activations on time. Reliability and on-time delivery of the bot is monitored and available 24/7.

- External benefit is customer service
- Internal benefit is increased operational reliability and stability.

Flexibility: 'Changing what we do'

External benefit: There's potential to expand the current journey and create new services that could leverage the current automation journey.

Internal benefit: Flexibility of the bot assists faster response times, eliminates wastage in changeovers as one continuous process, no hand offs required and maintains dependability.

Cost advantage: 'Doing things cheaply'

The bot provides a cost advantage as there is no wasted time or effort to correct mistakes. Admin overheads are reduced. Dependable operations satisfy the customer's needs and eliminate wasteful disruption as the bot will process requests as and when needed.

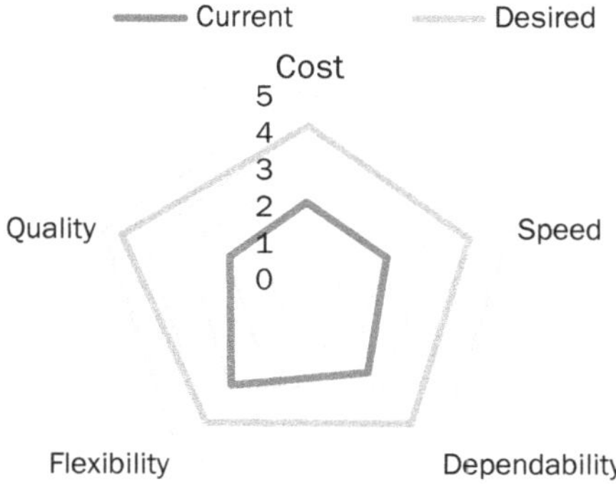

Figure 11.7 On-Biller Polar Diagram

The polar diagram represents the improvement of the operational benefits for speed, quality, dependability, flexibility and cost. This is achieved through a better customer experience journey, and improved efficiency through automation.

THE RESOURCES AND PROJECT PLAN

The Resources Required

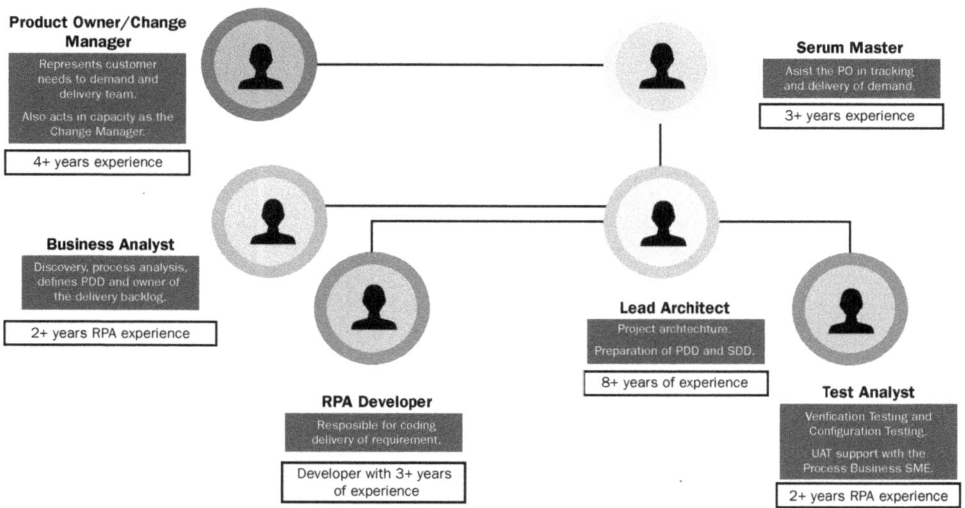

Figure 11.8 Delivery Resources

The resources required are a team containing our best people with a combined knowledge of transformation and automation experience. We understand the importance of governance and agility in execution and thinking hence our proposed structure and resource mix. The product owner represents the end customers' needs, in this case the on-biller, for whom this solution will benefit. The product owner also stands in proxy as a change manager who will assist in driving change and user acceptance to business. He enlists his requirements to the scrum master, who assists in the tracking of the demand delivery. The Scrum master liaises with the lead architect to obtain a technical design approval with the assistance of a business analyst, who completes a detail process document. This item is then added onto a delivery sprint with a developer for coding of the requirement. Once development is completed it is passed over to a test analyst for vigorous testing and to ensure the acceptance criteria have been met. Once user acceptance testing has been signed off with business, the process is production ready and can be moved into the production environment with our support team.

The Project Plan

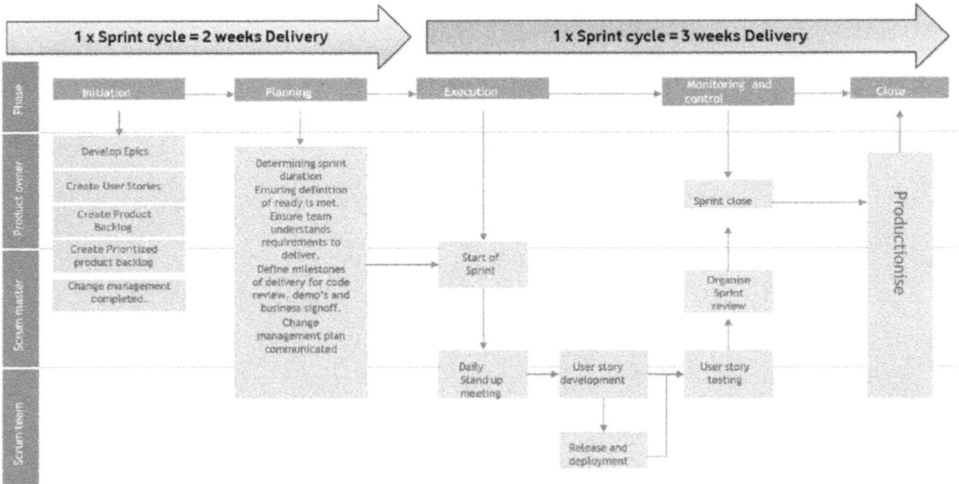

Figure 11.9 The Project Plan

The project plan has a five-week lead time for delivery. This consists of a two-week sprint cycle for initiation and planning to meet the definition of ready before development can start and to ensure the change management plan has been completed and communicated. The second sprint cycle consists of three weeks delivery for execution to completion due to the sising of development required. Here the actual development or coding of the bot takes place as well as user acceptance testing and demos to business before sign–off and production can be completed.

REFLECTION

We conclude that automation can be of great assistance to improve the subscriber activation of customers from the on-billers. The previous process only allowed for bulk uploads greater than 50 subscriber lines requests and a one-on-one manual processing. It was highlighted that capturing 50 lines manually would take from six to 11 hours. With automation, it would allow the specialists to be able to focus on less mundane, manual repetitive tasks. With robotics employed, it will allow for greater accuracy, reduced wait times and the ability to increase the capacity of the system. The organisation can further investigate an outsourced or insourced labour model for the project. Figure 11.9 shows the figures for the both the insourced and outsourced model.

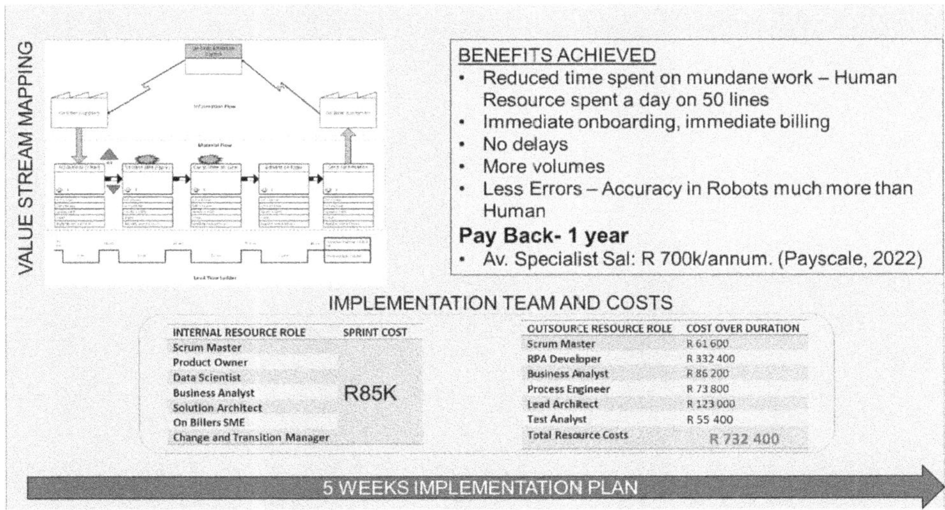

Figure 11.10 Reflection

Using the outsourced model, we estimate a payback period of over 1 year using our case where one specialist was hired. The average per annum pay was obtained from the PayScale data for a specialist (Payscale, 2022).

The SLA improved shifts from six hours per single manual subscriber activation to 30 minutes as well as for batch process with an SLA of 24 hours is reduced to 30 minutes. For the new process the transaction time is the same for single line subscriber activation or 50+ batch subscriber activations.

ACKNOWLEDGEMENT OF CONTRIBUTORS

- Kgaogelo Moloko
- Lesiba Ledwaba
- Maggie Govender
- Rezaan Marlie
- Weseela Nana

(All are affiliated to the Wits Business School, University of the Witwatersrand, Johannesburg).

REFERENCES

Boute, R. N., Van Mieghem, J. A. (2021, April 10). Digital Operations: Autonomous Automation and the Smart Execution of Work. Retrieved from https://papers.ssrn.com/sol3/papers.cfm?abstract_id=3400186

Payscale. (2022, May 11). Salaries in South Africa. Retrieved from https://www.payscale.com/research/ZA/Country=South_Africa/Salary

Slack, N. et al. (2017). Operations Management. In N. Slack, et al., *Operations Management*, 3rd edn (pp. 37–46). Cape Town: Pearson.

CHAPTER 12

Digitalising Operations at Park

INTRODUCTION

Park is a national and international site that celebrates the ideals of liberty, diversity and human rights. It is a cultural site that houses a museum and a memorial dedicated to honouring our heroes and heroines who contributed to South Africa's liberation struggle.

In the Park 2021/22 Action Performance Plan, their CEO cited:

> The financial sustainability of the Institution is a key risk and together with the impact of the national state of disaster and the nationwide lock down has necessitated the need to review the institutional plans to ensure that the plans respond to the COVID-19 pandemic and continued service delivery in the 2020/21 financial year.

Currently the level of operations at Park is very manual, there are multiple handoffs and information gaps. Below is a simple customer query where the customer is calling Park to find out if they will be able to purchase a ticket using Vodapay.

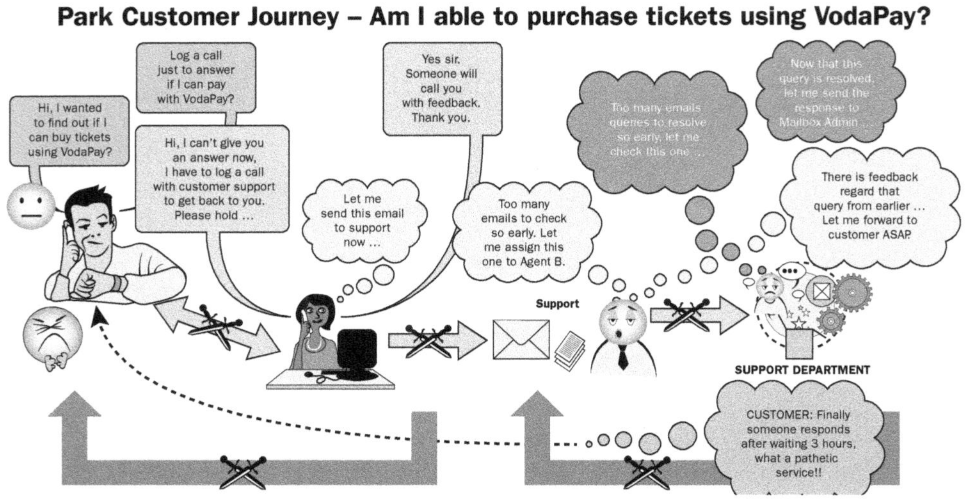

Figure 12.1 Rich Picture of Current Customer Inquiry at Park

As depicted in the image above, a simple process that should have been easily resolved took longer due to lack of basic knowledge and skills of the internal staff.

To get to the root cause of this problem, we used the 5 Whys methodology to formulate the problem statement for the above-mentioned scenario to ascertain why Park needs to optimise operations.

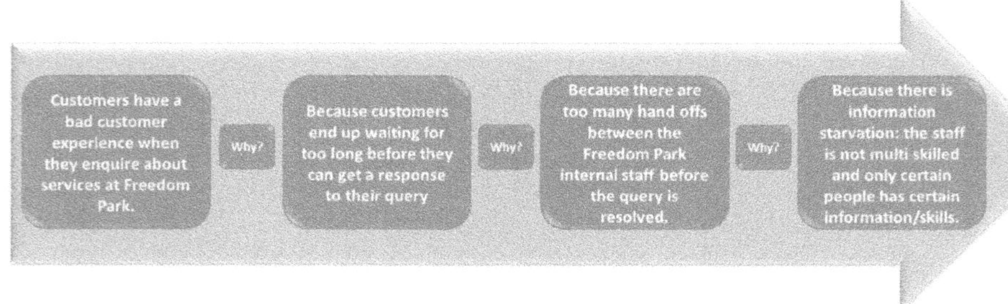

Figure 12.2 5 Whys Analysis of Park Customer Inquiry

CURRENT OPERATION PROCESS MAP

The current process map shows the steps followed when a customer calls Park wanting to know if they can pay with VodaPay to purchase entry tickets. When the customer calls, the receptionist answers to resolve the customer query. Due to information gaps in the process, she is unable to assist the customer and takes his details, creates a support ticket for the support staff and provides the customer with a reference number. Once the support staff has resolved the information gap, they will send an email to the customer with the relevant information.

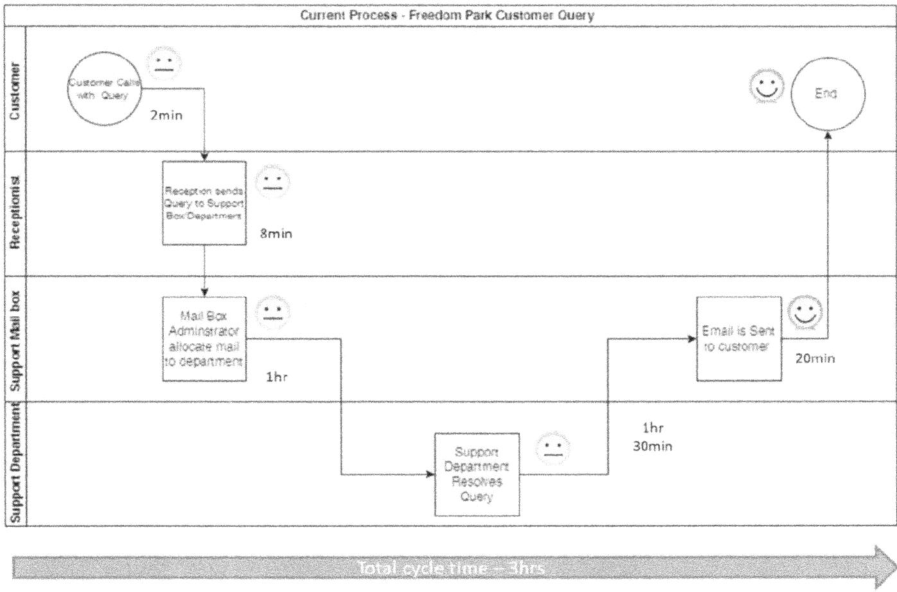

Figure 12.3 Current Process Customer Inquire Process Map

GAPS IN THE CURRENT PROCESS

The following gaps were identified in the current process:

- Process flow, slow lead and cycle time, slow resolution of inquiries, limited information flow
- Information gap, reception doesn't have the required information on hand, provided information is inconsistent and low quality
- No service request system, lost queries, no traceability on request
- No call centre system, calls are not logged and measured for first call resolution rate (FCCR), average handling time, repeat caller rate, call abandonment rate
- Poor customer experience, delayed responses (inefficiency and ineffectiveness), no customer satisfaction survey and tNPS.

PARK DIGITAL MATURITY

Park digital maturity is at the conceptual level based on the digital assets that they have and marks the starting point of the digital journey. The current digital maturity of Park is low, due to the high dependency on manual processes and, their current infrastructure is approaching end of life, posing cyber security and privacy risks.

As part of the operational process improvement journey, Park's digital journey will be improved by implementing SaaS cloud-based solutions, RPA, Big Data Analytics, Knowledge base and CRM.

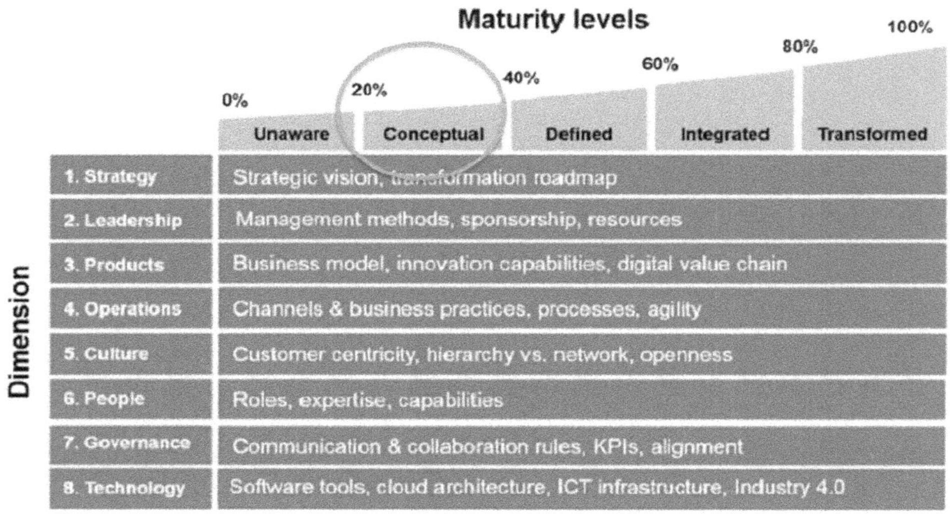

Figure 12.4 Park Digital Maturity

PROCESS OPTIMISATION AND SUCCESS CRITERIA

The current process was reviewed, optimised and streamlined. The gaps identified (see Figure 12.3) were addressed using digital solutions and faster process flow to improve the overall customer experience thereby optimising and improving the identified success criteria discussed below.

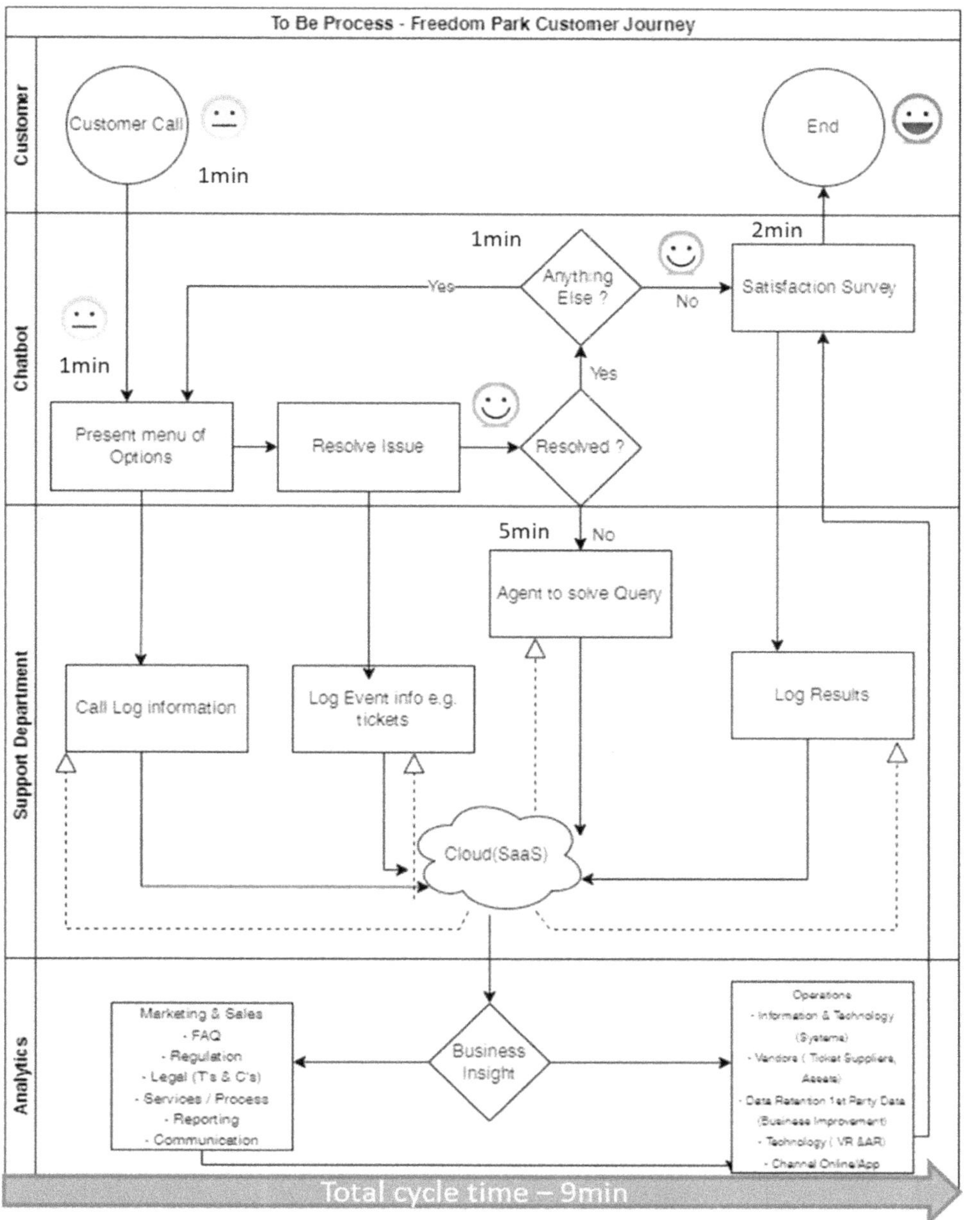

Figure 12.5 Future Process Customer Query Process Map

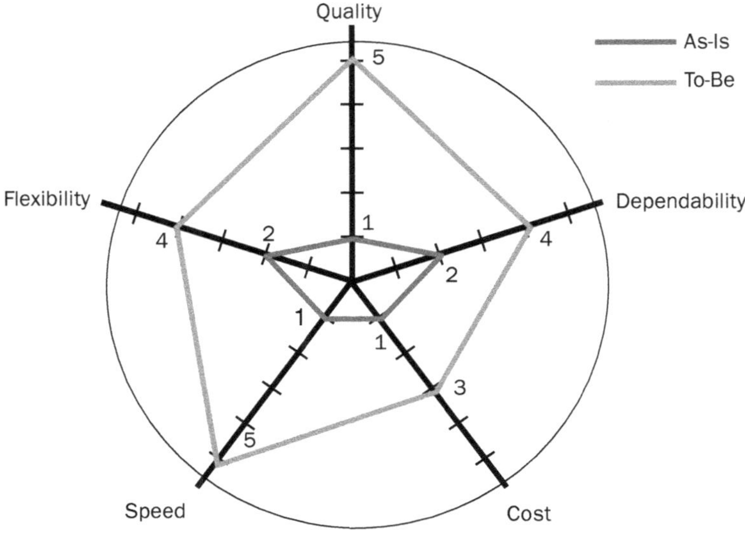

Figure 12.6 Polar Diagram of Park Customer Query

Reviewing the operational objectives using the current and future customer query operational process, the above Polar Diagram was completed. The rationale for the assigned ratings and the projected improvements are discussed in Table 12.1.

Table 12.1 Park DAS Analysis

Performance Objectives	Current Process	Future Process
Quality Measured using tNPS, repeat caller rate, call abandonment rate	Rating 1 • Poor Customer Exp., delayed responses (inefficiency & ineffectiveness), no satisfaction survey • No call centre system, calls are not logged and measured • Information accuracy is poor as it lives in people's heads	Rating 5 • Customer Survey at the end of the call to measure customer experience • Reduce repeat caller rate by ensuring customer are correctly serviced on their first call • Reduce call abandonment rate as Chatbot is available 24/7 • Information captured in knowledge base is key to the success of operation based on the ML Analytics
Dependability Measure using First Call Resolution Rate, Service request resolution	Rating 2 • Reception doesn't have the required information on hand, provided information is inconsistent and low quality	Rating 4 • Replace receptionist with a 24/7 workforce in the shape of an NLR chatbot exploiting customer-processing technologies viz Active (Mobile voice)

Performance Objectives	Current Process	Future Process
Cost Measure using cost in Rands per query, 1 is high and 5 is low	Rating 1 • Resource intensive (Receptionist, Support staff and mailbox administrator)	Rating 3 • Initial investment costs are high for system integration and training • Process cost of resolving a query significantly reduced • Continued Chatbot training cost incurred to resolve failed transactions
Speed Measured using cycle time, throughput time, average handling time	Rating 1 • Slow resolution of inquiries • Limited information flow	Rating 5 • Process flow improvements, lead and cycle times reduced as chatbot can directly resolve customer query • Exploit customer data in real time (in line with POPIA) to reduce cycle time • NLR chatbot can handle multiple requests in parallel preventing bottlenecks at reception and in the support department
Flexibility Based on analysis of the current and the future processes	Rating 2 • Inflexible enquiry process • No service request system, lost queries, no traceability on request	Rating 4 • Multi-option solution (can be traversed) • Handover solution to support staff if Chatbot unable to handle in real-time • Parallel resolution of inquiries and logging service request to the cloud • Chatbot integrated into multiple SaaS systems, Call Centre, Service Request, Knowledge Base, Customer Relationship for scalability and integration benefit

USE OF THE DAS MODEL

Park's operations are extremely manual with limited automation across the board. The Park board do, however, have high aspirations to improve their existing operations by using digitisation, automation and smart control rules to reduce repetitive work.

This will remove the high level of dependency on manual work and augment the support staff with smarter execution of mundane operational processes. The DAS framework defines different levels of maturity for Digitisation, Automation and Autonomous execution and Smart Controls. Park used the model to evaluate and map their current operations and future aspirational goals against the defined levels (Boute, Winter 2021).

Not only does the DAS framework act as an audit of current and future states, but it also helps companies decide what to do next. Park used this information to plan and map out their journey to digital operational excellence (Boute, Winter 2021). In the table you can see the assessment together with the supporting information. This is dealt with extensively in our report. Using the DAS model, the maturity of Park's current and future operations is assessed. For purposes of this report the customer query process depicted in Table 12.2 was used.

Table 12.2 DAS Framework To Assess Current and Future Operational Process Maturity

DAS	As-Is Process	To-Be Process
Levels of Digitisation	Level 1: Siloed applications • Email for communication between receptionist and support team. • Responses to customer are logged in event system. • No data analytics is done	Level 4: Cloud based enterprise solutions • VOIP call answered by bot on Call Centre system • Auto logging of event on ticketing system • Bot provides customer with required service • Loop until completed and surveys customer • Upload results of all interactions to SaaS systems Call Centre, CRM, eCommerce, Survey
Levels of Automation and Autonomy	Level 0: No automation • All processes manually executed by receptionist and support staff	Level 3: Automation with autonomous control in most environments • Fully automated chatbot resolving inquiries & service requests • Offer related and alternative services to upsell / x-sell while customer on call (tickets, t-shirts, etc.) • If support staff required, bot updates ticket, support staff have access at all hours via internet • Survey customer while on call • Apply machine learning to inform future interactions
Smart levels of Control Rules	Level 0: No feedback control • All processes manually executed by receptionist and support staff	Level 2: Explicit instructions contingent on multiple features • While machine learning is used to learn from past interactions to improve on future customer inquiries, the bot will still breakout to the human support staff under certain circumstances • Using results from previous break-out interactions to train bot future conversations • As bot learns human interaction is reduced

PERFORMANCE IMPROVEMENT ACHIEVED WITH DIGITISING THE OPERATION

Digital transformation is expediting the ability for physical and organisational boundaries to be broken to engage a real-time workforce, connect teams and drive collaboration. As per our new process, which introduces the SAAS Cloud infrastructure, Big Data, Chatbot, RPA, and driven by the need to monitor, control and protect against failures, ensure query fulfilment and high productivity, protect and upskill personnel, and do all this while leveraging enhanced cyber security architectures. Hereby, we seek to achieve operational excellence by continuing to accelerate Park's digital transformation, leveraging a common digital thread from engineering to operations that uses performance intelligence to improve agility, reliability and efficiency building operational resilience and sustainability (Resnick, 2021). Exceed customer expectations with tools that intelligently match customers to service providers based on prior experience, special qualifications and more.

RESOURCE UTILISATION

The Chairperson of Park cited in their 2021 report that resource mobilisation will be the focus for the FY21 term in order to grow the visitors' numbers who will consume the Park's products and services as well as to generate funds.

Financial / Funding	• Government Grants • Budget allocation • Generated revenue
Budget (R11m)	• SAAS – R4m • Resources (People) – 4 x 12m – R6m • Training (Re-/Upskilling existing people) – R1m
People	• Customer Support and IT / Cloud Operational Support • Management Staff • Project Resources (x4)
Know How / information	• Training: Reskilling and Upskilling of Support department and Operation support for SaaS technologies • Create / Capture IP into Knowledge Base system
Channels	• Self Service Voice Calls
Stakeholders	• Government, Sports and Culture • Museum Board and Benefactors
Information Technology	• Integrate existing IT into SaaS solution • Big Data Analytics – Improve decision making process

Figure 12.7 Project Resources

The above resources have been identified as required for the implementation of Parks Operational Efficiency programme, an initial capital investment of R40 million will be required for the first year. For a detailed discussion on Resource Utilisation see Figure 12.6.

The implementation of Operational Efficiency Programme will extend over a one-year period broken into four phases of three months each and iterative and incremental approach will be used to deliver measurable value to customers and Park at the end of each phase.

Figure 12.8 Park Operation Efficiency Plan on a Page

IN CLOSING

Surviving and thriving beyond the new normal will require manufacturers and processors worldwide to deploy solutions that sustain operations resiliently using common data to connect people, processes and assets that create a single version of the truth. To attain best-in-class performance in productivity, quality and delivery of services, Park embarked on a digital journey to transform and optimise their operations. This will be an ongoing journey for Park to maintain a competitive edge, operational excellence and technology leadership.

ACKNOWLEDGEMENT OF CONTRIBUTORS

- Tania Blaauw
- Vuyo Ndiko
- Hazel Digama
- Prince Kutama
- Potlako Mavundla
- Jaco Greeff- Cronje
- Tlotlego

(All are affiliated to the Wits Business School, University of the Witwatersrand, Johannesburg).

REFERENCES

Boute, R. N. (Winter 2021). Digital Operations: Autonomous Automation and the Smart Execution of Work. *MBR, 01*(01), 177–186.

CHAPTER 13

Digitalising a Fastfood Organisation

INTRODUCTION

The case study seeks to document findings and recommendations made through analysis of the Fastfood Company ordering process. Various tools were utilised to analyse the current process and products and provide guidance on suitable digital tools that can be used for the proposed process. The starting point was to understand the fastfood outlets' ordering process and time spent at each activity point. This analysis was mapped up using a process flow diagram, focusing largely on the walk-in process widely used by consumers across all Fastfood Company outlets. An additional value chain analysis was carried out as it directly linked to Fastfood Company's ability to efficiently service its customers. The notable lag times in the process were the time it takes to place an order and the order waiting time after confirming order, which are directly impacted by efficiencies of the internal process. A further analysis of Fastfood Company positioning was done using the product matrix. The outcomes indicated that the existing process is positioned further away from the natural line. This would be due to the inefficiencies in the current process with quality and speed in providing the final product to the client. This observation is further supported by the findings of the polar diagram, which notes quality and speed as concerns compared to well-established fastfood outlets like Nando's. As previously highlighted, the focus has been on the end-to-end walk-in process. Thus, a 4V Model was used to understand how walk-in ordering services are positioned in comparison to online services. The findings revealed that fast food used high levels for volumes and variety. However, it was felt that there is a need to improve quality and speed.

The final leg of the analysis looked at application of the DAS model, which provided an indication of Fastfood Company's current level of digitisation. The results indicate that Fastfood Company measured at level 1 for digital solution as online ordering process is the primary digital solution. It scored level 0 for automation, autonomy, and smart solution as most of its ordering processes are manual. As a result of the overall analysis the proposed solutions were mapped as a proposed process flow. The proposal was to fully roll out the use of digital self-service kiosks which would allow the customers to place an order and make payment themselves. Eliminating the use of receipts in phases is an additional proposal that will see the customer receive an SMS with an order code upon confirmation of payment. The introduction of these kiosks would allow the internal stuff to focus their attention on the kitchen processes, thus improving quality and speed. The additional digital solution proposed should be rolled out in phases at a later stage.

BACKGROUND OF FASTFOOD COMPANY

The Fastfood Company brand started in South Africa in the 1960s, establishing over 960 outlets locally. It has cemented itself as the one of the largest fastfood chains in the country, specialising in the mass production of fried chicken (SA, 2021).

Various macroeconomic factors have contributed to the success of Fastfood Company; adopting newer technologies for their workers has improved the staff working environment (Frue, 2019). Furthermore, Fastfood Company encourages all franchises to be compliant with the Occupational Health and Safety Act. To contribute to the reduction in Fastfood Company's environmental footprint, sustainable packaging options were introduced at most franchises (3SMedia, 2022). The company also replaced plastic straws and other plastic packaging with sustainably sourced alternatives.

The outbreak of the Covid-19 pandemic prompted the brand to place greater emphasis on utilising digital technologies to improve customers satisfaction and create new channels for connecting with consumers. Customers can now use various online platforms to place orders: these are Fastfood Company 'Click & Collect', Fastfood Company SA mobile app, delivery through Uber Eats and Mr Delivery (unknown, 2021).

While the digital platforms created convenience, a large portion of South Africans have maintained the traditional walk-in and drive-through options to place orders. The assumption is that the high unemployment rate in the country means individuals would choose to use their disposable income less on household essentials as opposed to data. A large majority of the South African population relies on public transport to commute home, thus a walk-in option would be viable.

As the digital era disrupts the traditional method of operating, it remains increasingly important for fastfood franchises to remain relevant and maintain a competitive advantage. The operations should ultimately create sustainable value for all its customers, while improving internal operational processes.

ANALYSIS OF FASTFOOD COMPANY CURRENT OPERATIONS

Fastfood Company Current Ordering Process

Figure 13.1 depicts the current ordering process for walk-in and drive-through at Fastfood Company outlets.

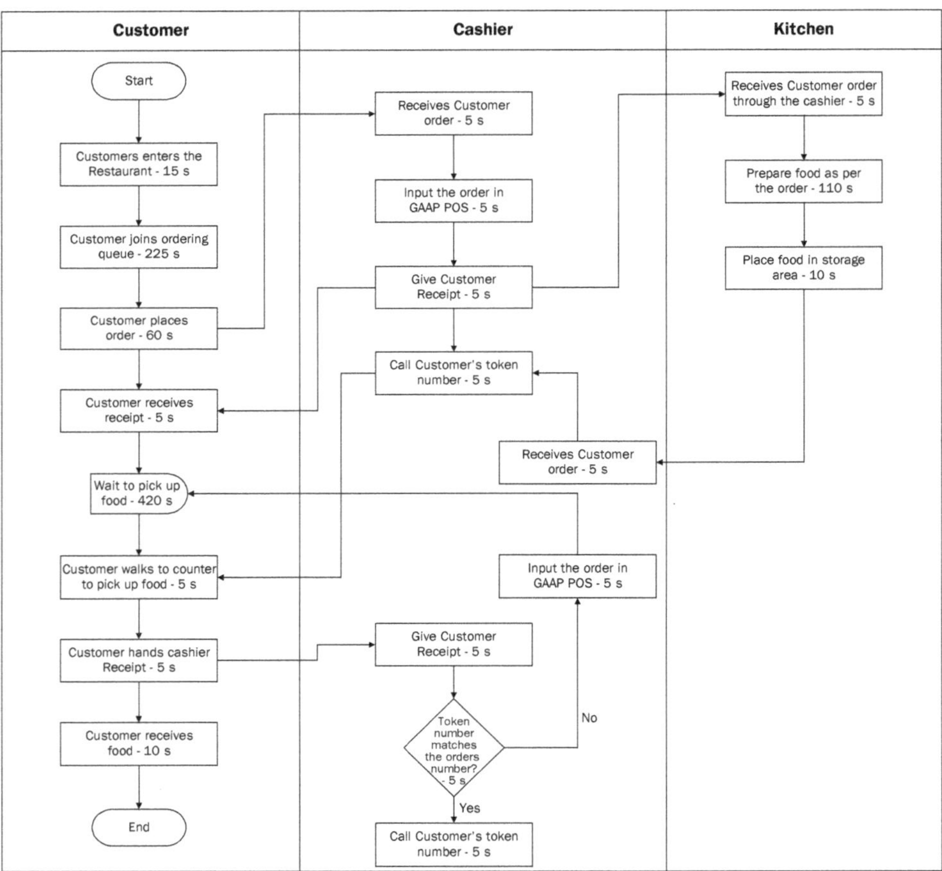

Figure 13.1 Fastfood Company Ordering Process Flow

Input—Output Model

Transformed Inputs

- Raw materials (raw chicken, vegetables, spices, flour, potatoes, drinks, etc)
- Information (cooking manuals, order information – in-shop/online, payments (online, cash,) etc)
- Customers (in-store customers/drive-through)

Transforming Resources

- Facilities (building, equipment, machines, etc)
- Staff (cooks, managers, facilitators, etc)

Transformation process(es)

- Cooking of meals
- Order processing
- Serving of meals to in-house customers
- Floor management
- Kitchen management
- Supply chain management
- Market and advertise products and
- Delivery services

Outputs

- Ordered food to customers (walk-in/drive-through/remote deliveries)
- In-house customer service

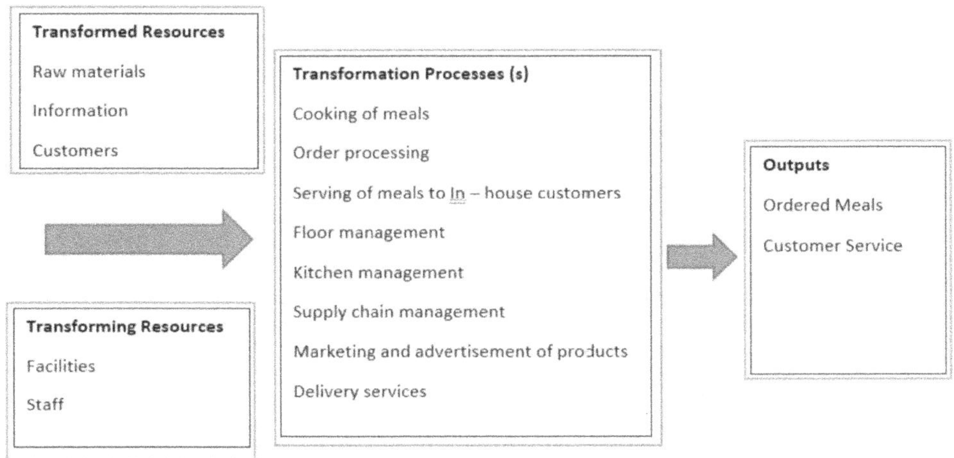

Figure 13.2 Input—Output Model

Value Stream Mapping

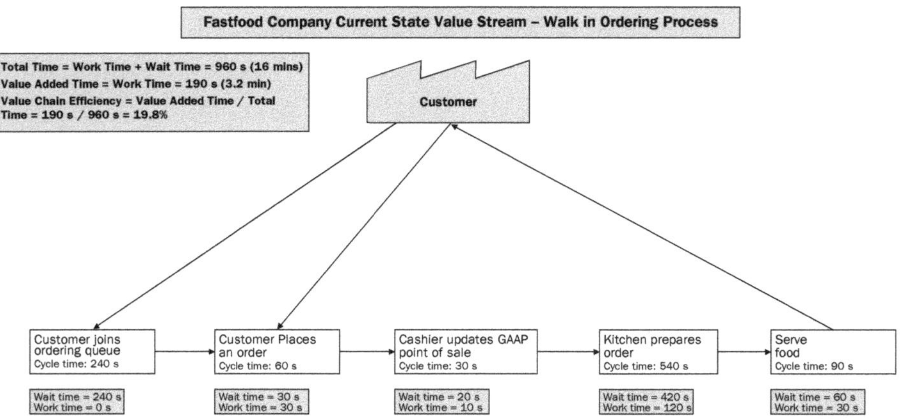

Figure 13.3 Value stream Map

Total Throughput Time: The Product-Process Matrix

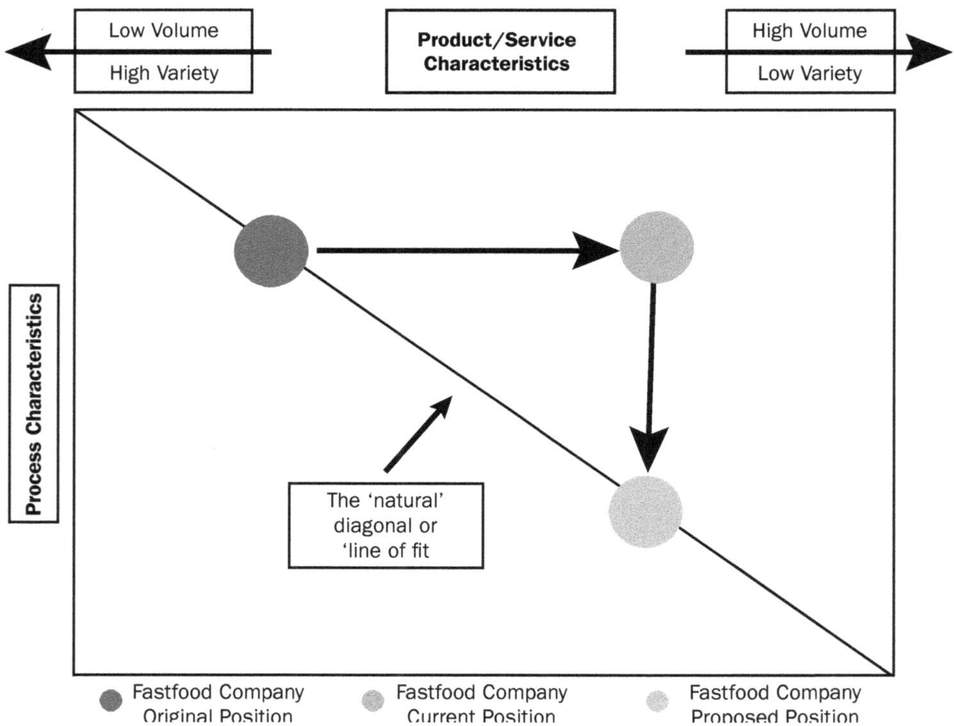

Figure 13.4 The Product Matrix

Looking at Fastfood Company's current position, the company falls under a quick fastfood service shop. It has high customer volumes, and it also has a variety of food offering, which cause the longer waiting time for food, especially during high demand times such as weekends, low quality of their food as customers are always complaining about the quality of the chicken, and unhappy customers when it comes to consumer service. Fastfood Company loses money due to low retention of customers caused by the bad service.

The current process is sitting further away from the natural line due to the inefficiencies of the current process affecting the quality and speed of their services they offer to the customer created by the variety of products available.

The proposed positioning of Fastfood Company calls for it to reduce its offerings by analysing the current data, to help guide them to streamline their product offering according to locations and popular meals so that customers can get the best quality and improve on time it takes to give customers their orders.

Volume—Variety 4V Model

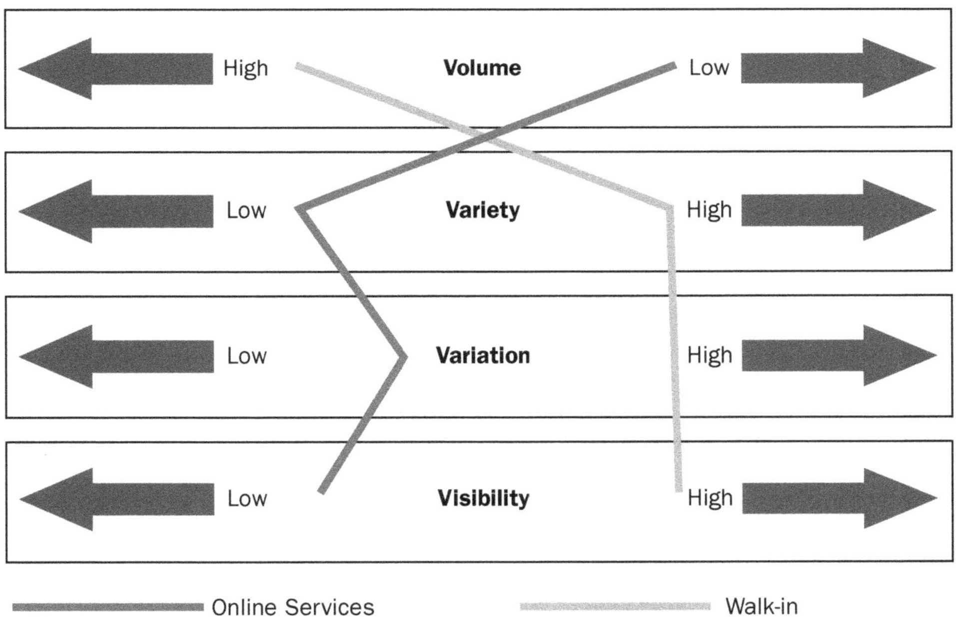

Figure 13.5 4V Model

Figure 13.5 shows the 4V Model (Volume, Variety, Variation and Visibility). The comparison is between the two ordering systems which are walk-in (Restaurant and Drive-thru) and Online (WhatsApp, UberEats, MrD, Fastfood Company website and app).

For the walk-in, the Volume is high as the majority of customers prefer going to the store to order their meals and low volume of online because many of their customers are not technologically advanced and don't have data and some customers have been getting a bad service experience.

For the online orders, the menu is different from the walk-in menu; not all products are available for ordering (eg ice cream) so it has a low variety.

The Variation of both the walk-in and online is high, especially at month-ends and during load-shedding and for online services, where customers wait for between 30 minutes and an hour to get their meals; for online orders they are out of drivers most of the time.

The Visibility for walk-in is high as it is a contact service, unlike the online one.

Fastfood Company Operations Performance — Polar Diagram

The Polar Diagram (Figure 13.6) represents the importance of performance objectives for Fastfood Company and Nando's.

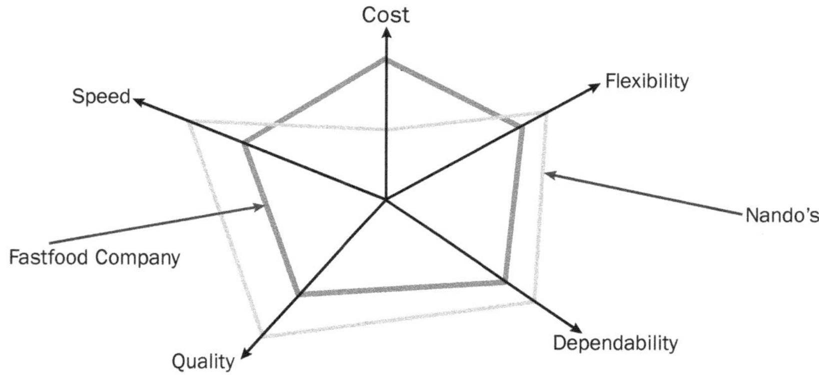

Figure 13.6 Polar Diagram

	Fastfood Company	**Nando's**
Speed	Drive-through orders relatively quick. Walk-in services depends on the number of clients in store.	Walk-in services depends on the number of clients in store. Drive-through options is limited.
Quality	Quality is inconsistent	Consistent quality across franchises
Flexibility	Menu rarely changes therefore not flexible	Menu is flexible in terms of flavour available and catering to health-conscious segment
Dependability	Delivery is relatively unreliable. In-store collection moderate.	Delivery is reliable. In-store collection moderate.
Cost	Low product pricing	High product pricing

PROCESS GAP ANALYSIS

Food Not Stored in Warmers When Customers Are not Around To Collect the Order

Due to Fastfood Company's being known to mostly have long lines in South Africa, a lot of customers prefer walking into the store, placing their orders then going out to do other activities. Unfortunately, this leaves the food cold as once the order is assembled it gets placed on a counter until the customer comes to collect.

Inability to Predict the Order Volumes (Variation Demand)

Predictive analysis is not used at Fastfood Company. For example, on weekends or at month end demand is expected to increase. However, they are always struggling with long queues during these periods due to not enough meat being cooked and not enough meals being prepared. Most of the Fastfood Company restaurants have been providing their services in their areas for years, yet they still struggle with managing demand. This affects speed of service.

The Inconsistent Quality of Cooked Meat

Different cuts of meat require different cook times. Fastfood Company currently cooks their pieces in bulk. For example, a drumstick is cooked together with a breast, leading to inconsistent quality. They separate their batches in three categories: large chicken pieces, wings and burger patties.

High Manual Ordering Process

The ordering process requires customers to walk in, join a queue to a cashier, and usually one or at most two cashiers are working, look through the screen or board to choose their meal, get a receipt, stand in another line for pick up, and only then they will get their food. Customers are usually required to wait until they interact with the cashier, only to find out that their meal of choice is not available.

Ice Cream Machine Occasionally out of Service

One of the biggest complaints from customers is that the ice cream machine always seems to be broken. This is not due to missing ingredients, but the machine not churning, etc. There is also no redundancy. Only one machine is being used to service all customers. When that one machine stops working, the entire ice cream or milk shake service line is cut, which leaves customer frustrated. There is also no upfront notice given to customers on the availability of the ice cream, until they get to interact with the cashier.

Paperless Order Receipt Method

Some customers place their orders and perform other activities while their order is prepared. The main problem would be where customers misplace their receipts, making it difficult for the cashiers to believe them when they come to collect their orders without the receipt. That experience of having to pay for another order because of the missing receipt can drive customers away.

Smart Customer Profiling

Some customers do not want to browse through the entire menu for them to access their favourite meals. They already know what they want, yet they have to browse through the entire menu before they get to their meal of choice. If Fastfood Company had better customer profiling, the ordering process would be simplified for returning customers.

Loyalty Rewards

Fastfood Company has lots of loyal customers who are not rewarded for their loyalty to restaurant. Loyal customers feel appreciated when they get rewarded for their loyalty. This helps to build long-lasting relationships between the business and customers. This can also help drive sales because customers will keep coming back to reach a specific target to get rewarded.

Customer Centricity

Customers need to login to Fastfood Company website and input their details to register the feedback, which is a lengthy process and not customer-centric at all. Customers do not want to go through the lengthy process to rate the service or provide their feedback.

CURRENT FASTFOOD COMPANY LEVELS OF DIGITISATION

A Digital, Automation and Smart (DAS) diagnostic framework will be used to determine the level of digitisation at Fastfood Company. The DAS model can be applied to a specific process or an entire value chain, against the three levels mentioned above. Due to the nature of the organisation chosen in this case study, Fastfood Company, involving customer interaction from the point of ordering through to the point of collection; there is an opportunity to gather data, which presents opportunities to personalise experiences and successfully address customer pain points in providing better products and services in real time.

In conducting the diagnosis, the focus will be on whether there is any digitisation of activities at Fastfood Company operations from the point customers order food, either online, walk-ins or drive-through. The second part will look at whether there is any automation of some activities, whether autonomous or human-controlled automation of processes and activities. Finally, a determination would be made of whether operations at Fastfood Company are fully automated and fully digitised.

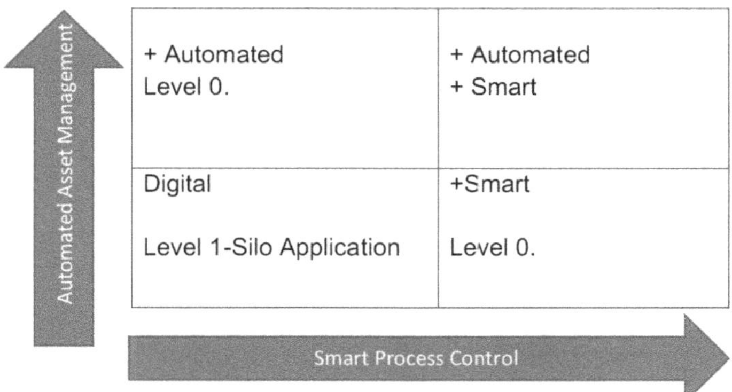

Figure 13.7 DAS Model (Boute & Mieghem, 2021)

Some digitisation has been implemented at Fastfood Company operations. A web-based application enables customers to order online and then collect from a specified store. Besides online ordering, the rest of the processes seem to be manual processes. There is no application of smart technologies such as robotic process automation or artificial intelligence.

FASTFOOD COMPANY DIGITAL, AUTOMATION AND SMART LEVELS

- Digital: level 1– Siloed application.
- Automation and Autonomy: Level 0
- Smart. Level 0

	Menu Browsing	Order placing	Order Payment	Order Confirmation	Order preparation	Order Collection
Digital						
0. Not computerized				X	X	
1. Siloed application	X	X	X			X
2. Enterprise data platform						
3. Internet-web-based platform						
4. Cloud-based platform						
5. Connected devices/mobile/wearable						
Automation & Autonomy						
0. No automation (no machine or bot)	X	X	X	X	X	
1. Automation with human control/supervision						X
2. Automation with conditional autonomous control						
3. Automation with autonomous control in certain environments						
4. Automation with full autonomy						
Smart						
0 No feedback control	X	X	X	X	X	X
1. Explicit instructions contingent on one feature						
2. Explicit instructions contingent on multiple features						
3. Machine learning						

Figure 13.8 Fastfood Company's Digital Operations Diagnostic Across the Value Chain

Digital

There's an option for digital payment method.
The display of the menu on screen.
The display of order status on screen.

Automation and Autonomy

Fastfood Company's processes are not automated except for the display of the order status.

Smart

Fastfood Company does not currently have smart technologies.

FASTFOOD COMPANY DIGITISATION

Contactless Payment

Contactless payment will enable customers to use Google Pay, Android Pay and other e-payment platforms when ordering food in-restaurant. This capability can be enhanced within the Fastfood Company self-service kiosks and be integrated with the point of sales systems in store. The POS systems or the self-service kiosks can be enhanced for the customer by displaying QR codes for e-wallets or enable NFC payment for customer using their cards. Customers can also be rewarded with points and bonuses within their Fastfood Company app after they have made their payment (Alper, 2020).

Paperless Receipt Integration with POS System

Customers can have the ability to obtain their paperless receipts that can be integrated with the Fastfood Company app and the store's POS system. The digital receipts will be forwarded to the customer's cell phone as soon as a sale is completed. The receipts will be stored in the cloud where they can be moved, verified, forwarded, or published (Letsebe, 2017).

AI Technology Enablement for Customer Interactions

From an AI integration perspective, Fastfood Company can implement conversational AI for customer interactions. This can be used for customer concerns, questions, and requests within the ordering process. Customer feedback can then be calibrated, and the customer could also chat on the Fastfood Company app or on the website with an AI bot. The AI bot could potentially answer customers questions, prompt more details, and direct the customers where applicable. If the AI bots are unable to solve the customers concerns or questions, then they can be redirected to a real staff member for better assistance. AI bots will free up staff members time so they can attend to other aspects of the business (Alper, 2020).

QR Codes Enablement on Various Channels

Fastfood Company can enable the QR code functionality by enabling customers to auto-scan on posters, tables, coasters, doors, or websites to allow customer access to online menus, order and pay without contact (Insight, unknown).

Digital Records and Data Analytics

Digitised records of the ordering process will assist Fastfood Company by automatically tags records (customer information, order history and time stamps) to provide an audit trail. Digitised records will be available in the cloud and therefore will enable easy access, require no physical storage, and provide opportunities to report and analyse data for management and continuous improvement purposes. Ordering record keeping, this will also enable Fastfood Company to be able to do personalised experiences for the customer (Perconte, 2021).

Fastfood Company To Implement a Food Ordering Management Platform

This platform will enable Fastfood Company to streamline their operations based on customer behaviour and attributes. It might link to the number of orders for a particular item or finding the least ordered dishes – digital management solutions allow them to make data-driven decisions. This, as well, includes effective inventory management to minimise food waste and identifying customer preferences. This digital platform assist Fastfood Company to improve their kitchen performance (Startus-Insights, Unknown).

Enhance Fastfood Company App Functionality: Driver Tracking for Delivery Services

From a Fastfood Company app perspective, all stakeholders involved in the delivery process can have a view of the deliveries.

This enables the stores to track drivers nearby, thus cutting down on delivery cost and time. Drivers can reach customers without much delay and customer can also keep track of their orders (Panchal, 2020).

PROPOSED ORDERING PROCESS (VALUE CHAIN AND POLAR DIAGRAM)

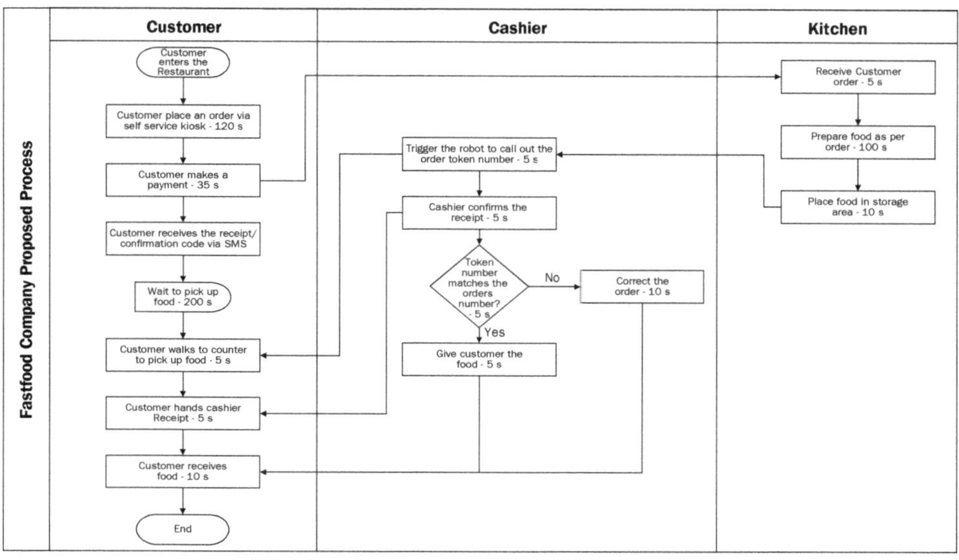

Figure 13.9 Proposed Process Flow

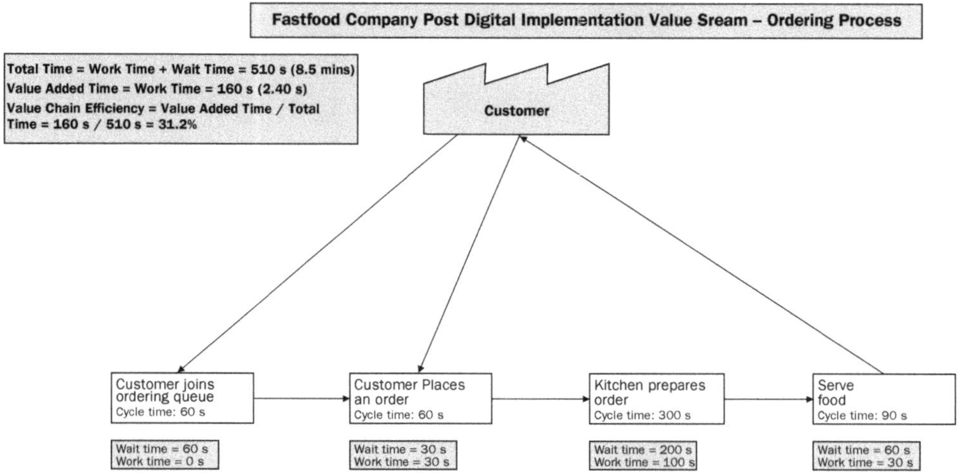

Figure 13.10 Digital Value Chain — Ordering Process

	Menu Browsing	Order placing	Order Payment	Order Confirmation	Order preparation	Order Collection
Digital						
0. Not computerized					X	
1. Siloed application						X
2. Enterprise data platform						
3. Internet-web-based platform						
4. Cloud-based platform	X	X				
5. Connected devices/mobile/wearable			X	X		
Automation & Autonomy						
0. No automation (no machine or bot)					X	
1. Automation with human control/supervision						X
2. Automation with conditional autonomous control	X	X	X	X		
3. Automation with autonomous control in certain environments						
4. Automation with full autonomy						
Smart						
0 No feedback control	X		X	X	X	
1. Explicit instructions contingent on one feature		X				X
2. Explicit instructions contingent on multiple features						
3. Machine learning						

Figure 13.11 Fastfood Company's Digital Operations Diagnostic — Post Implementation

Digital

Fastfood Company ordering and data warehouse will be cloud-based.

Automation and Autonomy

The addition of the kiosk will automate the ordering and payment process.

Smart

The new devices will help to collect and store the data for future usage to determine demand and construct new menus.

Polar Diagram — Post Implementation

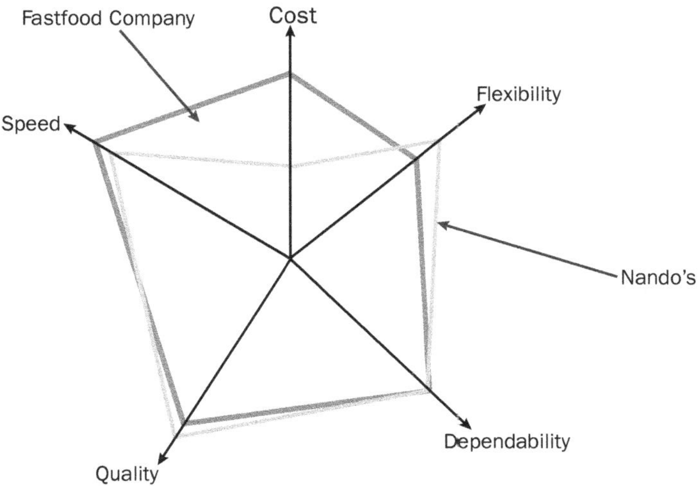

Figure 13.12 Polar Diagram — Post Implementation

The implications on the five performance objectives of the proposes solution that will improve activities in the walk-in ordering process.

Performance Objectives	
Speed	The introduction of kiosk will reduce the ordering time.
Cost	The introduction of paperless receipts will reduce cost overhead cost (receipt paper roll/ink).
Quality	Provide better quality products as transactions are taken care of by the kiosk.
Flexibility	Improve customer experience by introducing multiple payment methods.
Dependability	Stock optimisation based on the data accuracy.

IMPLEMENTATION PLAN

Activities	Timeframe	Cost Implications	Risk	Risk Mitigations
Self - Service Kiosk				
Full roll-out of self-service kiosk across all Fastfood Company franchises	6 months	R1,500 000	Load-shedding or road reduction	Generators on-site or investment in solar power for business continuity

Activities	Timeframe	Cost Implications	Risk	Risk Mitigations
Data Storage Platforms and Reporting Tools				
Data warehouse	6 months	R2 000 000	Data theft and corruption of data	Adequate cybersecurity measures in place
AI and Analytics tools (Off the shelf solutions)	3 months	R300 000	More time to implement than anticipated.	Proper definition of the business cases that needs to be solved and well-defined project planning
Staff – Training				
Training on use of kiosk	3 months	R3 000 per franchise manager	Staff resistance to use of kiosk	Change management to be rolled out 3 months prior to the implementation of the project and 3 months after post-implementation
Change management rolled out company wide	6 months	R3 000 per franchise manager		
Standardisation of cooking procedure (culture change)	1 year	R3 000 per franchise manager	Staff reluctancy and resistance	
Software Improvements				
Introduce voice command to the digital ordering screen (in-restaurant)	1 month	R2 400 per month	Voice command errors	Regular software updates to avoid errors from occurring
Investment in cybersecurity software	3 months	R40 000 per month (license fees)	Data theft and corruption of data	Adequate cybersecurity measures in place

RECOMMENDATIONS

Based on the analysis conducted of the ordering process of Fastfood Company, the key elements listed below have been recommended for implementation:

- Digitise some activities from ordering stage to the time when customer collects order.
- Invest in self-service kiosks to enhance the speed of delivery and minimise waiting time for customers.

- Invest in some Artificial Intelligence tools to enhance speed and accuracy of customer purchasing behaviour to enhance personalisation of the service to customers.
- Use data collected on demand variation to enhance the flexibility to speedily service customers without keeping them in long queues.
- Roll out training companywide to ensure all stakeholders are on board and are competent to use new digital tools.
- Reduce the use of paper slips by offering customers an option to receive their order numbers via SMS.
- Roll out change management workshops aimed at reaffirming importance of compliance with quality regulations, while encouraging staff members to buy into the use of kiosk.
- Recruit required skills to leverage the potential of the digital tools, such as Data Scientist.
- Install digital displays depicting orders numbers for customer to see when order is ready.

In conclusion, it is noted that although Fastfood Company has introduced online ordering and delivery platform, it still lags behind on digital transformation of its processes. The proposed solutions should be implemented in phases to obtain full benefits from the digital solutions. Management should remain committed to equipping their staff with adequate skills to effectively use the digital platforms. Fastfood Company has great potential to become a digitally enabled game changer in the field of fastfood.

ACKNOWLEDGEMENT OF CONTRIBUTORS

- Bridgette Lefifi
- Isaac Mkhabela
- Malekhase Moea
- Sinah Molepo
- Thandiwe Mkalipi
- Tshepo Lepota
- Tshepiso Matsena
- Tyla Janneker
- Xolani Mcunu

(All are affiliated to the Wits Business School, University of the Witwatersrand, Johannesburg).

REFERENCES

3SMedia. (2022, February 23). infrastructurenews. Retrieved from https://infrastructurenews.co.za/2022/02/23/Fastfood company-going-beyond-sustainable-packaging/

Alper, A. (2020, May 15). medium.com. Retrieved from https://medium.com/eatos/5-ways-to-digitize-your-restaurant-1789456e7737

Boute, R. N., Mieghem, J. A. (2021). Digital Operations: Autonomous Automation and the Smart Execution of Work. *MBR*, 177–186.

Frue, K. (2019, October 7). pestleanalysis. Retrieved from https://pestleanalysis.com/pestel-analysis-of-Fastfood company/

Insight, E. *hospitalityinsights.ehl.edu*. Retrieved from hospitalityinsights.ehl.edu: https://hospitalityinsights.ehl.edu/restaurant-technology-trends

Letsebe, K. (2017, August 02). *itweb*. Retrieved from www.itweb.co.za: https://www.itweb.co.za/content/JOlx4zMklEQq56km

Panchal, C. (2020, November 24). *theappideas*. Retrieved from theappideas.com: https://theappideas.com/5-different-ways-to-digitize-your-restaurant-in-2022/

Perconte, M. (2021, April 6). *trustplace*. Retrieved from trustplace.app: https://trustplace.app/blog/use-digital-transform-restaurant-operations/

SA, B I. (2021, April 27). *businessinsider*. Retrieved from www.businessinsider.co.za: https://www.businessinsider.co.za/Fastfood company-turns-50-in-south-africa-here-is-how-it-all-started-2021-4

Slack, N, Brandon-Jones, A, Johnston, R, Singh, H, & Phihlela, K. (2017). *Operations Management: Global and Southern African perspectives.* Cape Town: Pearson South Africa.

Startus-Insights. (Unknown, Unknown Unknown). *startus-insights*. Retrieved from www.startus-insights.com: https://www.startus-insights.com/innovators-guide/5-top-digitalization-solutions-for-restaurants/

unknown. (2021, October 4). *Mail&Gaurdian*. Retrieved from mg.co.za: https://mg.co.za/special-reports/2021-10-04-Fastfood company-celebrating-a-rich-heritage-of-spreading-finger-licken-goodness-in-south-africa/

CHAPTER 14

Digitalising the Transport Information System: A Perspective

BACKGROUND

Our syndicate chose the transport information system services as the processes we would like to conduct an assessment of and determine a digital operations model. We specifically focused on driving licence renewals, which is a particular point of frustration for many South Africans.

South Africans regularly complain about the slow process, the inconsistent service experience and the lengthy process and queues. There is overwhelming consensus that the process is highly inefficient and needs to be re-engineered to provide a seamless and efficient customer experience and eliminate frustration.

South African traffic management has gone through meaningful change over the past decade, having implemented the transport information system platform in 2007. They have subsequently been able to pull all drivers and vehicles licensing status onto one platform. Recently they have been able to incorporate some fines from specific municipalities and metropolitan cities. Not all fines are aggregated onto the system as some municipalities are not linked into the transport information system.

DMAIC

In order to streamline and optimise the existing process we have chosen to follow the DMAIC method to provide structure. The DMAIC assists identifying wasteful activities and the activities are streamlined.

Define

Process Map of the Current Operations

The current process is dependent on a number of manual resources required and physical infrastructure. The process starts off with a booking service that is performed online, with the next requirement being that the customer needs to come into the licensing offices to compete the renewal process. The process type is a service type offering and is a mass service, which has high volume and low variability processes.

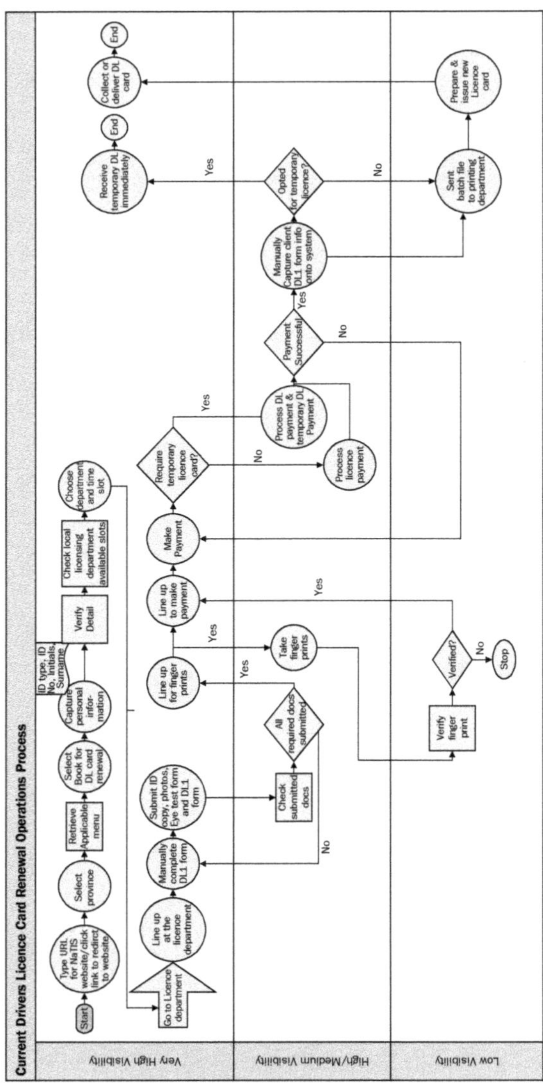

Figure 14.1 Current Driving Licence Card Renewal Process

236

Assessment of the Current Process

We have used the SIPOC tool to determine the Suppliers, Inputs, Process, Outputs and Customers (Table 14.1).

Table 14.1 SIPOC for Traffic Licensing Department

Suppliers	Inputs	Process	Outputs	Customers

• Traffic department
• Courier Company
	Receive information from applicant:
	• ID Type
	• ID number
	• Surname
	• Initials
	• Contact details
	• Address
	• Supporting documents:
	  – Copy of ID
	  – Photos
	  – Eye test
		• Access the transport information system
		• Check for available bookings
		• Apply for available booking
		• Go to licensing department
		• Submit supporting documentation
		• Line up for fingerprints
		• Complete DL1 form
		• Line up to make a payment
		• Request temporary licence card
		• Receive DL card
			• Completed application order/form
			• Temporary DL document
			• DL card
				South African citizens over the age of 18

Gap Analysis

- The current process takes two to three months from online booking to receiving your driving licence card.
- The process is cumbersome and South Africans dread renewing their licence.
- The slot availability is erratic and sometime means you have a licence that will expire before your new application.
- The queueing process is lengthy and usually involves having to book a day off from work. This could be costly.
- The process has many handoffs and the margin for error is significant.
- Process requires significant headcount resourcing and can be costly for the department.
- The process type is a service-type offering and is a mass service, which has high volume and low variability processes.

The current process can be considered as being not optimised or streamlined owing to the following:

- An inconsistent customer experience, which means you likely to get your driving licence issued anywhere between two and three months post booking.
- Customer frustration and lack of trust in the traffic authority is really high.
- There are no set SLAs for work to be done between departments.
- Manual handoffs between departments are fraught with errors and inconsistencies.

Voice of Customer (VOC)

Table 14.2 Voice of Customer (VOC)

Segment	Customer issue	Customer need	Critical To Quality (Customer requirements)
External	It takes too long to get a driving licence	Reduce the cycle time to renew a licence	2 weeks
External	It's always a struggle to get the slots	Applicants do not need to see the slots as they are doing the application online	Customer needs to do the application online, without having to go to the department – 10 minutes
External	Too many queues at the department	Reduce the queues	Do everything online - 10 minutes

Measure

Data collection plan – We used the data collection plan to systematically structure our data collection process. The type of measure for all the collected data is 'output'.

Table 14.3 Data Collection Measure

Measure	Type of Measure	Type of Data	Operational Definition
Total application processing time	Output	Continuous	The total time in minutes for the applicant to complete the form.
Total application processing time	Output	Continuous	The total time in days from when an applicant submits the application to when the DL card is issued.
Total number of received applications	Output	Discrete	The total number of submitted applications per day

Measure	Type of Measure	Type of Data	Operational Definition
% of defective incoming applications	Output	Discrete	Total number of unsuccessful applications received per day.
Response time for third party integration	Output	Discrete	The time it takes to get response from 3rd party system(s) in seconds.

Analyse

Value Stream Mapping Analysis

The value stream mapping analysis performed on the driving licence renewal process has determined that a total of 11 activities add no value. These activities are reflected and highlighted in amber below. We assessed the value stream according to three categories: information flow, the product flow as well as the time ladder.

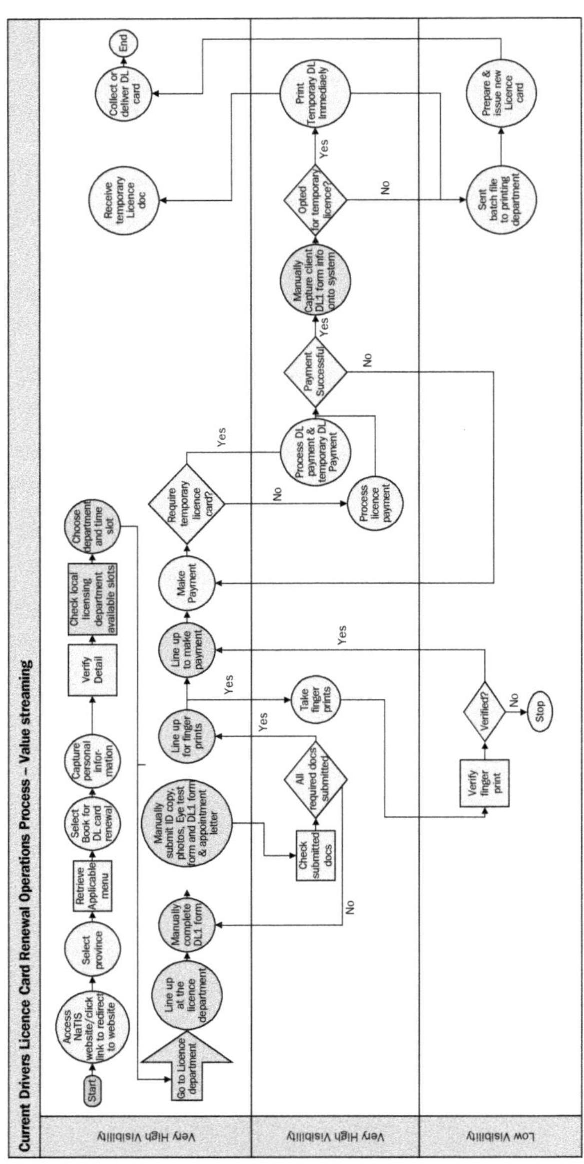

Process step	1	2	3	4	5	6	7	8	9	10	11	12	13	14	15	16	17	18	19	20	21	22	23	24	Total Steps	% of Total
Value-Added	★	★	★	★	★	★												★	★		★	★	★	★	12	50%
Non-Value Added							★	★	★	★	★	★	★	★	★	★	★			★					12	50%

Figure 14.2 Value Stream Mapping Analysis

The criteria and requirements for an optimal solution:

- The ultimate objective is to provide the solution in a manner that gives the client good customer experience and ensures that there is dependability in receiving their driving licence renewal card on time.
- The process must be **quality** controlled and have no failure points.
- The process should be efficient and effective and provide the customers with a driving licence in the fastest time possible.
- The solution should be cheaper as it eliminates costly expenses for the customer like travel, booking a day off, having to pay for photos etc.
- The solution should be flexible enough so that the client can renew his driving licence at any point of the day and not be subjected to a booking service that tells them when they can access the service.
- The convenience of being able to do the renewal from the comfort of the customer's home or mobile device is also important.
- The solution must be reliable and always on and be able to validate the client's profile as well as authenticate the client in a seamless and efficient manner.
- The process must be standardised and have little variability and variation.

Improve

Table 14.4 Solution Prioritisation Matrix

Solution Description	Root Cause Addressed	CTQ Impact (H, M, L)	Implementation effort (H, M, L)	Quick win (Yes, No)	Technology Required (Yes, No)
1. Applicant completes the form electronically	Cycle time Efficiency	H	H	No	Yes
2. Applicant uploads the supporting documentation online	Cycle time Efficiency	H	H	No	Yes
3. Applicant makes payment online	Cycle time Efficiency	H	H	No	Yes
4. Applicant can choose the delivery method	Cycle time Efficiency Effectiveness	M	H	Yes	No
5. Applicant can choose to print or email temporary driving licence	Cycle time	M	M	Yes	No

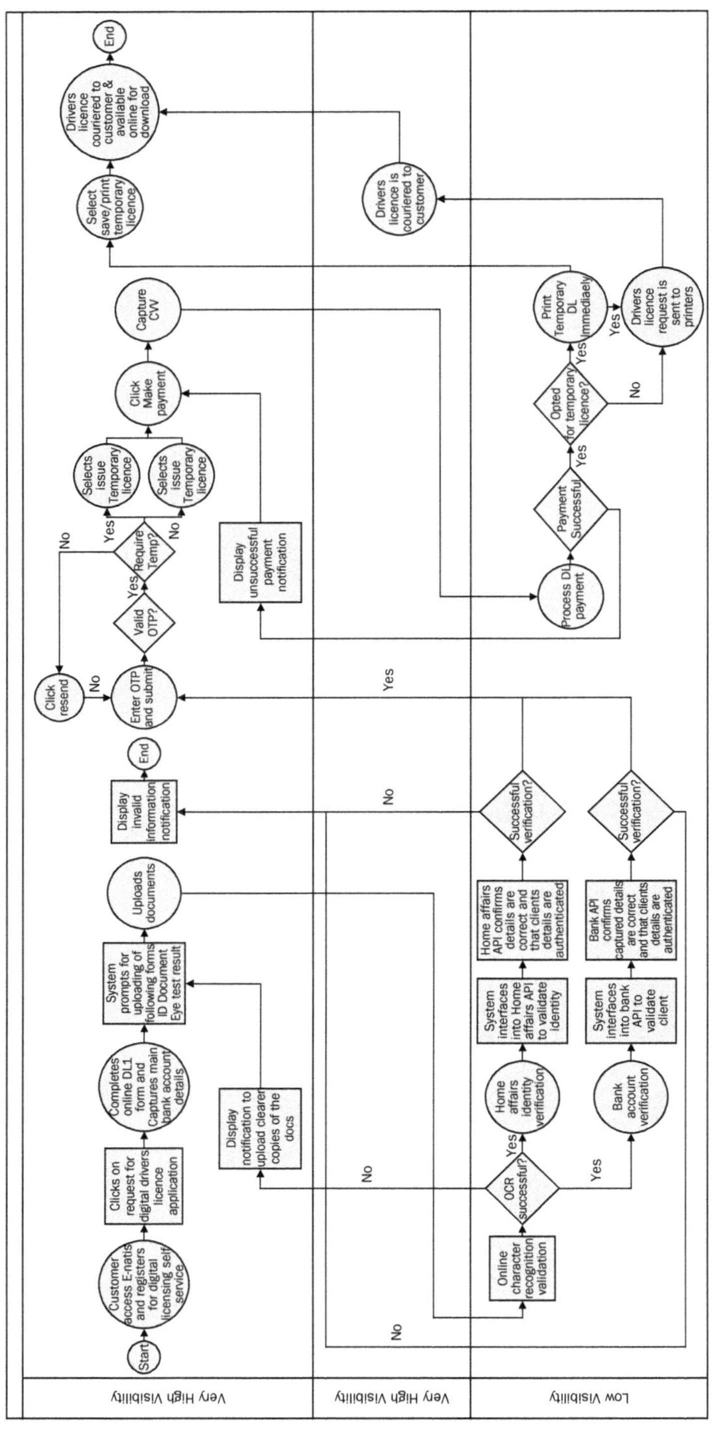

Figure 14.3 Future Digital Driving Licence Process (Future Mode Operation)

Non-value-adding process steps were removed from the process to ensure the improvement and optimisation of renewing a DL with the transport information system. The process is now streamlined, efficient and easier to manage.

Failure Modes and Effects Analysis

Table 14.5 Failure Modes and Effects Analysis

Item or process step	Potential Failure Mode	Potential Effects of Failure	Potential Causes	Current Controls	Recommended Action
Applicant completes the form electronically	Information not complete	Applicant unable to send application	Customer information not complete	Minimal	User friendly form and clear required information
System interfaces to Home Affairs API to validate identity	System could not validate identity	Applicant will not be able to continue with the application	ID number provided is wrong	Manual check	Prompt the customer to check if ID number provided is correct
Applicant makes payment online	System could not integrate to 3rd party	Applicant unable to make a payment	3rd party system down	Minimal	Send notification to System administrator to do 1st line test

Control

Table 14.6 Process Monitoring Plan

CTQ	Process Steps Where the CTQ is Measured	Data Collection Method	Data Collection Frequency	Owner Responsible for Collection
1	Applicant completes the form electronically	1. Application cycle time for internet will be collected through the traffic department order system 2. Query will be run each week to pull application data 3. All orders processed will be entered into the traffic department Quality Assurance Spreadsheet and control charts will be created	Weekly	Processing manager

CTQ	Process Steps Where the CTQ is Measured	Data Collection Method	Data Collection Frequency	Owner Responsible for Collection
2	After submission, applicant awaits a delivery notification	1. Application cycle time will be collected through the traffic department order system 2. Query will be run each week to pull application data 3. All orders processed will be entered into the TA Quality Assurance Spreadsheet and control charts will be created	Weekly	Processing manager

3.0 Digital Maturity Assessment

- Our assessment on the traffic department's digital maturity is that it has implemented an enterprise level platform (transport information system) across multiple areas and departments and has been able to collect and synchronise data across various activities e.g., vehicle data is aligned to driver information and fines information collected from various municipalities are now visible at vehicle and driver level countrywide.
- The management of this complexity would not have been possible without a sophisticated platform. This platform has been able to facilitate significant operational management benefit within the road traffic management centre. While the focus has been on integrating various functions and services, there has been a lack of services and online functionality to allow end users/consumers accessibility. The current transport information system capabilities are limited to calendar bookings for appointments and query logging.
- The ability to fulfil self-service functionality beyond that is non-existent. This does mean that the RTMC requires significant staff headcount and investment in physical infrastructure like buildings, office equipment etc.
- Our assessment is that RTMC would be considered at a digital maturity level 2, having met the requirements of a platform that can collect and synchronise data however; because of its very limited internet capability and online self-service functionality it does not meet the requirements to be considered for level 3.
- It is our considered view that RTMC has all the elements to pursue a digital transformation journey that would facilitate digital adoption of customer channels.
- We focused on driving licence renewals because the process is manual and cumbersome and has the most impact on being able to provide an efficient customer experience if digitised.

DAS FRAMEWORK MODEL

The DAS framework provides the organisation with an opportunity to assess its digitised process for efficiency. The current transport information system, although web-based, does not allow for end-to-end integrated automated and smart performance.

The proposed transport information system, which is a full end-to-end digital system, consists of digital, automated and smart integrations.

The proposed transport information system is classified as a connected devices/ mobile application due to its ability to permit users to interact remotely via an application interface. All that the client/user requires is internet connection and a mobile device or computer. The various steps of the online driving licence card renewal are automated without the need for human intervention. A user is required to input certain information and complete online forms directly on the platform.

Digital

Table 14.7 Digital Integration

	DIGITAL 0. Not computerised 1. Siloed application 2. Enterprise data platform 3. Internet web-based platform 4. Cloud-based platform 5. Connected devices/mobile/wearable
Online registration and selection of DL application	5
Completion of online DL1 form and captures main bank account details	5
Upload of ID copy and eye test results	5
Verification of uploaded documents (OCR)	5
Customer identity verification (Home Affairs)	5
Customer bank account verification (AVS)	5
Customer authentication via OTP	5
Selection of optional temporary licence	5
Select permanent DL	5
Payment	5
Generate digital temporary licence	5
Issue digital DL	5
Courier DL card	0

As stated above the proposed transport information system is a connected devices/ mobile application. Firstly, users with internet access can access the transport information system remotely on their smart phones/devices and computers. Secondly, it is interactive, because it utilises user input information such as login details and ID number to identify the user. Thirdly, it has an embedded online payment service, making the process of renewal easy and convenient. Finally, it is connected to third party apps, such as Home Affairs and bank APIs to perform validations.

Automation and Autonomy

Table 14.8 Automated Integration

	AUTOMATION & AUTONOMY 0. No automation 1. Automation with human control/ supervision 2. Automation with conditional autonomous control 3. Automation with autonomous control in certain environments 4. Automation with full autonomy
Online registration and selection of DL application	3
Completion of online DL1 form and captures main bank account details	3
Upload of ID copy and eye test results	3
Verification of uploaded documents (OCR)	4
Customer identity verification (Home Affairs)	4
Customer bank account verification (AVS)	4
Customer authentication via OTP	2
Selection of optional temporary licence	2
Select permanent DL	2
Payment	4
Generate digital temporary licence	4
Issue digital DL	4
Courier DL card	0

The transport information system platform can be classified as having automation with autonomous control in certain environments. The renewal process is highly automated, with the processes completed online, and eliminating manual checks or confirmations. The back-end system automatically reads, interprets and processes inputs. The key steps within the process are also autonomous to certain point, without requiring much human intervention. The human control/intervention aspect is only at the end of the process, where the driving licence card is printed. Limited human intervention is a good indicator of the value of automation, which means less human error and an increase in accuracy.

Smart

Table 14.9 Smart Integration

	SMART 0. No feedback control 1. Explicit instructions contingent on one feature 2. Explicit instructions contingent on multiple features 3. Machine learning
Online registration and selection of DL application	2
Completion of online DL1 form and captures main bank account details	2
Upload of ID copy and eye test results	3
Verification of uploaded documents (OCR)	3
Customer identity verification (Home Affairs)	3
Customer bank account verification (AVS)	3
Customer authentication via OTP	2
Selection of optional temporary licence	2
Select permanent DL	2
Payment	2
Generate digital temporary licence	3
Issue digital DL	3
Courier DL card	0

The transport information system platform has a level-2 Smart capability, with explicit instructions contingent on multiple features. The system is connected to other applications, such as Home Affairs and banks to verify ID numbers and other Personal Identifiable Information that clients have input. This creates a feedback loop for the system to authenticate the information, approve or reject the request. Incorrect information will prompt the system to flag the error and provide the user with an opportunity to input correct information. If the user again fails to provide the correct information or upload valid documents, the system will reject the renewal and the user will not be able to proceed to the next phase.

The system uses OCR to read and interpret the eye test results. It is configured with a range of algorithms that are able to distinguish between normal and abnormal test results. Abnormal results will prompt the user to state whether the test was conducted with the use of prescription glasses or not. If not, the user will be advised to purchase prescription glasses for driving, however, the user will be allowed to proceed to the next phase of the transport information system.

DAS CONCLUSION

With all this information gathered, it is clear that the transport information system is a viable and valuable option for digitising the driving licence card renewal process. It is efficient, convenient, easily accessible, automated and contains high degrees of autonomy. It is also affordable and less time-consuming. It is more valuable to have a mobile digital platform that is interactive than a manual process.

Based on the high scoring on digital levels, autonomy and automation, and smart capabilities, the DAS framework has assisted us to see the feasibility of digitising the driving licence card renewal process. All of these benefits are a 'click away' without users having to leave their homes.

PERFORMANCE IMPROVEMENTS ACHIEVED

The digitised process is a significant improvement from the previous manually intensive process. This is why:

- Overall process improvement has been achieved by reducing the number of days before a driver will receive his driver licence card. From two to three months has now been reduced to 10 days start to end.
- Overall manual handoffs have been reduced from 12 to two.
- Operational servicing times have been improved from a typical 8 am–3:30 pm working days only to always on 365 days a year 24 hours a day and every day of the week servicing.
- Client information is appropriately stored in a cloud-hosted database and can be retrieved instantaneously.
- Daily client servicing was capped at 130 clients per day per branch for a total

8 000 clients across the country; that capacity has now increased to potential of 300 000 clients per day.

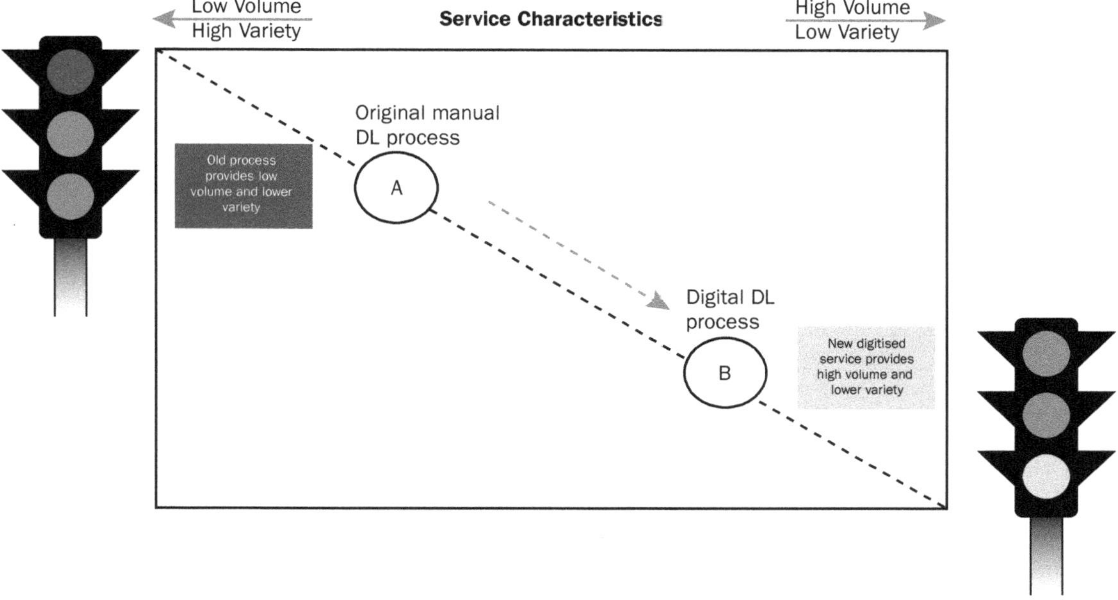

Figure 14.4 Comparing Old and New Processes

We compared the two processes against the polar diagram against the value benefits of speed, quality, dependability, cost and flexibility. The polar diagram below reflects the clear benefits that's the digitised process has over the comparable old manual process employed.

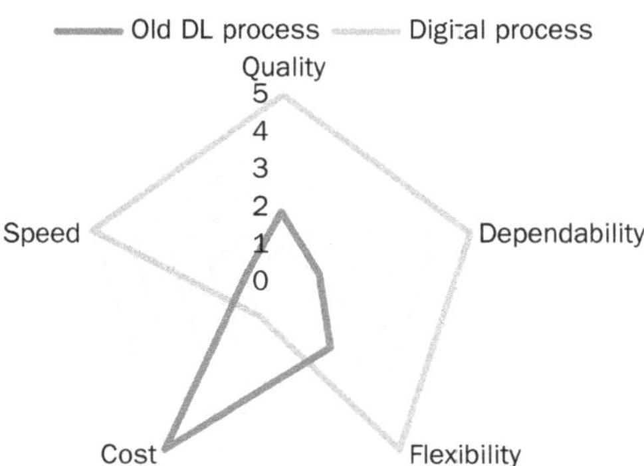

Figure 14.5 Polar Diagram Comparing Old and New Processes

249

Table 14.10 Resource and Project Planning Required to Implement the Process

Resources	Quantity	Total days required
IT and mobile app software developers	6	90 days
Project manager	1	90 days
Change manager	1	40 days
Business Sponsor	1	90 Days
QA testing	4	30 days
Business Analysts	2	90 days
Solution Architects	2	40 days
UX Designer	2	30 days
Product Manager	1	90 days

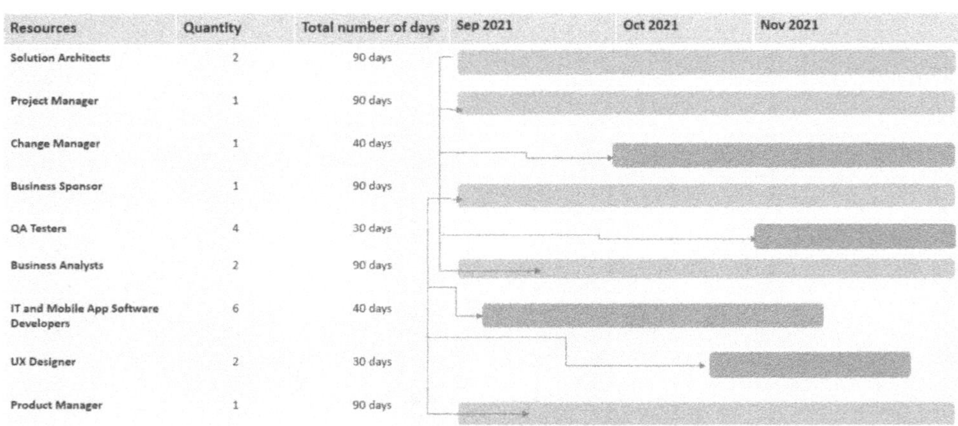

Figure 14.6 Project Plan (Gant Chart)

REFLECTIONS ON WHAT HAS BEEN ACHIEVED BY DIGITISING THE PROCESS

- The new and automated digital driver licence process is significant upgrade and improvement over the traditional process and alleviates a significant angst moment for South Africans and motor vehicle drivers. The operational improvement achieved is significant and provides significant operational savings to the Department of Transport.
- This saving will be seen in a reduction of staff required to service the operations and provides an opportunity to reduce physical brick and mortar buildings.
- The volume of driving licence applications can also be processed significantly faster which allows licensing department staff to focus on more complex

services. The model can also be replicated for other services like vehicle licence renewals.

- The overwhelming benefit, however, is provided to motor vehicle drivers as the process reduces time to receive a driving licence from an average of two to three months to receiving it within a week. Customers are also able to plan better as the new process is more consistent and the experience is standardised.

ACKNOWLEDGEMENT OF CONTRIBUTORS

- Justin Thomas
- Thobeng Choeu
- Mokgadi Molebatsane Tshenolo Malunga
- Maduo Lebakeng
- Leo Da Silva

(All are affiliated to the Wits Business School, University of the Witwatersrand, Johannesburg).

CHAPTER 15

Digitalising a Retailer

INTRODUCTION

Retailer has started looking at digital integration through its flagship store in Boksburg. However, there are some gaps in the optimisation strategy which we will highlight in this chapter.

PROBLEM STATEMENT

In order to clearly define any problems within Retailer, it is essential to look at the process of operations within the stores and ultimately its service excellence to its customers to deliver great value. According to new research on customer experience as the pulse of every business, it positions the customer as the one empowered as businesses try to delivery great customer experiences to drive loyalty and sustain a good revenue stream in the long run from the customer. Not considering the importance of a good customer experience is not an option anymore for businesses as competition is ever increasing and the voice of the customer is much louder in this digital age (Frichou, 2020).

It is also essential to look at the organisation from a SWOT analysis perspective. Look at the value-stream map to determine ways in which Retailer can isolate, communicate and quantify what the business is doing to add value versus what is done that creates waste. Thereafter we can look at gaps in operations and what can Retailer streamline to eliminate waste and increase productivity within the 118 stores.

Retailer is a strong brand and one of the leaders in the hardware industry. A major concern is the poor customer service rating received on HelloPeter, which indicated a bad trust index of 2.2 out 10. The business is struggling with providing a good consistent customer experience across all touchpoints of the business to exceed customers' expectations and needs.

Research indicates that keeping an eye on the entire customer journey and offering a superior service means the customer is more likely to keep doing business with you in the future (Frichou, 2020). Therefore, Retailer needs to address this problem head on.

SWOT

The table below helps us to pinpoint challenges and threats to the business of Retailer, together with its strengths and opportunities to help mitigate some of the problems within the business.

Strengths	Weaknesses
• Large variety of products • Part of the Massmart Group • Established brand • Large footprint • Multiple store formats eg Retailer express/ warehouse • Capital • Staff specialise in specific products • High barriers of entry into industry – few competitors	• Inconsistent customer service • Lack of product knowledge by staff • Complex culture within organisation • Unnecessarily complex/disjointed hand-off processes • Time-consuming • Difficult to find an item • Large variety of products with inconsistent store layout
Opportunities	Threats
• Create a mobile app • Improve the website UX and E-Commerce • Take part in machine learning exercise with Massmart to improve digital innovation • Expand partnerships with suppliers to provide better product/service offerings • Source local products • Display screens – improve sales experience • Self-service kiosks • Integration of online and physical shopping experience	• Tough competition • Price increases due to inflation • Global unrest – supply disruptions • Cybersecurity threats • Looting

VALUE-STREAM MAPPING (ANALYSIS) OF RETAILER

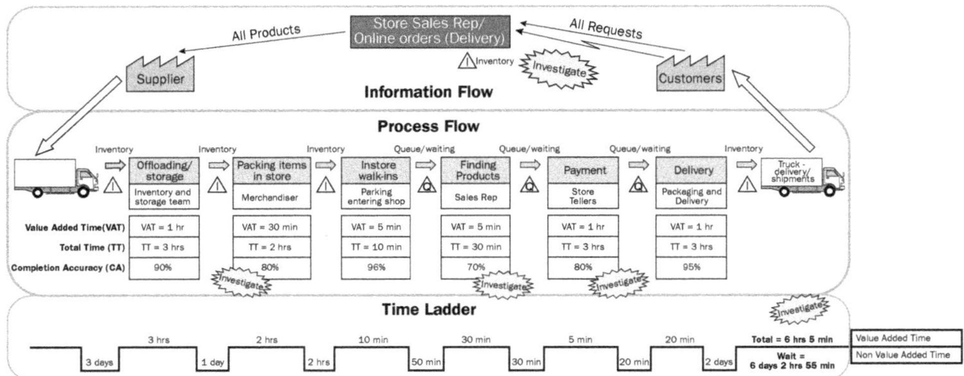

The purpose of this value-stream mapping analysis of Retailer is to assist us to identify and remove or reduce 'waste' in value-stream processes, therefore helping to increase the efficiencies given in the value stream of Retailer. The removal of waste is intended to increase productivity by creating leaner operations within the business, which in turn makes waste and quality problems easier to identify (Singh et al, 2011).

The value stream starts from the Information Flow, when a customer requests an order which is received by Retailer employees. Retailer then needs to ensure that inventory is in stock from its suppliers. The Process Flow then tracks how the customer gets the product they required. Lastly, the Time Ladder gives us an insight of the total time it takes to complete the Value-Added process time and Non-Value-Added Time which is wasted in the process.

Through the analysis it is evident that Retailer needs to investigate customer enquiries on inventory and, look at the completion accuracy percentage to mitigate any delays in getting the right items on shelves. Also it must investigate the delays experienced by customers to effectively find items in the store and the waiting period to pay for an item. And lastly it needs to investigate the overall waiting period to improve future processes for great costumer value (Hines & Rich,1997).

GAPS IN OPERATIONS

Organisational effectiveness can be dictated by how efficient the operational processes are in order to perform optimally. By making use of value-stream mapping, we could analyse the current state and design a future state of taking products/services from the beginning of a specific process until it reaches the customer. The value-stream map displays all critical steps in a specific process and quantifies the time and volume taken at each stage.

Using value-stream mapping, we were able to define the gaps in the operation of Retailer. These gaps refer to the difference between the current performance of a process and desired performance and they have a negative impact on the organisational bottom line.

From the value-stream mapping analysis of Retailer, the time ladder reflected a total of six days and two hours, 55 minutes of non-value-added time vs a total of six hours, five minutes value-added time for the entire process flow. The stages where we encountered longer waiting times are from truck deliveries to offloading and storing the products (two days), offloading to packing items in store (one day), and the delivery stage until the customer receives the product.

From the analysis, we were able to identify the stages where we could remove or reduce 'waste' to increase efficiency and productivity.

Gaps in operations

Streamline approach
- Customer service: Remove siloed ways of work in each department
- Upskill employees on the floor to be able to assist a client in any department still have product specialist
- Store layout: reconfigure the layout of the store to be easier to navigate

DIGITISING THE RETAILER OPERATIONS

Propose a fully integrated digitising operations solution based on an analysis of the identified case problem, incorporating key digitising operations principles, techniques and trends. The strategic intent of the solution should also be made clear.

DAS Model Framework

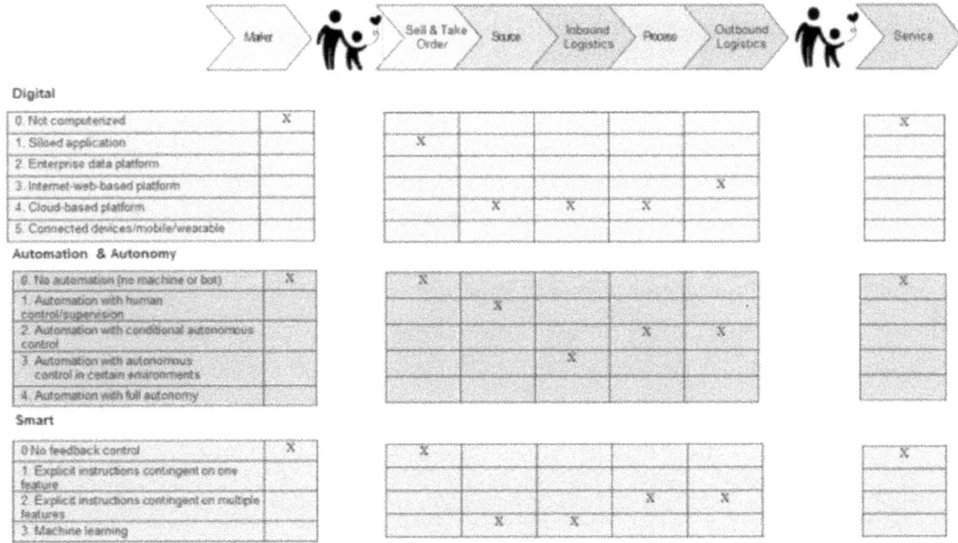

The DAS framework (Boute & Mieghem, 2021) is a useful diagnostic tool that was used to identify which processes in the company's workflow were supported by digital operations and which would benefit from further optimisation. The image above indicates our findings of the operation before digitisation. From this we can gather that some of the processes within the workflows are advanced in the digitising process and some need to be prioritised for digitisation. In our analysis we focused on the customer experience of the operation.

Market: We defined this as customer experience in the physical store interactions including all activities that take place from the moment the customer enters the Retailer premises. We noted that instore customer experience was sitting at a **Digital level** 1, **Automation level** 0 and **Smart level** 0, which is consistent with customer reviews gathered from Google Reviews and on Complaints Board.

Service: We looked at post-sales customer experience analysing whether Retailer was able to assess customer satisfaction through post-sales surveys or reviews. Post-sales customer experience was sitting at a **Digital level** 1, **Automation level** 0 and **Smart level** 0.

Below is a post-optimisation representation showing how the process would possibly score once proposed optimisation solutions have been implemented.

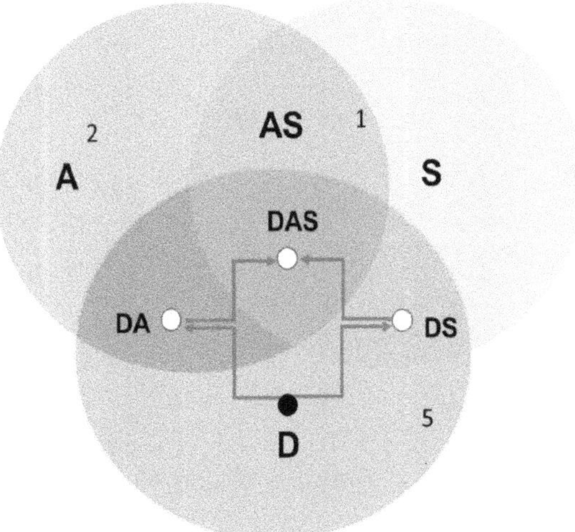

After analysing the data from the DAS model we concluded that we would need to digitise the customer's instore experience by implementing new technology and leveraging of existing ones. According to Moverstech (n.d) on the findings from a survey carried out by McKinsey and Company, an organisation can potentially see an increase in customer satisfaction of approximately 33% post-implementing digital services.

Digitisation Solutions

We propose upgrading existing technology like the Retailer website to enable customers to create a profile either online or through a kiosk instore. Once the profile has been created the customer will be able to add products to the wish list both instore and online. To improve the customer experience, we provided the customers with the ability to add products as they navigate through the aisles by scanning a QR code.

In addition, the customer will be able to upload a picture or make use of a generic picture to visualise the end result of renovating a specific space. For example, for bathroom renovations, the customer will be able to upload a picture of their bathroom and will be able to choose wall and floor tiles, other bathroom accessories/fixtures and even create a feature wall. During the design process the customer can capture the room's measurements; as the customer is choosing the products which they feel complement each other they will be provided with the cost of the products and will also be given a guide as to the quantity of the products that they should purchase (for example, tiles and tile cement).

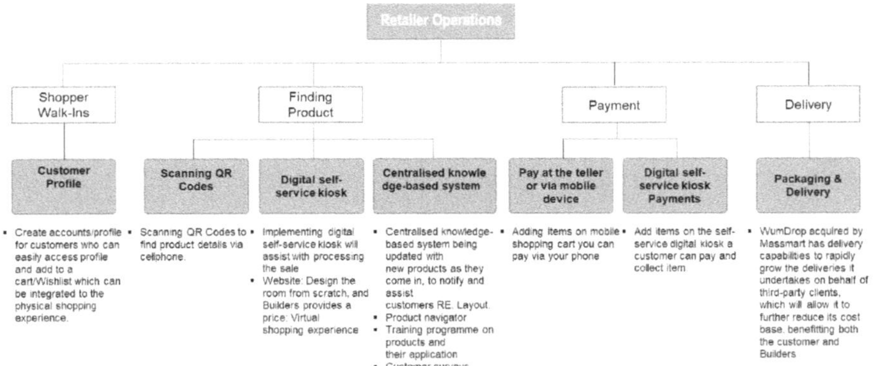

This digital solution provides a seamless shopping experience by introducing additional payment methods to the customer, who will have the option to pay for purchases from a mobile device, the kiosk or at the teller. Should the customer make use of the kiosk or a mobile device (accessing the online profile through the phone), it will save them time from waiting in the queues to pay. Once the payment has been concluded the invoice will be submitted to the Retailer team, who will have the products available for the customer at dispatch.

This digitised process saves time for new and repeat customers and creates an improved customer experience which could result in higher sales.

Performance Improvement

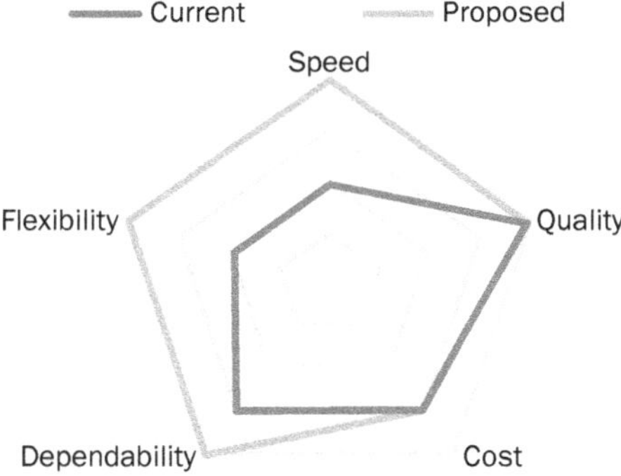

The structural, infrastructural, and technological design attributes are directly linked to the co-created purchase decision of a consumer (Wandi et al, 2021). The introduction of digitised solutions helps businesses realise a perspective shift in relation to their potential client base of customers that associate with a particular brand. That considered, through the introduction of the self-service kiosk in the market and customer feedback loops for the service element, we can formulate a process that is measurably quicker in capturing and executing sales. The efficiency in speed of sale and service will in turn allow for increased flexibility as staff will have greater capacity to assist with client queries.

By enabling clients to virtually create their environments or select any product, it places less reliance on staff to walk through every option with the client when coming to the purchase decision. Visual representations provide a consistent client experience which feeds into the dependability of the process as a client is not solely reliant on differing product knowledge and descriptive abilities which vary from salesperson to salesperson. Standardisation of the selection step while providing clear and accurate description of products and their application through a virtual means will lead to greater propensity for purchases and improve overall client satisfaction.

The technologies should help make it a memorable buying experience and the survey element will allow for positive reinforcement and assist with keeping employees motivated to maintain high quality levels and enhance the service reputation.

GOALS AND OBJECTIVES

Our aim is to streamline and digitise operations by automating systems and integrating the digital eco-system with the physical stores, which will improve the effectiveness of the business and ultimately improve the customer experience.

IMPLEMENTATION PLAN

Digitising the operational elements of Retailer will be accomplished by focusing on three main sections: marketing, customer services and processing orders.

Focus area	Time frame	Activity	Resources
Market • Customer service • Product knowledge	15 months	• Create accounts/profile for customers who can easily access profile and add to a cart/Wishlist which can be integrated to the physical shopping experience. • Scanning QR Code to get product details via cell phone. • Website: Design the room from scratch, and Retailer provides a price: Virtual shopping experience	• Website • App • Database • CRM
Sell & Take order • Waiting times • Disjointed process	18 months	• Implementing digital self-service kiosk will assist with processing the sale	• IoT • Kiosk • CRM
Service • Poor communication • Aftersales support	15 months	• Centralised knowledge-based system being updated with new products as they come in, to notify and assist customers e.g. Layout. • Product navigator • Training programme on products and their application • Customer surveys	• Customer Database • Product Database • RPA • CRM

Phase	Time Frame	Budget	Activity	Person responsible	Monitoring
Planning Platform Applications	6 months	R1,000,000	•Research market and competitors in industry Get information from all stakeholders	•Marketing	•Monitor if we are able to meet timelines
Development Phase Creating app for profiles & QR coding Cloud computing CRM VR website implem Instore kiosk	12 Months	R2,000,000 R3,000,000 R2,000,000 R1,000,000 R2,000,000 R10,000,000	•Develop the different technologies with the various stakeholders •Development of app including QR scan coding •Development of CRM system •Visit identified sites to do environmental mapping & to research individual stores for Bluetooth low energy beacons •Cloud computing service provider	Service Providers, who include software developers, business analysts, cloud architect, system administrator, graphic designer, network engineer, app designer	•Reaching project milestones
Testing Phase Phase 1 Phase 2	5 Months	R5,000,000	•Stress test the website •Test Kiosks	•Project manager	•Staging Site Browser testing Speeding testing Readability testing Regular feedback sessions Type of information gathered
Launch Phase 1 - platform Phase 2 - application	6 Months	R2,500,000 R2,500,000	•Run digital marketing campaign for targeted signed up customers •Launch of the kiosks	•PR Manager •Project manager	Use Digital monitoring tools

Risk Mitigation

The CRM implementation will enable Retailer to monitor whether the digitisation strategy implementation is on track. Measuring results at regular milestones, and to act when required, is pivotal in mitigating risk.

Proposed Strategy	Implementation Issues & Risks	Implementation Risk Management	Key Metrics	Timeframe			
				Q1	Q2	Q3	Q4
Digitising systems: Market	Insufficient information on the targeted market sector and winning clients over. Variety of clients who expect different types.	Improve R&D on new markets.	Increase of new customers.				
Digitising systems: Purchasing of Order	Load shedding. Technology not working. Customers and staff struggling to use the technology.	Training of staff. Service provider to assist with tech maintenance.	Reduced Kiosk down time. Customer engagement UI tracking. reduced number of support tickets logged with software provider				
Digitising systems: Service	Customers challenged by the technology.	Engaging with customers directly, via customer surveys and market surveys.	Customer reviews/ Google reviews, decline in Hello Peter complaints.				

CONCLUSION

Summary of Findings

The goal of digitising the identified Retailer operations would rely heavily on automation, integration, and innovation of processes. Marketing, customer service and order processing were identified to be the primary focus areas to be digitised.

It is evident from the SWOT analysis that Retailer does have shortcomings however, strengths and prospects to enhance business operations digitally outweigh the threats.

Specifically using lean-management methods, we were able to identify business process stages that remove or reduce 'waste' to increase efficiency and productivity. This way, the return on investment would be realised.

Key Implications

Digitising operations is not a simple task; however, when done right and at scale it yields impressive results. Retailer would need to invest in change management, skill sets (training), collaboration and other digital investments that create value. On the upside, this exercise can easily facilitate positive changes in their supply-chain strategy and endorse flexibility in the business operations environment.

Chances of Success/Failure

Considering the entity's digital maturity stage and digital capabilities, especially those already implemented at the Boksburg flagship store, there are great chances to expand and further integrate innovative digital solutions across all Retailer operations. Likewise, the proposed digital strategy underscores the feasibility of a successful digital transformation journey.

ACKNOWLEDGEMENT OF CONTRIBUTORS

- Sello Mkosi
- Chantel Naicker
- Avo Ndiko
- Phathu Nemukula
- Thireshni Sanasy
- Nolubabalo Silwana
- Siphamandla Msimang
- Dave Ntsangani

(All are affiliated to the Wits Business School, University of the Witwatersrand, Johannesburg).

REFERENCES

Armstrong, B., Lee, G. L. (2021). *Digital Business*, 2nd edn. Silk Route Press.

Creamer Media. (2019). Retailer opens flagship store in Boksburg. Retrieved from https://youtu.be/YvXHvDFKapo

Frichou, F. (2020, March 25). 5 Reasons why customer experience is the pulse of every business right now. Retrieved May 10, 2022, from https://business. trustpilot.com/reviews/learn-from-customers/5-reasons-why-customer-experience-is-the-pulse-of-every-business

Hines, P., Rich, N., Esain, A. (1999). Value stream mapping: a distribution industry application. *Benchmarking: An International Journal*.

Lasa, I. S., Laburu, C. O., de Castro Vila, R. (2008). An evaluation of the value stream mapping tool. *Business process management journal*.

Martin, K., Osterling, M. (2014). *Value stream mapping*. Estados Unidos de América: Shingo Institute.

Massmart Press Release (2019) Retailer debuts new store prototype at Retailer Boksburg. Retrieved ffrom https://www.massmart.co.za/Retailer-debuts-new-store-prototype-at-Retailer-warehouse-boksburg/

Moverstech. (n.d). Benefits of customer service digitization. Retrieved on May 11, 2022, from Benefits of customer service digitization - MoversTech CRM

Oba, P. (2022). Digitising Operations – Day 2 Slides. Retrieved from https://ulwazi.wits.ac.za/files/3266169/download?download_frd=1

Oba, P. (2022). Digitising Operations – Day 5 Slides. Retrieved from https://ulwazi.wits.ac.za/files/3266201/download?download_frd=1

Oba, P. (2022). Digitising Operations - Session 1 - Introduction 2. Retrieved from https://ulwazi.wits.ac.za/files/3266159/download?download_frd=1

Review Companies Online | Customer Service & Company Ratings | hellopeter.com. (2021). Hello Peter - Retailer Warehouse. Retrieved 10 May 2022, from https://www.hellopeter.com/Retailer-warehouse

Singh, B., Garg, S. K., Sharma, S. K. (2011). Value stream mapping: literature review and implications for Indian industry. *The International Journal of Advanced Manufacturing Technology*, 53(5), 799–809.

Staughton, R., Johnston, R. (2005), Operational performance gaps in business relationships. *International Journal of Operations & Production Management*. 25(4): 320–332.

Value-stream mapping. (n.d.). Retrieved May 11, 2022, from https://en.wikipedia.org/wiki/Value-stream_mapping

Van Wyck, J., Rose, J., Ahmad, J., Kupper, D. (2019, March 15). The How-To Guide to Digital Operations. Retrieved May 11, 2020, from https://www.bcg.com/publications/2019/how-to-guide-digital-operationss

Wani, D., Malhotra, M., Clark, J. (2021). Strategic Service Design Attributes, Customer Experience, and Co-Created Service Choice: Evidence from Florida Hospitals. *Production and Operations Management Society Journal*.

CHAPTER 16

Digitalising Operations in a Bank

INTRODUCTION

BBB Bank's Wealth Management division conducts a regular client payout operation where clients with share trading accounts issue instructions for the bank to pay out dividends from their trading account to a specified bank account. Clients expect the correct amount to be paid out on the instructed day reliably. BBB Bank strives to uphold its service level agreements and deliver on client expectations; however, currently they fall short of benchmarked operational excellence resulting on average 10% of instructions not processed on time and 8% processed with errors per month. Currently the process is conducted manually daily by a fully dedicated stockbroking administrator with validation and processing by the Finance Operations officer.

This chapter will seek to analyse the current processes and activities and identify opportunities to optimise and digitalise the operation in order to improve operational performance. The defined objectives are:

- Improve quality through ensuring accuracy of processing the request by reducing average monthly instructions processed with errors from 8% to 0%.
- Improve dependability of the operation by ensuring that payments processed on time is improved from 90% to 100%.
- Optimise speed of the operation by reducing the time taken to complete the operation from 5 hours to approximately 10 minutes.
- Improve cost efficiency by negating the need for an allocated resource with an annual remuneration of R250 000 p.a.
- Improve governance of the operation through enhanced data management practices.

The following improvements have been recommended in order to achieve the defined objectives:

1. Optimise the process by removing unnecessary steps, eliminating duplicate activities and running more activities in parallel.
2. Digitalise the operation to achieve a fully automated operation leveraging cloud to host data, system integration and straight-through processing.

The proposed solution results in the speed of the operation being reduced from five hours to approximately ten minutes ensuring 100% accuracy of processing consistently and on time. As a result of the operation being fully automated, the stock broking administrator will no longer be required to conduct the operation and can be reallocated to conduct more complex tasks or assigned to a different business unit and cost centre.

This solution will require nine months to implement and a project implementation team of all design, technical and management professionals will be appointed to execute the project. The key constraint that will need to be managed is the embedded culture of the division impacting their willingness to adopt the solution considering the perceptions around digitalisation leading to job losses. BBB Bank Group consists of the following frontline clusters: Corporate and Investment Banking, Retail and Business Banking, Wealth and Africa Regions. The group offers wholesale and retail banking services as well as insurance, asset management, and wealth management.

This report will seek to optimise and digitalise the regular client payment operation within BBB Bank Private Wealth. The objective of this operation is to process and execute standing client instructions to withdraw dividends from their share trading account into a specified bank account. This instruction includes when they would like to receive dividends payouts from their stock broking account as well as the amount they would like to receive. This operation is carried out daily assessing which customers need to be paid out every day and processing the operation.

BBB Bank's high level value chain has been described in Figure 16.1 below indicating where this occurs within the overall value chain.

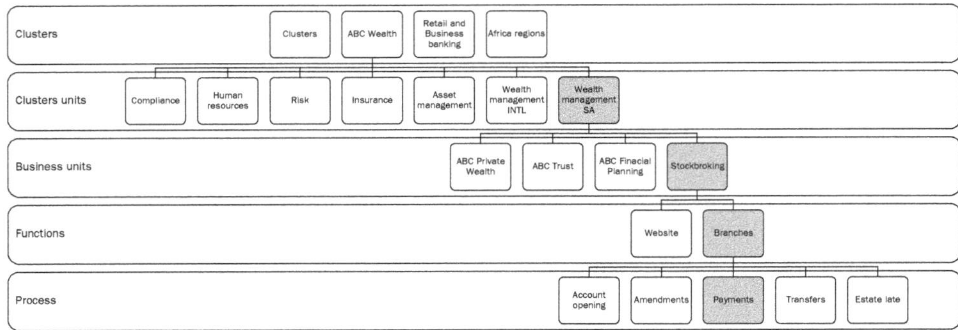

Figure 16.1: BBB Bank Group Value Chain

Figure 16.2 shows the input–output model associated with regular client payment operation being analysed conducted by the payments division.

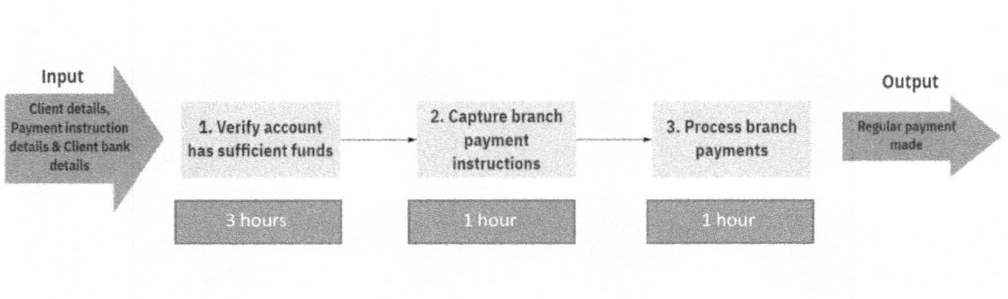

Figure 16.2: Operation Input–Output Model

PROCESS MAP

The existing processes and activities associated with the operation have been mapped as shown in Figure 16.3.

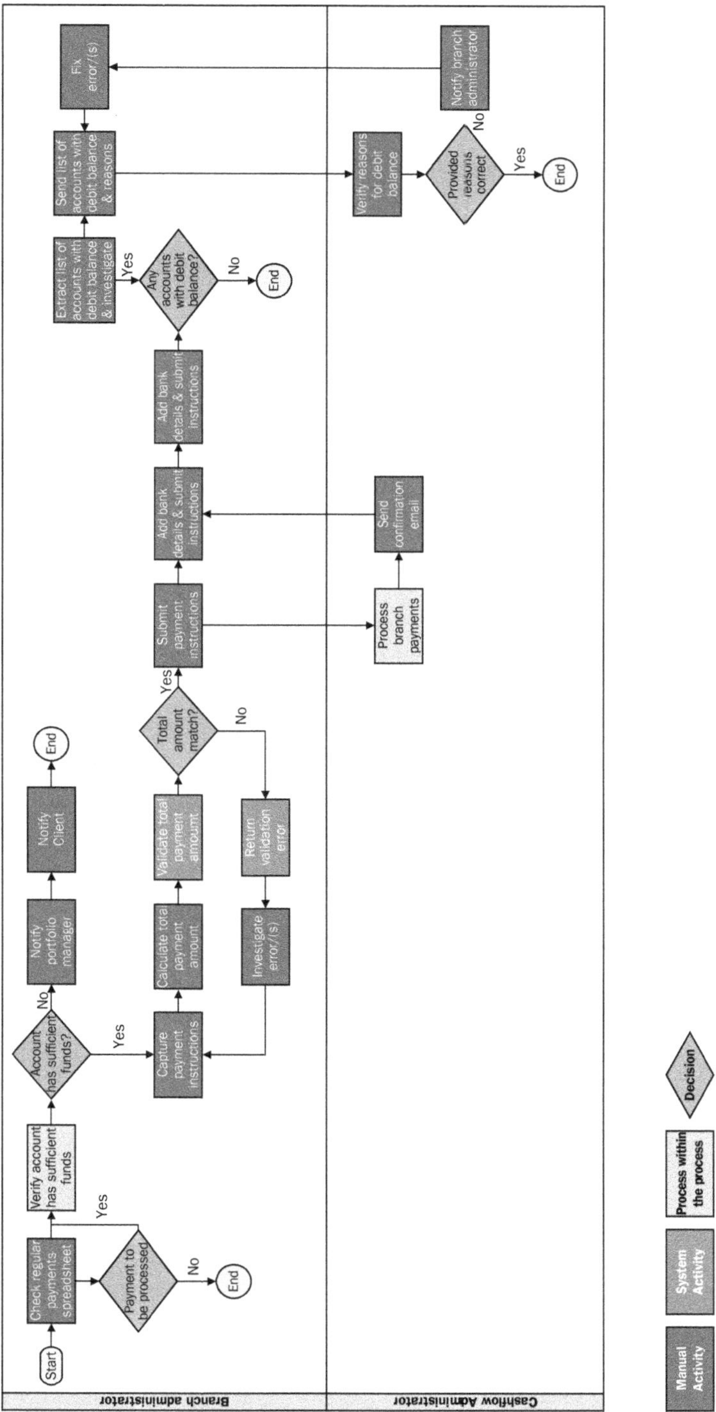

Figure 16.3 As-Is Process Flow Diagram

ASSUMPTIONS

The following assumptions pertaining to the optimisation and digitalisation of the operation have been made:

- BBB Bank processes 20–60 payout instructions per day on average.
- Currently the operation takes five hours to complete.
- Currently 10% of instructions are not processed in time per month resulting in late payments.
- Currently 8% of instructions are processed with errors.
- The existing stock broking administrator responsible for carrying out this operation spends 80% of the day conducting this operation daily.
- The existing stock broking administrator responsible for carrying out this operation receives an annual remuneration to the value of R250K PA CTC.
- On average time taken to respond to an email is ten minutes.

VALUE STREAM MAPPING AND GAP ANALYSIS

Value stream analysis has been conducted to identify current process inefficiencies and waste. The gaps identified have been detailed below:

1. **Duplicate capturing – There are four occasions in this process where instructions are captured:**
   - Clients capture their payment instruction details and send via email.
   - Instructions are recaptured by the stockbroking branch administrator into the regular payments spreadsheet on the shared drive.
   - On the day of processing instructions are recaptured onto the stockbroking portal.
   - On the day of processing instructions are recaptured again in the Broker Deal Account System (BDA).

2. **Quality – The manual nature of the execution of the process leads to errors**
   - The spreadsheet is manually updated by the stockbroking administrator when a client submits an instruction for a standing client payment. This sometimes results in errors where the amount to be paid out is captured incorrectly or the incorrect banking details have been captured.
     - No validation in place to check things like bank account details or branch code details.

3. **Long processing times – the operation takes five hours to complete**
   - Manual steps in the process result in long processing times; almost all steps are manual

- Emails between the stockbroking branch administrator and the cashflow administrator add to long processing times.
  - When the client payment instruction is on BDA, cash flow administrator (finance operations) sends an email to the stockbroking branch administrator informing them that the instruction is on BDA and they should go ahead and capture the bank details.
  - The stockbroking branch administrator sends an email with the list of accounts with a negative balance and the reason to the finance operations & master data. *The reasons given must be verified by these teams.*
  - In the list sent by the stockbroking administrator, if the wrong reason has been given, the cash flow administrator notifies the stockbroking branch administrator via email, advises them on what the correct reason for the negative balance is and asks them to update the email sent and re-send.

4. **Lack of information management**
   - The regular payments spreadsheet is stored on the shared drive accessible to everyone and there is a risk that anyone can edit it.
   - Management has no way to view audit trails or accurately determine the processing of these payment instructions. This is crucial when trying to create and maintain a pleasant client experience.
   - No reporting/difficult to draw out reports as payment information is captured on separate Excel spreadsheets and some comes through email or phones calls.

5. **Service level agreements not being met**
   - Due to long processing times because of duplication, back-and-forth with emails, at times increased volumes and constrainted resources some instructions miss the cut-off times and are not processed on the day the client requested.
     - The cut-off time for processing transfers from a fixed income portfolio is 11am.
     - The regular payments spreadsheet must be checked before the cut-off time (1pm) each business day.
     - The email to capture bank details on BDA must be sent by finance before the 2:30pm cut-off time to release payments.

6. **Unable to deliver best client service**
   - Wrong payment amounts are sometimes paid out due to capturing errors.

- Payments are sometimes paid into the wrong banking account due to capturing errors and no validations in place.
- Some payment instructions are sometimes paid out later due to missed cut-off times.
- Clients are only able to send instructions and receive support during standard working hours.
  - All of this results in bad client experience.

7. **Process efficiency constraints**
   - There is no standardisation around how instructions are submitted by clients, introducing inefficiency.
   - Process depends on the availability of the key role players.
   - Resources always must be allocated to run this operation.
   - Client capturing and submitting of instructions must occur within working hours for assistance by the staff.
   - There is no trigger to start the process daily; it is dependent on the availability of the administrator.
   - Activities in the processes are highly repetitive and resources allocated are forced to dedicate the majority of their time in the day to this operation.

PRIORITISED OBJECTIVES

The objectives of improving the processes associated with the operation being analysed have been defined in order to determine the scope of the process improvement:

a) Improve quality through ensuring accuracy of processing the request by reducing average monthly instructions processed with errors from 8% to 0%.
b) Improve dependability of the operation by ensuring that payments processed on time is improved from 90% to 100%.
c) Optimise speed of the operation by reducing the time taken to complete the operation from five hours to ten minutes.
d) Improve cost efficiency through by negating the need for an allocated resource with an annual remuneration of R250 000 p.a.
e) Improve governance of the operation through enhanced data management solutions.

Figure 16.4 shows the current operational excellence performance against benchmarks with competing financial institutions. This has been mapped specifically against Allan Gray, where this operation is fully automated. BBB Bank will seek to achieve the benchmarked performance.

Polar Diagram

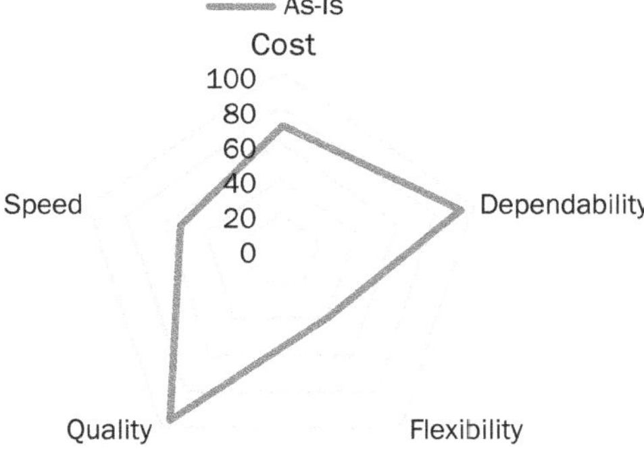

Figure 16.4 BBB Bank Current Performance

PROCESS OPTIMISATION

To optimise the process towards achieving the objectives, the following actions are recommended to optimise the current process eliminating waste:

AS-IS	Recommended optimisation
No standardisation around how instructions are submitted	Create a standard form that clients use to capture payment instructions
Daily checking of the spreadsheet	Set reminders for only the days where there are payment instructions. The branch administrator will only check the spreadsheet on the days where there are reminders set to do payments.
Duplicate capturing	Remove duplicate capturing by adding instruction submission interface/form on the Investments online website. When the instruction has been captured and submitted by the client on the stockbroking website, *the relevant back-end systems should be updated with the client's regular payment instruction.*
Manual steps in the process	
Back and forth with email	Automated notifications to different actors in the process. Integrate the systems involved in the process so they are *'aware of each other'*
Steps that are not necessary that can be taken out	Combine steps 4, 5 & 12 and these should all be done as one step in one system. Remove step 3 and let the administrator notify the client directly about insufficient funds.
Steps that can run is parallel	Run step 10 & 15 in parallel

Considering the nature of the operation, these actions will only result in a marginal improvement in the objectives defined:

* Only approximately 20% reduction in the speed of the operation is achieved.

In order to achieve the defined operational improvements set out in the objectives, digitalisation of the operation is proposed; however, it is necessary to evaluate the digital maturity of the business to understand the ability of BBB Bank to deliver a digital strategy for operations and achieve digital transformation objectives for the further optimisation and digitalisation of the operation.

BBB BANK DIGITAL MATURITY AND DAS ANALYSIS

The DAS framework has been used to assess BBB Bank's digital maturity and opportunity to digitalise the operation. This has been assessed based on the three control aspects of the model: digital, automation and autonomy and smart.

1. Digital:

It has been deduced that the 'As-Is' process is currently conducted as a siloed application within the Digital control as:

* Repetitive capturing is done by both the customer and branch administrator on different medium channels and formats.
* Manual transfer of data is inputted into the different systems which are not integrated for validation and verification checks.

In optimising the process, the workflow can upgrade to a level 2 digital process where the silos are integrated through the development of an enterprise data platform. This will eliminate the manual transfer of information and multiple verification checks.

Digital		
Description	As-Is Process	Optimised Process
0. Not computerised		
1. Siloed application	×	
2. Enterprise data platform		×
3. Internet-web-based platform		
4. Cloud-based platform		
5. Connected devices/mobile/wearable		

To reach a desired future state of level 3 (internet-web-based platform), all process workflows would need to be run off an internet web-based platform where the client payment instruction is done via a web portal and the back-office systems are integrated with the web portal for data sharing and processing.

2. Automation and autonomy

Within the As-Is process, there is no automation as the verifications, checks, and payment calculations are done by the branch administrator.

With the optimised process, the stockbroking system does the validation checks, the branch administrator fixes the errors if there are any and there is a handover process in parallel to the cashflow administrator to process payments resulting in reduced time and waste.

Automation & Autonomy		
Description	As-Is Process	Optimised Process
0. No automation (no machine or bot)	×	
1. Automation with human control/supervision		×
2. Automation with conditional autonomous control		
3. Automation with autonomous control in certain environments		
4. Automation with full autonomy		

The desired future state is a level 4 automation with full autonomy where the process runs automatically with no human intervention. This will result in faster processing time, reduced headcount costs for administrators, who can be allocated to more strategic and critical thinking roles within the organisation.

3. Smart

The digitalisation and automation of the process workflows does not guarantee that intelligence will be executed to ensure error free and accurate processing of data. It is therefore imperative to apply smart algorithms for optimisation and real-time processing. The As-Is process has no smart controls as intelligence cannot be applied to execute the work, there is no feedback control due to the lack of digitisation, automation, and manual interventions from humans.

In the optimised process, explicit instructions are followed by the branch and cashflow administrators as payment verifications and checks can only be made if all data entries are completed by the stockbroking portal and BDA system.

Smart		
Description	As Is Process	Optimised Process
0. No feedback control	×	
1. Explicit instructions contingent on one feature		×
2. Explicit instructions contingent on multiple features		
3. Machine learning		

The desired future state is smart level 2. In this instance, automation can be used to replace the human element to contact the customer to confirm the successful online payment instruction submitted by the customer, analyses and process the payment instructions.

PROPOSED DIGITALISATION SOLUTION

The proposed optimised and digitalised solution has been mapped below in Figure 16.5 with a description of the process.

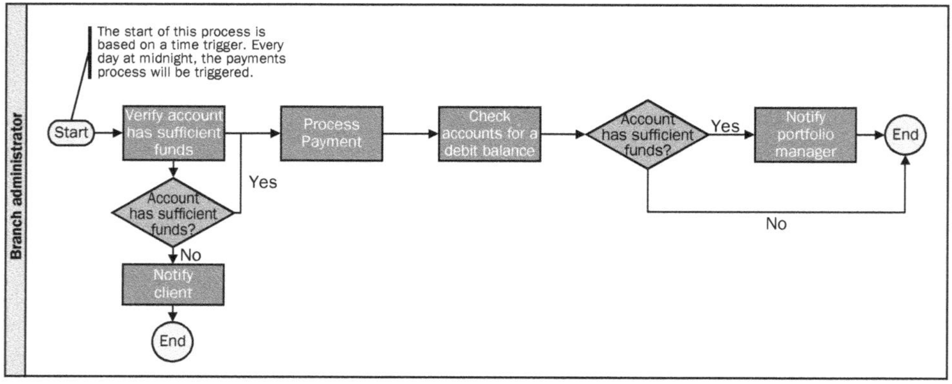

Figure 16.5 Optimised and Digitalised Process Flow Diagram

Description
Pre-condition – this must be done before the process is executed:
1. Client logs onto investments online website, captures & submits the regular payment instruction.
    a.   Client must select the account the payment should be made from.

b. The regular amount that should be paid out.
c. The account bank details the money will be paid into.
   i. As part of capturing the account bank details, a validation to check if the details captured are correct and belong to the client will be performed.
d. After successful completion of all mandatory regular payment instruction details, the client will submit this instruction online.
   i. On submitting the instruction, a message to approve and confirm that the client is the one submitting this instruction will be sent to the primary cell phone number on record and once accepted/approved the instruction will be successfully submitted.
e. The regular payment instruction is then saved to a backend system i.e. the instructions engine system.
f. A copy of the instruction submitted by the client is emailed to the client.

Digitalised regular payments process steps:

2. Based on an automated time trigger set on the instructions processing engine, every day at midnight the payments process is kicked off. This process includes the system:
a. Verify if an account has sufficient funds.
b. If NO, the payments process ends, and an automated notification is sent to the client affected notifying them that there are not enough funds in their share trading account.
c. If YES, then the system will continue and process the payment(s).
d. Once the payments have been successfully processed, the system will check for accounts with a debit balance (i.e. accounts that have a negative balance after the payment was processed.
e. If there are NO accounts with a negative balance, then this process ends.
f. If there are accounts with a negative balance, an automated notification is sent by the system to the portfolio manager and this process ends.

BENEFITS OF THE SOLUTION

The main objectives as outlined and discussed in preceding sections around key internal and external measures are achieved through the proposed solution, centred around process improvement, market-wide benchmarking and customer experience improvement. Below are some of achievements realised through the process overhaul.

1. **Speed**

   Reduction of waiting periods between the completion of tasks and in-process handover delays.

2. **Over processing**

   Reduction of over processing of data, capturing and analysis at multiple touch points in the process and converging the operation into a single system.

3. **Errors**

   Elimination of human verification and validation of payments

4. **Productivity**

   Re-allocation of the resources to strategic value adding business activities.

IMPACT ON PERFORMANCE

Proposed Digitisation	Improved performance objective	Quantified performance enhancement
1. Internet web-based platform where the client payment instruction is done via a web portal and the back-office systems are integrated with the web portal for data sharing and processing.	1. Quality 2. Flexibility	Enhances quality by 8% through the reduction of error of capturing of instruction and increases flexibility by 50% through the agility of the process for future change.
2. Full autonomy where the process runs automatically with no human intervention	1. Speed 2. Cost	Full autonomy will result in a 30 times faster processing time as well as reduced headcount costs for administrators who can be allocated to more strategic and critical thinking roles within the organisation resulting in a long-term reduction of cost of 90%.
3. Automation can be used to replace the human element to contact the customer to confirm the successful online payment instruction submitted by the customer, analyses and process the payment instructions.	1. Cost 2. Dependability 3. Quality	Autonomous process decreases cost through re-allocation of the resources to strategic value adding business activities (contributing to the long-term reduction of cost), increases dependability through on time payment processing as well as increases quality through the accuracy of processing requests and reduction of error, all resulting in the achievement of the prioritised objectives.

Polar Diagram

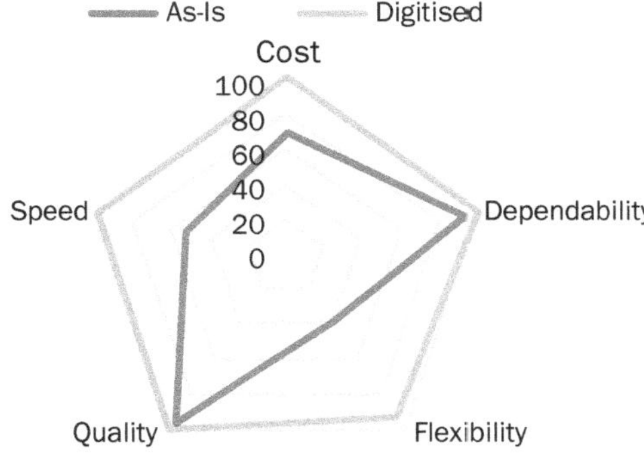

RESOURCES AND PROJECT PLAN

The following resources are required to digitalise and automate the payment instruction process.

1. Sponsor
2. Solutions Architect
3. Developers
4. Infrastructure Engineers
5. Business Analyst
6. Quality Engineer
7. Project Manager
8. Change Manager
9. Supervisor
10. Services Support

Project Implementation Plan

The following implementation process will be followed to automate our digitised process:

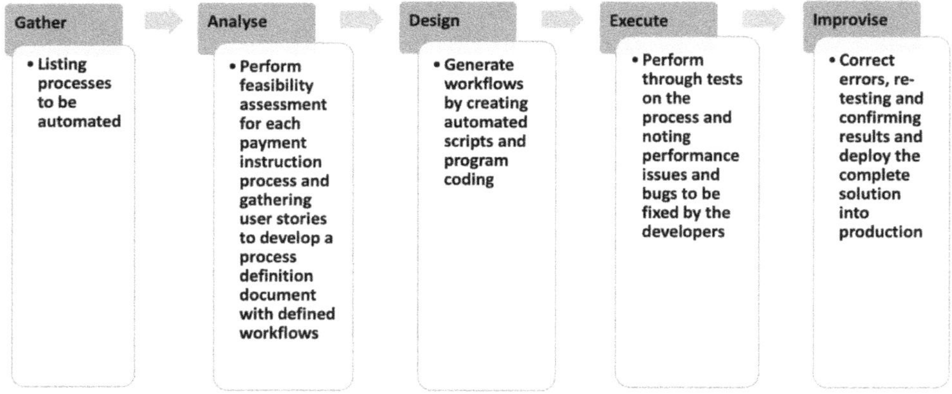

High Level Project Plan

Figure 16.6 Implementation Plan

The following organisational challenges have been identified as part of the implementation and will need to be mitigated to ensure a smooth deployment.

Challenges	Mitigations
Siloed Implementations	Early involvement, alignment, and collaboration of the development team with IT Infrastructure and Security to ensure a seamless deployment and integration of systems.
Existing and Legacy IT Infrastructure Constraints	Maintain a centralised IT infrastructure to ensure synergy between development implementation process requirements and the enterprise IT infrastructure.
Employee Resistance	Active change management and continuous communication to be put in place to ensure employee buy-in and a smooth transition. Upskilling and training of employees to be conducted.
Cost Implications	Bank BBB will choose the correct solution to implement and handle the process automation in-house to reduce capital costs.

CONCLUSIONS

This investigation sought to improve the operational performance of the regular client payout operation. Optimisation of the process did not significantly impact the performance of the operation as a result, a digitalised solution was developed which achieved all objectives defined. While there is a once-off cost associated with implementing the solution, Bank BBB will break even on the investment within two years based on the savings to be achieved by negating the need for a fully dedicated administrator receiving remuneration of approximately R250 000 per annum. BBB Bank will need to implement change management to ensure that the solution is adopted by the internal staff.

ACKNOWLEDGEMENT OF CONTRIBUTORS

- Amandla Mtimkulu
- Daniel Dorfling
- Langa Dube
- Maame Tabiri
- Monde Nkwenkwe
- Reeme Bohloa
- Sebongile Dumako

(All are affiliated to the Wits Business School, University of the Witwatersrand, Johannesburg).

REFERENCES

Cybiant, L. M. S. (2020). Robotic Process Automation Implementation Roadmap. October 20.

Dongre, R. (2021). BLOG, ROBOTIC PROCESS AUTOMATION, RPA:Considerations/Challenges for successful RPA Implementation. June 24.

CHAPTER 17

Digitalising Printing Press *eGazette* Section

INTRODUCTION

In each country, government has an official way of communicating with the public and in South Africa they do so through the *Government Gazette* published by the printing press. 'The Government Printing Works (GPW) is a government component reporting to the Minister of Home Affairs; with oversight by the Parliamentary Portfolio Committee on Home Affairs. It specialises in the printing and development of security media, including ballot papers, voters roll, passports, visa, birth certificates, educational certificates, smart identity documents (ID) cards, examination materials, *Government Gazette*s and a wide range of other high security printed media' (Government Printing Works, 2018). The *Government Gazette*s are periodical publications authorised to publish public and legal notices. Proclamations by the President, regulations and notices in terms of Acts, company registrations are some of the notices published in gazettes. Dissemination of accurate information is important and must be done in a timely manner hence effective operations management is at the core of publishing gazettes. In the printing press the *Government Gazette* is processed and published in the Origination Division by the *eGazette* section. The *eGazette* section will be the focus of this chapter.

For organisations to prosper, operations management is vital as it boosts efficiency within a production facility as it manages operation and processes within an organisation (Planet Together, 2018). Brandon-Jones, Slack, & Johnston (2013) describe Operations Management as exciting, important and challenging. It is important because it is likely to improve customer service and efficiency simultaneously. Equally, it is exciting as 'it is at the centre of so many of the changes affecting the business world – changes in customer preference, changes in supply networks brought about by internet-based technologies, changes in what we want to do at work, how we want to work, where we want to work, and so on' (Brandon-Jones, Slack, & Johnston, 2013). Lastly it is challenging as it is the operations manager who'll be responsible for making changes in response to changing customer demands. The managers must be creative in finding solutions to 'technological and environmental challenges, the pressures to be socially responsible, the increasing globalization of markets and the difficult to-define areas of knowledge management' (Brandon-Jones, Slack, & Johnston, 2013).

One way that operations managers can make changes in response to customer demands is through automating processes, where computer-controlled devices and electronics undertake control of processes. The aim of automation is to boost efficiency and reliability while removing the need of performing repetitive and rule-based tasks.

Background

Operations management in the *eGazette* section improved efficiency, customer service as well as the cost of producing notices. This was done by automating internal processes resulting in reduced input resources. Input resources that were reduced include human resource costs through overtime that was eliminated, manufacturing costs as time of production and paper usage was reduced, to name a few. The printing press *eGazette* section is responsible for publishing different types of gazettes which include Tenders, Legal notices, Ordinary and Extraordinary gazettes etc. The employees in this section are responsible for the quality check of all notices received, i.e. to check whether:
* the notices meet the business rules (if mandatory fields are completed on forms and if proof of payment is attached with the quotation);
* if the information is captured correctly by the system; and
* all notices are proofread before publication to ensure that the copy from the client and what will be published is the same.

This section was automated in 2015 where all manual processes were digitised. Initially clients used to submit hardcopies of their notices and the section would have to type all the notices into the system, additionally do quality check as described above. When it was automated, forms for each type of notice were created and published on the company website where clients would download, complete the forms and send them to the section for publishing. Automation improved the process as typing of notices internally was eliminated and improved efficiency as the section only had to focus on the quality of the notice resulting in an improvement in the turnaround time for publication and the cost of producing the notices.

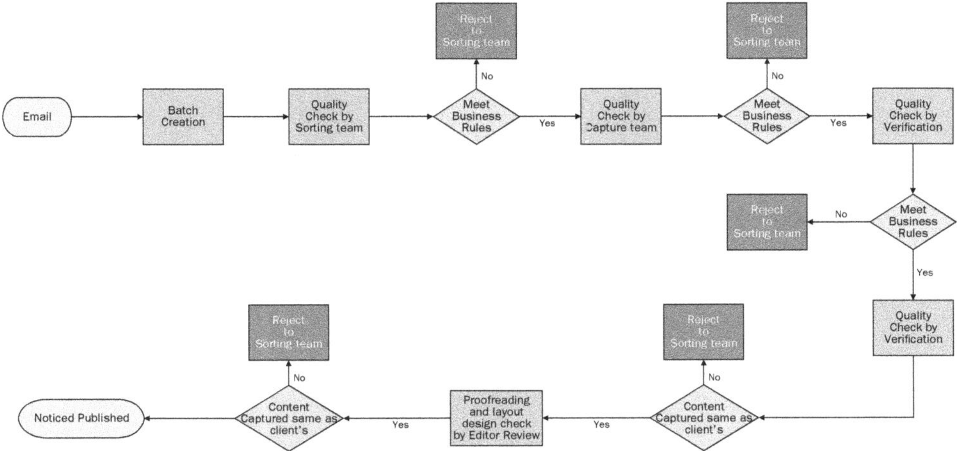

Figure 17.1 Current Publication Process of Notices (Source: Odwa Sigodi)

Aim of the Assignment

Review and critique operations management strategy and the objective function of printing press *eGazette* section as well as find ways on how the section can be automated further.

PROBLEM STATEMENT

Technology and digital services have played a major role in improving customer service as it has improved turnaround time of processes as well as immediate access to products and services; however, it has changed customer behaviour. Customer expectations have risen, and they expect service to be provided when they want it, regardless of the time (Iyoob, 2017). Digitising internal processes of the *eGazette* section had its benefits as stated above; however, new challenges were identified, ie:

- Client expectations regarding service increased as they expected a shorter turnaround time.
- Clients used the same proof of payment for different notices, this was realised after the notice is published.
- Regarding internal processes, complacency from employees has been identified due to the repetitive nature of the process.

THEORETICAL FRAMEWORK

Dhoul (2019) defines Operations Management as 'chiefly concerned with planning, organising and supervising in the contexts of production, manufacturing or the provision of services. It is delivery focused, ensuring that an organisation successfully turns inputs to outputs in an efficient manner. The inputs could represent anything from materials, equipment and technology to human resources such as staff.' Therefore, 'an operation's function is concerned with getting things done by producing goods and services for clients' (Dhoul, 2019). To be able to manage operations, an operation's strategy is needed as it guides the organisation on the direction to take in day-to-day activities as well as long-term goals. Day-to-day activities of an organisation are within the operation's function, which makes correlation between the strategy and operations of an organisation important as it will determine success of the organisation in the long-term. Thus, consistency between short-term activities of operations and long-term strategy is key to achieve competitive advantage. Implementation of the operations strategy is critical as noble plans without action are futile.

Operations processes may be similar in transforming inputs to output; however, their characteristics differ in several ways in creating the output. These characteristics are known as the 4Vs (Brandon-Jones, Slack, & Johnston, 2013):

- The *volume* of output: is prevalent where tasks are repeated, employees work with standard procedures, machinery or processes will be specialised for production of that specific product or service and this will result in low unit costs.
- *Variety* of output: For variety organisations need to be flexible in their offerings and this flexibility is characterised by matching needs of customers. Due to complexity of customising products and services to customer needs, this may lead to high unit costs.
- *Variation* in the demand of output: Organisations need to be able to predict demand by customers and plan for their operation in accordance to those demands. Therefore, flexibility will be needed in such organisations to cater for customer needs during the peak times and off-peak times. During peak times, the cost per unit may be high.
- The 'degree of *visibility* which customers have of the creation of their output' (Brandon-Jones, Slack, & Johnston, 2013). In this dimension value-added services are directly experienced by customers. There's low tolerance for waiting and customer contact skills are needed to offer satisfactory service to manage customer perceptions. Variety is high as each customer's needs may be unique.

When organisations strategise for operations, they must ensure that they choose characteristics that are in line with the product or service they offer. For example, an organisation with mass production will be characterised with 'high volume, low variety, low variation and low visibility' (Brandon-Jones, Slack, & Johnston, 2013), whereas in a customer-processing operation volume will be low, with 'high variety, high variation and high visibility' (Brandon-Jones, Slack, & Johnston, 2013).

Sustainability of organisations is dependent on operations management; when it is done effectively, it will result in a triple bottom line, ie:

- The social bottom line: where an organisation has a connection with the society they operate in but also balance that with direct internal consequence, which is profit. At an individual level, the organisation should ensure that it devises jobs and work patterns that will allow employees to contribute their talents stress free (Brandon-Jones, Slack, & Johnston, 2013).
- The environmental bottom line: where organisations take into consideration the effects of their business on the environment (Brandon-Jones, Slack, & Johnston, 2013). Paper usage has decreased drastically in the section since the inception of *eGazette*.
- The economic bottom line: where operations managers should ensure that they use operations resources effectively. To achieve this, they must control costs, increase revenue, reduce risks, make effective investments and grow long-term capabilities (Brandon-Jones, Slack, & Johnston, 2013).

At a day-to-day level of operations, however, 'there are five basic performance objectives that apply to all types of operation' (Brandon-Jones, Slack, & Johnston, 2013). These are:

- Quality: by 'doing things right by providing error free' products fit for their purpose to customers (Brandon-Jones, Slack, & Johnston, 2013);
- Speed: strive for speed advantage by increasing availability of products at the expected time (Brandon-Jones, Slack, & Johnston, 2013);
- Reliability: by ensuring that delivery promises made are kept (Brandon-Jones, Slack, & Johnston, 2013);
- Flexibility: ability to change and fast enough to meet customer demands. Operation's activities may need to be changed to cope with unexpected circumstances (Brandon-Jones, Slack, & Johnston, 2013); and
- Cost-effectiveness: 'Produce goods and services at a lower cost that will enable them to price appropriately for the market' (Brandon-Jones, Slack, & Johnston, 2013).

Mastering these five operations objectives will result in operations excellence as process efficiency will result in lower costs, lower operational risks will result from reduced errors, higher capacity utilisation results in lower capital requirements, revenue will be secured through repeat business where service is enhanced and lastly opportunities for process learning will result in capabilities for future innovation (Brandon-Jones, Slack, & Johnston, 2013).

In the process of reducing input resources in operations, organisations have taken up automation as an option. Automation is defined as 'the technique, method, or system of operating or controlling a process by highly automatic means, as by electronic devices, reducing human intervention to a minimum' (Dictionary.com). The emphasis of automation is on 'sustained performance: efficiency, productivity and reliability' (Guglielmelli, 2014). Areas that usually get automated are high-volume and highly repetitive processes, high-value processes such as money processes and those that create better customer experience as well as high-stakes processes. Automation tends to substitute labour but on the other hand it does complement labour as it simplifies business processes, increase productivity as well as change in demand for labour e.g. new skills may be created. Therefore, in the implementation of automation, while processes are improved, change management must be done concurrently to ensure that labour is not drastically affected by it. One way of doing this is through lean synchronisation where 'flow of items (materials, information or customers) that constitute services and products always delivers exactly what customers want, in exact quantities, exactly when needed and exactly where required in the lowest cost possible' (Brandon-Jones, Slack, & Johnston, 2013). The focus of this concept is on eliminating waste while meeting demand with perfect quality. Its philosophy is defined by three issues:

- Continuous improvement: where you discover new ways to improve.
- Eliminate waste: where you eliminate activities that don't add value.
- Involvement of everyone: which encourages problem-solving by the team, enriching jobs, rotating jobs and multi-skilling. This inspires engagement, 'personal responsibility, and ownership of the job' (Brandon-Jones, Slack, & Johnston, 2013).

Therefore, lean synchronisation in the implementation of automation highlights that loss of employment is not the aim of automation but to improve business processes while multi-skilling employees.

ANALYSIS OF CURRENT PRINTING PRESS OPERATIONS

The *eGazette* section has a strategic objective of co-ordinating and distributing 'government information in accordance with quality and delivery specifications' (Government Printing Works, 2018). Operations in the section generates gazettes through the input-transformation-output process by changing inputs into outputs (Brandon-Jones, Slack, & Johnston, 2013). The **Input** resources comprise:

* Transformed resources is information (notices) from clients which is edited and published by the department in respective gazettes.
* Transforming resources is the staff and the software used to process the notices.

The **transformation process** of notices goes through different teams in the section where they do the quality check and proofreading.

Lastly the **Output** are the notices published in respective gazettes, eg all tender notices published in one gazette.

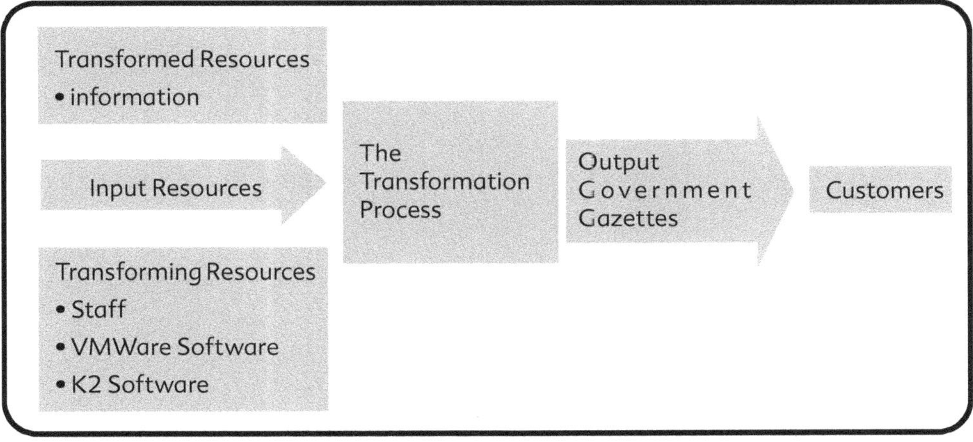

Figure 17.2 Operations Input Resources and Outputs (Source: Odwa Sigodi)

In the production of gazettes the **volume** of notices is high and the implications of that include repeatability of tasks by employees, the standards/business rules are set which should be met for each notice received and these notices are processed in specialised software (Kofax & K2). This results in low unit costs.

Variety, however, is low as the notices are published in precise gazettes on a set date of publication, which results in limited flexibility.

Variation in demand is also low due to standard times of publication with cut-off times given to clients.

The **visibility** dimension is also low as there is less exposure in the information-processing operations.

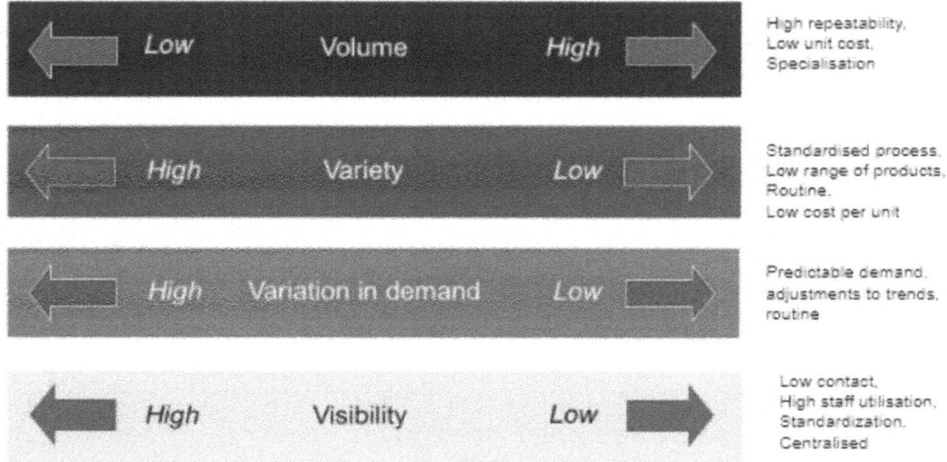

Figure 17.3 Typology of Operation of the *eGazette* Section (Source: Odwa Sigodi)

FINDINGS AND RECOMMENDATIONS

Operations in the *eGazette* section meet the operations performance objectives. The focus in the production of gazettes is on quality, reliability and cost effectiveness. Given that there are cut-off times for submission of notices and set dates for publication, speed may not be emphasised in the internal processing of notices, if processing is within the turnaround time. However, through enquiry emails received from clients to check the status of their notice, the section will have to improve on this. Due to the autonomous nature of the section, flexibility is also not important but in situations where there is an urgent gazette that needs to be published it is done so through the 'extraordinary gazette' and where needed cut-off times are not enforced.

As noted earlier, client expectations about the turnaround time have increased. They expect immediate response on the status of their notices as well as confirmation that it will be published. In instances where notices do not meet business rules, notices are rejected back to the client. This can result in clients missing the publication of that week, if they don't receive a rejection email quickly. To remedy this, the section could be automated further by introducing a submission process for notices through the website and a mobile application. In this process, clients will be responsible for the quality of their notice, request a quotation and make immediate payment online. A notice submitted this way can bypass the first and the third section and thereafter go through to the final quality check and proofreading sections (see Figure 17.1 for the current process).

As indicated in the problem statement, the repetitive nature of internal processes makes employees complacent. Quality check is sometimes compromised by teams, most especially at the beginning stages of the process as they expect other sections to do due diligence. The new process will reduce complacency and increase accountability in sections, as each employee that processes a notice will ensure that notices are processed right the first time. With automation, there are always concerns that jobs will be lost. Taking lean synchronisation into consideration, instead of a terminating employment, the new process will provide multiskilling as employees in the affected sections will be cross-trained on all sections. Customer needs must be considered when automating; there are customers who will be enthusiastic about the new process but there will be a few that still prefer the current process. Therefore, the two processes can run concurrently until such time when all customers use the website and mobile platform. The proposed process (see Figure 17.4) has an implication of reducing workload from the Sorting and Verification teams if clients use the website and mobile application for submitting notices. Thus, job rotation will occur as employees in the Sorting and Verification teams will have to work in the other sections when there is demand.

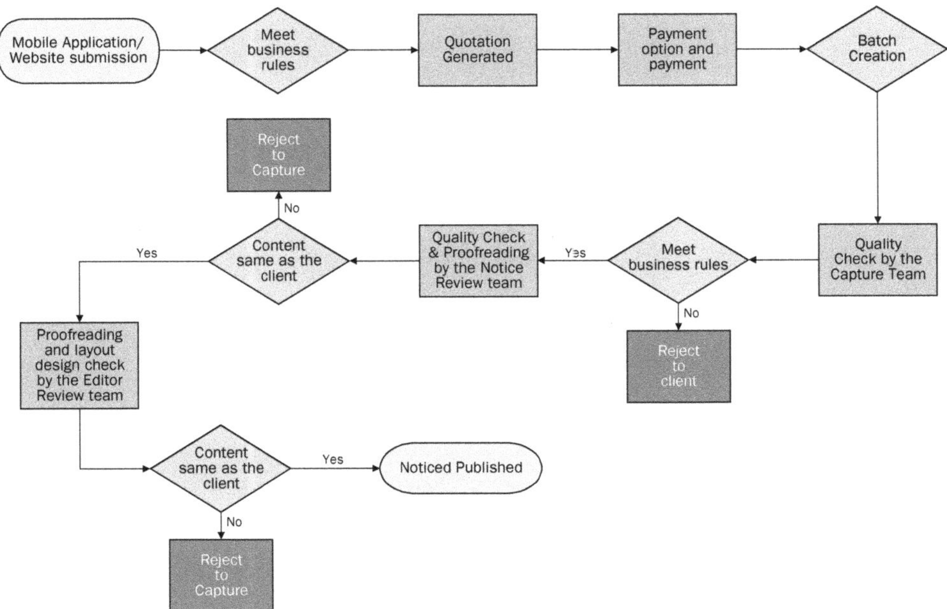

Figure 17.4 Proposed New Process for *eGazette* (Source: Odwa Sigodi)

The payment issue identified in the problem statement where clients use the same proof of payment for different notices will be resolved since clients will make immediate payment with the 'proposed process for *eGazette*'. However, some clients will prefer the current process. To mitigate this problem, automation of the accounting system may be needed for fast and efficient tracking. Xero acounting software, for example, runs on the cloud, allowing unlimited users to have access from different devices at any time. It needs to be connected to the bank account and it can match up quotations/invoices with amounts deposited into the bank account. It can generate invoices and send them to clients for immediate payment. It can connect to different types of job tracking, business applications, point-of-sale, customer relationship management system etc (Xerox, 2019). It has features to run every part of business e.g. keep accurate records, keep watch on business health, information security, bank reconciliations etc. There's no installation needed, it offers free upgrades and all information is backed up automatically.

CONCLUSION

Operations management is vital for businesses as it has 'potential to improve efficiency and customer service simultaneously' (Brandon-Jones, Slack, & Johnston, 2013). It is at the centre of many changes affecting the business world and operations managers must be creative in finding solutions for the changes needed. Operations management's aim is to ensure that input resources are transformed into output efficiently. Therefore, the transformation process of input resources must be in line with the output characteristics (the 4Vs) of products and services the business wants to offer. This can result in sustainability of the business through achieving the triple bottom line, i.e. 'the social bottom line, environmental bottom line and economic bottom line' (Brandon-Jones, Slack, & Johnston, 2013). The business goals, however, can only be realised if 'five performance objectives (quality, speed, reliability, flexibility and cost-effectiveness)' are applied at day-to-day operations (Brandon-Jones, Slack, & Johnston, 2013). Mastering these objectives will result in lower costs, lower operational risks will result from reduced errors, higher capacity utilisation results in lower capital requirements, revenue will be secured through repeat business where service is enhanced and lastly opportunities for process learning will result in capabilities for future innovation (Brandon-Jones, Slack, & Johnston, 2013).

Automation is one of the solutions operations managers must consider when improving business processes as it boosts efficiency and reliability as it removes repetitive and rule-based tasks. When implementing automation, change management must be part of the process to reduce negative effects on labour. Lean synchronisation is an option to consider in the automation process as its philosophy is on the elimination of waste, continuous improvement while involving everyone.

ACKNOWLEDGEMENT OF CONTRIBUTOR

* Odwa Sigodi

(Affiliated to the Wits Business School, University of the Witwatersrand, Johannesburg).

REFERENCES

Brandon-Jones, A., Slack, N., Johnston, R. (2013). *Operations Management.* Italy: Pearson Education Limited.

Dhoul, T. (2019, January 10). Top MBA. Retrieved from https://www.topmba.com/mba-programs/what-operations-management

Dictionary.com. (n.d.). Dictionary.com.

Government Printing Works. (2018, August 3). Government Printing Works. Retrieved from http://pmg-assets.s3-website-eu-west-1.amazonaws.com/Government_Printing_Works_Annual_Report_2017-2018.pdf

Guglielmelli, E. (2014). What is automation. *IEEE Robotics & Automation Magazine*, 93.

Iyoob, J. (2017, December 19). *Technology And Its Impact On Consumer Behavior.* Retrieved from https://www.etechgs.com/blog/customer-service/technology-impact-consumer-behavior/

Planet Together. (2018, December 12). *Planet Together.* Retrieved from Planet Together: https://www.planettogether.com/blog/functions-of-operations-management

Xerox. (2019). *Xerox.* Retrieved from https://www.xero.com/za/features-and-tools/accounting-software/

CHAPTER 18

Digitalising Room Service

EXECUTIVE SUMMARY

This chapter has chosen the hotel industry as one of the most important components of the wider service industry, catering to customers who require overnight accommodation and holidays for family and friends. It is closely associated with the travel and hospitality industries, although there are notable differences in scope. The chapter allows readers to learn more about the hotel industry and its services to those other service industry sectors, and breaks down the current process of hotels/restaurants for the guest that requests a stay or accommodation. The assignment is based on the Digitising Operations Guideline (the DAS model). We will begin to analyse the case and demonstrate knowledge of digitising the hotel's operations to make it more efficient as a business and maintain high customer satisfaction, and where applicable we will demonstrate the use of the DAS model.

It then focuses on how to streamline the processes that are currently at play and ensure a good return on investment by ensuring hotels (e.g., Holiday Inn, City Lodge, and Protea hotels) continue to provide quality, timely and cost-effective services for visiting guests. The chapter will be engaging more specifically on the following topics/questions:

- Do a process map of the operation.
- Carry out value stream mapping (analysis).
- Identify any gap through an analysis of the problem and come up with a proposed solution to solve the problem.
- Check if the process is optimised/streamlined.
- Check for digital maturity of the business.
- Justify the use of the DAS model to digitise the operation.

- Digitise the operation (carry it out).
- Check whether performance improvement has been achieved by digitising the ops.
- What resources and project plan will be required to achieve this?
- What are the key milestones for revenue, profits, growth, and customers?

PROBLEM STATEMENT

a) Market gap
    Restaurants need new software solutions but are using old or outdated tools and services.
b) Customers
    Inflexibility, lack of simplicity, and efficient services for customers who are visiting hotels.
c) Financials
    High inventory and operational costs due to old and outdated methods/tools.
d) Quality
    Delayed orders
    Waiting time too long
    Manual processes prone to error
e) Usability
    Lack of digital technology in the whole process
    Lengthy times in between the process
    Lack of automation of the check-in process
    Used cutlery left unattended on trays after guests finished eating

CURRENT BUSINESS PROCESS

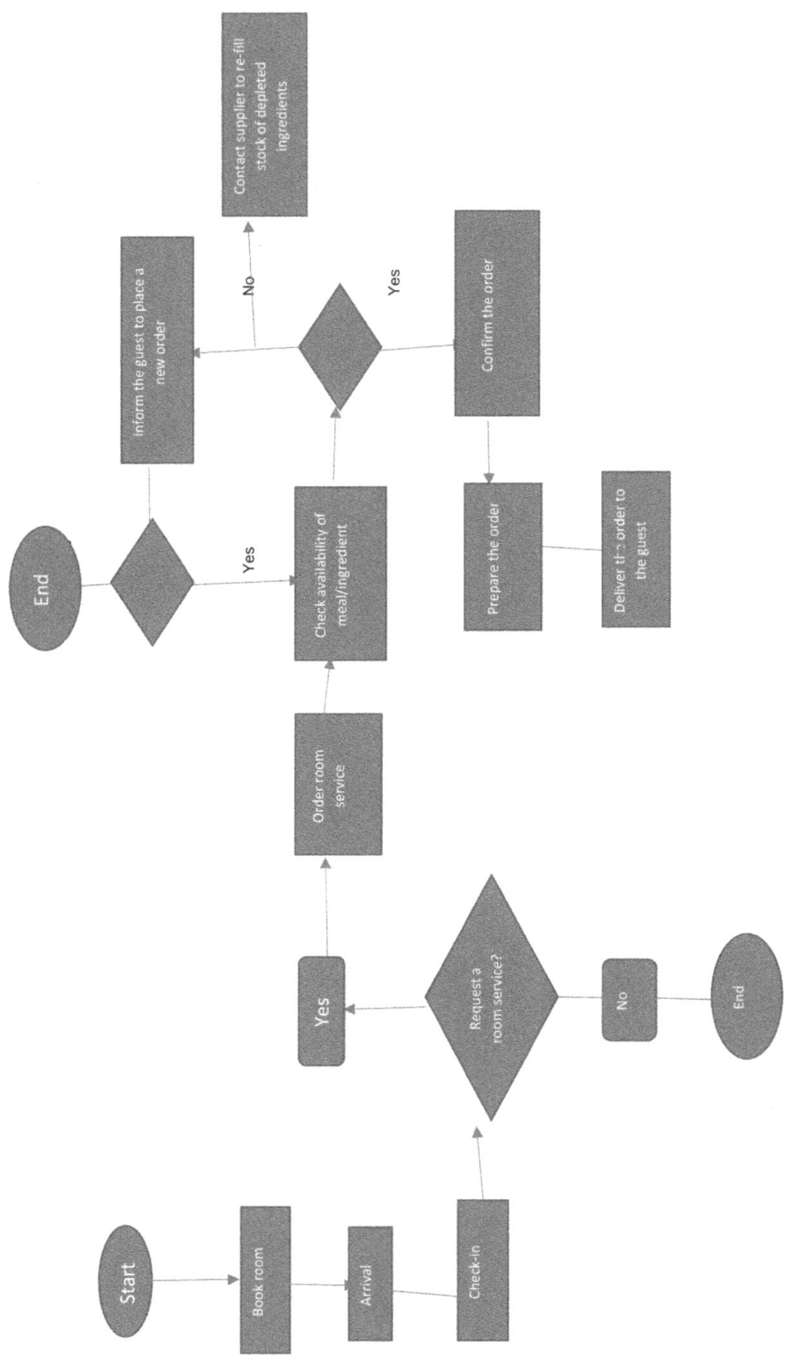

Total Cycle Time: 1H 56 Min

VALUE STREAM MAPPING (ANALYSIS)

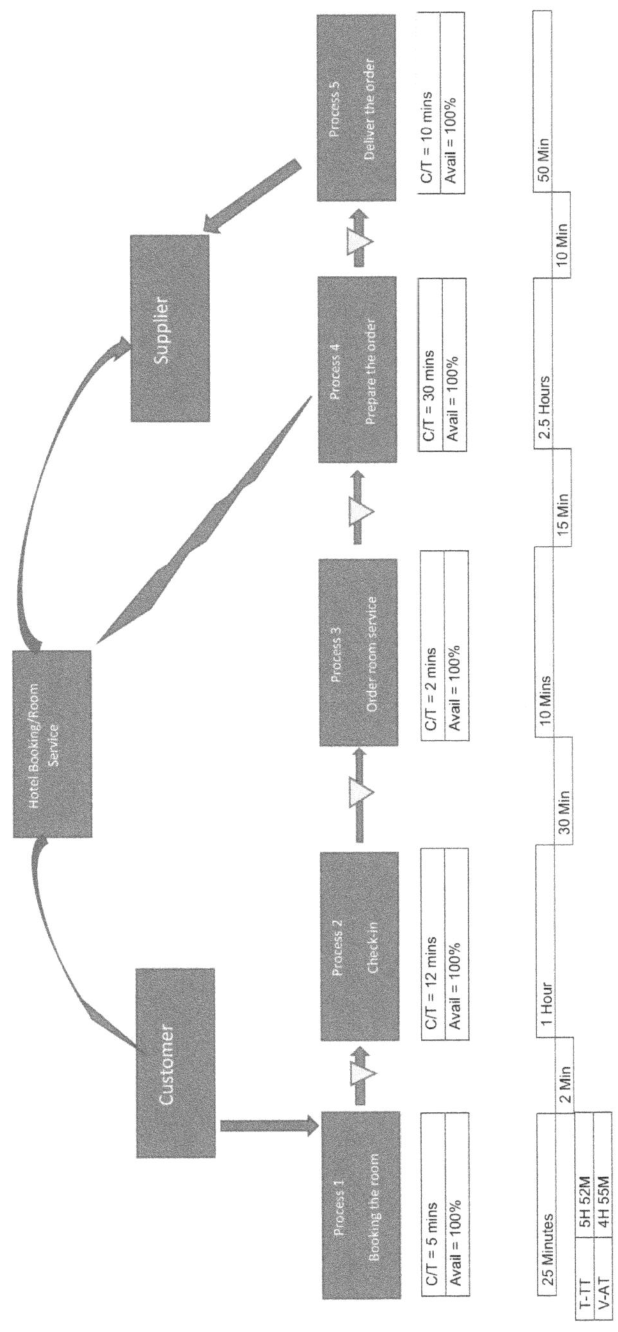

- *Calculations based on five customers at a time*
- *Total wait/wastage time is 57 minutes*

Table 18.1 Market Gaps, Proposed Solution and Benefits

Gaps:	Proposed solutions:	Benefits
• Lack of digital technology in the whole process • Shorten the times in between the processes • Automation of the check-in process • Used cutlery left unattended on trays after guests finished eating.	• Check-in using smartphone (IoT sensors at the doors) • Digitise room-service services using an app/smart device (Ordering food, miscellaneous services) • Digital menus of the restaurant within the vicinity. • Room service payments must be authorised by the main guest. • Sensors installed on the trays and will send a notification to the kitchen to be automatically removed.	• Reduce turnaround times. • Ensure that on first contact the quality is correct. • Measure speed and efficiency in check-in. • Reduce maintenance and utility costs. • Using Big Data from information captured on the mobile application performance could be measured and errors/shortcomings could be corrected/enhanced.

IS THE PROCESS OPTIMISED/STREAMLINED?

The digital level is at 0 as the processes are mostly analogue (eg, a guest needs to phone the reception and the order must be written down and taken to the kitchen to be completed). In autonomy and automation, it's at level 0 due to all the manual actions involved. For Smart, the process is at level 0 due to fact that there are no feedback controls in place for the environment. Hence this process is not streamlined or optimised.

THE DIGITAL MATURITY OF THE BUSINESS

The industry is currently in its earlier adaptors phase in terms of digitalisation. It is currently in level 0 of digital operations regarding the DAS framework. We are aiming for digital level 4, where it will be cloud-based, and the industry will be brought closer to the 4IR.

THE DAS MODEL TO DIGITISE THE OPERATION

To raise this aspect of the hospitality industry to allow for growth in the digital environment, incorporate automation of repeatable and manual tasks, and provide smart operations.

As the current state of the room service aspect is not digitised, the aim is to introduce a cloud-based app that will increase the user experience by allowing them to request services/meals via the app and make this process less manual and remove the admin tasks associated with ordering room service.

Automation will be in the form of RPA, to capture the orders from guests and relay it to the cooking staff to complete the order and then for the delivery staff to get it to the guest.

The Smart operations will be to collect data on guests, to check when and what specific guests order to build profiles that can then be used to market specific offerings (e.g., the specials hotels are offering) to guests.

To be able to implement these necessary improvements to reduce manual action, and waste and proactively perform stock taking, the use of the DAS model to assess the current state is necessary.

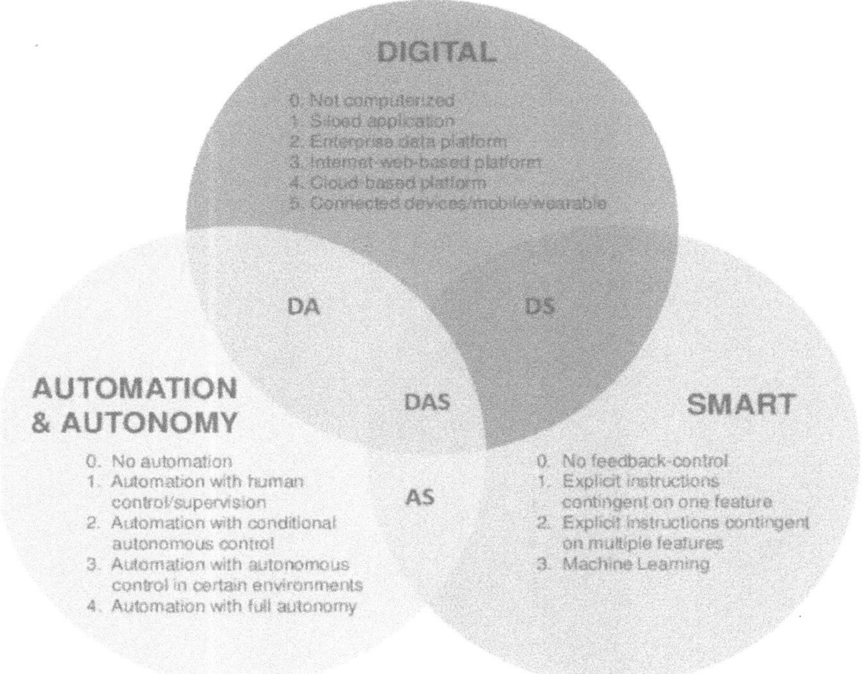

Current state	Future state
Digital = 0	Digital = 4
Automation/Autonomy = 0	Automation/Autonomy = 2
Smart = 0	Smart = 2

DIGITISE THE OPERATION (CARRY IT OUT)

The process has been streamlined through the digitisation of the other processes (i.e., digital booking of room service and a digital menu to select from and confirm the order), this will save a substantial amount of time for the customer and cut off paperwork for the hotel. This will help the hotel to work efficiently in delivering room service and avoid unanswered calls to the reception, which can lead to unhappy customers.

a)   The customer will book a hotel room, pay and confirm online.

b)   The customer will arrive at the hotel and check in; on check-in, the customer will receive a smart device with a digital key and a room service menu, plus digital menus of the restaurant within the vicinity (IoT sensors at the doors).

c)   The customer can then proceed to order room service (ordering food, miscellaneous services) whenever they want, and it will be done.

d)   The orders of room service payments must be authorised by the main guest and will be digitally received from the reception and carried out for the customer.

e)   Sensors installed on the trays will send a notification to the kitchen to be automatically removed.

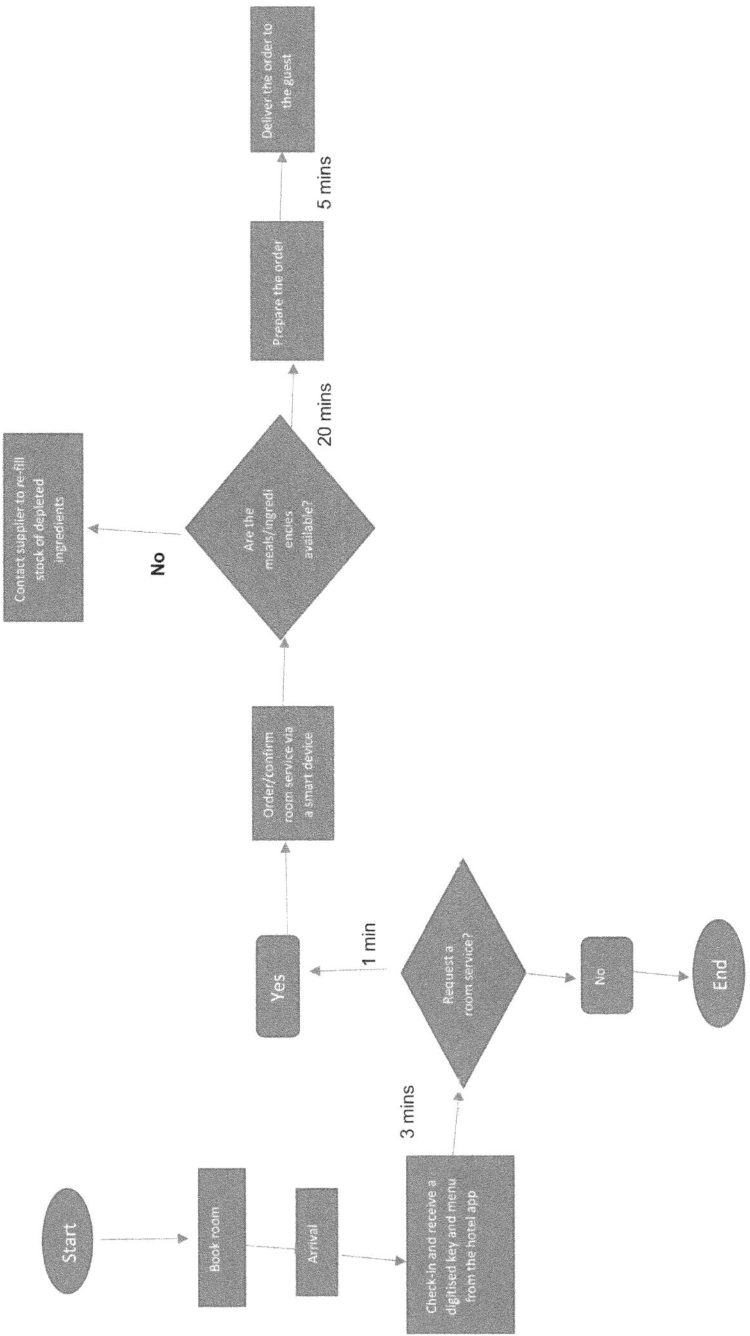

- *Calculations based on five customers at a time*
- *Total wait/wastage time is 4 hours, 45 minutes*
- *Total cycle time: 2 hours, 20 minutes*

PERFORMANCE IMPROVEMENT AFTER DIGITISING THE OPERATION

The performance has greatly improved through the streamlining of the processes by digitising parts of the process to efficiently and speedily deliver room service to the customers. Before the improvement, the process was cumbersome with a lot of activities to go through for the customer to get their order. Below is the list of the improvements made:

- Digitised keys with IoT sensors installed on doors to allow more secure rooms to put customers at ease without worrying about lost or misplaced keys.
- Digitised menu for room service with access to another restaurant within the vicinity to allow the customer to have a variety of food and encourage customers to come for more visits.
- Paperwork/printing of menus and bills will save the hotel costs of paper and printer resources time and allow a speedy response to customers' requests.
- The hotel reception responds to requests more speedily and leaves a happy customer who's more likely to come back and recommend the hotel to friends and family.
- The total time saved for the operation is one hour twenty-eight minutes per person, therefore the digitised operation was significantly optimised.

RESOURCES AND A PROJECT PLAN

Resources would include tangible, which look at the external appearance and facilities. Intangible is the way in which a customer/guest experiences and uses services and human, which anticipates and develops the present and future employee needs.

Tangible	Intangible	Human
Property (Hotel) Financial (Working capital) Capital from investors as well as the hotel's managing board Hotel facilities	'The potential for profit' trademarks, copyrights, patents Brand name – Like Sun International Hotel affiliations and associations Supplier & partner relationships Robust technology and skills Culture Customer relationships Data Concierge service Valet service Amenities and room service Valet service Amenities and room service	Skills – Chefs, porters, marketing and reception staff Innovative management Productivity Culture alignment Motivation & commitment

Critical Success Factors

Critical success factors are the areas in which a business must excel to survive in the marketplace. Critical success factors include/cover, however not limited to, what the customer wants, how the company survives competition and risks, and how one could use the resources to achieve, maintain and sustain operational excellence.

What do customers want?	How do firms survive competition	Key success factors
• Accessibility • Low room rates • Convenience • A home away from home • Simplicity • Personalised services • Brand appeal	• Keeping operation costs low • Keeping product pricing low • Product simplification • Quality delivery of products and services • To be successful hotels need to compete on an international level • Awareness of what other hospitality firms are doing internationally and what they are doing to attract new customers and loyalty	• Cost efficiency • Location • Global outlook • Quality management • Flexibility • Brand reputation
Actions from the CSFs	**Key metrics and targets**	**Risks**
• Market research to get regular feedback on products and services • Staff/Guest feedback on how to streamline and improve services and products	• Food delivery on time • Getting through the service centre the first time • 100% success rate on room service • Reduced waiting period on making orders • Percentage return on loyalty	• Regulation due to ownership of customer data and privacy

Project Plan on a page							
Task number	Task name	To be assigned to	Start Date	Complete Date	Duration	Dependencies	Status
1	Set kick-off meeting	S Brown	24/05/2022	24/05/2022	1 day		Not yet started
2	Agree on objectives	S Brown	25/05/2022	25/05/2022	1 day	Task 1	Not yet started
3	Detailed Requirements	P Ndlovu	26/05/2022	28/05/2022	3 days	Task 2	Not yet started
4	Hardware Requirements	R Green	01/06/2022	04/06/2022	4 days	Task 3	Not yet started
5	Final Resource Plan	S Brown	01/06/2022	04/06/2022	4 days	Task 3	Not yet started
6	Staffing for the project	S Brown	04/06/2022	18/06/2022	10 days	Task 4 & 5	Not yet started
7	Technical Requirements	R Green & P Yell	20/06/2022	22/06/2022	3 days	Task 6	Not yet started

Project Plan on a page							
8	Testing	R Green & P Ndlovu	23/06/2022	29/06/2022	5 days	Task 7	Not yet started
9	Additional Development (if any)	R Green & P Yell	30/06/2022	09/07/2022	8 days	Task 8	Not yet started
11	Pilot	P Ndlovu	30/06/2022	23/07/2022	17 days	Task 7	Not yet started
12	Pilot sign-off and implementation of the solution	P Ndlovu & S Brown	25/07/2022	TBA	TBA	Task 7	Not yet started

REFLECTION OF WHAT IS ACHIEVED/GAINED

In conclusion, this review is based on the hotels like City Lodge, Protea hotel, and Holiday Inn, to name a few but where 4IR technology is not adopted or is at an early adoption phase. The adoption of digitisation will improve the customer experience as well make these hotels front runners in the hospitality industry and increase variation.

The adoption of digitisation will improve the customer experience as well as allow the company to meet the five Operations Performance Objectives:

- Dependability – Digitised keys with IoT sensors installed on doors to allow more secure rooms to put customers at ease without worrying about lost or misplaced keys.
- Flexibility – Digitised menu for room service with access to another restaurant within the vicinity to allow the customer to have a variety of food and encourage customers to come for more visits.
- Quality – The hotel reception responds to requests more speedily and leaves a happy customer who's more likely to come back and recommend the hotel to friends and family.
- Costs – Reduction in printing and updating Room Service menus. There will also be a decrease in card printing and activations, thereby allowing the reception staff to focus on guest needs.
- Speed – No delays in waiting in queues at reception as the checking in will be digitalised.

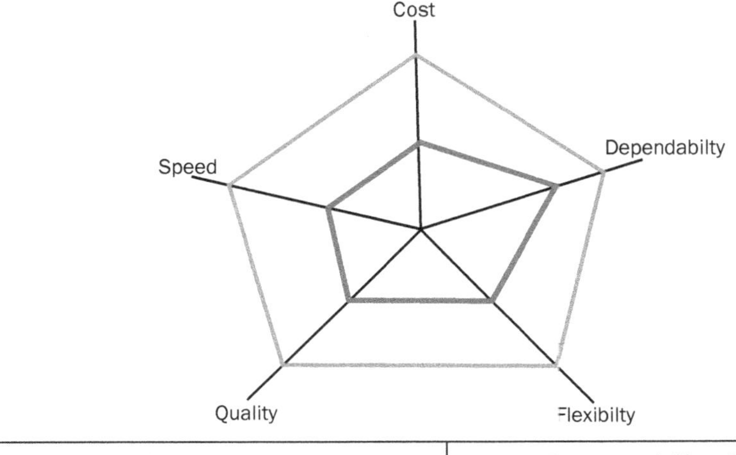

Current state −	Future state (with optimisation) −

ACKNOWLEDGEMENT OF CONTRIBUTORS

- Nicolette Shanand
- Beauty Nhleko
- Kumaran Pillay
- Progress Sethunya
- Tshepo Mazibuko
- Dineo Motlhamme

(All are affiliated to the Wits Business School, University of the Witwatersrand, Johannesburg).

REFERENCES

Cook, Y. (2019, August 28). What is the intangible product of the hospitality industry? – Richardvigilantebooks.com. Retrieved from https://richardvigilantebooks.com/what-is-the-intangible-product-of-hospitality-industry/

G. S. (2021, November 29). Hotel Digital Room Service System. Retrieved from https://www.linkedin.com/pulse/hotel-digital-room-service-system-govind-soni-/

Huebsch, R. (2016, October 26). Environmental Conditions in the Hospitality Industry. Retrieved from https://smallbusiness.chron.com/environmental-conditions-hospitality-industry-35257.html

Moqups App. (2022). Retrieved from https://app.moqups.com/4SqhEGIMwryApsaATsGfnVCRC5zjhSQ5/edit/page/aa9df7b72

O. (2022, March 26). Hotel Automation: Everything the Modern Hotelier Needs To Know. Retrieved from https://operto.com/hotel-automation/

ResearchGate. (2008). Find and share research. Retrieved 2022, from https://www.researchgate.net/

ResearchGate. (2008a). The DAS framework of Boute and Van Mieghem 2021. Retrieved 2022, from https://www.researchgate.net/figure/The-DAS-framework-of-Boute-and-Van-Mieghem-2021-evaluates-the-levels-and-reach-of-a_fig1_348378168

Revfine.com. (2022, February 19). Hotel Industry: Everything You Need to Know About Hotels!. Retrieved from https://www.revfine.com/hotel-industry/

Smartsheet. (2022). Work Collaboration Software & Solutions | Smartsheet. Retrieved from https://www.Smartsheet.Com/

Vora, S. (2018). The Right Way to Order Room Service at a Hotel. *The New York Times.* February 1. Retrieved from https://www.nytimes.com/2018/02/01/travel/room-service-tips.html

Digitalising the Food & Beverages Manufacturing Sector Education and Training Authority (FoodBevSETA) Grant Process

INTRODUCTION

The training authorities were established in South Africa to manage skills development requirements and needs of the economy. These government entities promote, facilitate and incentivise skills development by identifying skills gaps and fulfilling training requirements. There are twenty-one training authorities that cover linked sectors of economic activities, which are mandated to put the National Skills Development Plan (NSDP) into practice.

Each training authority identifies the skills needs of its sectors that include learnerships, apprenticeships, internships and diverse types of learning programmes. Training authorities then co-ordinate skills development and training to meet them in collaboration with companies and accredited training providers, moderators and assessors. ˙

Food & Beverages Manufacturing Sector Education and Training Authority (FoodBevSETA)

FoodBevSETA's function is to promote, facilitate and incentivise skills development in the food and beverage manufacturing sector. As indicated in Figure 19.1, FoodBevSETA is made up of three core business divisions:
i)   Research, Planning and Monitoring & Evaluation
ii)   Learning Programmes and Strategic Projects
iii) Education and Training Quality Assurance (ETQA).

Figure 19.1 FoodBevSETA High Level Functional Structure

PROBLEM STATEMENT

This chapter focuses on the Learning Programmes and Strategic Projects division of FoodBevSETA, concentrating on two of their key processes, Mandatory Grants (MG) and Discretionary Grants (DG), that form the core of operations. We will evaluate these business processes and their efficiency in light of FoodBevSETA's strategic objectives and where possible make recommendations to streamline these processes for improved efficiency and shorter lead times.

PROBLEM ANALYSIS

Gap Analysis

FoodBevSETA operations and process workflows were reviewed and interviews were conducted over teams with three different Senior Managers (SMs) from the core business divisions. Below are some of the gaps we observed in FoodBevSETA's operations and processes.

Challenge/Gaps	Impact on Operations	Consequence to FoodBevSETA
Inefficient processes	Most FoodBevSETA processes and operations are manual and prone to human error	Execution requires a lot of human resource investment.
		Critical activities end up being done more than once to correct errors (*costly and time-consuming*). • Regulatory compliance is compromised, e.g., Company registrations, Accreditations and Tax compliance checks are all done manually. • Training programmes proposed vs FoodBevSETA strategic targets needs to be verified manually in DG.

Challenge/Gaps	Impact on Operations	Consequence to FoodBevSETA
	Operations data is sitting in different non-integrated locations	This poses difficulties in reporting and there is a high risk of incorrect reporting.
	Fraud detection and prevention controls difficult to implement	High inefficiencies as it takes about 4 months for FoodBevSETA to process (evaluate, adjudicate and award) DG applications after the window closes.
Loss of important documents	FoodBevSETA gets physical documents via couriers	Sometimes training provider's contracts and learner documents get lost during physical handling (courier, handling at FoodBevSETA)
Ineffective controls for Learner validation	This poses a risk of impersonation	• No means of validating learner class attendance. • Learners can be enrolled in more than one training programme at a time without being detected. • Learners can enroll in more than one training programme to benefit from stipends. • Ghost learners: the deceased are used as active learners to benefit from stipends.

Process Map As-Is MGs

• MGs are allocated and paid to levy-paying employers who are registered in terms of the Skills Development Levies Act. The process map of issuing MGs is shown in Figure 19.2.

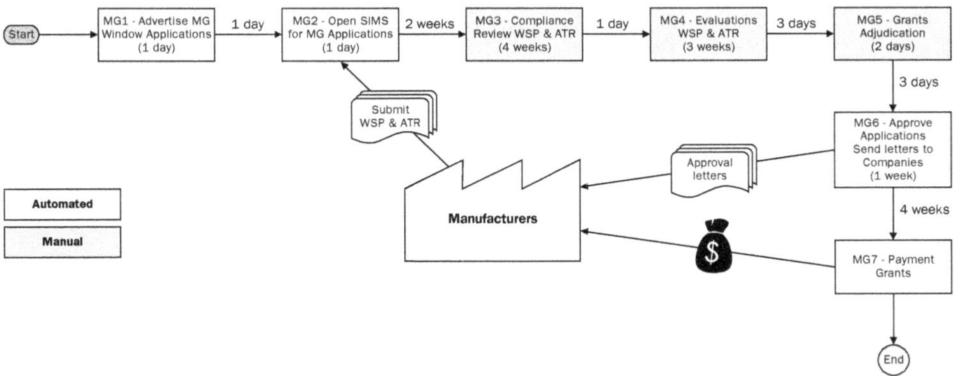

Figure 19.2 Process Map As-Is MGs

Process Map As-Is DGs

• DGs are allocated and paid to encourage any stakeholder to contribute towards skills development. The process map of issuing DGs is shown in Figure 19.3.

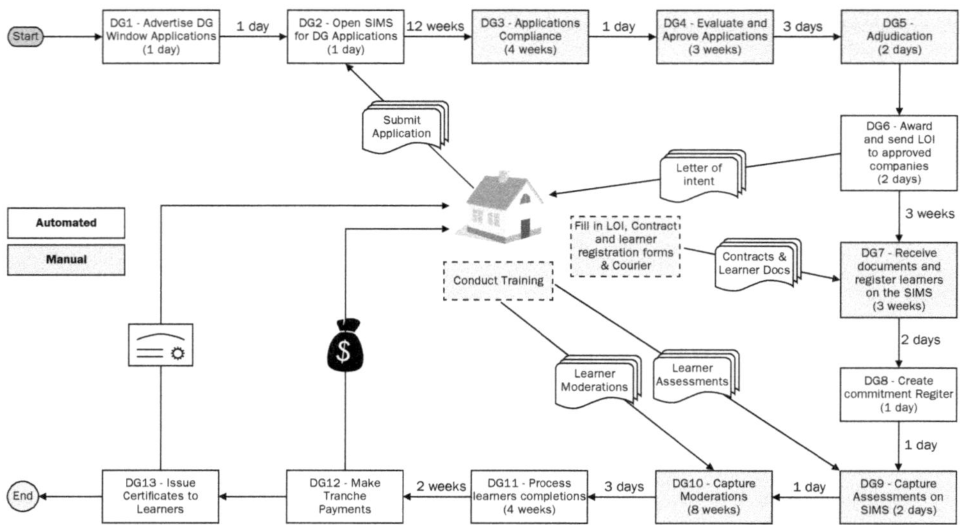

Figure 19.3 Process Map As-Is DGs

Value Stream Mapping Analysis MGs

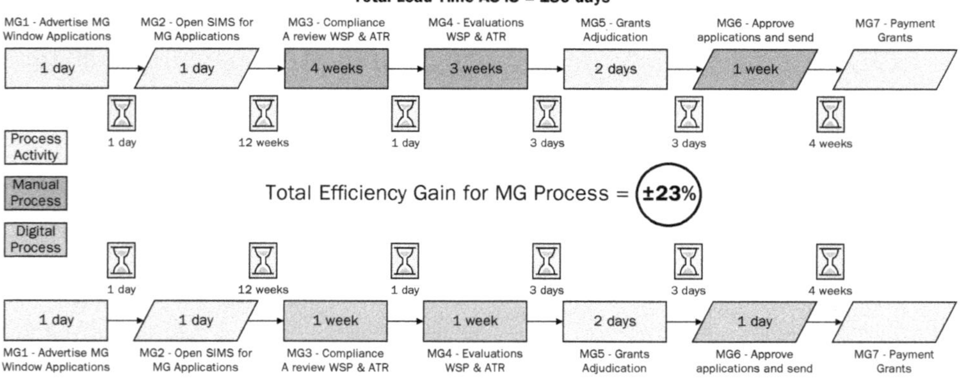

Figure 19.4 Value Stream Mapping Analysis MGs

Value Stream Mapping Analysis DGs

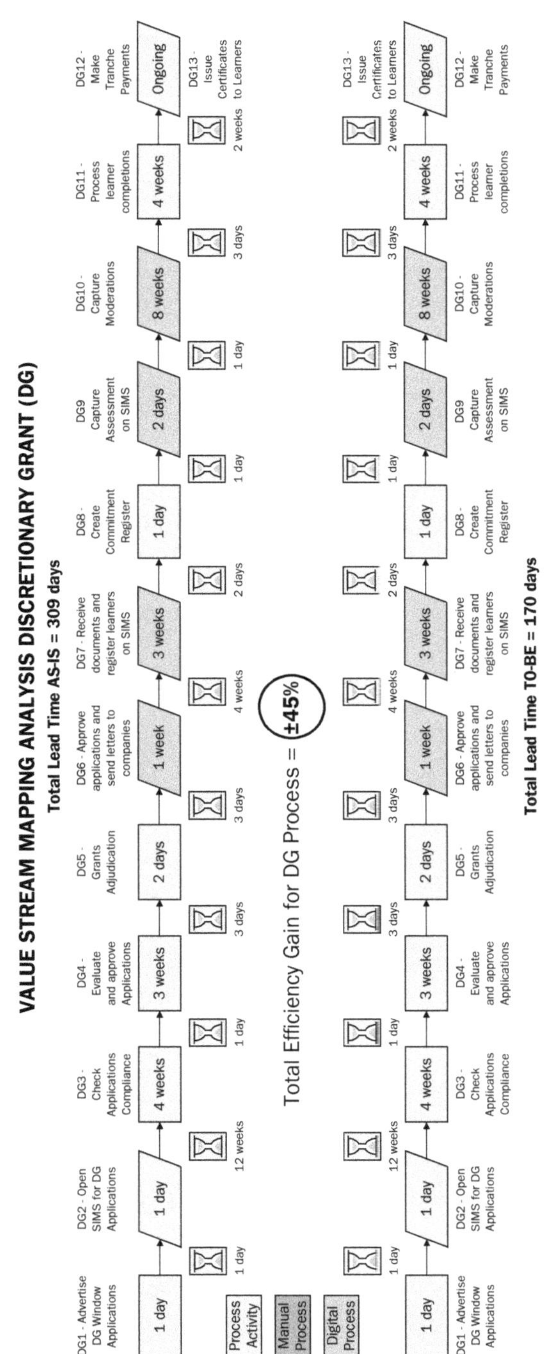

Figure 19.5 Value Stream Mapping Analysis DGs

With reference to Figures 19.4 and 19.5, we used our proposed recommendations to play out how the processes of MGs and DGs could look if our recommendations were realised.

For MGs (Figure 19.4), all three of the manual processes could potentially be automated, and this yields a very healthy 23% improvement in the lead time of the process.

For DGs (Figure 19.5), six processes could potentially be automated, and this yields an impressive 45% improvement in the lead time of the process.

FoodBevSETAs efficiency (especially for DGs) echoes into the food and beverage sector. By meeting or exceeding their targets of bringing more skilled and competent people to the sector quicker, with more efficient approval of training applications from training providers, the industry can address the consistently high demand for food and beverages, which has become much more pronounced with the advent of the Covid-19 pandemic.

Assessment of FoodBevSETA against the Six Operational Excellence Principles

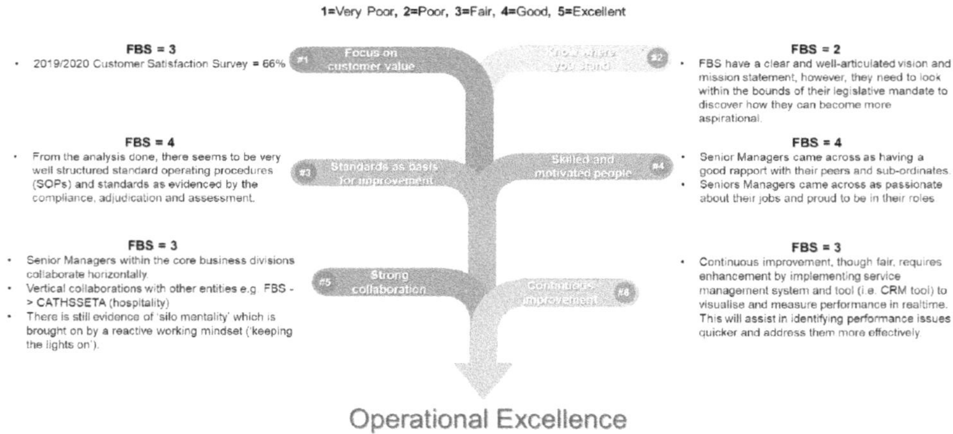

Figure 19.6 FoodBevSETA Operational Excellence Principles

FoodBevSETA Operations Performance Objectives As-Is

The evaluation of the operations performance objectives for FoodBevSETA follows and the pivot diagram is shown in Figure 19.7. The rating is done with the 5-point Lippert scale given below.

> 1=Very Poor, 2=Poor, 3=Fair, 4=Good, 5=Excellent
>
> **Quality (1/5):** Manual processes make it difficult to eliminate mistakes.
>
> **Speed (2/5):** Manual processes and non-integrated systems make efficiency and speed difficult.
>
> **Dependability (4/5):** In conjunction with flexibility, dependability should be high if FoodBevSETA are as rigid about delivery.
>
> **Flexibility (2/5):** Period for applications for MGs and DGs are prescribed and regulated and cannot be changed. Policies not flexible as they are guided by statutory requirements.
>
> **Cost (1/5):** FoodBevSETA is not executing its operations cheaply because of inefficient processes e.g. re-doing work more than once due to errors

Figure 19.7 FoodBevSETA Performance Objectives

Digital Maturity of FoodBevSETA

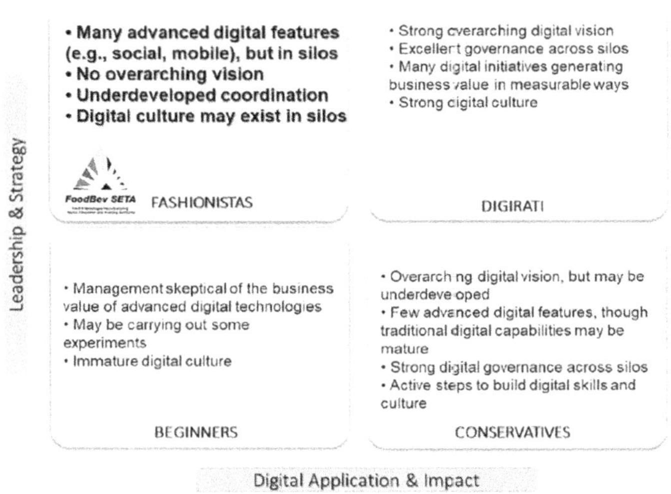

Figure 19.8 FoodBevSETA Digital Maturity

We rated FoodBevSETA in the category of 'Fashionistas' in terms of digital maturity. The reasoning behind our rating is as follows:

- Based on the interviews that we carried out with the three SMs from the three core divisions of FoodBevSETA (Figure 19.1), we found that they are extremely keen on using digitalisation and automation to improve their operational efficiency.
- FoodBevSETA have begun automating some of their processes (see Figures 19.2 and 19.3), however it does not seem that there is well a plan/roadmap that is co-ordinated and prioritised and executed in a structured way.
- FoodBevSETA's vision statement is very clear: 'To have sufficient and appropriate knowledge and skills available in the Food and Beverages Manufacturing Sector.' However, our view was that it does not talk to the future.
- The insert in Figure 19.9 is from the FoodBevSETA website, and gives an indication that FoodBevSETA is committed to digital (4IR) for itself and for its stakeholders.

Figure 19.9 FoodBevSETA Website Insert

Source: http://www.foodbev.co.za/

THE DAS FRAMEWORK

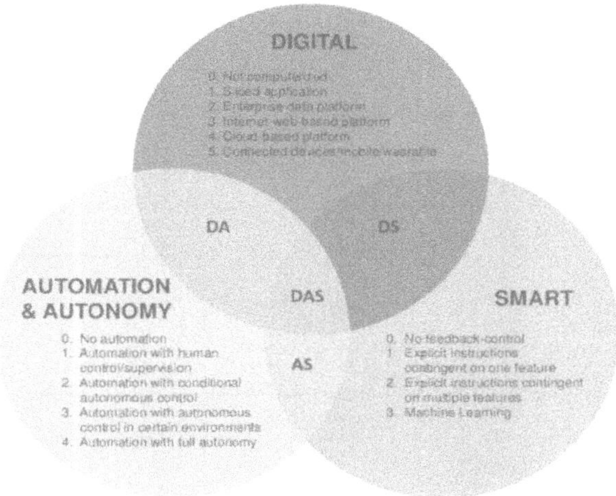

Figure 19.10 DAS Model

Source: Boute and Van Mieghem (2021)

From the three dimensions of Digitisation, Automation and Smart execution (DAS) model in Figure 19.9, the FoodBevSETA process and their associated tasks have been tallied appropriately, more especially looking at the As–Is scenario. Processes that are currently manual require to be digitalised and those processes that are digitalised require to be taken a step further to Automation and Autonomy. Either being Digital or Automated, appropriate levels have been allocated to process tasks.

Process MG

Process Task	Digital, Automated and Autonomous, Smart (DAS) Choices
MG1 – Advertise MG Window Applications	A1
MG2 – Open SIMS for MG Applications	A2
MG3 – Compliance Review WSP & ATR	D2
MG4 – Evaluations WSP & ATR	D2
MG5 – Grants Adjudication	D2
MG6 – Approve applications	A2
MG7 – Send approval letters	A1
MG8 – Payments Grants	A1

Process DG

Process Task	Digital, Automated and Autonomous, Smart (DAS) Choices
DG1 – Advertise DG Window Applications	A1
DG2 – Open SIMS for DG Applications	A2
DG3 – Check Applications Compliance	D2
DG4 – Evaluate and Approve Applications	D2
DG5 – Grants Adjudication	D2
DG6 – Award and Send LOI to approved companies	A1
DG7 – Receive documents and register learners on the SIMS	D3
DG8 – Create Commitment Register	A4
DG9 – Capture Assessments on SIMS	D2
DG10 – Capture Moderations	D2
DG11 – Process learner completions	A1
DG12 – Make Tranche Payments	A1
DG13 – Issue Certificates to Learners	A1

PROPOSED RECOMMENDATIONS/IMPLEMENTATION PLAN

Proposed Recommendations

1. **Improve Training Provider Application Compliance Checking**
   - If direct interfaces are created into SARS and Home Affairs respectively, then tax compliance status of a training provider can be verified instantaneously, as well as ID verification of learners. This would save a lot of manual work and human errors.

2. **Improve Training Provider Application Evaluation**
   - The 'digital system' should be able to screen skills training programme applications against FoodBevSETA's strategic programmes and shortlist those that are relevant and reject those that are not e.g. requiring 100 artisans as chefs and not as food technologists. This will have a significant reduction in manual processing.

3. **Improve Training Provider Application Approvals**
   - On the system, award letter is automatically generated and sent to company (MG & DG).
   - System automatically sends a contract to the training provider for sign-off (DG).

4. Improvement Learner Registration

- DG: contract-linked training plan, learners must be registered directly on the FoodBevSETA system. The training provider can be coaxed to do this quickly, as it is in their best interests.

Implementation Plan Deliverables	Task/s	Resources Required	Time Frame / Assumptions
Improve Application Compliance Checking	Initiate project to create interfaces to SARS and Home Affairs	EXCO Senior Management IT Project Management	±3 months
Improve Application Evaluation	Initiate project to put into place 'digital system' with screening functionality (possibly via RfP process)	Senior Management IT Project Management Supply Chain Management	±6 months Management commitment and CAPEX budget approval
Improve Application Approvals	Additional requirements for customisation once 'digital system' is ready.	Senior Management IT Finance for Business case	±2 months after 'digital system' is ready. Any additional funding required is made available.
Improve Learner Registrations	Additional requirements for customisation once 'digital system' is ready.	Senior Management IT Finance for Business case	±2 months after 'digital system' is ready. Any additional funding required is made available.

SUMMARY AND CONCLUSION

FoodBevSETA faces three main challenges, ie inefficient processes, ineffective learner validation controls and unreliable document management process. These have negatively affected FoodBevSETA efficiency and effectiveness as key processes are manual and prone to human error and tend to lead into fraud and learner impersonation that costs the organisation.

FoodBevSETA is not fully digitally mature, although there is huge potential to make key operations more mature. This exercise discovered that ten Discretion Grant and three Mandatory Grant process steps are manual and need to be automated to improve efficiency. We recommend that all the identified manual processes be automated. For Mandatory Grants this will reduce total inefficiencies from 180 days to 139 days, (23% improvement), and for Discretionary Grants from 309 days to 170 days (45% improvement).

The next step is that FoodBevSETA put together a cross-functional project team that will implement the proposed operations improvements that deliver automation of Grant Application Compliance, Grant Application Evaluation, Grant Application Approvals and Learner Registrations processes. The chances of being a successful are extremely high as the FoodBevSETA management and teams are keen to improve their operational efficiencies.

ACRONYM LIST

BCCS: Baking, Cereals, Confectionery & Snacks
DAS: Digital, Automated and Autonomous, Smart
DG: Discretionary Grant
DHET: Department of Higher Education and Training
ETQAs: Education and Training Quality Assurance bodies
FoodBevSETA: Food & Beverages Manufacturing Sector Education and Training Authority
MG: Mandatory Grant
NSDS: National Skills Development Strategy
QCTO: Quality Council for Trades and Occupations
SETA: Sectoral Education and Training Authority
SM: Senior Managers
SOPs: Standard Operating Procedures
TVET: Technical and Vocational Education and Training

ACKNOWLEDGEMENT OF CONTRIBUTORS

- Tendani Mudau
- Godfrey Chisanga
- Siyabonga Dyosiba
- Thabo Serame
- Donald Dandawa
- Uvarajan Naidoo

(All are affiliated to the Wits Business School, University of the Witwatersrand, Johannesburg).

REFERENCES

Boute, R., Gijsbrechts, J., Van Mieghem, J. (2020). Digital Lean Operations: Smart Automation and Artificial Intelligence in Financial Services. *SSRN Electronic Journal*. 10.2139/ssrn.3747173.

https://www.dhet.gov.za/SitePages/SkillsDevelopmentNew.aspx#

http://www.foodbev.co.za/

http://www.foodbev.co.za/storage/app/media/Annual%20Performance%20Plan%202020_21.pdf

http://www.foodbev.co.za/about-us/mission-and-vision

https://www.scaledagileframework.com/operational-value-streams/

https://nationalgovernment.co.za/units/view/228/food-and-beverage-manufacturing-industry-sector-education-and-training-authority-foodbev-seta

https://www.semanticscholar.org/paper/73792ad4a5df07ccb48b42599bef1383712f6671

Six principles for operational excellence: https://www.gwynt.eu/en/6-principles-for-operational-excellence/

Slack, N., Brandon-Jones, A., Johnston, R., Singh, H., Phihlela, K. (2017). Chapter 4: Process design. In *Operations management: Global and Southern African perspectives*, 3rd edn. Cape Town: Pearson South Africa.

CHAPTER 20

Digitalising Administration in a Leading Business School

BACKGROUND

BS is the graduate school of a leading university, according to the Global Universities in Africa report (US News, 2022). According to the 2020 review, the school's vision is to be recognised as one of the best business schools in Africa chosen by employees, society, students, government and businesses. BS offers tailor-made programmes, seminars, and different postgraduate programmes and aims to produce future leaders of Africa (BS Year in Review, 2020). This study looked at BS administration's digital maturity by assessing students' journey life cycle, from application processes, admissions, registration, academic programme and until the students graduate.

INTRODUCTION TO INNOVATION IN THE STUDENT LIFE CYCLE

Learning has changed the growth of technology. Technology has forced universities to use innovative ways when they interact with students from the application process until they graduate (Vita et al, 2020). Even though innovation is not new, in recent years it is happening at a faster rate and it is forcing higher education institutions like BS to keep abreast with the market and equip themselves with digital skills, innovative systems and improved processes (Paap & Katz, 2004).

Many institutions have ignored the impact innovation can bring in the student life cycle; rather they are still trapped in the traditional ways of doing things. This report unpacks the current state of BS admission processes, identifies gaps in the current process and comes up with the proposed solution by optimising the current processes and operations.

PROCESS MAP

Current/As-Is Process

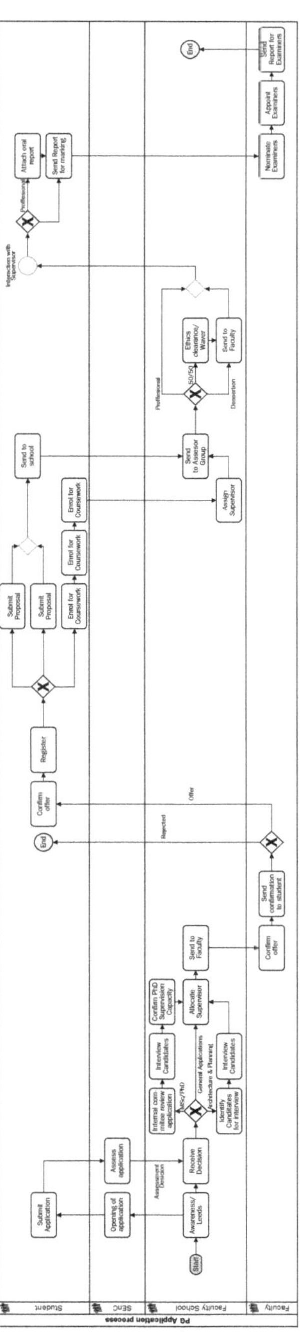

Figure 20.1 BS AS-Is Process

319

The process shown in Figure 20.1 is triggered when the Faculty promote the opening of their programmes and this is normally done through posters and publishing the information on the website. The Student Enrollment Centre (SEnC) will activate the opening of online application forms for student to begin their applications. Using the online platform, students will complete and submit their applications.

SEnC will assess the submitted application based on the rules, and then forward it to BS for decision-making. Depending on the admission level the applicant is applying for, BS will either interview the applicant, or allocate the supervisor provided the school has supervision capacity. If the school does not have supervision capacity, they will then allocate the supervisor at a later stage. The school will then forward their decision to the Faculty.

The Faculty will confirm the decision made by the school and inform the applicant (offer/reject).

If an applicant receives an offer, they will be informed of the registration process. Upon registering, the student will have to submit the research proposal and send it to the school for processes such as research topic submission and approval, allocation of a supervisor, and ethics clearance/waiver.

If the student passes all the processes, the next step will be to interact with the supervisor to complete the research report. Once the research report is complete, it will be sent to the Faculty for marking and examination.

The process will end when the student receives the final marked research report.

VALUE STREAM AND GAP ANALYSIS OF BS

The current BS student application, admission and registration process takes approximately eight months for a student to be successfully registered and two months to be allocated to a supervisor after registration. It takes an additional two months for students to receives the exam results for each registered module.

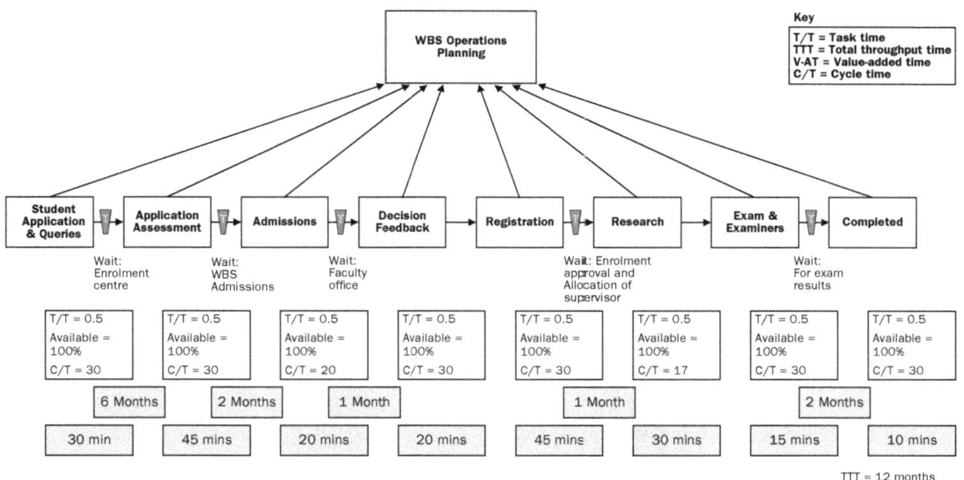

Figure 20.2 Value Stream Mapping

While analysing the process, using the Lean method depicted in Figure 20.2, repetitive steps, barriers and actions that are not bringing value to the student administration were identified and shows that only 10% of the activities are value-add whilst 90% of those activities are non–value-add as shown in Figure 20.3.

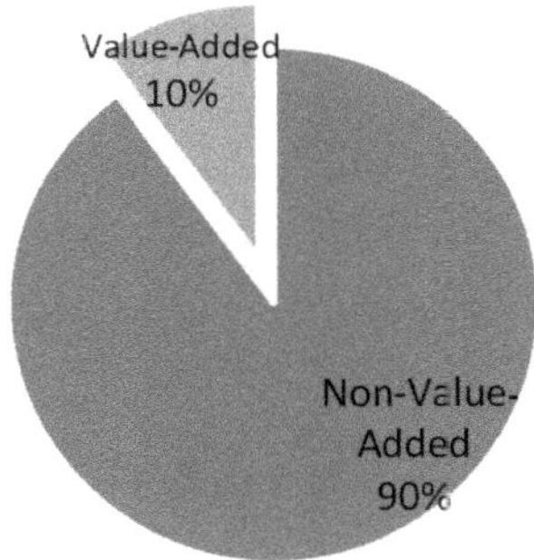

Figure 20.3 Value-Added vs Non-Value-Added Activities

Using the Digitised, Automated and Smart (DAS) model (Boute & van Mieghem, 2021) shows that some activities can be optimised to improve the student journey.

To eliminate delays and improve student experiences, BS should consider investing in technology such as robotic process automation (RPA), which is a software technology that makes it easy to build, deploy, and manage robotics (UIPath, 2022) and Artificial Intelligence (AI), which is a computer algorithm that simulates learning (Armstrong & Lee, 2021). Automation of the application assessment, admissions and registration stages will halve the total throughput time to less than four months.

Reliable data, security and data quality are a prerequisite for digital, automation and smart operations (Boute & van Mieghem, 2021). Implementation of a cloud-based data warehouse platform will centralise student information.

BS may also consider investing in internal digital skills development and capabilities to prepare the organisation for a data-driven culture and ensure that there is leadership support for the implementation of the new technology direction.

BS 5 PERFORMANCE OBJECTIVES

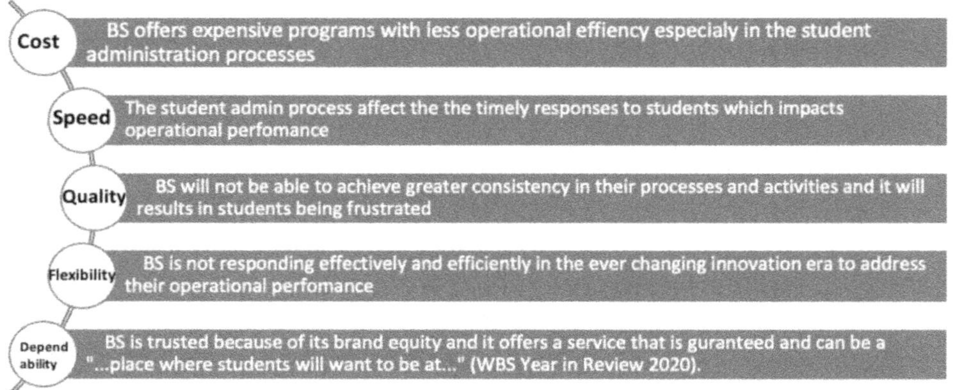

Figure 20.4 5 Performance Objectives

- **Cost** – BS has a lot of student enrolments and their programmes cost above average compared to other institutions. However, their operational efficiency is lacking – especially the student administration process.
- **Speed** – the response to applications and admin queries is inefficient. There are a lot of bottlenecks in the admin process, which cause unnecessary delays. This results in students being allocated to incorrect modules, blocks, and delivery module methods, ie, FT (Full Time), PT (Part Time) and online.
- **Quality** – given the inefficiencies in a speedy response to student queries, this has negatively impacted the operational performance of BS despite its good academic reputation.
- **Flexibility** – the current BS operation process is not flexible. The admin process is a rigid 'tick-box' procedure that does not accommodate anomalies

in student circumstances, thereby failing to meet individual student needs. In an era of hyper-personalisation that is enabled by digital technologies, BS fare incredibly low on flexibility.

- **Dependability** – historically, BS has held high brand equity with programmes, processes and academic staff that are closely equivalent to Ivy League institutions (Study portals, 2022). However, over the past couple of years, this brand equity is being eroded by operational inadequacies, albeit being able to retain academic excellence to some extent.

BS OPERATIONS VS UCT GBS AND GIBS

The 4Vs methodology in Figure 20.5 depicts BS in comparison to peer institutions such as UCT GBS and GIBS.

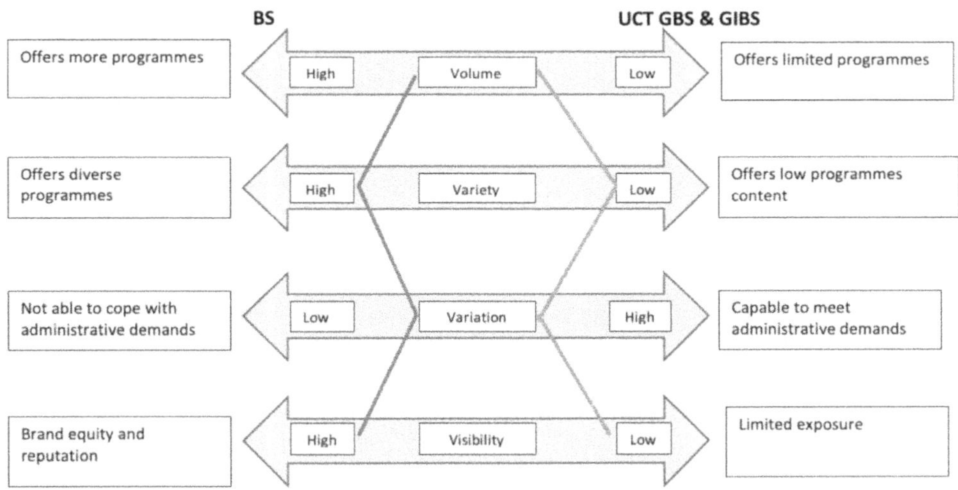

Figure 20.5 4Vs

- **Volume** – BS offers a wide bouquet of academic programmes in comparison to its peers. This means the number of student enrolments is higher for BS. Inadvertently, this compromises the student admin process as it gets overwhelmed by the number of students. There does not seem to be a rigorous cap on student enrolment per programme intake thus overloading the enrolment process and compromising the quality of service offered.
- **Variety** – BS offers a wide variety of short courses, post-graduate, Executive and Leadership programmes. It is ahead of its peers by offering revolutionary programmes such as Digital Business for NQF (National Qualification Framework) levels 8, 9 and 10, which is tailor-made for the 4IR.

- **Variation** – BS is not capable of coping and meeting students' administrative demands due to the number of student intake. This results in BS not being able to accommodate the norm students' administrative requests.
- **Visibility** – BS is highly ranked compared to its peers. According to a ranking and survey done by Global Employability, directors and recruiters consider BS graduates to be the most employable in South Africa because they are taught by academics that are experts in their fields (Faro, 2021).

The polar diagram in Figure 20.6 below is used to measure the operational performance of BS, UCT GBS and GIBS in the student administration processes.

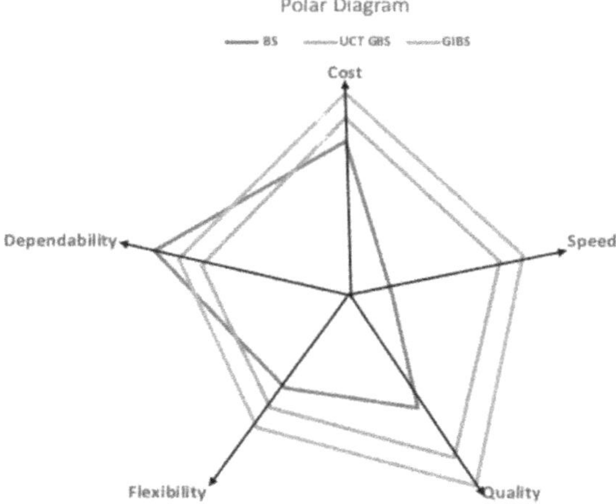

Figure 20.6 Polar Diagram

UCT and GIBS perform well in the areas of speed, quality and flexibility and we see an increase in their operational costs.

Looking at dependability, we see BS having the upper edge, the reason being their trusted brand.

DAS MODEL

DAS framework is used to assess the current state of BS online operations and the entire value chain in terms of activities and interactions with students, using the three dimensions of digital, automation and smart. DAS will also help BS to determine where they want to be in the future.

Institutions are established to provide teaching and learning to satisfy the needs of students they serve. In the twenty-first century, universities are facing a great many challenges from the changing needs of the students, volatile operating environment, fierce competition, and even substitute of their services (OECD, 2015). Boute & Mieghem (2021) argue that by digitising operations, organisations may replace manual work with enhanced automation and smart control algorithms to determine how work must be executed intelligently to improve efficiency, productivity, and customer experience. By augmenting human work with digitising, BS can improve the quality, speed, variety, variation, and visibility of its operational services. Using the DAS model, BS can identify or map functions that can be performed using other technology enablers like AI and RPA. Figure 20.7 below depicts the functions that can be optimised using the above-mentioned technologies and assist with BS digital maturity.

Digital

Education Market	Awareness and Students Applications	Application review/pre-selection	Student admission	Course delivery & Library Access	Assignment & Exam	Graduation & Alumni
0. Not computerised		X		X		X
1. Siloed applications				X		
2. Enterprise data platforms						
3. Internet-web based	X				X	X
4. Cloud-based		X		X		
5. Connected devices						

Automation & Autonomy

Education Market	Awareness and Students Applications	Application review/pre-selection	Student admission	Course delivery & Library Access	Assignment & Exam	Graduation & Alumni
0. Not automation	X	X	X	X	X	
1. Automation with human supervision						X
2. Automation with conditional autonomous control						
autonomous control in certain environment						
4. Automation with full autonomy						

Smart

Education Market	Awareness and Students Applications	Application review/pre-selection	Student admission	Course delivery & Library Access	Assignment & Exam	Graduation & Alumni
0. No feedback control	X	X	X	X	X	X
1. Explicit instructions contingent on one feature						
2. Explicit instructions contingent on multiple feature						
3. Machine learning						

Figure 20.7 DAS Model

According to McKinsey (2021), maturity of the available digital technology, data integration, and organisational setup determines the level of personalisation that an organisation can provide as a starting point. The BS application process is partially matured because some of the processes, such as the selection of students based on meeting the admission criteria, is still done manually through selection committees.

Secondly, the graduation proceeding is still mainly done physically, although the option of online graduation was made possible during the Covid pandemic.

The selection and admission of students can be automated with the use of

RPA technology that is supervised for final decision. The RPA can then provide feedback and communication updates to respective students about the outcome of their applications.

There is ongoing concern about handling of queries and turnaround time to provide updates. BS needs to invest more on Chatbots to automate the enquiry process to speed up responses and improve customer experience. From the above-mentioned analysis, BS is at level 3 when measured on the maturity scale, and they need to strive for continuous improvement on their digital processes.

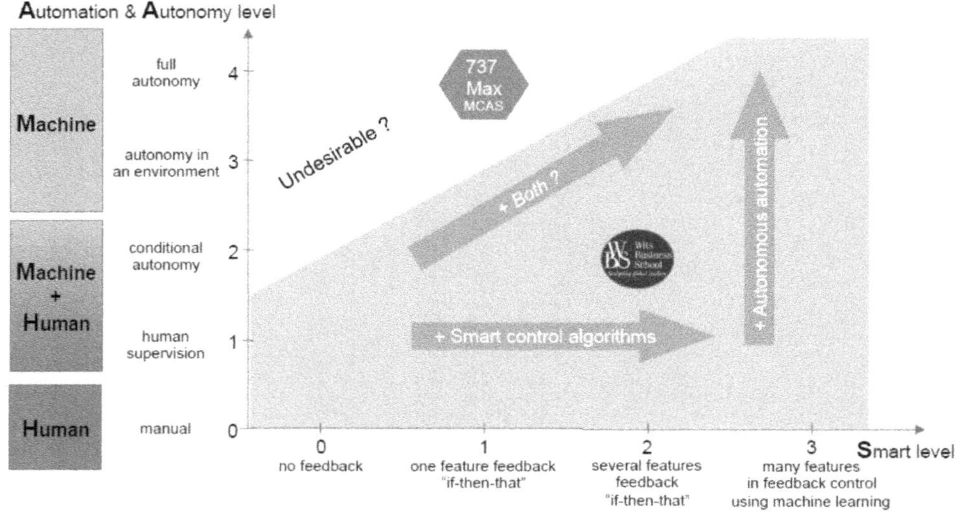

Figure 20.8 Automation and Autonomy Level. Source: Boute & Van Mieghen

FUTURE OF BS OPERATIONS

According to Deloitte 2019, smart operations rely on a diverse stack of technology capabilities that must have the layers of channels, analytics and automation, data platforms, integration, enterprise applications infrastructure, security and risk.

The interaction with students from application to graduation requires efficient operations to render a superior student experience. This can be achieved through optimising operations by deploying automation, autonomous and intelligent technology in their operating and value chain process.

The deployment of autonomy automation on level 2 of the vertical axis is recommended where RPA can process inputs such as enrolment requirements for entry to certain programmes.

Should the RPA not be able to process the information, it must alert and request human intervention. BS is recommended to deploy smart technology such as AI with several features at level 2 on the horizontal axis to make decisions and provide feedback. Smart level 2 must be able to determine and select the best students and identify organisations that are interested in enrolling their staff.

To achieve this, Table 20.1 outlines the areas and techniques that BS needs to adopt.

Table 20.1 BS Areas of Improvement

EPIC	Functional Areas	Proposed technology solution
Queries	Queries	Leads to direct/Google Analytics, Chatbot, AI
Application Process	Application process	Cloud, RPA, AI, Chatbot
	Application assessment	RPA, AI
	Decision feedback	RPA, AI
	Admission	RPA, AI
	Registration	Cloud
Research Journey	Enrolment and allocation of supervisor	RPA, AI
	Research Proposal Approval	AI
	Assignments/Exams	AI
	Research journey and interaction with supervisor	RPA, AI
Internal/External Stakeholders	Allocation of examiner	RPA, AI

IMPLEMENTATION PLAN

Ismail & Manso (2018) contend that agile methodology employs processes and procedures that seek to improve project delivery, reduce cost and increase speed system development. Using agile project delivery methodology, BS can launch a programme that will consist of four projects. These will be:
- Queries
- Application Process
- Research journey
- Internal/External stakeholder

With the agile methodology, these projects can be executed sequentially and broken down into smaller components which will enable a quick to market.

Agile methodology involves continuous collaboration and engagement with project stakeholders. This method is currently the most preferred method of delivering IT (Information Technology) projects due to its flexibility and ease of change to customer requirements.

Figure 20.9 outlines the execution roadmap that BS can follow to achieve the set objectives which will improve the student journey experience with the business school.

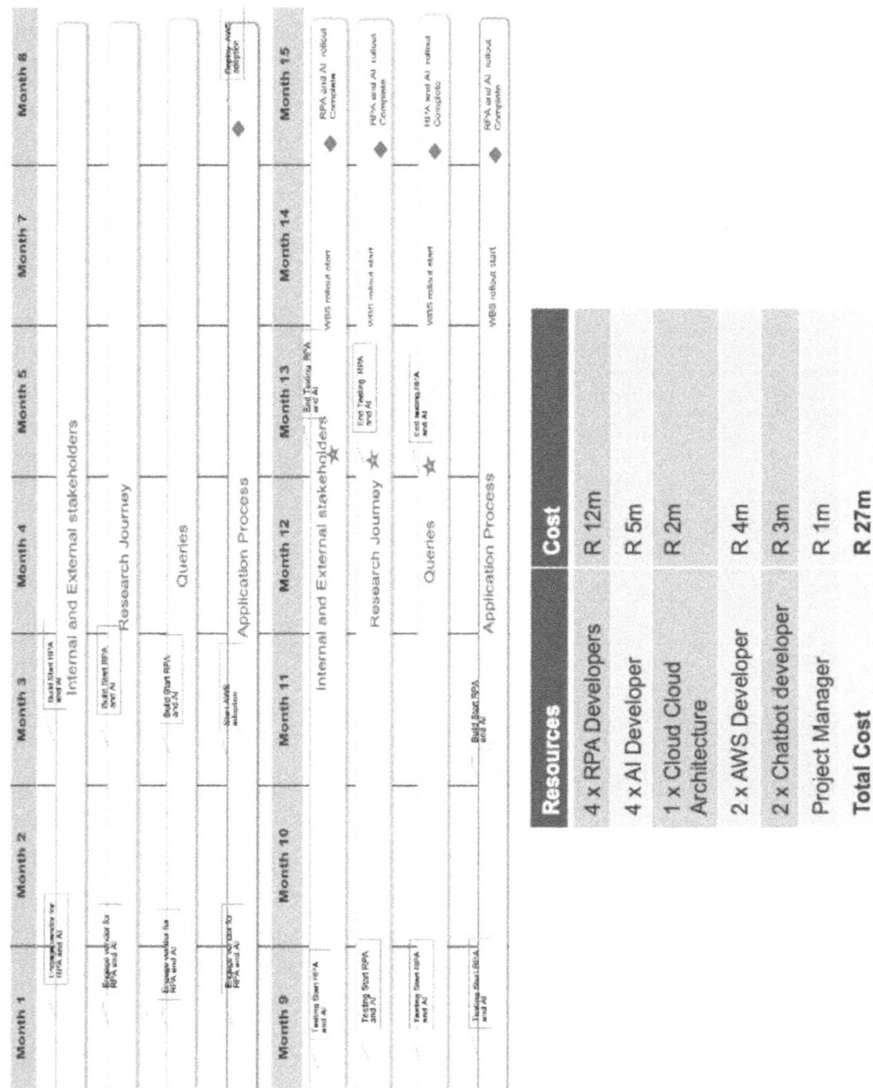

Figure 20.9 Implementation and Resource Plan

SO WHAT?

The primary objective of optimising the operations with digital technologies is to improve student journey experience and become no 1 on the university ranking index in Africa.

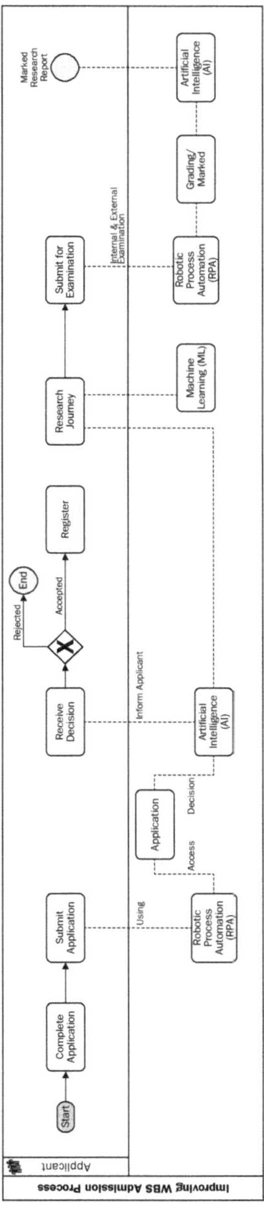

Figure 20.10 New Optimised Process Model Reduction of Cost; Operational Excellency and Operational Flexibility

329

EPIC	Process	Current Throughput Time	Current Value Added Time	Proposed Technology solution	Optimised Throughput Time	Optimised Value Added Time
Application Process	Application submission	-	30 minutes	Cloud, RPA, AI, Chatbot	-	30 minutes
	Queries & Application Assessment	6 months	45 minutes	RPA, AI	30 days	10 minutes
	Admissions	2 months	20 minutes	RPA, AI	5 days	10 minutes
	Decision feedback	1 month	20 minutes	RPA, AI	3 days	10 minutes
	Registration	-	45 minutes	Cloud	-	10 minutes
Research Journey	Enrolment and allocation of supervisor	1 month	30 minutes	RPA, AI	5 days	20 minutes
	Assignments/Exam & Examiners	2 months	15 minutes	AI	10 days	5 minutes
Total		TTT= 12 months	V-AT = 3 hrs 35 mins	-	TTT= 2 months	V-AT = 1 hr 40 mins

Figure 20.11 New Optimised Throughput and Value-Added Times

The above table depicts the total throughput time for the proposed system. Value-Added time will also be reduced from four hours to two hours. This implies that the proposed solution will bring desirable digital operational improvements for BS.

The proposed solutions will enable BS to respond to student dynamic needs efficiently, thereby improving student experience, service effectiveness and BS ranking. The student administration process will be flexible to accommodate anomalies in student circumstances. The cost of implementing the proposed solution is high in the short term but, in the long run, the cost of student administration operations will reduce (Ernst & Young, 2011). This will allow additional human resources to be optimised and reskilled in other value-added services.

ACKNOWLEDGEMENT OF CONTRIBUTORS

- Andene Mwambetania
- Katlego Khoetha
- Meshack Majola

- Tendai Masaure
- Zanele Mgoza

(All are affiliated to the Wits Business School, University of the Witwatersrand, Johannesburg).

REFERENCES

Armstrong, B., Lee, G. (2021). *Digital Business*, 2nd edn. Silk Route Press.

Boute, R., van Mieghem, J. (2021). Digital Operations. *Autonomous Automation and Smart Execution of Work*, 01.

Deloitte. (2019). *The next-generation connected campus.* Deloitte Development LLC.

Ernst & Young. (2011). *The digitization of everything: How organisations must must adapt to changing consumer behaviour.*

Faro, T. (2021). 5 Reasons To Study At Wits University. Retrieved July 22, 2022, from https://www.careersportal.co.za/education/universities/5-reasons-to-study-at-wits-university

Ismail, M., Mansor, Z. (2018). Agile Project Management Review. *Challenge and Open Issues*, 24(7).

McKinsey & Company. (2019). *Digital service excellence: Scaling the next-generartion operating model.*

OECD. (2015). *Students, Computers and Learning: Making the Connection.* Paris: OECD.

Paap, J., Katz, R. (2004). Anticipating Disruptive Innovation. *Research- Technology Management.* 47:5, 13–22, DOI: 10.1080/08956308.2004.11671647, 13–22.

Studyportals. (2022). What are Ivy legue Universities and why should i care? Retrieved July 19, 2022, from https://www.mastersportal.com/articles/1958/what-are-ivy-league-universities-and-why-should-i-care.html

U.S News. (2022). 2022 Best Global Universities in Africa: Retrieved July 20, 2022, from https://www.usnews.com/education/best-global-universities/africa

UiPath. (n.d.). Robotic Process Automation (RPA). Retrieved July 21, 2022, from https://www.uipath.com/rpa/robotic-process-automation

University Guru. (n.d.). Business schools in Johannesburg, South Africa Rankings. Retrieved July 19, 2022, from https://www.universityguru.com/business-schools-johannesburg

Vita, S., Rega, A., Mennittto, L. (2020). 'TED' Teaching Educational Device. *A digital tool to educational practice for special needs.*

WITS BUSINESS SCHOOL. (2020). *2020 Year in Review.*

CHAPTER 21

Conclusion

Operations play a major role in the success of modern organisations. With the advent of the fourth industrial revolution, operations have transformed into digital, autonomous and automated, and smart. Modern organisations are using the latest technologies to plan, run and manage their operations. Another factor fuelling the digitalisation of operation is Industry 4.0 implementation. This has transformed modern organisation operations by improving the levels of interconnectivity among products, people, processes, services and equipment, big data analytics, as well as both horizontal and vertical integration of value chains. It has further resulted in competitive advantage through enhancement of operational performance such as reduction in cost, quality improvement, shorter lead times and improving customer satisfaction. However, modern organisations are finding it difficult to digitise their operations in the absence of standard frameworks. The purpose of this book has been to compile practical case examples in digitalising the operations so that readers can understand through practical scenarios how to digitalise the operations.

This book consists of 19 case study examples on digitalising operations. These are illustrative cases and analysed for academic insights. We believe these cases will help the students to gain insights to understand the concept of digitalising operations. Further, the methodical analysis followed in this case can be used as a guideline to digitalise the operations.

The case in Chapter 2 was devoted to solving the patients' problem and making their visit to the hospital easier. The performance objectives of the proposed operations ensured that the costs of providing health care to patients are kept low by limiting supply chain irregularities and wasteful expenditure. Speed will be enhanced to ensure that waiting times are reduced – this will be achieved by speedy movement of required materials, data and decision-making. Using the feedback received the care provided to patients can be kept consistent with their expectations. The operations will be flexible to adapt to the changing requirements of the patients. The proposed digitalisation of operations will also ensure timely delivery of services as promised to the patients.

Chapter 3 was dedicated to studying an electoral commission and how it can be improved through digitalisation. The proposed system of digitalising was targeted for e-voting as it improves the efficiency of the electoral process. The chapter further discusses how globally electronic voting technology intends to speed the counting of ballots, reduce the number of staff needed to count votes manually and provide improved accessibility for voters. The case further concludes by stating that the investment in this new system is expected to pay off in the long term, as running expenses are anticipated to decrease significantly and save time and costs for the current and future voters of South Africa.

Chapter 4 was committed to operations optimisation for handling insurance claims. The chapter proposes to redesign an existing insurance company claims process. Insurance companies remained reliant on cumbersome and time-consuming documentation workflows for a considerable amount of time. These procedures resulted in less efficient management throughout the lifecycle of the claim, leading to longer open claim periods, less accountability, and less precise claim data. The South African financial services industry has evolved and is now focused on eliminating time-consuming manual labour and lengthy workflow obstacles. The paradigm shift is that processes should serve the users (administrators) rather than work against them. This change presents numerous advantages. The case conducts a comprehensive analysis of the current claims process's design and operation was performed followed by a proposed redesign of the business claims procedure has been developed. The proposed claims process demonstrates an operational enhancement to achieve the desired objectives.

Chapter 5 explicates the digitalisation of the Post Office. The proposed solutions will be able to drive down operational costs and increase revenue opportunities by reducing waste in the process and automating workflow and tasks. These solutions will be scalable to reduce disruption to the operations. The customer's experience will be enhanced through actively managing detractors and keeping the customer informed in real-time throughout the delivery journey. Finally, digitalising operations will allow employees to focus more on strategic work. The solution will create value optimisation and drive costs down, improve the customer experience by keeping customers informed in real-time, further improving turnaround time by reducing waste and automating repetitive work.

Chapter 6 expounds the practical case of digitalising operations for a property management company. The commercial property industry has been drastically impacted by recent macroeconomic factors. This has necessitated the need for improvement in the customer experience. Property managers have had to adjust and move forward. Increased flexibility and adaptability are required. Currently, the property leasing process is time-consuming and highly manual and well primed for digital improvement. The key finding when analysing the current process was that there is a lot of wasted time in between processes (non-value-added time). In addition, processing time was very long for certain steps, in particular, the lease negotiation and contracting processes. The case recommends that XYZ company go through a lean transformation to streamline and enhance its processes. As mentioned, XYZ manages every rental property manually, utilising a variety of disconnected technologies like email, phone calls, paper, physical signing and delivery. Through the case analysis and suggestions, XYZ can improve operations and increase efficiency through digital transformation. Digitisation will strengthen XYZ's business processes, functions, and procedures through performance improvements to enhance overall results as outlined in the five objectives. This case makes an important point that before embarking on any digital transformation strategy, it is vital to first understand the business processes and identify potential wastage or ineffective steps. By improving the processes and implementing new technologies, reskilling should be considered to effectively utilise the current workforce whose functions may have become superfluous. The case concludes by stating that digitalisation is a continuous improvement process and by applying the principles of operations management, XYZ can ensure they are ready to adapt and move forward into the changing business world.

Chapter 7 illuminates a detailed analysis of coal value chain operational optimisation and digitisation using a case study of the electrical utility service provider. The cases propose that BPR and automation process will ensure that the company can improve visibility and effective management of the Primary Energy Value Chain while maturing its Digital, Automation, Autonomous and Smart levels. The case further suggests that these proposed improvements will impact the department positively.

Chapter 8 is devoted to digitalising driving licence renewal operations analysis and improvement. The case is analysed in detail making use of the 4Vs (volume, variety, variation, visibility). This is used as a guideline to assess the performance of operational processes and to categorise product/service types. This is then followed by a detailed recommendation on how these can be optimised using digital technologies. The process is analysed before and later, after digitisation, to test for optimisation in cost and efficiency.

Chapter 9 explains a practical case of digitalising a leading fast-moving consumer goods manufacturer. The case uses lean techniques such as Value Stream Mapping and the Five Whys, to identify the opportunities to eliminate waste and improve time in the value stream and customer experience. Further, they offer solutions for the FMCG company as to how to digitise the operations so that the organisation can reduce waste in the value streams, increase the quality of the delivery process, and optimise fleet operations which in turn reduces fuel and other operational costs, reduction in inventory by applying a Pull System using data collected from across the value stream, and planning for the future using the DAS model which can introduce further benefits and increase digital maturity of RBB.

Chapter 10 gives details about a practical case of digitalising public hospitals in South Africa. The case delves into pressing and operational issues affecting public healthcare operations in South Africa through digitisation and standardisation of the admission and medical records process on a centralised management system across public hospitals in the country. Through the analysis of value streaming the process map, they were able to identify the inefficiencies as time was getting wasted while patients are waiting due to lack of standardised admissions procedures as well as lack of integrated systems to store and provide patients information. They propose to tackle the process inefficiencies through process redesign, making use of emerging technologies and standardising some of the work procedures along with some of the emerging technologies such as RPA, Cloud Systems, biometrics and facial recognition which is important for mitigation and speed improvement in bottleneck areas and thereby reducing inefficiencies.

Chapter 11 makes clear how to digitalise billing operations in a telecommunication service provider. The case concludes that automation can be of great assistance to improve the subscriber activation of customers from the on-billers. The previous process only allowed for bulk uploads greater than 50 subscriber line requests and one-on-one manual processing. It was highlighted that capturing 50 lines manually would take between six and 11 hours. With automation, it would allow the specialists to be able to focus on less mundane, manual repetitive tasks. With robotics employed, it will allow for greater accuracy, reduced wait times and the ability to increase the capacity of the system. The organisation can further investigate an outsourced or insourced labour model for the project.

Chapter 12 describes the digitalisation process of Park, which is a national and international site that celebrates the ideals of liberty, diversity and human rights. The case identifies existing gaps in operations such as slow lead and cycle time, slow resolution of inquiries, limited information flow, information gap, reception doesn't have the required information on hand, provided information is inconsistent and low quality, no service request system, lost queries, no traceability on request, no call centre system, calls are not logged and measured for first call resolution rate (FCCR), average handling time, repeat caller rate, call abandonment rate, poor customer experience, delayed responses etc. The case further proposes solutions by digitalising the operations.

Chapter 13 justifies digitalising the operations of a fast food organisation. The starting point was to understand the fastfood outlets ordering process and time spent at each activity point. This analysis was mapped up using a process flow diagram, focusing largely on the walk-in process that is widely by consumers used across all company outlets. An additional value chain analysis was carried out as it directly linked to the company's ability to efficiently serve its customers. The notable lag times in the process were the time it takes to place an order and the order waiting time after confirming the order, which is directly impacted by the efficiencies of the internal process. Further analysis of company positioning was done using the product matrix, the outcomes indicated that the existing process is positioned further away from the natural line. This would be due to the inefficiencies in the current process which is quality and speed in providing the final product to the client. This observation is further supported by the findings of the polar diagram which notes quality and speed as a concern in comparison to well-established fastfood outlets like Nando's. As previously highlighted in prior paragraphs, the focus has been on the end-to-end walk-in process. Thus, a 4V Model was used to understand how walk-in ordering services are positioned in comparison to online services. The finding showed that walk-ins maintained high levels of volume and variety which supports the need to improve quality and speed. The final leg of the analysis looked at the application of the DAS model which indicated the current level of digitisation and how it can be improved.

Chapter 14 vindicates the digitalisation process of the transport information system. The case proposes a new and automated digital driving licence process over the traditional process. The operational improvement provides operational savings to the Department of Transport.

This saving will be seen in a reduction of staff required to service the operations and provides an opportunity to reduce physical brick and mortar buildings. The volume of driving licence applications can also be processed significantly which allows licensing department staff to focus on more complex services. The model can also be replicated for other services like vehicle licence renewals. The overwhelming benefit, however, is provided to motor vehicle drivers as the process reduces the time to receive a driver's license from an average of two to three months to receive it within a week. Customers are also able to plan better as the new process is more consistent and the experience is standardised.

Chapter 15 supports the digitalisation of a retailer. The case uses digitising retailer operations using automation, integration, and innovation of processes. Marketing, customer service and order processing were identified to be the primary focus areas to be digitised. It is evident from the SWOT analysis that

336

retailer does have shortcomings, however, strengths and prospects to enhance business operations digitally outweigh the threats. Specifically using lean-management methods, the case was able to identify business process stages that remove or reduce 'waste' to increase efficiency and productivity.

Chapter 16 is devoted to digitalising bank operations. This case sought to improve the operational performance of the regular client payout operation. Optimisation of the process did not significantly impact the performance of the operation, as a result, a digitalised solution was developed which achieved all objectives defined. While there is a once-off cost associated with implementing the solution, Bank BBB will break even on the investment within two years based on the savings to be achieved by negating the need for a fully dedicated administrator receiving an annual remuneration of approximately R250 000 per annum. BBB Bank will need to implement change management to ensure that the solution is adopted by the internal staff.

Chapter 17 explains digitalising the printing press *eGazette* Section. The government gazettes are periodical publications authorised to publish public and legal notices. Proclamations by the President, regulations and notices in terms of acts, and company registrations are some of the notices published in gazettes. Dissemination of accurate information is important and must be done promptly hence effective operations management is at the core of publishing gazettes. The case analysis of the existing operations and proposes digital solutions to mitigate the inefficiencies in the current processes.

Chapter 18 illuminates digitalising the room service in a hotel. The case analyses room service operation and proposes a digital solution to improve the same.

Chapter 19 proposes to digitalising the food & beverages manufacturing Sector education and training authority (FBS) grant process. FBS face three main challenges, ie inefficient processes, ineffective learner validation controls and unreliable document management process. These have negatively affected FBS efficiency and effectiveness as key processes are manual and prone to human error and tend to lead to fraud and learner impersonation that costs the organisation.

FBS is not fully digitally mature, although there is huge potential to make key operations more mature. This exercise discovered that ten Discretion Grant and three Mandatory Grant process steps are manual and need to be automated to improve efficiency. We recommend that all the identified manual processes be automated. For Mandatory Grants, this will reduce total inefficiencies from 180 days to 139 days (23% improvement), and for Discretionary Grants from 309 days to 170 days (45% improvement).

The next step is that FBS put together a cross-functional project team that will implement the proposed operations improvements that deliver automation of Grant Application Compliance, Grant Application Evaluation, Grant Application Approvals and Learner Registrations processes. The chances of being a success are extremely high as the FBS management and teams are keen to improve their operational efficiencies.

Chapter 20 expounds on digitalising administration in a leading business school. The case proposes optimising the operations with digital technologies to improve the student journey experience. The proposed solutions will enable BS to respond to student dynamic needs efficiently, thereby improving student experience, service effectiveness and BS ranking. The student administration process will be flexible to accommodate anomalies in student circumstances. The cost of implementing the proposed solution is high in the short term but, in the long run, the cost of student administration operations will reduce (Ernst & Young, 2011). This will allow additional human resources to be optimised and reskilled in other value-added services.

For the benefit of the readers, we summarise the steps used to digitalising the operations

1. Prepare a detailed problem statement by incorporating the needs of all stake holders especially customer and market needs.
2. Draw the high-level process map of the process which you are intending to digitalise.
3. Carry out a value stream analysis to understand the value creation process.
4. Streamline the process by reduction of non-value-added activities.
5. Draw the current performance objective function.
6. Check the digital maturity of the business.
7. Identify the state of Digital, Autonomous and Automation and Smart levels within the value stream.
8. Determine the end state of Digital, Autonomous and Automation and Smart levels by considering the customer needs, market needs and organisational strategy.
9. Propose solutions using digital technologies to reach the end state and chart the technology management plan.
10. Evaluate resources required in terms implications in cost, technology management, change management and secure top management buy in.
11. Re-evaluate the future state in terms of Digital, Automation and Autonomy and Smart levels.
12. Compare the performance objectives using polar diagram before and after.
13. Devise project plan and implementation strategy by taking care of all stakeholders.

14. Digitalise the operations.
15. Monitor the performance objectives continuously for sustaining the operations.

We hope this compilation of practical case examples for digitalising the operations has expanded your line of thinking as regards how to digitalise the operations and what benefits can one reap with digitisation. Digitalising operations is a continuous journey, and it has to be pursued in cyclical and progressive manner.